JINNEALOGY

JINNEALOGY

Time, Islam, and Ecological Thought
in the Medieval Ruins of Delhi

ANAND VIVEK TANEJA

STANFORD UNIVERSITY PRESS

STANFORD, CALIFORNIA

Stanford University Press
Stanford, California

©2018 by Anand Vivek Taneja. All rights reserved.

 Awarded the Joseph W. Elder Prize in the Indian Social Sciences by the American Institute of Indian Studies and published with the Institute's generous support.

AIIS Publication Committee:
Susan S. Wadley, Brian A. Hatcher, Co-chairs
Joyce B. Flueckiger, Pika Ghosh, Mytheli Sreenivas, Ramnarayan S. Rawat

Printed in the United States of America on acid-free, archival-quality paper

Library of Congress Cataloging-in-Publication Data

Names: Taneja, Anand Vivek, 1980– author.
Title: Jinnealogy : time, Islam, and ecological thought in the medieval ruins of Delhi / Anand Vivek Taneja.
Description: Stanford, California : Stanford University Press, 2017. | Series: South Asia in motion | Includes bibliographical references and index.
Identifiers: LCCN 2017012270 (print) | LCCN 2017014062 (ebook) | ISBN 9781503603950 (e-book) | ISBN 9781503601796 (cloth : alk. paper) | ISBN 9781503603936 (pbk. :alk. paper)
Subjects: LCSH: Jinn—India—Delhi. | Islam—India—Delhi. | Muslim saints—India—Delhi. | Islamic antiquities—India—Delhi. | Islam—Relations—Hinduism. | Delhi (India)—Religious life and customs.
Classification: LCC BP63.I42 (ebook) | LCC BP63.I42 T363 2017 (print) | DDC 297.3/9095456—dc23
LC record available at https://lccn.loc.gov/2017012270

Typeset by Bruce Lundquist in 10.75/15 Adobe Caslon

CONTENTS

LIST OF ILLUSTRATIONS

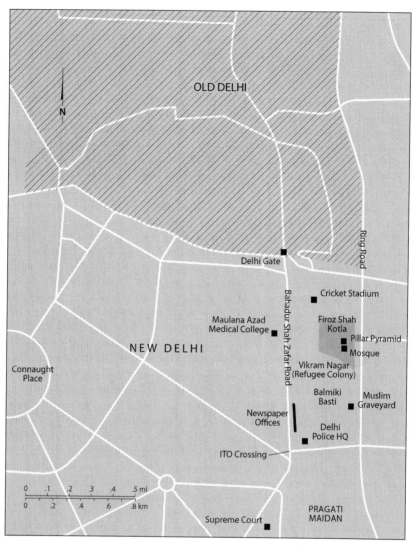

OLD DELHI

N

Ring Road

Delhi Gate

Cricket Stadium

Maulana Azad
Medical College

Bahadur Shah Zafar Road

Firoz Shah
Kotla

Pillar Pyramid

Mosque

NEW DELHI

Vikram Nagar
(Refugee Colony)

Connaught
Place

Balmiki
Basti

Muslim
Graveyard

Newspaper
Offices

Delhi
Police HQ

ITO Crossing

0   .1   .2   .3   .4   .5 mi

0   .2   .4   .6   .8 km

PRAGATI
MAIDAN

Supreme Court

MAP 1. *Firoz Shah Kotla and its surroundings.*

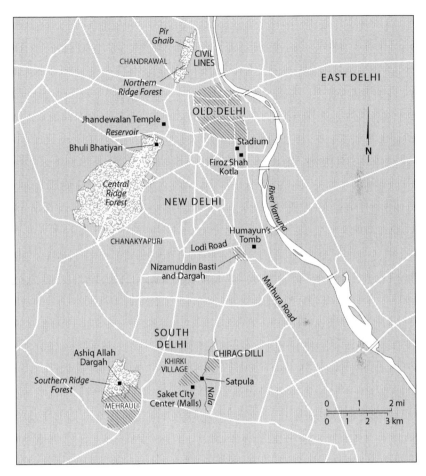

MAP 2. *Some of the places discussed in this book.*

ACKNOWLEDGMENTS

Tera tujh ko saunp de kya lagat hai mor? If I return to you what is yours, then what is left of me? In the writing of this book, I have accrued too many debts to ever account for in full measure.

Columbia University was a generous intellectual home. I continue to learn much from every interaction with Partha Chatterjee, and his intellectual generosity and openness remain a model for me, as does his engagement with subaltern politics. Brinkley Messick, with his kind and rigorous mentorship, made sure that I became an anthropologist of Islam as well as an anthropologist of South Asia. Michael Taussig's experiments with "ficto-criticism" and his deep engagement with Walter Benjamin underlie pretty much every page of this book. Manan Ahmed Asif's example as a public intellectual and his engagement with "futures past," as well as his practical life-advice, have been crucial to my work and thought since we first became friends through the blogosphere in 2005. Carla Bellamy's deep engagement with dargah culture and her support and encouragement throughout my fieldwork have had an enormous impact on my work and thought. I also learned enormously from Nadia Abu El Haj, Severin Fowles, Elizabeth Povinelli, Zoe Crossland, Jyoti Hosagrahar, Nathaniel Roberts, and Shahid Amin. Conversations with Frances Pritchett, and her weekly Ghalib gatherings, made Columbia an even more hospitable space once I returned from fieldwork.

The research and writing of this book would not have been possible without the *rahnumai* of many friends. Bhrigupati Singh was with me when I first noticed the dargah of Nanhe Miyan at Mandi House Circle. His work continues to inspire my own, and our disagreements merely prove how productive and provocative his thinking is. Nauman Naqvi, the original *gharib nawaz*, opened up worlds of thought and emotion with every conversation we shared outside Butler Library, and in some sense, this book continues our conversations. Pasha Mohamed Khan shared his extensive knowledge of Islamic lore and literature and guided me to medieval sira literature, thus providing a genealogy to *jinnealogy*. Raghu Karnad's curiosity and enthusiasm propelled much of my field-work. Kaushik Bhaumik's thoughts about cinema and religion have been hugely productive for my own. Siobhan Lambert-Hurley's groundbreak-ing work with Muslim women's autobiographies opened my eyes to what I might have missed otherwise. Abhishek Kaicker's historical work on early modern Delhi has provided important insights into my ethno-graphic engagement with the contemporary city. Joel Lee's warmth and hospitality, and his engagement with the question of "untouchable reli-gion," have been a model of *gharib nawazi*. Amaar Abbas introduced me to the mysteries of Mehrauli. Sarover Zaidi guided me to crucial contacts in Begampur. Naib-ul-Haq Qasimi's generosity opened up entire worlds for me in Old Delhi and in Uttar Pradesh. Conversations with Narayani Gupta, Kai Friese, Farid Nizami, Nayanjot Lahiri, Swapna Liddle, Rana Dasgupta, Ravi Sundaram, Sohail Hashmi, Shahid Amin, and Sunil Kumar were crucial to my understanding of the deep historical trans-formations and contemporary discontents of Delhi. Jayant Tripathi and Ratish Nanda shared their valuable insider information into the politics of heritage in Delhi and opened many doors that would otherwise have remained closed.

The research for this book was made possible through the generosity of Columbia University, the Wenner-Gren Foundation for Anthropological Research, and Vanderbilt University. The writing of several drafts of this book has been made possible through the generosity of Severin Fowles and Ellen Morris, Pooja Dodd, and the Robert Penn Warren Center for the Humanities at Vanderbilt University, each of whom provided beau-tiful spaces to think and write in. In the process of writing I benefited immensely from the initial reading of Maheen Zaman, Owen Cornwall, and Taymiya Zaman, whose enthusiasm propelled me through several drafts. Avtar Singh's push to make my research accessible resulted not just in an article but in a form of writing. Sean Dowdy's enthusiasm about *jinnealogy*, Giovanni da Col's insights, and the anonymous reviewers from HAU have contributed a great deal to my shaping of Chapter 1.

Jennifer Fay gamely ploughed through an early and unwieldly draft of Chapter 2 and gave terrific insights that have improved it tremendously. Conversations with Manan Ahmed, Radhika Govindrajan, Nancy Lin, and Anna Gade have deeply shaped Chapter 6. The thinking about Islam in this book has been greatly shaped by the "Local Islams" workshops at Vanderbilt and the yearlong Sawyer Seminar "Vernacular Islams Beyond the Arab World." The workshops and the seminar facilitated wonderful and remarkably productive conversations, which have been greatly productive for my thinking and writing. In particular I would like to thank my colleagues Tony Stewart, Richard McGregor, and Samira Sheikh, whose intellectual engagement and generosity have been models of collegiality. I would like to thank Mathangi Krishnamurthy, Margrit Pernau, Anna Gade, Alireza Doostdar, Yunus Dogan Telliel, Roanne Kantor, Audrey Truschke, Kalyani Menon, Irfan Ahmed, and Aarti Sethi for giving me the opportunity to present my work at some remarkable conference panels and to initiate some remarkable conversations. I would also like to thank Ravi Sundaram, Arthur Dudney, Mahesh Rangarajan, Gautam Bhan, Pankaj Jha, Akbar Hyder, Azfar Moin, Kathy Ewing, Sean Pue, Karen Zitzewitz, Sarra Tlili, Emilie Townes, Ali Asani, K. Sivaramkrishnan, Erik Harms, Audrey Truschke, Kabir Tambar, Ann Grodzins-Gold, Daniel Gold, Hayden Kantor, Ifthikar Dadi, Teena Purohit, Farina Mir, Alaina Lemon, Alireza Doostdar, Muzaffar Alam, CM Naim, Tyler Williams, Liz Chatterjee, Naisargi Dave, Sandra Bamford, Girish Daswani, Katie Kilroy-Marac, Brian Larkin, Durba Mitra, Gigi Dopico, and Barry Flood. Their hospitality and generous engagement with my work gave me the opportunity to present my work to diverse audiences, and the conversations that followed have influenced my thoughts in perceptible and imperceptible ways. Farina Mir's graduate seminar read the manuscript a few weeks before submission, and their insights have been enormously helpful in shaping its final form. I would like to thank Salman Hussain and Janaki Phillips in particular for their careful engagement.

This book comes out of a deep engagement with the city and the people of Delhi. I would like to thank all my friends and acquaintances at Firoz Shah Kotla, many of whom readers will encounter in the pages that follow, for so generously letting me into their gatherings and into their lives. I would also like to thank everyone at Sarai-CSDS, the research and practice space in Delhi, which first pushed many young people to engage deeply and critically with the city they live in. As a recent panel of wonderfully diverse and resonant papers at the Madison South Asia conference proved—with presentations by Aarti Sethi, Debashree Muhkerjee, Lawrence Liang, and myself—the intellectual energies first produced in that basement space in Rajpur Road continue to expand outward into the world. I would also like to thank my undergraduate teacher at Ramjas College, Mukul Mangalik, for actively encouraging my academic interests and for serving as a model of what passionate teaching can be. Ranjani Mazumdar, Shohini Ghosh, and Sabeena Gadihoke at MCRC, Jamia Millia Islamia, taught me to think about, and think with, images.

In Delhi the friendship of Bonojit Hussain, Tara Basumatary, Aditi Saraf, Kai Friese, Shivam Vij, Sarover Zaidi, and Laurent Gayer (now in Paris) have sustained me through fieldwork and beyond. In New York Eric Beverley, Nabil Ashour, Arunabh Ghosh, Amiel Melnick, Bina Gogineni, Jon and Cristina Carter, Samita Sinha, Suzanne Schulz (on her occasional visits), Lynn Berger, and Julia Fierman saw me through the writing of early versions of this work. I would like to thank Sarah Vaughn, Matt West, Kaet Heupel, Sophia Stamatopoulou-Robbins, and especially Seema Golestaneh and Darryl Wilkinson for years of camaraderie. In Nashville Ken McLeish and Juliet Wagner made the process of writing less lonely, and Riyaz Latif and Pratim Sengupta and our late-night *adda* sessions were truly inspirational. The generous friendship of Divya Kannan, Tariq Thachil, Piyali Bhattacharya, Jennifer Fay, Bryan Lowe, Andy Hines, Keegan Finberg, Carwil and Sophie Bjork-James, Dana DeLoca, and Odie Lindsey made sure that I stayed sane through the combined pressures of teaching, writing, and child-care. The EOS gatherings put together by Beth Conklin prompted both conviviality and ecological thought, as did "The Contemporary in Theory" seminar organized by Ben Tran and Alex Dubilet. Radhika Govindrajan and Dan Birchok have been friends beyond geography and have gone above and beyond the call of duty, painstakingly reading the entire manuscript and improving it vastly with their insightful comments and suggestions. Taimoor Shahid generously helped with the proofreading.

Carla Bellamy, Manan Ahmed, Christian Novetzke, and Laurent Gayer generously read and commented on early drafts of the book proposal. I would like to thank Thomas Blom Hansen for his enthusiastic support of the manuscript at Stanford University Press, and Jenny Gavacs for her early shepherding through the editorial process and for her careful editorial suggestions on Chapter 4. I would also like to thank Christophe Jaffrelot and Ann Gold—the no-longer anonymous reviewers who chose to reveal themselves to me—for their support of and thoughtful comments on the manuscript. I would like to thank Kate Wahl, Olivia Bartz, Marcela Cristina Maxfield, and Anne Fuzellier Jain at the Press for their prompt and helpful communication through the production process, and Joe Abbott for his eagle-eyed copyediting. I would also like to thank the publications committee of the American Institute of Indian Studies for awarding this book the Joseph W. Elder Prize in the Indian Social Sciences. I hope the book lives up to the promise they saw in the manuscript.

An earlier, shorter version of Chapter 1 was published in 2013 in *HAU: Journal of Ethnographic Theory* as "Jinnealogy: Everyday Life and Islamic Theology in Post-Partition Delhi." Some of the material concerning Chandrawal village and Pir Ghaib in Chapter 2 was originally published in *The Indian Economic and Social History Review* (*IESHR*) in the 2012 article "Saintly Visions: Other Histories and History's Others in the Medieval Ruins of Delhi." A section of Chapter 5 was originally published in my essay "Saintly Animals: The Shifting Moral and Ecological Landscapes of North India," in *Comparative Studies of South Asia, Africa and the Middle East* in 2015. I wish to thank the publishers and the journals for permitting me to reuse the material. I would like to thank the National Library of Australia for access to the 1945 map of Delhi detailed in Chapter 1, the Alkazi Collection of Photography for permission to use the image of Pir Ghaib in Chapter 2, and the Victoria and Albert Museum for permission to use the film publicity material in Chapter 2.

Finally, family: As in this book, family extends far beyond merely biological kinship. I would like to thank Kaustubh Chakraborty, Gaurav Pant, and Sumit Roy for maintaining our friendship over the years across disparate geographies. Annie Sengupta, Anjali Sengupta, Salil Chaturvedi, and Monika Kshatriya for adopting me and other mutts into their open hearts and homes. My siblings—Maneesha Taneja, Suveesha Taneja, and Aman Taneja—for all the years of laughter through thick and thin. Ashutosh *bhai* for always being calm in the midst of the madness—and for the awesome mutton. My parents, Vinod and Dipali Taneja, for always being there and for the values they have always stood by. My new family in the United States, who have adopted me wholeheartedly: Rahim Rahemtulla, Abeer Hoque, Mona Karim, and my brothers Philip Alban and Daanish Masood. My wife, the writer Sheba Karim, for our amazing journey together, for being the editor of my life and soul and of several drafts of this book. And finally, I would like to thank our daughter, Lillah, who brings such joy to the world even in these dark times. And I look forward to the light that is yet to come.

Nashville, July 2017

JINNEALOGY

WALKING AWAY FROM
THE THEATER OF HISTORY

Kho'e hue jahan ka chehra pehen ke aun
Mitti men teri utrun tab kya pehen ke aun?

Shall I come wearing the visage of a lost world?
How shall I dress when descending into your clay?

—Riyaz Latif

In October 2012 a man went to watch a play in the ruins of Firoz Shah Kotla, a rather apposite location. Firoz Shah Kotla is a fortified palace-complex built by the cousin and successor of the infamously cruel Sultan Muhammad bin Tughlaq (r. 1325–51), the protagonist of Girish Karnad's *Tughlaq*, the play being staged.

The man left the performance midway. In contrast to the illuminated stage he'd just left behind, the path out of the ruins was dark and eerie, framed by the jagged silhouettes of tall, crumbling walls rising against the light-polluted sky of the city beyond. As he neared the exit, he passed an alcove lit with candles where a few people were huddled in prayer. Here, he heard a voice, bodiless but resonant, and came to a halt. The voice was responding to the pleas (*fariyad*) of the people gathered there, but no one else seemed to hear it. His hair stood on end, listening to the voice from the invisible, but he was unafraid.

. . .

The ruins of Firoz Shah Kotla are located near the center of modern Delhi, the capital of the republic of India, and a vast metropolitan area that is home to more than sixteen million people. If you were to walk into the ruins on a Thursday afternoon, you would soon pass an alcove on your right, in what remains of a massive masonry gateway, thronged

1

with women and a few men praying, lighting candles, and depositing petitions. If you were to ask someone, you would be told that this is the place of Nanhe Miyan. If you were to probe a little further, you would be told that Nanhe Miyan is a *wali*, a Muslim saint, who is also a jinn, a spirit made of smokeless fire. Nanhe Miyan is one of several jinn-saints venerated at different spots among the ruins of Firoz Shah Kotla, a place where religious practice has emerged outside of and parallel to existing institutional structures. It was at the alcove of Nanhe Miyan that Santosh Mishra had stopped, heeding a voice no one else could hear, while walking away from the staging of *Tughlaq*.

Girish Karnad wrote *Tughlaq* as an allegory for national disenchantment in the 1960s. The play plots the descent of an idealistic and intelligent ruler into the cruelty and madness for which the historical Sultan Muhammad bin Tughlaq is infamous. The play, translated into several Indian languages, continues to find resonance with viewers and readers more than fifty years later. Santosh Mishra's story of his first encounter with the jinn-saints of Firoz Shah Kotla is an invitation to a radically different allegory: walking away from a familiar spotlit history of kings and statist dramatis personae toward another kind of relation to the past anchored in this ruinscape, to open oneself to the small voice of history,[1] eloquently whispering in the dark.

The unfolding of this allegory, and its intricate connections to life in the contemporary city, is the concern of this book.

. . .

The idealism of the postindependence Nehruvian era gave way, from the mid-1960s, to a darker time of betrayed hopes, floundering social policies, and growing militant unrest. The central government was widely perceived as increasingly corrupt, venal, and autocratic. It was the tragedy of the present that led playwrights like Karnad to interpret the past as ironic prelude. This despairing vision of the past found a home in the ruinscape of Delhi in 1974, when Ebrahim Alkazi's adaptation of Tughlaq was staged in the Purana Qila (Old Fort), two miles south of Firoz Shah Kotla. The ruins of the sixteenth-century fort served as a backdrop to a remarkably contemporary political fable: a year after the Purana Qila staging, Prime Minister Indira Gandhi declared the Emergency, a period of the suspension of electoral democracy and the rule of law that lasted nearly two years—the prime minister as Tughlaq.

A few months after the end of the Emergency of 1975–77 Firoz Shah Kotla came to prominence as a religious site in both popular memory and archival records. Many of those who come to Firoz Shah Kotla, both Hindu and Muslim, are from the areas worst affected by the excesses of the Emergency: the working-class Muslim and Dalit neighborhoods of Old Delhi, targeted by the state for evictions, forced sterilizations, and demolitions. Yet their relation to the past, among these ruins, is not one of despair but of hope and healing. They write their petitions to the jinn-saints among these Tughlaq ruins in a form reminiscent of the *shikwa*, a Perso-Islamic legal form of directly addressing one's plaints to the sovereign, prominent in the political theory of the Delhi Sultanate. In the dreams and visions that direct them to these ruins, they see Muslim saints wearing archaic robes, harking back to the medieval past. They make themselves at home in a monumental ruinscape of vast, cool underground chambers and thick masonry walls, glimmering monolithic pillars, and tall Islamicate arches—architecture far removed experientially from the cramped, boxy, ill-lit, flimsy, and often airless dwellings in which the majority of Delhi's population now lives.

As Santosh Mishra once did, let us walk away from the theater of history, from its all-too-familiar plots. The actors may wear the robes of the past and perform in the ruins of a medieval fort, but the story of political corruption and excess is the story of today, offering a vision of history that takes the modern state as its subject, viewing the past as a mere prelude to the tragic inevitability of the present. Let us return to the shadows, away from an all-too-familiar spectacle, until we, too, are stopped in our tracks by a voice, a voice that speaks of other relations to the past: the past not just as what was but as what could have been, and could be again;[2] the past not as past and dead but as full of concepts and potentialities for *life*, for the present and the future.[3]

In Chapter 2 I show how those who come to Firoz Shah Kotla and petition the jinn-saints embody such a relation to the past. They do not remember the singular cruelty of Muhammad bin Tughlaq but, rather, enact the normative political theology of Indo-Islamic kingship, in which any subject could present a petition before the king and expect justice to be done.[4] In a time when the postcolonial government's relation to its poorer subjects is mediated by layers of bureaucracy, and characterized by a plenitude of hostility and a scarcity of care (Tarlo 2003; Gupta 2012), the religious act of petitioning a jinn-saint in the ruins of a sultan's palace is also political—reimagining the subject's relation to the state.

. . .

The letters written to the jinn-saints enact an intimate sovereignty, as I show in Chapters 2 and 3, a paternalistic government whose justice reaches far beyond the categories of care imposed by the postcolonial state on its subject populations. In this the religious practices at Firoz Shah Kotla are more radical than the "politics of the governed" on which Partha Chatterjee (2004) focuses. Chatterjee argues that in political society, collectives organize themselves into populations—categories of subjects whose biological care is the goal of colonial (and postcolonial) governmentality—and thus turn the logic of governmental classification and enumeration into a moral imperative for care. The letters written at Firoz Shah Kotla, by contrast, imagine a far more intimate and individualized relation to sovereignty. And while populations and communities have been empowered in colonial and postcolonial India to "colonize the life-world of the individual" (Das 1995, 16), the letters deposited and the stories told at Firoz Shah Kotla imagine a justice that allows for the undoing of the often oppressive norms of family and community and allows women and men to make ethical choices that contradict societal morality: a Muslim woman, for example, articulating her love for a Hindu man.

. . .

How can we recognize as ethical the articulation of desires that contradict social norms? How do we understand the articulation of such nonnormative desires in a religious space where religion is widely considered, in both academic and commonsensical understandings, to be the source and staunchest upholder of communal morality? In asking these questions, this book enters the terrain of the anthropology of ethics and freedom (Laidlaw 2002, 2013) in Chapters 3 and 4, and it brings the concerns of this literature into conversation with the anthropology of Islam. This is, of course, an ongoing conversation but one that has been dominated by "virtue ethics" (Mattingly 2012), focusing on the deliberate cultivation of virtuous selves through bodily practices such as veiling (Mahmood 2005) and sermon audition (Hirschkind 2006), and adherence to strict moral codes. The practices of piety studied in Mahmood's and Hirschkind's seminal books, as representatives of this literature, focus on Islamic revival movements in Egypt, movements that focus on what Shahab Ahmed (2016) has called *prescriptive* authority, finding (and following) norms for pious behavior within the limits of the righteous examples of the Prophet Muhammad and the earliest followers of Islam. So even though the literature on virtue ethics in Islam is concerned with the cultivation of moral selves, this ethics looks a lot like following rules. There is no room in such an understanding of ethics and its relation to religion for understanding much of what we see at Firoz Shah Kotla, where people act in ways that constantly challenge and contradict normative morality. Men and women mingle and talk and laugh easily with each other; Muslims and non-Muslims freely interact and eat together; and jinns are treated and petitioned as saints, saints who are asked to bless interreligious unions: none of this fits with ideas of pious behavior if *prescriptive* morality is taken to be the norm for Islamic ethics.

And what we see at Firoz Shah Kotla is not exceptional: much of everyday life in the Muslim world, the *ordinary ethics* (Lambek 2010) by which life is lived, does not fit the models of pious selfhood or moral rule-following of Islamic revivalist piety (Al-Mohammad and Peluso 2012). This has led to an "anthropological divide" between the study of revivalist and "everyday" Muslims (Fadil and Fernando 2015), with the everyday being marked, in Fadil and Fernando's reading of the work of Schielke (2009), for example, as the site of resistance to pious norms or, in other words, of *impiety*.

But rule-following and modes of self-cultivation based on "pious imitation" of the *salaf* have not been the only norm for Islamic ethics, historically speaking. Shahab Ahmed (2016) criticizes modern academic understandings of Islam for focusing only on "prescriptive authority" in the formation and transmission of the Islamic "discursive tradition" (Asad 1986) and ignoring "exploratory authority" in the constitution of the tradition. By exploratory authority, Ahmad alludes to the historical freedom of Muslims to explore a multiplicity of truths and values, which he extrapolates from the literary and poetic self-expression of Muslims in what he calls the "Balkans-to-Bengal complex" from the fourteenth century to the nineteenth—literature and poetry such as the *divans* of Rumi and Hafez, which are in no way inseparable from "religious" life. Muslims could experiment with religious truth, and ideas of pious behavior, because they were not just bound to follow the "text" of the Quran and the hadith as interpreted into codes of pious behavior by jurists but had the potential to access the "pretext" of the revelation: the revelatory potential of the invisible (*ghaib*) realm that was manifest not just in the seventh-century Quran but in continuing potentials for poetic inspiration, mystical experience, and philosophical insight, which, as Ahmad points out, have had a far greater role in Muslim religious life and ethical self-expression, historically speaking, than "the mimesis of a pristine time of the earliest generations of the community (the *salaf*)" (S. Ahmad 2016, 81). Ahmad's opening up of the academic understanding of the Islamic discursive tradition to include the exploratory dimensions of Islamic piety ties in well with Amira Mittermaier's (2012) critique of the paradigm of self-cultivation in the anthropology of Islam. Mittermaier calls attention to the limitations of this paradigm, with its "emphasis on intentionality and deliberate action [that] obscures other modes of religiosity that center neither on acting within nor acting against but on being acted upon" (2012, 247). Mittermaier's work (2011) focuses on the power of revelatory dreams in everyday life in Egypt and the ways in which dreams not only challenge the idea of the individual, bounded, rational subject but also open up ethical potentials for dreamers that challenge and exceed reformist ideals of pious behavior and normative morality. Following Ahmad and Mittermaier, we can see the everyday not as impious but as charged with the potential of revelation and hence of ethical expressions not necessarily constrained by legalist understandings of sharia. It is such an everyday, shot through with the ethical urgings of dreams and visions, and the affective charge of the jinn, that one encounters at Firoz Shah Kotla.

And here we encounter ethics not as rule following or as technologies of self-making but rather as a set of *qualities* (Lambek 2015). The ethical qualities encountered and exemplified at Firoz Shah Kotla are *gharib nawazi* (hospitality to strangers), which I write about in Chapter 3, and nonpatriarchal fatherly affection, which I write about in Chapter 4.

The jinn-saints of Firoz Shah Kotla are antipatriarchal father figures, perceived as the fathers of daughters, not of sons, and women far outnumber men in this space. In patrilocal and patriarchal North Indian culture, the *babul*, the father of the daughter destined to go away to another, is a figure of unconditional childhood affection and intimacy. To articulate desires that contradict the normative morality of family and community, Hindu and Muslim women—and the men who love them—come to pray to and petition the jinn-saints at Firoz Shah Kotla.

What makes Muslim saints become such antipatriarchal figures for women and men across religious divides, when the image of Islam, in the contemporary mediascape, is so thoroughly oppressive, especially of women? The antipatriarchal potentialities of Islam, which coexist with the patriarchal juridical consensus, center on the popular memory of the Prophet Muhammad, and his relations with the women in his life, especially the loving relation with his daughter Fatima. In Chapter 4 I show how these memories have continued as affective and ethical potentialities in the popular realm, especially through the figures of jinns and *paris* (fairies) linked to Fatima. These are figures celebrated in eighteenth-century *rekhti* poetry, poetry written by men but celebrating urban femininity, and the early modern vernacular cityscape (Argali 2006; Vanita 2012). In the corpus of this poetry Nanhe Miyan's name recurs often.

.   .   .

Rekhti poetry virtually disappeared from the canon of Urdu poetry after the debacle of 1857. The failure of the widespread rebellion of that year, and its brutal and vengeful crushing by the British, was seen as a civilizational defeat, especially by the Muslim elite of North India, particularly those belonging to Delhi. In looking for causes for their defeat, they turned upon their own culture and religion, looking on them anew through the lenses of the conqueror (Vanita 2004, 2012; Pritchett 1994).

Now they, too, saw their culture as inferior to the culture of the victorious British: too irrational, too effeminate, too sensual. Rekhti poetry was censured as both symptom and cause of this degeneracy, and both this poetry and the world that it celebrated—the world of desiring women, the world of the affective pulls of jinns and *paris*, sanctified through rituals—were seen as uncivilized and un-Islamic and were excised both from the corpus of Urdu poetry and from the reformist and revivalist visions of Islam then taking root in colonial India. These visions were part of the modern paradigm of distinguishing true (religion) from false (superstition), a distinction inseparable from the effects of colonial power and epistemology (Asad 1993; Josephson 2012; Ramberg 2014). For revivalist Islam, as for Hindu, Christian, and Buddhist reform, "Only some ways of talking with and relating to gods and spirits qualify as religion, as a modern category of human experience and practice. . . . The understanding presumes a divide between the territory of the human and the realm of the transcendent and dematerialized divine" (Ramberg 2014, 15).

The *imams*, the officially appointed leaders of prayers in mosques, to whom I spoke, including the imam of the mosque at Firoz Shah Kotla, had adversarial reactions to the sanctification of the jinns at Firoz Shah Kotla and to the practices of veneration and petition related to them. They dismissed these practices and beliefs as ignorant, misguided, and superstitious—as not-quite-acceptable in the fold of Islam. If we were to follow a dominant strand in the academic study of Islam, then we, too, would have to recognize these practices as not-quite-Islamic: for here Islam is recognized only in the ways those authorized to interpret it—learned, seminary-trained men such as the imams, familiar with the foundational texts of scripture and law—choose to define "correct" Islamic practice. But what are now seen as deviant practices, such as attributing saintliness to jinns, spread across a vast geography from Morocco to India (Westermarck 1926). These are not "local" deviations, then, but an entire popular strand of Islamic thought and life that, in conversation with foundational texts and figures but unconstrained by the patriarchal assumptions undergirding modernist understandings of sharia, gives us an Islam of plenitude, of enormous potentialities for ethical life.

This parallel Islamic discourse is accessible not only to Muslims but also to non-Muslims. This discourse, and the potentialities it holds open for ethical life, spreads not just through mosques, and the texts and discourses of religious leaders, but through voices and visions, stories and songs, and even cinema: Bombay cinema is a popular cultural form renowned for its "Muslimness." It is an industry whose commercial products of popular entertainment, directed at a majority non-Muslim market, are often replete with Islamic theology and ethics (Kesavan 1994; Bhaumik 2001; Bhaskar and Allen 2009). There are intricate connections and parallels between the mise-en-scène of Bombay cinema and the religious landscapes and dreamscapes that I encountered in Delhi. In cinema and dream, and in the often dreamlike space of Firoz Shah Kotla, people move through architectural forms closely associated with the medieval Muslim past, encountering figures dressed in garb that would not have been out of place in a seventeenth-century Mughal miniature. Both in cinematic stories and in people's narratives of their lives, the passage through these ruins, whether singular or oft recurring, is fundamentally transformative of the self and its relation to the world.

Santosh Mishra's halting at the alcove of Nanhe Miyan, hearing a voice from the unseen, is not a singular story. Nor is the story he tells of the subsequent changes in his life and in his sense of self. It is popular common sense at Firoz Shah Kotla that more Hindus come here than Muslims do. And many of those who come here, both Hindu and Muslim, come after encountering the saint in their dreams, an encounter that leads not just to the instrumental resolution of problems but to significant changes in their affective lives and ethical choices.

What do the jinn-saints whisper to them among these ruins, and in their dreams?

The jinn-saints, I would wager, speak of and speak to a deep history that constitutes the North Indian self, a self far older than the Partition based on the incommensurability of Hindu and Muslim. They whisper of a past of the Sufi ethic of *gharib nawazi*, hospitality to strangers, which made Sufi shrines places of hospitality, open to all. They speak, as I show in Chapter 5, of the long histories of translation that have made Islamic ideas and concepts an indistinguishable part of Indic life and ethics. They speak of the history of Sufi theological concepts such as *fana*, the annihilation of the self, opening up possibilities for everyday life: the disentangling of the self from caste and familial identities and obligations (identities empowered and not dissolved by the politics of the postcolonial state). They speak of Islam as an ethical *inheritance* and not a religious *identity*, the inheritance of a premodern past shared by Muslims and non-Muslims.

.   .   .

This inheritance should not have survived. After 1857 the British actively worked to destroy the memory of Mughal sovereignty and demonize the history of Muslim rule (Chatterjee 2010a; Ernst 1992, 18–22). This project fed into the construction of communalism from the late nineteenth century onward and contributed to the growing violence and distrust between communities (Pandey 1990), culminating, in a sense, in the mass violence and demographic shifts of Partition, which saw millions of people uprooted from their intimate geographies, including the majority of Delhi's Muslims.[5] Partition violence saw the destruction of scores of Muslim shrines and tombs in Delhi, erasing a shared sacred geography virtually overnight. The post-Partition, postcolonial Indian state, haunted by the specter of Hindu right-wing violence, operates in a mode of *archival amnesia*, actively working to forget all ways of being, all claims to belonging, all landscapes and property claims that preceded its inception in 1947.

In contrast, as I show in Chapter 1, in the stories told at Firoz Shah Kotla, and in other parts of Delhi, jinns are linked to deep time, connecting human figures thousands of years apart. In these stories long-lived jinns serve as interlocutors connecting figures as distant in time as Moses, Jesus, and Muhammad or, in a story directly linked to Firoz Shah Kotla, the Prophet and the famed theologian Shah Waliullah of eighteenth-century Delhi. In these stories jinns are the figures of the transmission of memory beyond all possibility of human history. These stories became increasingly popular in post-Partition Delhi, as did the public veneration of jinn-saints at Firoz Shah Kotla. The popularity of jinns, and their links to deep time, increased in a city whose landscapes, public life, and archives were increasingly marked by the deliberate forgetting of a past—the pre-

1947 city—barely a generation old. The jinns are figures, we could say, of *apotropaic mnemonics*, magical figures of memory who serve as an antidote to the magical amnesia, the sleight of hand, of the postcolonial state, which makes things disappear not by keeping them out of its archives but by making them disappear within.

. . .

The literature of political theology has been primarily concerned with the secularization of theological concepts and hence the movement, we could say, of theological concepts into the (ostensibly secular) domain of the political (Agamben 1998; de Vries and Sullivan 2006). At Firoz Shah Kotla we see the ways in which the political, the ways in which people interact with and are affected by the postcolonial state, influences the theological. While the letters written to the jinn-saints are reminiscent of the medieval *shikwa*, they are often photocopied multiple times, and deposited in different niches and alcoves all over the ruins, as if addressed to the different departments of a modern bureaucracy. The letters are almost always accompanied by a clearly legible and detailed address and, increasingly, with photographs.

These letters written to the jinn-saints create an unusual archive of the struggles and desires of subaltern life in the contemporary city, voices otherwise unheard by families, by the media, by the government. It is a unique autobiographical archive, especially of women's voices in the contemporary city. By photographing some of these letters in situ over the years, I have preserved a tiny fragment of this transitory archive. I say "transitory" because at irregular intervals these letters are taken down, swept into piles by the workers of the Archaeological Survey of India (henceforth ASI), and burned.

Firoz Shah Kotla and hundreds of other medieval structures have been in the custody of the ASI since the early twentieth century. Their coming into the custody of the ASI happened at the same time as the landscapes of Delhi were being radically transformed to build New Delhi after 1911, the new imperial capital of British India. This was not a coincidence. In Delhi the ASI was tasked with preserving medieval remains as scenic *backdrop* to the new British imperial city. But to preserve this ruinscape as merely backdrop meant divorcing it from the thick texture of everyday life, rituals, excursions, and stories that connected the ruins to the lives of people from urban Old Delhi, as well as those from the surrounding villages, many of which had been nestled among these ruins for hundreds of years. It was proposed in 1914, for example, to turn Firoz Shah Kotla into a scenic park with curving drives, amenable to automobile tours, and cover its walls with ivy, so it would resemble an English castle, "back home." But to achieve this, the ASI first had to erect a fence around Firoz Shah Kotla to prevent the newly unauthorized entry of natives, who were wont to do all sorts of unseemly things among the ruins, such as hanging out, using the ruins as a short-cut to get to the river, and treating some parts of the ruins as sanctified spaces (CCO, f166/1914).[6]

In the years after 1911 the built remains of precolonial Delhi became spaces of political contestation between the imperial government, symbolized by the ASI, and the people of Delhi (Rajagopalan 2016). The ASI wanted to preserve the ruins as mere backdrop, "dead" in the parlance of the ASI's 1923 conservation manual, whereas the people of Delhi wanted to reclaim the ruins as spaces of life—both religious and secular. This struggle imbued the ruinscape of Delhi with an unprecedented agency. The ruins of the premodern past now became embodiments of the precolonial, places where the lost lifeworld of Muslim rule became *present*. In the Urdu literature produced in Delhi after 1911, both antiquarian and literary, these ruins were written of in a language of mystical vision and presence hitherto encountered only in religious contexts. Each stone and brick of the ruinscape of Delhi, to paraphrase Rashid-ul-Khairi (one of the elegiac Urdu writers of the early twentieth century), was now imbued with the sanctity of Muslim saints and the sovereignty of Muslim kings (Rashid-ul-Khairi 2010, 62–63).

This complete identification of the *asar-e qadima*—the traces of the ancient, as these premodern ruins and buildings were collectively known in Urdu—with Muslim lifeworlds took a dark turn in 1947, when hundreds of historic mosques and shrines in Delhi were attacked and badly damaged in post-Partition violence. These spaces, now alive with Islam, had to be destroyed or converted in acts of subjugation, in ways that paralleled the violence being inflicted on the Muslim population of Delhi. Many mosques were converted into temples overnight by placing idols inside them. This served as a precedent for placing idols inside the Babri Masjid in Ayodhya in 1949, a mosque built in the time of the first Mughal emperor, Babur (r. 1526–30), a figure metonymic in the Hindu right-wing imagination with Muslim iconoclasm and Mughal oppression (Lahiri 2012). Erecting a temple at the site of this mosque became a rallying cry for the Hindu right-wing in the late 1980s, who finally succeeded in demolishing the mosque in December 1992, inaugurating a subcontinent-wide spate of riots and violence, the unfinished business of Partition.

.   .   .

In the years after 1947, as I show in Chapter 7, the medieval mosques and shrines under the custody of the ASI were obsessively patrolled and protected, much more so than in the colonial era, and no religious practice was allowed in them. They were now rendered "dead" in the parlance of the ASI, and all efforts were made to prevent these buildings—now referred to by the generic term *monuments*—from returning to life. This was part of the contradictory nature of post-Partition India—an ostensibly secular country but one in which public life was now dominated by (upper-caste) Hindu self-assertion and the always lurking threat of Hindu right-wing violence. The identification of the ruinscape of Delhi with Muslim lifeworlds made it impossible for them to remain as "living spaces" in the new dispensation. The monuments had to be preserved, as part of the "built heritage" of the secular nation-state, scenic backdrops to the progress of the nation, but were increasingly removed from the realm of everyday life and religiosity (Kavuri-Bauer 2011). The policies and laws of the postcolonial state became necrophiliac with respect to the monuments of the Muslim past—able to love and care for them only as corpses. Restoring these monuments to the religious life of Muslim communities became an important aspect of Muslim politics in the late 1970s, after the end of the Emergency, and into the 1980s (H. Ahmed 2014). The revival of religious practices at Firoz Shah Kotla can be linked to this political moment, which succeeded in returning several "protected" mosques in Delhi to their former character as spaces of prayer. But the antagonism between Muslim religious practice and ASI conservation has never quite disappeared, and it still plays out at Firoz Shah Kotla and other sites.

. . .

In the contemporary lexicon of the ASI, the term *life* is associated solely with religious practice. But at Firoz Shah Kotla we see the flourishing of life in much more varied forms. Firoz Shah Kotla is now a zone of zoological density and diversity in the life of the city. Fish swim in the waters of the *baoli*, the deep circular stepwell still plentiful with water. Colonies of black ants prosper on the flour offered outside their burrows and on the sweets offered to the saints in the underground chambers here. Pigeons flock to the grain scattered for them every day, and kites gather to feast on the meat thrown to them. In the subterranean passages and chambers dense clusters of bats hang from the ceilings, chittering and squeaking over the heads of pilgrims while flying through clouds of smoke and incense. Cats were so plentiful that newcomers to the site often asked if this is where they could find the *billiyon ka mazar*, the shrine of the cats. The stories of old-timers are replete with encounters with snakes in the basement chambers and passages. As jinns are renowned to be shape-shifters, these birds and animals, especially the cats and the snakes, are seen as embodying the saints.

The equivalence of Muslim saints with animals, while novel in the densely human landscapes of postcolonial Delhi, also draws on a rich, if minor, tradition of seeing animals as ethical exemplars and moral agents in both Islamic and Indic traditions (Taneja 2015). As I show in Chapter 6, the emphasis on the animality of the jinn-saints in this space, and the kindness shown to animals here, serves both as a critique of the anthropocentric worldview of reformist Islam and as a memory of sacrality in the premodern city, where the experience of the sacred was connected, across communities, to the ecology and topography of the city. In the eighteenth-century Persian account of Dargah Quli Khan, the *barakat* (blessings) of the saints were indexically connected to the greenery of orchards and forests, the fragrance of flowers, and the healing powers of the waters of Delhi's streams and wells. The sanctity of saints was deeply intertwined with the pleasure of wandering among the greenery and the potential for affective and physiological transformation that resulted from opening one's sensate self to the ecological.

In the colonial city the connection of saints and gods to the city's ecology was gradually disrupted, a disruption that was accelerated by the massive growth of the postcolonial city. Saintly graves were disconnected from gardens and orchards by acres of brick and concrete. Tanks were filled up to make way for new homes and markets. Wells ran dry as groundwater was depleted by overuse. Once-sacred streams were fouled with sewage. New gods came to Delhi, gods of a more transcendent provenance, unconnected to the vanishing local sacred geography or, in the case of Islam, new, more transcendent ways of imagining and relating to the one God.

Paradoxically, the ASI, so committed to prohibiting religious practices in the monuments it protects, has ended up preserving older possibilities of the sacred in the city, thanks to its conservation (and horticultural) practices. As no new construction is allowed at monuments under its authority, ruins preserve not only older architecture but also an older embedding in the ecological, impossible to find at "living" religious sites, which are built over now with concrete and marble. And the horticultural practices of the ASI, creating gardens and lawns amid its ruins, approximate the dargah spaces of an older Delhi, where the shrines of saints were integrally connected to gardens, spaces that gave respite from the "vain agitation" of the city (Wescoat 1996).

. . .

Firoz Shah Kotla is a space of uncommon harmony in the contemporary city: between humans and nonhumans, men and women, Hindus and Muslims, high caste and low. Yet it is also a site marked and shaped by conflicts: between the post-Partition state and the city of Muslim memory that it inherited, between differing visions of Islam, between elite conservation philosophy and popular religious practice.

The elite relation to the ruins of Delhi, like the ASI's, has been one of admiring the ruins as background, with no real relation to the life of the city. The medieval ruins of Delhi, deeply tied to Islam, also index other times, other forms of sacrality, and other property rights and claims on Delhi's land. Their presence is deeply discomfiting to the elite residents of modern Delhi—overwhelmingly Hindu and Sikh—many of whom live in South Delhi, dense with the remains of medieval cities. They wish the ruins to remain as dark, picturesque backgrounds—akin to the follies, the *faux* ruins that dot English estates—but dread their return to (religious) life, for who knows what other claims might come back to life along with the monuments?

By their very presence these ruins ask, Who owns this city and the land it stands upon? They are the remnants, and reminders, of the complex of ritual practices, customary rights, and property regimes that still have unresolved claims on the modern city. They index a fundamental instability underlying the fabric of the modern city, much of it built in the last seventy years but atop a lived geography hundreds of years older. This is a question never adequately addressed in the often violent expropriations that followed the transition from Mughal to British rule in 1857, the building of New Delhi in 1911, or the Partition in 1947. The legacy of these unanswered questions haunts the modern city in the form of property litigation—litigation, for example, between the ASI and the Waqf Board over the custodianship of monuments. Muslim mosques, shrines, and graveyards are *waqfs*, endowments given in perpetuity that cannot be bought or sold. The Waqf Board is the legal custodian of waqf properties and hence has claims to recognition as the rightful custodian of the many historic mosques and shrines currently under the control of the ASI. The ASI disputes this.

For the elite of Delhi, the majority of whom have formed relations to Delhi and become owners of property here only after 1947, the ruins, as reminders of the older landscape of Delhi, carpeted over by their homes, are deeply disturbing spaces (Dasgupta 2014, 194–95), largely ignored and avoided. The discomfort around these ruins only increased with the legal necromancy practiced by the ASI around these "dead" monuments. In 1992, perhaps in an attempt to contain the fallout from the politics around the Babri Masjid, a new ordinance was passed, prohibiting any construction within a one-hundred-meter radius of a monument protected by the ASI. In subsequent years this made the dead, darkening, disused medieval mosques of Delhi into an active, threatening force in the life of the city. For all areas within a one-hundred-meter radius of any protected monument—several hundred acres of prime real estate in the most elite and commercially vibrant parts of the city—were now out of bounds for any new construction. Hundreds of cases of demolitions, evictions, and litigation followed—the apogee of the dark enchantment wrought by the postcolonial state on the precolonial landscapes it inherited.

. . .

Another vision of conservation has been growing and taking root in the city in recent years, carried out by secular conservation architects and funded by the philanthropy of the Aga Khan. In my conclusion I turn to this view, which seeks not just to restore the architectural beauty of monuments treated shabbily by the ASI but to reconnect them to the life of the city. This has meant not only a growing tolerance for religious practices at historical monuments but also an active embrace of people living with and in medieval monuments in the area around the famous Sufi shrine of Nizamuddin and an active promotion of events such as Sufi devotional songs at monuments. But this is not the only way in which these monuments are being reconnected to the life of the city. In this new paradigm these buildings are also sought to be restored to their ecological significance—to situate them once again amid gardens and waterways and birdsong, as they originally were—and thus to make these ruins an integral part of improving the city's quality of life. This quality of *life* is imagined not just in terms of improving human aesthetics and values (the beauty of these buildings and their gardens) but in terms of an increasing plenitude of life, beyond the human—the return of bird habitats, for example, and the increase in the number of trees and green spaces.

Here we have a secular conservation movement whose aims look remarkably similar to religious practices at Firoz Shah Kotla, which have reimagined this ruin as a space where human and nonhuman life come together. I believe that this points us toward the possibility that enchantment—the taking of the natural world to be full of value, and making moral claims upon us (Bilgrami 2006, 2014)—can be both secular and religious.

The ASI wishes to see the material world under its jurisdiction as "dead," devoid of religious life and significance. But the new conservation paradigm sees these buildings as full of not just aesthetic values but also moral values and possibilities of life: human, animal, and vegetal. This is an enchanted view of these buildings and their role in the life of the city, and it is in this enchanted view that I see the potentialities of rapprochement between the seemingly incommensurable worlds of elite conservation and subaltern religious practice. Will these potentialities be actualized? That remains to be seen, but in keeping with the joyous possibilities of life I have encountered among the ruins of Firoz Shah Kotla, this is the note of hope on which I conclude this book.

CHAPTER 1

JINNEALOGY

Archival Amnesia and Islamic Theology
in Post-Partition Delhi

I'm everything you lost. You won't forgive me.
My memory keeps getting in the way of your history.

—Agha Shahid Ali

TWO AFTERNOONS AT FIROZ SHAH KOTLA

May 2007. A Thursday afternoon at Firoz Shah Kotla (fig. 1). Looking
out from atop a three-story stepped-pyramid among the ruins, I can see a
cricket stadium to the north. Beyond it lies Old Delhi. To the west I see
the high-rises around Connaught Place. To the south lie a refugee colony,
a row of newspaper offices, and the headquarters of the Delhi Development Authority. To the east is an indoor stadium, the new Delhi State
Assembly, and a strange counterpoint to the tall monolithic pillar that
rises from the roof I stand on: the smokestack of a thermal power plant.
This pillar dates back to the third century BCE and is inscribed with
the edicts of the Buddhist king Ashoka. When it was brought here and
installed in the 1350s by Sultan Firoz Shah Tughlaq, this palace complex
was new, as was the city of Firozabad surrounding it. The forty-foot-tall
monolithic pillar, incised with ancient script, is still smooth and polished
after more than two thousand years, glinting in the sun.

Next to me, a young girl reaches her hand through the metal grills
that surround its base, attempting to touch the pillar, and asks the *Lat
Wale Baba*, the saint of the pillar, to turn her father away from alcohol
and make him a Muslim who observes the five daily prayers. *Mere papa
ko namazi bana do, Baba.* Inside the ruins of this structure, beneath this
pillar, people throng dimly lit chambers. They deposit letters of supplica-

FIGURE 1. *Firoz Shah Kotla on a Thursday afternoon. Photo by author.*

tion addressed to the same Lat Wale Baba. Such letters, often photo-copied, are found in niches and alcoves all over the extensive ruins of Firoz Shah Kotla. The letters form a strange and transient archive of the challenges and pathos of life in Delhi: a chronicle of loveless marriages, alcoholism, unemployment, disease, promises broken, debts unpaid, love unrequited.

Later that afternoon, I am at a tea shop in Vikram Nagar, the post-Partition Punjabi refugee settlement immediately south of Firoz Shah Kotla, the southern walls of the fortification extending into the settlement. I am talking to a shopkeeper who says he was born in Firoz Shah Kotla, when it was still a tent city inside the main citadel, before people were relocated to this more permanent settlement just outside the walls. I ask him if people prayed at the pillar when he was a child.

"Pray?" He is indignant. "We used to go piss on the pillar when we were children," he says. "All this business started when Laddu Shah came here, after Sikandar Bakht became a minister in 1977. There was no worship here before that."

· · ·

January 2008. Another Thursday afternoon. I do a circuit of Firoz Shah Kotla, following the usual route people take. I begin near the main entrance, at a wall darkened by candle soot and incense, the remains of a gateway into the inner parts of the citadel. This is the place of the jinn known as Nanhe Miyan (Little Mister). I pass the old *baoli* (stepwell), now closed after a man drowned in it last year. Next I come to the pyramid-like structure atop which stands the pillar. Then I head to a dark basement passage under the fourteenth-century mosque adjacent, where there are seven vaulted chambers. People traverse this passage, entering each chamber, turn by turn. The air is thick with incense and bodies and the echo of murmuring voices and the squeaking of bats and the whirring of their wings overhead. Here the only light is from flickering candles, so the people thronging the space are apparitions, appearing and disappearing spectrally through the thick fog of incense. After I have visited all seven chambers, the incense overwhelms both smell and vision. When I emerge, blinking, into the sunlight on the other side, my ears accosted by the clamor of traffic on the Ring Road, it's as if I have reentered the world after a long, inexplicable absence.

I walk to the far side of the mosque, where there's a hole in the wall. The wall is thick, rough chunks of stone held together by mortar. The hole is near its base, jagged and irregular, the stones that once sealed it lying in a nearby heap. It's large enough for an adult to squeeze through but not without some contorting. I get in line and await my turn. People wait for heads to emerge from the hole, help pull them back into the daylight, and then pass through the hole, into the darkness on the other side. The hole seems smaller when you're up close, the wall about six feet thick. I am grateful that I'm not claustrophobic. Suddenly the passage opens into something only slightly wider. I swing down, able to stand upright again, and find myself standing on a narrow, steep staircase, with a few inches of clearance for my shoulders and the top of my head. The way down is lit by a few flickering candles. The stone chills my bare feet. I descend, turn a corner, and enter a vast, many-arched underground hallway. There are perhaps fifteen other people in the expansive gloom, lit only by the occasional candle and a weak glimmer of sunlight entering through a chink overhead. At the far end of this subterranean space is a large cluster of candles and incense sticks where people stand, hands raised in prayer, eyes closed, facing a blank wall covered with shiny green sheets of offering.

Those who walk ahead of me stop occasionally and bow briefly to spaces in the walls and say, "Salam Alaikum," conversationally addressing entities neither they nor I can see.

A man stands at the top of the stairs, helping the less agile through. As I wait for a lull in the traffic, we talk. I ask him about the hole. "The archaeological people had blocked it up last year," he says, "but some boys opened it up again on the night of Shab-e Qadr."[1] Outside, in the vast grounds of this ruined fourteenth-century palace complex, AK Kaul, the Circle Officer of the Archaeological Survey of India (ASI) in charge of Firoz Shah Kotla, walks around the grounds. He takes pictures of "violations" with his digital camera, as proof to show to his superiors. For AK Kaul the prayers, the candles, the offerings, the letters, and the distribution of food within this space all violate ASI policy. When I asked him about his work here that afternoon, Kaul said something to the effect that he was posted here because he is not afraid of trouble and that he will stop "these people" from destroying this place.

Taslimuddin Khan, the imam of the mosque, tells a rather different story. According to him, it is Kaul and the "Archaeology Department" who have been willfully trying to profane a functioning mosque for years now, with no respect for the "sentiments of the community." "They provide no amenities," he says. "Instead, they try to obstruct prayer here in every way they can." In his account, for a long time now there's been a constant low-intensity war between the ASI and Muslims.

Squeezing out of the hole, back into the early waning sun of Delhi's winter, I find that Firoz Shah Kotla seems less like a war zone and more like a carnival. In the manicured lawns stretching between the various tumbledown bits of ruin of this former palace are hundreds of people, basking in the winter sunshine, queuing up for food being served, talking, laughing, relaxing after doing their rounds of the dark and inaccessible and frightening parts of these ruins. I return to a small group of people I befriended last summer, joining their circle on the grass. They are in their forties and fifties and sixties, and most of them have been coming to Firoz Shah Kotla for around two decades.

I tell my friends about my experience going through the hole. Akhtar tells me about the time, not so long ago, when many other subterranean chambers and passages were open (they have since been closed by the

ASI) and he had gone down to that same cavernous hall, and seen a row of tall figures in white, standing still, facing the wall. But when he turned around, the figures were gone.

NEW SAINTS IN AN OLD CITY?

Though Firoz Shah Kotla is a historic place, most of those who come here today do not think of it as a citadel or a historical "monument." The word *monument*, which has passed into common Hindi-Urdu usage in Delhi, is a vexed one. It implies that the structure in question is merely a secular space of scopic pleasure, meant to be looked at by tourists and visitors, and is not, and should not be, a place of active worship and veneration.[2] This understanding of the term *monument* comes from ASI policy, which distinguishes between "living" structures (those in regular religious use) and "dead" ones (those that are not). Postcolonial ASI policy favors protecting and conserving "dead" monuments and actively discourages monuments from coming "alive." But despite the informational boards around Firoz Shah Kotla, despite the structures and grounds here being under the jurisdiction and control of the ASI, most people who come here think of the site as a sacred *dargah*, or Muslim saint shrine. Firoz Shah Kotla is a very unusual dargah in the contemporary landscape of Delhi. Most dargahs are built around the sacred grave of a Muslim holy man.[3] Most dargahs, in Delhi and elsewhere, are bright spaces of marble and limewash, embodying the light of the saints buried within them (Ho 2006, 83–84). But Firoz Shah Kotla is a ruin, the time-darkened remnants of a medieval sultan's palace. There are no venerated graves or *mazars* here in these vast ruins, at least none that are visible. Among the congregants of this dargah there is an abiding insistence that what matters here is not graves but *jinnat ke asarat*, the influences/effects of the jinn.[4]

In Islamic cosmology jinns are a separate species of being, different from and older than humans. "He [Allah] has created man from dry clay and created the jinn from smokeless fire and made them invisible to the eyes of men" (Ashour 1986, 1). Formed of a completely different substance than humans, they are also said to be physically stronger and to have the ability to shape-shift and travel vast distances very quickly. Like humans, and unlike angels, they exercise free will and can choose between good and evil. Jinns are mortal, like human beings, but live far longer lives; some of the jinns alive today are counted among the *sahaba*, the companions of the Prophet Muhammad, having seen him personally and heard his recitation of the Quran.[5]

Human relations with the jinn, whether based on fear or intimacy (and often both), are widespread in the Islamic world, but they are, even in the case of named jinns like Aisha Qandisha of Morocco, usually seen as different from, though dependently linked to, the shrines and veneration of human saints (Crapanzano 1981; Spadola 2014). At Firoz Shah Kotla, however, the jinns *are* the saints—in the ways they are talked of and talked to and in the rituals of their veneration. How do we understand the popularity of jinn-saints in a city full of *human* saints, arguably the most sacred city in Indian Islam, known as *bais khwaja ki chaukhat*, the threshold of twenty-two saints? While evoking precolonial traditions of intimacy with jinns and spirits, the dargah of jinn-saints and its traditions of veneration nevertheless represents something new in the theological landscape of Delhi. Firoz Shah Kotla became a popular (as opposed to marginal) shrine in 1977, a few months after the end of the Emergency of 1975–77. I believe its emergence is intricately entwined with the transformations of the city's spiritual and physical landscapes, the massive erasures and displacements that shape the terrain of everyday life in the postcolonial city. The association of this space with jinns was not always benevolent, though the jinns at Firoz Shah Kotla are now understood to be (mostly) benevolent Muslim saints. The ruins of Firoz Shah Kotla used to be a space of danger, to be approached with caution (Kakar 1982, 27–28), even in the memories and accounts of people who come here regularly now. As Emilio Spadola (2014) points out, "As ambivalent figures of danger and power, difference and disruption, jinns and jinn-rites are conventionally tied to the danger and difference of socially marginal Muslims" (8). How, and why, have the jinns become saints in postcolonial Delhi?

Stefania Pandolfo, in her work on the conflicting and overlapping regimes of postcolonial psychiatry and the "cures of the jinn" in Morocco, thinks of the cures of jinns as another language, as it were, "other vocabularies of being, alterity and loss" (2009, 77)—a language that holds open the possibility of bearing witness. "The space of the cure addresses an affliction which is singular, but which is also a symbol that speaks of a collective condition, and a history: healing, and the sickness itself, are a kind of bearing witness" (2009, 82). Similarly, I see the presence of the jinns in the ruins of Firoz Shah Kotla, and the rituals of their veneration, as a poetics of bearing witness to the postcolonial condition of everyday life in Delhi.

In the stories told about jinns in contemporary Delhi, long-lived jinns act as transmitters of authority and blessings, connecting human beings who are centuries and millennia apart in time. This superseding of human chains of genealogy and memory by the *other-temporality* of the jinn is what I call *jinnealogy. Jinnealogy*, as I define it, is a theological orientation that encompasses the registers of ironic commentary, counter-memory, and apotropaic magic. The stories of jinn eyewitnesses who remember events and people from centuries ago are ironic commentary on the impossibility of human memory and on the destruction of the intricate webs of genealogy, memory, and belonging connected with Muslim saint shrines in the pre-Partition city. As Veena Das (2007, 162–83) has shown, the illegibility of the state's actions is central to the magic of the state in the lives of its citizens. As I show here, the illegibility of the state's archive, its will to *forget*, is also crucial to the illegibility of the state. Jinnealogy challenges the magical amnesia of the state by bringing up other temporalities, political theologies, and modes of witnessing against the empty, homogeneous time of the bureaucratically constituted present.

THE UNMARKED GRAVES OF FOOTSTEPS

> *. . . Jo mere tere shehr ki*
> *Har ik gali men*
> *Mere tere naqsh-e pa*
> *Ke benishan mazar hain . . .*

> . . . In every street
> Of your city and mine
> There are the unmarked graves
> Of your footsteps, and mine . . .

—Faiz Ahmed "Faiz"

The "unmarked graves of . . . footsteps" is a phrase that brings together the seemingly disparate elements of the ephemerality of everyday life and more "solid" memorials, such as graves and tombs. But graves and footsteps are not so easily separated. The destruction of Muslim tombs and saintly graves in post-Partition Delhi is intricately connected to the discriminations, deprivations, and aporias that mark everyday Muslim life in post-Partition Delhi.

What matters at Firoz Shah Kotla, many insist, is not graves but *jinnat ke asarat*, the influences/effects of the jinn. The insistence on the *absence* of sanctified graves at Firoz Shah Kotla is significant precisely because saintly graves have played such a crucial part in the landscape of Delhi—the threshold of twenty-two saints—as sites of the intertwining of sacrality and everyday life, of memory and community. Muslim saint shrines, built around the graves of holy men, serve as spaces of memory and belonging, connecting local communities, both Muslim and non-Muslim, to memories of the distant places from which the saints came, as well as embedding the saints in local sacred geographies and local histories (Green 2012). In the theological articulation of the importance of graves and grave visitation in the Indian Muslim tradition, as exemplified by Ahmad Riza Khan of the *Ahl-e Sunnat wal Jama'at* (also known as the Barelwi *maslak*), graves are important because they are sites of *presence*. The spirits of saintly Muslims are present at the site of their graves. The saintly dead can hear the living and can communicate with them; there is an interactive relationship between the dead and the living at the site of the grave (Sanyal 1996, 118–19).[6] Saintly graves are thus spaces of complex interplay between the historical and the sacral. These are spaces where communities are formed, people's everyday troubles are recounted, rituals are elaborated and transmitted, family genealogies are recorded, and stories are told. They are also spaces of connection to the spirits and the memories of the sacred dead.

Delhi's intertwined tapestry of memory and sacrality, linked to the graves of Muslim saints, was utterly torn apart by the violence of Partition. The enormity of the violence done in 1947 and its aftermath, while a story oft-told, bears repeating. Some twenty thousand Muslims were killed in the violence that began in September 1947, and by the time of the 1951 census, 3.3 lakh (330,000) Muslims of the city had left for Pakistan (Pandey 1997; Zamindar 2007, 5, 21). The size of the exodus gives us some sense of the scale of the violence, which did not stop with the taking of Muslim lives or the looting and destruction of their personal property. Muslim dargahs and tombs were viciously attacked, including four of the most ancient and venerated dargahs of Delhi: Qadam Sharif in Paharganj, Qutub Sahib's dargah in Mehrauli, the dargah of Chiragh Delhi, and the dargah of Sultan Ghari in Malakpur Kohi, as well as smaller dargahs, many of which were the focus of local veneration. In almost all cases the violence targeted the grave; many of the reports of the damage speak of the effacement of gravestones and the destruction of the decorative *jali* screens surrounding the graves. Some of these tombs and dargahs were also monuments protected by the ASI. A disconcertingly thick file is available in the Delhi State Archives, entitled "Damages Caused to and Occupation Taken of Protected Monuments During Disturbances and Thereafter" (DCO, f5/1947). Below are some extracts:

> The terracotta Jalis fixed around Roshan Ara's tomb at Delhi were found broken on the 8th October 1947. The Lamp Stone of marble at the grave head was also found dislodged. Attempt to dismantle the stone pavement was also made by the miscreants. . . . Now [two days later] the marble grave itself has been broken down and pieces appear to have been removed to an adjoining well. Not only stones have been broken but the miscreants have dug into the closed vault last night. . . . If such acts of vandalism continue then the monuments will be pulled down in no time. The inspection of the monument this afternoon reveals that the people in the locality are thinking of converting the place into a Gurudwara or temple.

> Beautiful stone jalis around the Tomb of Shah Alam at Wazirabad were found broken by my havildar on the 10th October 1947. On an inspection it was found that besides this damage the grave of the Saint had also been demolished. The Mimber in the adjoining mosque was also found dismantled and all stones uprooted. The inscribed plaster medallions were found to have been scraped off the walls and completely destroyed.

> At the 14th century monument of Pir Ghaib on the Ridge near Hindu Rao's hospital, the grave of the saint has recently been demolished. . . .

On the road from New Delhi to Mehrauli there is a village by the name of village Adchini. There is in this village the tomb of the mother of Hazarat Khwajah Nizamuddin Auliya. . . . A few days ago I happened to visit this tomb and found that the grave stone had been removed and the ground had been leveled. The compound of the shrine is being used by the villagers for stabling their cattle and storing cowdung.

. . .

As Vazira Zamindar's (2007) work shows, Partition was not a singular event but rather the inauguration of a structure of dispossession, displacement, and amnesia. The "Long Partition" continued to affect the Muslims of Delhi long after the events of 1947, being entrenched in the laws and policies of the postcolonial state, systematically eroding Muslim rights of property and citizenship.

When I first met Nasim Changezi in 2010, he was one hundred years old. He lived in Pahari Imli, a street in one of the Muslim-dominated residential areas of Old Delhi, south of the Jama Masjid. Long retired from government service when I met him, he and his son had started the Shah Waliullah Library, a single room that served both as a study space for local men and women and as an extensive and eclectic collection of thousands of books, as well as some quite rare manuscripts in Urdu, Persian, Arabic, Hindi, and English.

Nasim Changezi consciously played the part of the memory-keeper of Old Delhi, single-handedly fighting the effects of Partition on the landscapes of the city's memory. During one of our interviews he was in a strange mood. His constant refrain that day was, "*Ab kaun batayega?*" (Who will tell you now?) This refrain punctuated his rambling narratives, narratives that dealt mostly with the postcolonial transformation of Delhi and Partition violence. One story was about the tank outside Ajmeri Gate—filled up in the 1950s to make a market for refugees from Punjab—where delicious water chestnuts once grew and where, as part of the annual enactment of the Ram-Lila, the annual Dushehra reenactment of Lord Ram's life, Ram and Sita were rowed across the tank in a boat. *But who will tell you all of this now?*

He pulled out *shajras* (family trees) that stated his lineage from Adam down to himself and showed how he was intimately linked to many of the prominent families of Delhi—*But who will tell you this? Who has these documents now?* He told the story of his family documents. Many were kept in Bharatpur, where his grandfather was a minister of that kingdom and where he had looked at many of these documents as a boy. In 1947 mobs burned their house and destroyed their records, and nothing was left. "There were documents going back to Mughal times," he said, "written on gold edged paper. Who can tell you of these things now?"

Nasim Changezi told me a story that underscored his indispensability in a city where memory has died. Five or six years ago the cricket ground north of Firoz Shah Kotla was being renovated. In the course of the renovation they tried to cover over an old grave near one of the gates. Ten thousand people from Old Delhi attended a massive protest against the effacement of the grave. In the meeting that followed with the government, the local MLA (Member of the Legislative Assembly) called on Nasim Changezi to testify to the importance of the grave and the necessity of keeping it intact. According to Nasim Changezi, he told them what he knew, that the grave was that of Amir Panjakash, the great calligrapher of Mughal Delhi. The grave was left undisturbed.

ARCHIVAL AMNESIA

Oral testimony was needed to preserve the grave of a calligrapher, a man who produced documents for a living. Nasim Changezi's story is deeply ironic. Why did a then ninety-five-year-old man have to be dragged into this dispute to give oral testimony about the grave of a well-known calligrapher? Surely, there should have been documents?

The absence of documents in the story of an attempt to save a Muslim grave from effacement tells us something about the relationship of the postcolonial Indian state to the Islamic landscapes it inherited. Haunted by the anti-Muslim violence of Partition, the state wished to forget all Muslim presence and its Islamic past. This will to forget, as incomplete and contested as it is, is crucial to understanding the "magic" of the postcolonial state. The forgetting was attempted in many different ways. One way, as Nasim Changezi's story shows, was by attempting to efface and remove signs of Muslim presence from the landscape. Another way, attested to by the lack of documents in his story, was the cultivated amnesia of bureaucratic archives toward the memories of everyday life.[7] By this I mean not just access to the archives but the very organization and epistemology of the postcolonial archive, which made it well-nigh impossible to turn to the state to verify histories of presence, practice, and belonging.

To illustrate what I mean, let me recount my own experience of working with the records of the Archaeological Survey of India. Accessing government documents relating to protected monuments in Delhi proved to be the most challenging aspect of my research. First, I met with a flat-out refusal to access any files related to Delhi's monuments from the then superintending archaeologist of the Delhi Circle of the ASI. His reasons? "Those files have notings [notations] in them. They can be used by antisocial elements, antinational elements."

Strangely enough, among the "antisocial" and "antinational" elements he was afraid of getting their hands on these notations was the Delhi Waqf Board, which is actually a government body that includes among its office-bearers elected Muslim members of the Delhi Legislative Assembly, as well as Muslim officers of the Indian Administrative Service (IAS). Waqf is technically a form of property dedicated to God (and, in the language of the Central Waqf Act of 1954, given to the Muslim community for religious purposes) in perpetuity and is not transferable. Many of the mosques under the custody of the ASI in Delhi are also claimed by the Delhi Waqf Board. Under various acts passed by the colonial and postcolonial government, the Delhi Waqf Board is the ultimate custodian of all mosques and other waqf properties in Delhi, even those "protected" by the ASI or the State Department of Archaeology. Legally, there is no contradiction here. A protected building, under the 1904, 1958, and now 2010 Ancient Monuments Acts, is one that is protected irrespective of the proprietorship of the building. A building can, without contradicting the law in any way, simultaneously be in the custody of the Waqf Board, open for worship, and protected by the ASI. But the ASI has a policy of excluding the Waqf Board and Muslim worshippers from sites under its protection, a conflict alluded to by the superintending archaeologist's use of the terms *antisocial* and *antinational* to identify the Delhi Waqf Board.

I happened to run into a lawyer for the ASI at a book launch, who found my project interesting and gave me the names of people in the Survey's national headquarters to call. Even with this high-level introduction, and with all my credentials as a research-scholar from an Ivy League university, it took me more than a month of phone calls and visits to get what turned out to be only two weeks of access to the record room, which was in deep and entropic disorder. There was no catalog, and the files were piled haphazardly in bundles with no appreciable system of organization. My process of research in my two weeks in the record room became what I can only characterize as "random access": I would literally pull down a bundle of files from the shelves where they were stored with no visible attempt at chronological or thematic organization, remove the years of dust with a dust cloth that I'd started bringing with me, untie the knot that held what were often completely disparate files together, and start looking until I found something of interest. The files, of course, had their own complex system of numbering and notation, a form and custom of numbering that still continues in the ASI and in other government departments and agencies, but this system vanished completely when it came to the archiving of the files.

Two weeks after I started accessing the archives, I was told that my use of the archives was strictly unofficial, merely a favor, and had led to some displeasure among other senior officials and that I had to stop visiting the record room. It seemed that the ASI's archive was not an archive of authorized memory but of authorized forgetting, where files, once consigned to dust and darkness, were never to reappear in public, not even as diminutive flickers from academic footnotes. The authorized forgetting that characterized the ASI's archive was present not just in the impenetrability of the bureaucracy or in the disorder of the record room but also in the files themselves. This became clear to me when reading the postcolonial files I found in the record room in conjunction with the colonial files I read in another archive, the Chief Commissioner's Office Records stored in the Delhi State Archives.

In 1977 a certain Syed Ali Wajid wrote a letter to the ASI complaining that Survey staff were interfering with people's veneration at the shrine of Syed Jalaluddin in Firoz Shah Kotla. He claimed that the veneration had

been going on for more than a century. The officials of the ASI, instead
of investigating the actions of their employees, launched an inquiry into
the veracity of the claims made by the complainant. The dominant tone
of the file is surprise and annoyance, caught completely unawares by the
seemingly sudden eruption of "religious practice" at Firoz Shah Kotla on
their watch.[8] What was remarkable to me in reading the file was that in
the course of their investigation, officials of the ASI never once took re-
course to their own records, relying instead on various oral accounts and
published sources, *outside* the institutional archive and its system of files:

> I asked Shri Dikshit to send a person to the dargah of Nizamuddin to find
> out the relationship of Syed Jalaluddin with Shaikh Nizamuddin. The Dar-
> gah records could not furnish any information on Syed Jalaluddin who was
> not related to Shaikh Nizamuddin.
>
> I went through Zafar Hasan's description of monuments at Kotla Firoz
> Shah and memoir of Archaeological Survey of India no. 52 on Kotla Firoz
> Shah by J.A. Page. None of them contains any reference to Syed Jalaluddin in
> connexion with Kotla Firoz Shah.
>
> Not finding anything to support the claim of the votaries I asked Shri
> J.A. Chishti (R.O.) to consult *Asar-i-Sanadid* [written in Urdu]. The report
> of Shri Chishti who consulted other books as well is placed below. From the
> report it may be seen that Syed Jalaluddin's grave was near Turkman Gate.
> In view of the above facts it is essential to stop the present practice of paying
> homage immediately.[9]

All the works mentioned in the letter are published and widely circu-
lated books and records, present in libraries and bookshops rather than
archives. These are public rather than institutional documents, and the
ASI's turning to these records rather than to its own files indicates an
aporia in institutional memory. But in the Chief Commissioner's Office
Records, archives of the colonial government, there are copies of a detailed series of correspondence with the colonial ASI relating to Firoz
Shah Kotla when, under its jurisdiction, renovation and excavation began
there in 1914, which reveal not only that there was a steady trickle of
people constantly passing through Firoz Shah Kotla but also that practices of veneration (like sticking coins to the wall) that are seen today

were also seen back then (CCO, f166/1914). But as file 24/76/77 M(T) in the Archaeological Survey's record room reveals, no one in the ASI bothered to look at the files in their own record room, where a duplicate file of this correspondence surely exists or once existed. The ASI's head-quarters have been located in the same building since the 1940s.

An even more striking case is that of the protected Qudsia Bagh Mosque. On June 30, 1983, in the case of *Muntazima Committee Masjid Qudsia Bagh, Delhi versus the Union of India and Others*, the order passed by District Judge Jagdish Chandra declared, "There is no prima-facie evidence of the existence of any recognized religious usage or custom in regard to the holding of prayers or other religious ceremonies in the Mosque in question."[10] But there was evidence in the colonial archive of the mosque having been used as a worship site even after its declared pro-tection by the ASI, with the active engagement (if not outright approval) of the colonial ASI. In 1929 the Qudsia Bagh Mosque was under the unofficial management of the Anjuman Mooayyed-ul-Islam, a Muslim charitable organization that, under an agreement with the Delhi Gov-ernment in 1924, had taken over the administration of formerly derelict mosques under the protection of the ASI.[11]

Why did none of this evidence come to light in the case of *Muntazima Committee Masjid Qudsia Bagh, Delhi versus the Union of India and Others*, and countless other such cases, where the ASI denied the prior religious use of monuments not on the basis of marshaling positive evidence, as it were, but based entirely on the lack of evidence? Why was evidence needed in the first place to prove the existence of prayer in a mosque, a structure whose very raison d'être is worship? What made it impossible for the state and the judiciary to acknowledge or remember the usage of medieval monuments as living spaces of worship and veneration?

LAWMAKING VIOLENCE

To answer this question, let us return to 1947 and the violence of Par-tition, inextricably bound to the birth of the new nation-state, when the violence forced the abandonment of these "monuments" as sites of prayer. In his essay on the critique of violence, Walter Benjamin writes, "If, therefore, conclusions can be drawn from military violence, as being primordial and paradigmatic of all violence used for natural ends, there is inherent in all such violence a lawmaking character." The state "fears this violence simply for its lawmaking character" (Benjamin 1986a, 283).

The violence of Partition as it played out in India was motivated by a Hindu-majoritarian desire to remove all signs of Muslim sovereignty and belonging from India. This was a violence that the state could not (or did not) control, despite its avowed secularism. The specter of uncontrollable violence, foundational to the beginning of the new state, now haunted all government actions and social relations. The history of state and society in postcolonial India could well be the story of trying to accommodate the lawmaking violence that the state recognized it could not monopolize. This is reflected not only in the denial of Muslim claims to worship in monuments rendered "dead" by postcolonial policy but also in the erasure of Muslim graves, mosques, and shrines, spaces of living Muslim memory, from the landscapes of the new nation-state. It is easy enough, then, to speak of the Waqf Board as "antinational" because it remembers (and, unfortunately, wishes to revive) forms of property and customary usage far older than the nation-state and its ideal Hindu citizens.

Some of the most eloquent documentation of the erasures of Delhi's landscape can be found in Maulana Ata-ur-Rahman Qasimi's book *Dilli ki Tarikhi Masajid* (The historic mosques of Delhi) (2001). Qasimi writes about how not just homes and shops and businesses but tombs and graveyards were taken over by the Custodian (of Enemy Property) and sold to Hindu and Sikh refugees for throwaway prices. But the most startling picture that emerges in his book is that of a city of modernist planning (as exemplified by the DDA, the Delhi Development Authority), which sees itself as completely at odds with the Islamic landscape it has inherited and does its best to completely efface.

> After 1947 the sequence of occupation of Waqf Lands was started in Delhi under Jagmohan's governorship. It was Jagmohan's advice that wherever there is an old Muslim graveyard or empty Waqf land a DDA board should be put up on it, and so the DDA people put up their boards and prohibit the burial of the dead and to make their occupation secure they enclose the space with walls and to get rid of the graves with great wisdom they plant trees. Slowly

the trees go on covering the graves and finally these graves are leveled and this becomes a declaration that this is not the Waqf property of Muslims but the property of the administration. (Qasimi 2001, 35–36)

The graves disappear, and Delhi becomes primeval: "virgin" territory for development. Qasimi tells us the anecdote of Maulana Azad (who was the education minister[12] at the time and the only Muslim member of the central cabinet) trying to intervene with Prime Minister Nehru against the destruction of tombs and graveyards going on in Delhi, to which Nehru is said to have replied, "Maulana, half of Delhi is graveyards and mosques. Our schemes will fail if we don't have room to build" (Qasimi 2001, 37). Qasimi gives a striking account of a buried Tughlaq-era mosque in the grounds of the Lalit Kala Akademi (Academy of Fine Arts) in New Delhi. He was in a car with some other Muslim religious scholars. As they approached the former location of the fourteenth-century mosque he had heard so much about, he asked one of his older colleagues if he knew where the mosque used to be. They stopped the car and got out. "While indicating a mound in the enclosure of the Sahitya Akademi and the Lalit Kala Akademi they said the Tughlaq mosque is buried inside this mound and that trees have been planted all around the mound" (Qasimi 2001, 44). When the plans for the Lalit Kala Akademi were drawn, the area of the mosque fell into the plans and the DDA wanted to destroy it. Maulana Azad intervened and said that the mosque should not be destroyed at any cost. "After long arguments and debates it was decided that the walls and domes of the mosque be covered with rubble and a platform be built there" (Qasimi 2001, 45).

In the pre-Partition Delhi Guide Map (1945), the mosque still stands in the angle of Firozshah Road and Lytton Road, in a large vacant lot full of tiny, penciled trees (see fig. 2). Now, even the mound is gone. A gallery annex was added later to the Lalit Kala Akademi. The Akademi was built in 1954, less than a decade after Partition and Independence, as one of a whole series of cultural institutions built in the area now known as Mandi House Circle, institutions built to nurture and showpiece the modern cultural efflorescence of the new nation-state. A medieval mosque had no place here.

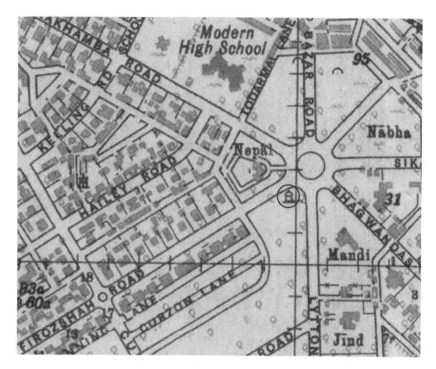

FIGURE 2. *A pre-Partition map of the Mandi House area. Source: Survey of India (1945),* Delhi Guide Map, *National Library of Australia, nla.obj.234365732.*

JINNEALOGY

Today, a stone's throw from where the mosque used to be, next to a defunct fountain and diagonally across from the Mandi House Circle, is a *mazar*, a venerated grave in the middle of the broad pedestrian pavement (fig. 3). The mazar is covered with asbestos roofing and marked off by small iron rails. A signboard says that it was established in 1966. The name of the saint present here is Nanhe Miyan Chishti. According to Anwar Sabri, the old caretaker of this mazar, Nanhe Miyan Chishti is a *rahmani* (merciful) *buzurg* (elder), from the Qadiri Sabri *silsila* and a disciple of Gharib Nawaz Muinuddin Chishti of Ajmer. Anwar Sabri reassured me, even before my asking, *"Aapka qayam yahin hai, original hai, banavati nahin."* (His place is here, it is original, not made up.)

A *qayam*, a place where one is established, is not necessarily a grave. Anwar Sabri said that when he started taking care of the place more than forty years ago, it was nothing more than a hole in the ground. He raised the earthen grave and whitewashed it every week. He was a painter with the Delhi Development Authority, and he supplemented his income with modest commerce by the side of the grave, selling incense and sweets and sheets for offerings at the grave, and by repairing bicycle punctures. He claimed that since he started taking care of the grave there have been no accidents at the Mandi House Circle, where seven roads come together. The municipal authorities often gave him trouble, not wanting him or the grave here, and he has spent at least one night in jail. But the baba appeared in a dream to an engineer with the New Delhi Municipal Corporation, who was planning a "beautification" of the area that would lead to the demolition of the grave to make way for a fountain. After the baba, the saint, appeared in his dream, the engineer begged his forgiveness, moved the fountain in his plans to accommodate the grave, and even presented the shrine with bags of

FIGURE 3. *The dargah of Nanhe Miyan Chishti, Mandi House Circle, New Delhi. Photo by author.*

cement to make the grave *pakka* (permanent). This is his biggest miracle, Anwar Sabri said, for the mazar not to be reduced to dust where so many others have been.

Other devotees, many of them Hindu, have provided a water tank, marble, and iron railings, solidifying the dargah's hold on its small patch of pavement. "Many of the devotees, including many actors and staff from the nearby National School of Drama, have been coming here for the past thirty years," Anwar Sabri said.

Nanhe Miyan is also the name of the first jinn-saint one encounters on entering Firoz Shah Kotla. His special place is a small alcove just off what would have been a large entry gate into the citadel. Nanhe Miyan was a name well known in eighteenth-century Delhi and Lucknow, as Intizar Hussain recounts:

> There were some special named jinns who had achieved a lot of fame among the ladies. They were Shah Dariya, Shah Sikandar, Zain Khan, Sadar e Jahan, Nanhe Miyan, Chahaltan; but the most fame was achieved by Shaikh Saddu. Mention of this can be found in the satire of Sauda [1713–81]. Rangin [1755–1835] has also given a reference to this.
>
> *Kisi ko ji se hai ikhlas Shaikh Saddu se*
> *Kahe hai aap ko Nanhe Miyan ki haram koi*
>
> Someone is sincerely devoted to Shaikh Saddu with their life.
> Someone calls themselves the intimate of Nanhe Miyan.
>
> It seems that the fame of Shaikh Saddu and Nanhe Miyan was from Delhi to Lucknow. (Hussain 2003, 115–16)

The poets that Hussain mentions were famous for their *rekhti*, poetry written in stylized imitation of "women's speech" and often ethnographically documenting their desires, lifeways, speech patterns, and beliefs (Argali 2006; Vanita 2012). This poetry had its heyday in late eighteenth- and early nineteenth-century Delhi and Lucknow. In the second half of the nineteenth century, rekhti poetry was censured by the reformist Muslim intelligentsia, who also attempted to repress the practices seen in rekhti, like the veneration of the jinn and the *pari* (fairies). Both these repressions can be linked to the debacle of 1857–58, when the widespread rebellion against the British East India Company was brutally crushed. British vengeance was particularly hard on the North Indian Muslim elite, whom they saw as being primarily responsible for the rebellion. The Muslim elite, in turn, saw 1857 as a civilizational defeat and started looking at Muslim cultural practices to find reasons for their downfall. Rekhti poetry was almost immediately identified as one of these cultural practices. The Urdu critic (and inventor of the modern Urdu canon) Muhammad Husain "Azad" had this to say about rekhti in 1880: "This invention [i.e., rekhti] should be considered one cause for the effeminacy, lack of ambition, and cowardice that developed in the common people" (Azad, *Ab-e Hayat*, cited in Vanita 2004, 44).

Altaf Hussain "Hali," among the greatest littérateurs of Urdu after 1857, famous among other things for the *Musaddas* (a.k.a. The Ebb and Flow of Islam), wrote the book *Majalis un-Nissa* (Gatherings of women, c. 1875) to educate *ashraf* Muslim girls to be better Muslims and better women. The didactic content included warning them against the religious practices of the lower-class women they would encounter in domestic life:

> Sitting with such people, how can one pick up any civilized manners? Indeed, you might learn a new religion which is unique in all the world, a strange sort of faith which you won't find mentioned in the Quran or the *hadith*. . . .
>
>   . . . In times of trouble, such people abandon God and call upon Allah Bakhsh, or sacrifice a goat to Shaikh Saddu or a cow to Sayyid Ahmad Kabir. In some places they pray to Bale Miyan or to Nanhe Miyan or ask for Darya Khan's intercession. Whomever you meet is obsessed with spirits or with the evil eye.
>
>   . . . These customs . . . are mainly found among ignorant and illiterate people. (Hali 1986)

Hali's disparagement of the practices of jinn veneration was not singular. For many strands of Muslim thought and practice that emerged in the aftermath of 1857, jinns were troublesome. The *nechari* (natural) school of thought exemplified by Sir Syed Ahmad Khan, committed to making Islamic beliefs commensurate with modern scientific rationalism, denied the existence of jinns and angels. "He [Syed Ahmad Khan] explained the Quranic assertion regarding the existence of jinns as being a reference to 'uncivilized people' or to man's propensity for evil" (Koshul n.d., 9). The Deobandis, committed to a more "traditional" Islamic ontology, did not deny the existence of jinns. "Deobandis, however, feel that Muslims risk angering God with their excessive reliance on jinn, angels and saints, for it is God alone who ought to be relied on" (N. Khan 2006, 244). In Deobandi thought and practice jinns are to be avoided and exorcised and are mostly considered malevolent. Even at Firoz Shah Kotla, the imam of the mosque insisted on the marginality of jinns to the sanctity of the space.[13] The insistence on the presence, saintliness, and efficacy of the jinn that I witnessed was often articulated in opposition to the imam.

.   .   .

One of the most tantalizing stories I heard about Firoz Shah Kotla came from Nasim Changezi. His memories of the ruin go back to his childhood and youth, the 1920s and 1930s.

"I used to go to Firoz Shah Kotla all the time," he said, "all alone, when people wouldn't dream of going there even during the day in groups of less than four or five" (he claimed he had been going there since 1921, which would have made him about eleven or twelve years old on first visit). It was wild and overgrown and terrifying in those days.

He used to be a *pehelwan* in his youth, a wrestler, and would go there alone to do his exercises. His parents knew that he used to go to Firoz Shah Kotla, "so they told me that when you oil yourself, don't slap your thighs hard; otherwise the people who live there [*wahan jo log rehte hain*, i.e., the jinns] will think you are attacking or challenging them."[14] He also used to go to Firoz Shah Kotla to go fishing, for until the 1920s the river ran close beside the ruin. One day he was passing through the chambers under the mosque, on his way to the river, when he found a big basket lying in one of the chambers; the basket was full of oranges, bananas, and packets of sweets from the famous Ghantewala sweetshop. He took the basket to what he calls the zanana [women's] chambers to the south of the mosque and left it there and carried some of the packets of sweets home. The next day, when he returned to the ruins, the basket was gone, and he heard a voice saying, *Ap ke ghar men to hamara bahut criticize*[15] *hai, aur ap hamara saman le ga'e?* [There is a lot of criticism of us in your home, and yet you took our stuff?]. He climbed up and looked around, but there was no one there. He climbed up the stairs to the top but didn't see anyone.

What are we to make of this story, of the basket of sweets, of the disembodied, mocking voice among the ruins? Although Nasim Changezi's family recognized the existence of jinns (and their presence at Firoz Shah Kotla), they did not recognize the possibility or, rather, the validity of their veneration, so much so that Nasim Changezi stumbled upon what was obviously a basket of offerings and failed (or refused) to recognize it as such, at least in his telling of the story. The next day, a disembodied voice chided him about his family's critical attitude. When I questioned him about the criticism the voice referred to, he answered evasively. "My family knew that I go there daily. So if I bring something from there, which I have never brought before, they understood that I had brought it from Firoz Shah Kotla." Then he started talking of his own travails with jinns, nightly troublesome encounters that would wake him from his sleep and which started after the incident at Firoz Shah Kotla, including what he describes as a forty-five-minute wrestling bout with a jinn that had pinned him down on his bed.

Nasim Changezi told all his stories with an air of pride. He had lived to be a centenarian, in reasonably good health, with a long memory and lucidity intact. But in his story of the vanished basket and the ghostly voice at Firoz Shah Kotla, I detected a boyish regret. His dragging the basket to another place among the ruins and leaving it there sounds like a child hiding his unexpected treasures. His reluctance to talk about what happened when he took the sweets home, except that they knew that he had brought them from Firoz Shah Kotla, indicates perhaps that he got a dressing down for indulging in the ignorant, superstitious practices of venerating the jinn. His returning to Firoz Shah Kotla to find the basket gone, a voice chiding him about his family's punctiliousness,[16] and the subsequent nightly visits by jinns (which stopped after he told his father about them) indicate a boy deeply haunted and unhappy about a loss that he can't quite comprehend but remembers vividly and can describe to a curious ethnographer more than eighty years later as if it happened yesterday. What else vanished for him with that basket of fruit? Perhaps the possibility of intimacy, rather than antagonism, with the world of the unseen?

In Nasim Changezi's account of the jinns, he emphasized their potential for evil and methods of protection against them. Yet the story he told me from Firoz Shah Kotla was one not of malevolence but of playfulness, which comes across much better in Urdu. *There is a lot of criticism of us in your home, and yet you took our stuff?*

. . .

In the 1960s and 1970s the name of Nanhe Miyan reappeared in the landscape of Delhi, at the shrine of Nanhe Miyan Chishti and at Firoz Shah Kotla. But the customs related to jinns in Delhi had changed. Nanhe Miyan and all the other named jinns used to be venerated in domestic spaces, in ceremonies held in private gatherings (Jaffur Shurreef 1832, 384–89), as Rangin documents in the glossary of women's idioms accompanying his *divan* of rekhti poetry: "*Baithak* ([A] Sitting): They spread a clean carpet and after bathing and washing they sit on it and Miyan Shaikh Saddu or Miyan Shah Dariya or Sikandar Shah or Zain Khan or Nanhe Miyan or the fairies or Bi Bachri come upon their head [possess them]" (Argali 2006, 32–33).

Now Nanhe Miyan is a public saint, claiming space and presence in the reconfigured landscapes of the postcolonial city, not restricted to sittings in domestic spaces. How do we understand the return of the jinns to prominence in the post-Partition city and their transformation into public saints, when there exists such a strong oppositional discourse against intimacy with them, similar to discourses in Morocco (Pandolfo 2009; Spadola 2014), where there has been a shift in Islamic revivalist discourses and their attendant models of personhood, malady, and cure toward emphasizing the malevolence of the jinn and foreclosing the potentialities of benevolence?

To understand this presence, I turn to stories of jinns circulating in Delhi. One of the most popular books about jinns published in Delhi, a book that many people immediately referenced when I mentioned that I was interested in jinns, is a book that could be characterized as an anti-jinn polemic. *Jinnat ke Purasrar Halat* (The mysterious affairs of the jinns) was first published in the 1950s and has since become a bestseller for the Old Delhi–based publisher Astana Book Depot, going into several reprints a year, according to the publisher.[17] The book is written by a *mufti* associated with Deoband who wishes to warn and empower men against the wiles of Satan and the jinn.[18] Mufti Shabbir Hasan Chishti states in the introduction, "For the Muslim public, rather, for the information of all the children of Adam, and for the betterment of their condition, in this book there is such an unvarnished account (*kacha chitha*) given of the mischief making of Iblis (Satan) and the jinns that reading it will force you to think about what weapon to use to overpower such an enemy of humanity" (Chishti n.d., 9).

But even in this book, the malevolence of the jinn is not the only theme. The book also has a benevolent role for the jinn in establishing connections between prophetic figures centuries apart in time. Jinns allow for the transmission of knowledge and traditions beyond all possibility of human memory:

The Prophet's meeting with the great grandson of Iblis [Satan]

Hazrat Abdullah bin Umar has narrated from his father, Hazrat Umar Faruq—I was sitting with the Prophet on one of the hills of Tahama when an old man presented himself in front of the Prophet and saluted him. Huzur [the Prophet] answered and said, Your voice and accent seem to be those of the jinn. He answered, I am Hama bin [son of] Him bin Laqis bin Iblis. Huzur asked, What is your age? He answered, At the time when Qabil [Cain] killed Habil [Abel] I was 43 years old. . . .

. . . In the age of Hazrat Nuh [Noah] I used to live with Muslims in a mosque. . . . I had told Hazrat Nuh that I was a part of the gathering of the killers of Habil bin Adam [Abel, son of Adam]. I desire God's forgiveness. Will God accept my repentance? Hazrat Nuh said, God is forgiving and merciful. Get up and do *wuzu* and offer two prostrations [of prayer]. I acted on Hazrat Nuh's advice and I hadn't yet lifted my head from the prostration when Hazrat Nuh said, lift your head from prostration, your repentance is accepted. . . .

. . . I often used to go on pilgrimage to see Y'aqub [Jacob]. I was with Yusuf [Joseph] in the place of his captivity. I used to meet Ilyas [Elijah] in the wilderness. . . . I have seen Hazrat Musa [Moses] too. He educated me in the books of the Old Testament and told me that when you meet

Hazrat Isa [Jesus] give him my regards. I conveyed Hazrat Musa's greetings to Hazrat Isa. Hazrat Isa told me that when you meet Muhammad,
you should convey my greetings to him. It is the narrator's statement that
when he heard this, Huzur [the Prophet] started crying and said, May salu-
tations keep reaching Isa. And till the world exists O Hama, may there be
peace upon you. You have fulfilled what was entrusted to you. (Chishti n.d.,
199–201)

I found the same anecdote in an English translation of Ibn Kathir's
(1301–73) fourteenth-century Sira of the prophet (Ibn Kathir 1998),
which read remarkably close to my translation of the same anecdote from
Urdu but with two crucial differences.[19] First, Ibn Kathir's text gives us
a long *isnad*, or chain of transmission, that Chishti does not reproduce.
Second, whereas Chishti doesn't express any doubts about the veracity of
this hadith, Ibn Kathir adds several caveats to his narration:

> The hafiz Abu Bakr al-Bayhaqi gave here a very strange hadith—one indeed,
> that was either objectionable or fabricated. However, its source is a cherished
> one. And I wish to report it just as he did. It is strange to come from him.
> (Ibn Kathir 1998, 4:132)

In translating this fourteenth-century account in the mid-twentieth
century, Chishti seems to amplify a logic already inherent in the story:
the superseding of human transmission of memory by the longevity of the
jinn—or what I have called jinnealogy. The memories of jinns, who live far
longer than human beings, stretch back several generations of human history. They can connect individuals hundreds of years apart instantaneously,
bypassing human institutions of memory and generations of transmission, short-circuiting genealogy (gray, meticulous, and patiently documentary)[20] into electrifying jinnealogy. Another jinnealogical story that is
quite popular in Delhi, many versions of which were recounted to me in
the course of my fieldwork, is linked directly to the mosque at Firoz Shah
Kotla. The version of the story given below is a compression from the oral
account of Chand, the son of Laddu Shah, the figure to whom the current
popularity of Firoz Shah Kotla as a dargah is usually attributed. (I explore
the biography of Laddu Shah in more detail in Chapter 2.)

The story goes that Shah Waliullah, the famous theologian of eighteenth-century Delhi, was once praying in the mosque at Firoz Shah Kotla when he saw a snake approaching him. He killed the snake with a stick. That night as he was sleeping, he was carried back to the court of the king of the jinns in the ruins of Firoz Shah Kotla, where the king told him that he stood accused of murder. He had killed the son of the king of the jinn, who had taken the form of a snake. In his defense Shah Waliullah quoted a hadith (saying) of the Prophet, saying that it was perfectly legitimate to kill a dangerous creature approaching you if you are praying. Had he known that the snake was actually a jinn in disguise, he would have done no such thing. The king asked the gathered jinns if what Waliullah said was true. An old jinn said, "Yes it is true. I have heard it myself from the lips of the Prophet." The old jinn was a *sahabi*, a companion of the Prophet by virtue of being a Muslim who had met the Prophet in his lifetime. Owing to his interaction with this old jinn, Shah Waliullah gained the stature of one of the Tabi'un, those Muslims who were born after the Prophet's death but had met one of the sahaba, the companions of the Prophet. The whole thing happened, in the explicit logic of Chand's version (and other versions) of the story, precisely because Allah wanted to raise the stature of Shah Waliullah.

Jinnealogy makes it possible for Shah Waliullah to overcome the thousand years between his life and that of the Prophet's and become one of the Tabi'un, the best generation after the companions of the Prophet. Shah Waliullah, of course, is the founding father, as it were, claimed as such by all the major revivalist traditions in modern Indian Sunni Islam (Sanyal 1996, 35–41). His being raised to the status of Tabi'un thanks to the jinn is an about-turn of sorts from the criticisms of jinn veneration growing in reformist discourses in the late nineteenth and early twentieth centuries. In his book Chishti even gives us an anecdote about jinn students studying at the famous reformist seminary, the Dar-ul-'Ulum Deoband. The fey, shape-shifting jinns, in this story, are disciplined into obedient transmitters of tradition:

Jinn also study at the Dar-ul-'Ulum Deoband. From the verbal accounts of some professors . . . I learned that jinns also study at the Dar-ul-'Ulum

Deoband. One night, around midnight, when Hazrat Maulana Habib ur Rahman Sahib, the *mohtamim* of Dar-ul-'Ulum was patrolling the campus, he saw two young snakes fighting and playing with each other in a locked room. Books lay open in front of the snakes. On seeing this, he immediately scolded them and said—is this a time to study or to fight? Upon hearing this, those two snakes instantly came back to regulation human form and started apologizing and swore that God willing, we will not give you an occasion for complaint again. (Chishti n.d., 150)

THE POLITICAL THEOLOGY OF EVERYDAY LIFE

In Delhi after 1947, the jinns become public saints and are recast as authoritative transmitters of Islamic tradition. Gods wax and wane (B. Singh 2011; 2015, 164–96). What might the waxing of the jinn-saint in Delhi tell us about the human condition in Delhi? How are these different forms of life intertwined? In what ways is popular theology tied to everyday life?

All this business started when Laddu Shah came here, after Sikandar Bakht became a minister in 1977. The year 1977 seemed like a significant date to me, on what was one of my first visits to Firoz Shah Kotla, because it was the year the Emergency ended. The Emergency was a twenty-month period of formally undemocratic rule imposed by the government of Prime Minister Indira Gandhi between 1975 and 1977. While the impact of the Emergency varied across regions and classes, it was a period of chaos for the lower classes of Old Delhi, predominantly Muslim and lower caste. It was a period of increased police brutality, coerced sterilizations for men, the violent demolitions of houses and shops, and the forced relocation of people to slum settlements across the river in Old Delhi. In the elections that marked the end of the Emergency in 1977, Indira Gandhi's government was defeated, and an anti-Congress coalition government came to power. Sikandar Bakht, mentioned by the man from Vikram Nagar, was a Muslim minister in this government.

Surely, there was a connection between the traumas of the Emergency, which disproportionately affected the Muslim and Dalit working class of Old Delhi, and the emergence of popular veneration at Firoz Shah Kotla, a place close to, and closely connected with, the Old City? Perhaps there is such a connection. Both the Vikram Nagar shopkeeper's words and the

ASI's files point us back to 1977 as the year that popular veneration takes off here, in the months after the end of the Emergency. And there is a strong geographical correlation between where those who come to Firoz Shah Kotla reside—Old Delhi and East Delhi—and the areas affected by the Emergency. Old Delhi was where homes and shops were bulldozed and people displaced; *Jamna par* was where they were resettled, eastward across the river. But no one *inside* Firoz Shah Kotla, including those who claim to have been coming for two or three decades, ever spoke to me about the Emergency, even though stories of state violence, injustice, and demolitions often cropped up in conversations. Perhaps because as the work of Emma Tarlo suggests, the Emergency, which seemed exceptional to the middle classes of India because of the curtailment of civic freedoms and the imposition of order, was not exceptional at all for the city's marginalized working classes: "The Emergency was not an isolated disruptive force in people's lives. It was located after and before other critical events. For some, these other events made the Emergency seem little more than just one in a long series of violent disruptions. For others, more recent losses had encouraged the elaboration of a narrative of oppression which formed a contiguous chain of suffering linking the past to the future" (Tarlo 2003, 136).

What can be said with more certainty is that the emergence of Firoz Shah Kotla as a newly popular religious space in the landscapes of Delhi is connected to the larger Muslim politics of Delhi in the 1970s. As Hilal Ahmed's (2014) work shows, a new kind of Muslim political discourse appeared in Delhi in this decade. The notion of "Muslim heritage," particularly control over Indo-Islamic heritage sites, emerged as the most fundamental Muslim political demand, overshadowing issues such as the protection of Urdu and the Muslim personal law (H. Ahmed 2014, 139). Grassroots organizations such as the *Masjid Basao Kameti* (Rehabilitate the Mosques Committee) were formed in the late 1970s in Delhi to restore the religious status of nonfunctioning historic mosques—or "dead" mosques—protected by the ASI. One of the first mosques the committee rehabilitated was barely a few hundred meters from Firoz Shah Kotla, now known as the Bhuri Bhatiyari Masjid (137). The Masjid Basao Committee was also involved with restoring prayers at Firoz Shah Kotla (Vij 2009), though popular memory here focuses on the figure of Laddu Shah.

Ahmed argues that what we see in the struggle for control over Muslim heritage spaces in the 1970s is the political construction, by Delhi's Muslim elite, of the memory of a royal Muslim past. This allowed for the articulation of a collective dignity for India's Muslims and defined the collective political interests of a single Indian Muslim community (H. Ahmed 2014, 282). But in the veneration of the jinn at Firoz Shah Kotla, I see not just the creation of a political collective to bargain for rights with the postcolonial state; I see religious life making possible a reimagination of the very terms of politics.

At Firoz Shah Kotla people write letters to the jinn-saints and deposit them in various niches and alcoves. As when applying to a government office, these letters are often photocopied. Multiple copies of the same letter can be found in various niches and alcoves all over the ruins, as if they are applications sent to the different departments of a modern bureaucracy. The letters are almost always accompanied by a clearly legible and detailed address, and increasingly, with photographs. Sometimes letters are written on photocopies of voter ID cards, the most ubiquitous (until recently) form of government-issued ID for working-class people (fig. 4). The desire for justice, even from the jinns, cannot be fulfilled, in the age of *Aadhaar*,[21] without submitting the data needed to be recognized as a citizen of the state.

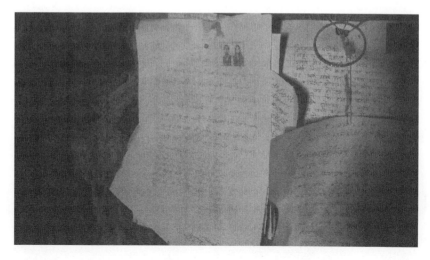

FIGURE 4. *Letters deposited at Firoz Shah Kotla. Photo by author.*

One cannot help but see parallels between the bureaucracy of the jinns and the bureaucracy of the Indian government, where, as Akhil Gupta's (2012) work shows us, the sites of governmental care for the populace are also sites of structural violence against the poor. Fear, and the overcoming of fear, is an integral part of the experience of Firoz Shah Kotla, especially in the dark subterranean chambers below the mosque, which are unlike any other dargah space that I know of. On Thursday afternoons these subterranean spaces, lit only by the flames of candles dimly visible through the thick fog of incense, are otherworldly spaces of sensory disorientation, even terror. The vertigo and terror of these intimate yet otherworldly spaces, so central to people's experiences of this site, where bat wings and bureaucratic forms and saintly presence are encountered in a sensorium of smoke and darkness, tell us something about the threats and possibilities that underlie, and often burst forth into, everyday relations with the state in Delhi.

But the relationships between people and the jinn-saints do not just mirror people's relations with the contemporary Indian state: they reimagine them. A recurring phrase I heard at Firoz Shah Kotla was *Mujhe pehle yahan aa kar bahut dar lagta tha* (I used to be afraid when I came here). The past tense is important. In people's accounts the initial fear of coming here was eventually replaced by a deep intimacy with the baba.[22] People petition the *sarkar* or government of the jinns about their most intimate problems, in the ruins of a palace, a premodern space of sovereignty, while using the bureaucratic forms and mechanisms of the modern state. In this, the religious practices at Firoz Shah Kotla are more radical than the "politics of the governed" that Chatterjee (2004) focuses on in his eponymous book. Chatterjee argues that in political society, collectives organize themselves into populations—categories of subjects whose biological care is the goal of colonial (and postcolonial) governmentality—and thus turn the logic of governmental classification and enumeration into a moral imperative for care. The letters written at Firoz Shah Kotla, by contrast, imagine a far more intimate and individualized relation to sovereignty, different from the logics of colonial and postcolonial governmentality.

Gods wax and wane. We should not mourn their passing. Impermanence and forgetting are essential to religious life, to make way for the new (B. Singh 2011, 441–43; 2015, 164–98). But what to make of the waxing jinn-saints of Firoz Shah Kotla, who bring a theological and political newness to the religious landscape of Delhi but who are nevertheless figures of *memory*—witnesses to times and lives impossibly remote? I believe that it is significant that the stories of the jinns told and retold in post-Partition Delhi, in both popular theological literature and in oral narrative, are linked to jinnealogy, to the transmission of knowledge not dependent on the institutions and genealogies of human memory. For in Delhi jinns are present in the blank spaces of the map, where the plans of the bureaucracy, the verdicts of the judiciary, and the illegibility of the postcolonial state's archive coincide to create vast erasures of the city's topographies, both lived and remembered.

Of all the names of the jinns recounted in rekhti poetry, only the name of Nanhe Miyan is now prominent in the landscapes of Delhi. Nanhe Miyan. *Little Mister*. The small voice of history, perhaps? In the stories of the encounters of jinns with the Prophet Muhammad and with Shah Waliullah there is an insistence on the jinn being a *historical* witness. The connections that the jinns make between figures separated by centuries and millennia are not connections made possible by the ontological realm of the *barzakh*, by dreams and visions, but by the sheer longevity of the lives of jinns. The insistence on jinnealogy, on connections between figures centuries apart made possible by eyewitnesses, is best exemplified by the story of Zafar Jinn in contemporary Indian Shia discourse. In this story Mir Babbar Ali Anis (1803–74), the famed *marsiya* writer, meets the aged and venerable Zafar Jinn in Lucknow. Zafar Jinn, according to tradition, was an eyewitness to the battle of Karbala (680 ACE). Mir Anis used Zafar's accounts of what really happened at Karbala to write his famed *marsiyas*, elegies to the martyrdom of Hussain and his companions. These marsiyas, which have canonical status among South Asian Muslims, are thus not acts of historical imagination and interpretation but eyewitness documentary evidence ("The Real Story of Zafar Jinn").

The jinns alert us to new temporalities brought into being by the postcolonial state. We now live in times where what we were eyewitness to has become the unimaginably distant past, impossible to verify through human memory or government documents.

Our time has become the time of the jinn.

CONCLUSION: THE TEMPORAL MAGIC OF THE STATE

In May 2014, a few days before the election results that brought Narendra Modi and the right-wing Bharatiya Janata Party (BJP) alliance to power with an overwhelming majority, the journalist Tavleen Singh (2014) wrote:

> Modi is seen as the magician who can make these things happen, with the flick of a wand, if he is given the chance to be the prime minister. . . . What is sad is that the only group of Indians who are not participants in this outpouring of hope and aspiration are Muslims.
>
> For them, the mood is sullen and scary. Wherever I have gone during the campaign, I have made it a point to seek out Muslims to understand why what happened in Gujarat in 2002 resonates so much more with them. . . . I have stopped in small villages in Bihar and Uttar Pradesh and asked why the absence of electricity, clean water and roads should not be as important to them as it is to their Hindu brethren and I have asked the same questions of mullahs in urban mosques. Everywhere, there has been a standard answer. Modi cannot be trusted because of what happened in 2002. . . .
>
> Later, when I have come home and pored over my notes, I have been intrigued not just by the sameness of the answers but by how much harm Muslims could be doing themselves by *remaining stuck in a time warp* that could perhaps be no longer relevant [my emphasis].

In February 2002, when Modi was the chief minister of Gujarat State, a systematic pogrom was launched against Muslims in Gujarat, which led to the gruesome and violent deaths of thousands of Muslims and the displacement and destruction of property of tens of thousands more. Twelve years later, in 2014, there was a constant reiteration of the theme, exemplified by Tavleen Singh, among those who wished to see Modi elected prime minister: *2002 was a long time ago. We need to move on.*

What kind of temporality does Tavleen Singh inhabit in which remembering the gruesome state-condoned violence that happened only twelve years before, and wishing to make political decisions based on that remembrance, becomes *remaining stuck in a time warp*? This is the ideal of postcolonial time, I would argue, time in which the future is only imaginable if we break completely from the past. Postcolonial time is secularized messianic time, a time of the radical abolition of tradition and history.[23]

This was a temporality that did not just appear in the lead-up to Modi's election in 2014 but was a time first inaugurated in India in 1947, with the radical uncertainties and resultant violence that inaugurated the simultaneous partition and independence of the country, a time that has since been assiduously maintained by the state through apathy and archival amnesia.

Sultan Ghari, the venerated tomb of Sultan Iltutmish's eldest son, is the oldest Muslim tomb in India, dating to the early thirteenth century. Records of its veneration go back at least as far as Dargah Quli Khan's *Muraqqa-i Dehli* (1993) from the mid-eighteenth century. The tomb was vandalized during Partition violence in 1947. Several years after this destruction, in 1955, the Jamiat-Ulema-e Hind, an organization of Islamic scholars, wrote to the Ministry of Education, wanting to get the tomb repaired and renovated in time for the upcoming *'urs*, or death anniversary of the saint.[24] Following orders from the ministry, the Survey promptly repaired the tomb within two months and then wrote to the ministry:

> The work of reconstructing the graves has been satisfactorily completed as far as warranted by the existing evidence and by the drawings available in the Department. The Protected Monument is in good condition, and no further repairs are necessary....
>
> ... It is noted that an Urs is going to be held at the monument from the 16th–18th July, 1955. *The monument has been a dead and deserted one for a long time, and no Urs has been held in the past.* There is, therefore, no justification for the use of the monument for such purposes. (my emphasis)

In looking at the "existing evidence and drawings available in the Department," the archaeologists seem to have pointedly ignored the report on Sultan Ghari by S. A. A. Naqvi, published in *Ancient India*, the journal of the Archaeological Survey of India, in 1947, which clearly states, "His tomb is even now regarded as sacred by the Muslims and every year on the seventeenth day of the month of *Ziq'ad*, his 'Urs or anniversary is celebrated and the shrine is thronged with pilgrims" (S. Naqvi 1947, 5–6).

How did the eight years between 1947 and the publication of the Archaeological Survey's own report become the *long time* in which the monument had "been a dead and deserted one" in the ASI's 1955 estimation? The lawmaking violence of Partition inaugurated an entirely new relationship of the archive to everyday life, a new sense of time and of history. In this new temporality of the nation-state Muslim time was firmly in the past, the *once upon a time* of fairy tales. Muslims had no claims to the present (or to presence) in the homogeneous time (and space) of the new nation-state. *Maulana, half of Delhi is graveyards and mosques. Our schemes will fail if we don't have room to build.*

Das writes of the "illegibility" of the (Indian) state, which allows its "double existence . . . between a rational mode and a magical mode" (Das 2007, 167). Das focuses on the illegibility of the state's actions, but what we have with the state's archives is an illegibility of the state's memory, a will, as I have argued, to *forget*. In the case of Firoz Shah Kotla and the Qudsia Bagh Mosque, spaces that had been used for prayer within living memory, the ASI argued (and continues to argue) that there was no evidence that these spaces had ever been used for prayers since their "protection," or official custodianship, by the government/ASI. In the case of the Qudsia Bagh mosque the court agreed with the ASI. *There is no prima-facie evidence of the existence of any recognized religious usage or custom.*

What is clear from both of these cases is that the ASI's record room was never called on to furnish any evidence in either of these (or several other cases). The state makes the papers, the only form it considers to be of evidentiary worth, vanish within the archive, hidden by dust and entropy, destroyed by insects and neglect. The archives had been rendered illegible by the state's will to forget.

The forgetting enshrined at the heart of the postcolonial archive is central to the illegibility and paradox of the state, its sleight of hand if you will. The state dismisses claims based on lived experience unless they can be supported by documents. But the documents disappear within the archives of the forgetful state. The state demands magic from its subjects to miraculously provide the proof that the state does its best to hide and make invisible. This contributes in no small measure to the particularity, transience, and irregularity of associations between state and local actors, mediated by graphic artifacts, in the functioning of postcolonial bureaucracy in Pakistan (Hull 2012, 20), in contrast to Max Weber's (1978, 988) understanding of files creating a system of institutional stability and bureaucratic memory. It is no wonder, then, that "documents produced by the state were invested with magical powers ... [and that] that view was held by all subjects of the state" (Gupta 2012, 212).

In the month after Narendra Modi came to power as the prime minister of India, the Ministry of Home Affairs destroyed more than 150,000 files in a "cleanliness drive." Orders are said to have been received straight from the prime minister's office (Prabhu 2014).

· · ·

Yeh insaf ki jagah hai (This is a space of justice) is a phrase I have often heard to characterize Firoz Shah Kotla. In this space of justice people deposit photocopied petitions that form a strange and transient archive of everyday lives in the city, their problems and sorrows, their hopes and disappointments. The image I have of this space of justice, from all the narratives I have heard, is something like this: on Thursday nights, when the people have left and the ruins of this medieval palace are deserted again, the jinns return to read petitions that people have left behind, a transient archive of the city's pain. This is the image of justice that persists among people at Firoz Shah Kotla, an image whose veracity they insist on despite open hostility from secular state agencies (the ASI), as well as "establishment" religious figures (the imam of the mosque). What does it mean for the working-class poor of Delhi to make this insistent turn to the jinns for justice?

In the histories of the postcolonial city there is no room for what those who come to this dargah have witnessed, what they have suffered, the stories they remember, the landscapes they revere. The jinnealogical story linked to Firoz Shah Kotla insists that the jinns who pass judgment are also witnesses—*witnesses to other times, to other modes of being*—like the *sahabi* jinn who witnessed the life of the Prophet. If Firoz Shah Kotla is a court, a space of justice, then perhaps the turn to the jinn is an insistence on the veracity of other times, of other modes of being, of other forms of justice, against the magical amnesia of the state.

CHAPTER 2

SAINTLY VISIONS
The Ethics of Elsewhen

Hai ghaib-e ghaib jisko samajhte hain ham shuhud
Hain khwab men hanuz jo jage hain khwab men

What we think is witnessing
is the hidden, hiding.
They are yet dreaming
who have awakened in a dream.

—Mirza Asadullah Khan "Ghalib,"
translation by Pasha M. Khan

The new, dialectical method of doing history presents itself as
the art of experiencing the present as waking world, a world
to which that dream we name the past refers in truth.

—Walter Benjamin

THAT WHICH WAS NAMED DELHI

The Pakistani writer Intizar Hussain begins his unique literary history of Delhi, *Dilli Tha Jiska Nam* (That which was named Delhi), by invoking the memory of an evening "two or three years after Partition":

> To tell the truth, it's just one of Delhi's evenings that has made me crazy, obsessed. This melancholy monsoon evening revealed itself to me for the space of a breath, and then vanished. . . .
>
> This was an evening two or three years after Partition. I had reached Delhi after a lot of effort. When we set foot in that celebrated passage that leads to the dargah of Hazrat Nizamuddin Auliya, the two times were meeting [it was dusk]. But the crowds that were usually present, with the scraping of shoulder against shoulder, were missing. Outside the dargah, the usual crowd around the shops selling roses, incense and candles was also nowhere to be seen. Silence had spread its encampment. From somewhere a group of

three qawwals appeared, harmoniums around their necks. They put the harmoniums down, and began singing immediately:

Ghar ghar men udasi chhayi hai, Shabbir Madina chhor chale

In every house sadness has spread, Shabbir [Hussain] has left Madina. . . .

We listened to them for a little while and then came outside. . . . Rewati said, Did you know that Ghalib's mazar is here as well? Let's go there. And so we got off the narrow path and started walking amidst tall grass. Janamashtami[1] had passed, and the grass had grown green and tall from the showers of [the months of] Sawan and Bhadon. In the middle of this grass a ruined platform came into view. Around it was a tumbledown enclosure wall. Inside, three graves in a ruinous condition. One of them was Ghalib's grave. I read the fatiha. Then we started walking through the tall grass again. Silence was all around. Only a peacock's call coming from afar broke this silence. After which the silence deepened even further. A couplet of Amir Khusrau's which I had just read at his tomb started whirling in my head:

Gori sovi sej pe aur mukh par daro kes
Chal Khusro ghar apne sanjh bhai chun des

The fair one sleeps upon the bed, her hair veiling her face.
Khusrau leave for your own home, it is dark now in this country.

After this I had to wait for thirty years to go to Delhi. Then somehow an opportunity to make a trip to this settlement presented itself. One trip. Then a second trip. Then a third trip. On every trip I made sure I visited the street of Nizamuddin Auliya. But now the whole map of the place had changed. Crowds. Shoulder scraping against shoulder. In every shop heap after heap of rose petals. Pushing and shoving to cross the threshold of the shrine to reach the tombs. And oh, the platform with Ghalib's grave vanished. The grass extinct. Now there was a wide platform of marble here. Beautiful filigree screens all around it. Inside, a grave made of marble. Right next to it, an imposing Ghalib Hall. On every visit the crowds seemed denser than the last time. And every time I badly missed that monsoon evening and that ruined grave falling apart amidst the tall grass. Oh Lord, where did that evening go and hide and where did that grave disappear to? Where should I look for it? (Hussain 2003, 6–7)

This was an evening two or three years after Partition. I had reached Delhi after a lot of effort. Intizar Hussain returns to Delhi as a man uprooted. He is only a temporary visitor, who will have to wait thirty years to visit again, which is what makes his account of these few moments even more compelling, because in these few sentences he describes a rootedness that is extraordinary. If we think of history, of the accumulation of the past as the soil, the ground that we stand on in the present, then compared to our shallow presentist experience of any given moment, Intizar Hussain describes a deep *fullness of time*, being present to many times at once. He stands in post-Partition Delhi and listens to the *qawwals* sing the seventh century, the impending martyrdom of Hussain at Karbala. He prays at the grave of a nineteenth-century poet of Delhi, and as he turns away, he remembers the melancholic verse of a poet from the thirteenth century, mourning the death of his beloved Nizamuddin. But the fullness of his time is not just that of history but of natural history: the weather, the seasons, the tall grass of Janamashtami, Krishna's birthday and the end of the monsoon, the call of the peacock. The fullness of his time is that of being present to landscape and human history indistinguishable from each other, as Ghalib's grave is almost lost in its green, vegetal surround—*history merging into the setting.*[2]

Every time Intizar Hussain returns to Delhi, he misses the *ruination* of Ghalib's grave, its almost vanishing into the tall grass of the late monsoon season. Ghalib's grave, now covered with a resplendent marble canopy and standing within a paved courtyard, no longer gives a sense of other times. It belongs, like the rest of Nizamuddin, to the rushed time of the contemporary city, with its bustling crowds, shoulder scraping against shoulder. Intizar Hussain did not mention that it is no longer possible to hear the call of peacocks in the passage leading to the dargah, for there is too much traffic on Mathura Road now to hear anything but the din of air-horns.

Delhi is a busy city, a frantic city, a city whose public life is characterized by rush and hustle. The city's traffic epitomizes the experience of time in the contemporary urban environment. Millions of cars and motorcycles now crowd the roads of Delhi, and thousands of new vehicles join the streets every day, offering the promise of velocity, of reaching one's destination faster. Horns honk at the slightest of delays or signs of slowness. While stopped, as people frequently are, at red lights and in traffic jams, FM radio provides a nonstop stream of fast-paced chatter and music and aspirational advertising. Time races on in Delhi, and people try desperately to catch up.

Naseer Bhai told me about the first time he came to Firoz Shah Kotla. He had to go to Dhaula Kuan, he said, and there was a traffic jam on the Ring Road, so he decided to turn right from Raj Ghat and take the inner route via ITO and India Gate. The traffic was jammed up there too. Stuck in crawling traffic, he saw a sign for Firoz Shah Kotla and decided to escape the traffic for a while and explore the place. He peeled away from the traffic on Bahadur Shah Zafar Marg, parked his vehicle, bought a ticket from the ASI booth, and walked into the ruins. "That must have been ten-thirty or eleven in the morning," he said. "The next time I looked at my watch, it was two o'clock." He thought of leaving then but couldn't. *Man hi nahin kiya jane ko* (I didn't feel like leaving). It was after five when he finally left. Being at Firoz Shah Kotla rendered the rushed time of the city irrelevant, made Naseer Bhai stop looking at his watch. Now he comes to Firoz Shah Kotla every morning and feeds the fish in the baoli. In many other stories I heard at Firoz Shah Kotla, people would leave the drudgery and frustrations of their workday midway to come to spend afternoons there. Manohar Lal, whom we will meet later in this chapter, remembers that the first time he came to Firoz Shah Kotla was in the morning, and he had no idea of the passing of time till the *maghrib azan*, the call for sunset prayers, sounded in his ears.

Much has changed in Delhi since Intizar Hussain's lost evening two or three years after Partition, but the insights his poetic prose provide are ever more relevant. The ruins of Delhi are spaces where the turbid flow of time in the city deepens and slows,[3] spaces where time is no longer measurable by clocks, each second discrete from the next. Rather, in the relative depth and stillness of time in these ruins, one is made aware of how the past and future eddy and swirl into the present. This experience of the stilling and deepening of time, the not needing to check watches and clocks, makes these ruins *thresholds of time*, spaces where one can be present to multiple orders of temporality, like looking down through shifting, refracting layers of water and seeing rippling images of fishes and ferns and the stones at the bottom, rising up through our own spangled, shifting reflections.[4]

One evening at Firoz Shah Kotla an employee of the ASI, who has been posted on duty to many of Delhi's medieval monuments, told me that in all the old monuments of Delhi, not just here but *sare kilon men*, in all the forts (including the seventeenth-century city wall of Old Delhi), there are *buzurgon ke saye*, the shades of Muslim holy men. You see them not just at night but also in the day. Then he proceeded to tell me the story of two women workers of the ASI who had disrespected the *buzurg* by urinating inside the fort, and how just before they were struck by mysterious illnesses as retribution, they had seen the buzurg, dressed in white clothes and with white turbans, the traditional attire of Muslim religious figures. "But," he said, "if you don't disrespect them, there is no harm to anyone." ASI officials are happy and prosperous and in no trouble with the courts or the police, and that is a big thing these days. The buzurg bless those who serve at the forts.

The story of the women urinating is telling. The women are punished for treating these medieval ruins as profane spaces, for not recognizing their sanctity.[5] In the account of the ASI employee, who identified as Hindu, all medieval fortifications in Delhi associated with Muslim rule are sacred spaces, blessed by the presence of holy figures. But don't these ruined fortifications belong to the medieval period, the dark ages of Indian history, when Hindus were subjugated under the iron hand of Muslim rule? At least so goes academic history written by the British and much hate-filled nationalist-popular history as it is written now (Chatterjee 2010a; Ernst 1992, 18–22; Pandey 1994). Firoz Shah Kotla was built by a Muslim sultan, the cousin of a man with a reputation for inhuman cruelty. And yet the majority of those who come here are non-Muslim, according to the assessment of the regulars here, both Hindu and Muslim. And the image they have of the medieval is completely different from the one historiography would have us expect. All these fortifications, places of war and soldiery and royal courts, now under the jurisdiction of the secular ASI, are haunted by the images, by the presence of Muslim holy figures, a presence that is a blessing for those lucky enough to live, or work, within medieval walls.

These dream-images have a radically different relation to time and remembrance than the discourses of the past constructed by national-colonial histories, where the past is merely prelude to the inevitability of the present (Asif 2013). Colonial historiography constructed Muslim rule in India as simultaneously cruel and effete, to make the colonial moment of its writing, the ongoing British conquest and subjugation of India, seem both inevitable and necessary. Hindus have always fought against Muslim oppression in nationalist historiography written in post-Partition India, thus portraying the birth of two separate and hostile nation-states as historical inevitability. The images of the past seen among the medieval ruins of Delhi, in ritual and dream, point to a different relation of past to present. The saintly visions that persist among the ruins, through indexing other potentials of the medieval than those remembered by national-colonial historiography, destabilize the time of the present, the inevitability of things as they are in the here and now. This destabilization, the presence of multiple pasts in the time of the present, is important for the remaking of individuals and communities, the potential for alternative futures. Hearing the call of the peacock at Ghalib's grave allows Intizar Hussain to be rooted, if even for a moment, in a landscape and a history that the Partition of India had made him an alien to.

Dreams and visions of saints, as Amira Mittermaier's (2011) work on dreaming in contemporary Egypt has shown us, are conceptualized as coming from an Elsewhere, not from inside the individual unconscious but from outside the subject. But the persistent connection between these visions and medieval ruins in Delhi indicates that these visions are also linked to *elsewhen*, times other than the contemporary moment. Here the past exists as a field of potential—*what could have been and what could be again*—which destabilizes the inevitability of present states of affairs. Saints present among ruins gained prominent followings, as I explore in this chapter, after periods of colonial and postcolonial state violence.

Ruins serve as thresholds of multiple temporalities not just in dreams and visions but also in ritual and in cinema. In each of these modes, ruins hold open ethical potential, the possibility of transformation of current states of affairs for both individuals and communities. I briefly analyze each of these modes of multiple temporality in this chapter and end with some thoughts on the persistent connection of Islam to the precolonial *elsewhen* in the dreamscapes and landscapes of contemporary North India.

THE ELSEWHEN OF RITUALS

> Whose are the stately whitewashed tombs? The Sufi saints. Whose
> are the dark abandoned tombs? Kings unknown. The contrast is
> vivid and dramatic.
>
> —Carl Ernst

Carl Ernst poses these questions, and their answers, while imagining a traveler looking down on the sanctified landscape of Khuldabad, a prominent Sufi center in the Deccan, but these questions could be asked of almost any Indo-Islamic landscape in contemporary India. It is only the tombs, and the memory, of Muslim saints that continue to be venerated and renovated by local communities, whereas the memories of Muslim kings have faded away now, a forgetting epitomized by the darkness and dilapidation of royal tombs.

At Firoz Shah Kotla we see a somewhat different paradigm; here, a dark, abandoned royal palace becomes a site of veneration. It is precisely this darkness and ruination of Firoz Shah Kotla, which index its disjuncture from the time of the contemporary city, that make it a sacred space. The king is still unknown here. Almost none of the regulars here have heard of, or speak about, Sultan Firoz Shah Tughlaq, during whose reign this citadel was constructed. But despite this absence of "historical consciousness," people's ritual relationships with this monument indicate a remarkable connection to the medieval (what I think of as the) past.[6] Take the case of the letters deposited to the jinn-saints at Firoz Shah Kotla.

In the account of the historian Muhammad Qasim "Ferishta," at the beginning of Firoz Shah Tughlaq's reign, the sultan installed a marble plaque near the center of the newly constructed mosque at Firoz Shah Kotla, on which the following was inscribed: "I have taken pains to discover the surviving relations of all persons who suffered from the wrath of my late Lord and master, Mahomed Tughlak, and . . . have caused them to grant their full pardon and forgiveness to that Prince in the presence of the holy and learned men of his age, whose signatures and seals as witnesses are affixed to the documents . . . which have been procured . . . and put into a box . . . and deposited into a vault in which Mahomed Tughlak is entombed" (Page 1937, 9).

The importance of documents, letters of forgiveness with the seals of spiritual authority, to guarantee the salvation of Muhammad Tughlaq's (r. 1325–51) soul is strikingly apposite, given the importance of letters in the accounts of his cruelty. The Moroccan traveler and *qadi* Ibn Batuta, who served in the court of Muhammad Tughlaq for several years, tells us:

> One of the most serious reprehensions against the Sultan [Muhammad Tughlaq] is that he forced the inhabitants of Delhi into exile. The cause of it was this. They used to write letters containing abuses and scandals, and they would seal the letters writing on the cover—"By the head of his Majesty none except he should read the letter." These letters they used to throw into the council chamber in the course of the night. When he tore them open he found abuses . . . so he resolved to lay Delhi waste. (Ibn Batuta 1976, 94)

We know from Ibn Batuta (1976, 84) again, prior to his telling us of the desolation of Delhi, that on two days a week Muhammad Tughlaq used to sit personally for *an nazar fil Mazalim* (the consideration of injustices) in a large open hall. In this he seems to have been following the exhortations of the eleventh-century Persian scholar and statesman Nizam al-Mulk Tusi, who wrote in his *Siyasat-Nama* (*The Book of Government*), "It is absolutely necessary that on two days in the week the king should sit for the redress of wrongs . . . to give justice, and listen to the words of his subjects with his own ears, without any intermediary. It is fitting that some written petitions should also be submitted if they are comparatively important, and he should give a ruling on each one" (Nizam al-Mulk 1960, 14). This legal form of direct access and complaint to the king was known as the *shikwa*, a word that still carries the connotation of grievance or complaint in modern Hindi-Urdu. On those two days, only four chamberlains, or *hujjab*, stood before the king, including the sultan's cousin (and later successor) Firoz Shah Tughlaq. If they did not accept the shikwas (complaints), the petitioners could then address the complaints directly to the sultan (Ibn Batuta 1976, 84).[7]

Matthew Hull (2012, 88–104) alerts us to the rooting of contemporary subcontinental practices of submitting petitions to the bureaucracy in precolonial South Asian political traditions. But even with such continuities in mind, to find petitions that are strangely resonant of a fourteenth-century legal form being deposited in a fourteenth-century Tughlaq palace more than five centuries after its initial abandonment is striking. At Firoz Shah Kotla we see the past manifest in ritual while being absent in narrative or "historical consciousness." How do we understand the fact that although the geographies of the city are drastically altered, and the history of the city barely remembered by those who come here, they are engaging in a practice remarkably similar to one extant in the fourteenth century? How did these rituals reemerge in the last quarter of the twentieth century? And how were they transformed into this new ritual form, where multiple photocopies of letters addressed to jinns are deposited in many alcoves across the ruins? Why did this writing of letters to jinns in a new-old legal form in the ruins of a medieval palace become a fitting ritual action for thousands of people in late twentieth-century Delhi?

.   .   .

Ritual, Seligman et al. (2008) argue, is subjunctive, imagining and ordering the world *as if*, in opposition to the way its practitioners know the real world to be. There is incongruity, rather than coherence, "between the world of enacted ritual and the participant's experience of lived reality" (20). Ritual performs the way the world could be, the way the world *should be*, as opposed to what it is.

Yeh insaf ki jagah hai (This is a space of justice), people say of Firoz Shah Kotla. The ritual of depositing letters in these ruins posits a world where the sovereign is still personally obliged to read every petition addressed to him. This contrasts sharply with most people's actual experience of government, marked by police violence and extortion, rampant corruption, the inaccessibility of higher officials, and the disappearance of documents. The presence of the jinn-saints in the ruins of a fourteenth-century royal palace, a location of precolonial Islamic sovereignty, is an image, a counter-memory of precolonial ideas of justice "flashing up" against the violence and illegibility of the postcolonial state.[8]

The characterization of Firoz Shah Kotla as a space of justice is shared with other dargahs and mazars across the subcontinent. They are part of a larger ritual vocabulary that Carla Bellamy (2011) refers to as "dargah culture," the unique culture of shrines identified as "Muslim holy places," which are also open to non-Muslims for prayer and supplication. Such shrines are usually (but not always) built around the grave of a Muslim holy man and are revered by Muslims and Hindus. Justice, in Bellamy's analysis, is central to the understanding of the ritual and efficacy of Muslim holy places. As her work on the shrine of Husain Tekri Sharif shows, the legitimacy of Muslim shrines continues to derive from their use of court symbols and legal language. Pilgrims (non-Muslim and Muslim) are still healed in the modalities of justice by bearing witness to what has been done to them and by having their testimony witnessed by both fellow victims and saints. Dargahs, as Bellamy notes, continue to offer pilgrims a means to seek justice and judgment with real-world consequences.

This unique culture is linked to what Muzaffar Alam (2004) has called "the Sufi intervention" in the politics of premodern Indian Muslim states. To simplify Alam's thesis, the Islamic polities of premodern India dealt with the "problem" of having a largely non-Muslim population by following political theory with an expansive understanding of sharia, inclusive of the laws and lifeways of other communities. In the Indian subcontinent this political theory was closely linked to articulations of the Islamic philosophy/theology of *wahdat al-wujud*, the unity of all being, usually traced back to Ibn 'Arabi; and the Sufis who believed and practiced this doctrine (which made them stand in opposition to more sectarian understandings of Islam) also made a deliberate intervention in politics from the thirteenth century onward, giving an ethical direction to the state, orienting it to a justice commensurate with their political theology. Alam's thesis is the most elegant historical explanation for why the ritual and built forms of Sufi dargahs are so similar to those of premodern royal courts; and why, as Bellamy notes, the healing power of dargahs is (still) linked to ideas of justice and judgment, even for non-Muslims. The legalistic nature of dargah rituals, rather than just making parallel claims to sovereignty (Eaton 2003), was always subjunctive, enacting justice as it *should be*, not necessarily as it was.[9] An anecdote reproduced by Muzaffar Alam from the *Akhlaq-e Jahangiri*, a treatise on ethics for rulers written in the reign of the seventeenth-century Mughal emperor Jahangir, illustrates this:

> Dular, the eunuch, the *hakim* of Panipat, had imprisoned a Hindu on the pretext of a crime then released him on payment of a huge sum. But the *hakim* . . . pressed for more money. The Hindu then fled and took shelter in the hospice of the Shaikh [Sharaf al-Din]. When Dular heard about this, he insisted that the shaikh hand over the fugitive and threatened him with dire consequences. . . . The shaikh did not budge. Subsequently, the hakim decided to ride to the hospice. . . . But no sooner did he enter the threshold of the hospice than the hakim was thrown from his horse's back . . . and instantly killed. . . . The shaikh did not touch him; he had simply hit the wall with his prayer carpet when he noticed Dular entering. . . . And then he wrote to the Sultan: "Brother 'Ala al-Din Khalji, keeper (*shahna*) of Delhi territory, accept greetings from Sharaf of Panipat, and then note that I have slapped Dular and sent him up to the sky. He had turned insane and had begun giving trouble to the people of God. Send another person here as soon as you get this letter or else the *shahna* of Delhi will also be dismissed. (Alam 2004, 73–74)

. . .

The coming of the British colonial regime severed the connections between Muslim piety, Sufi ideals of justice and ethics, and the practice of law (Kugle 2001; Liebeskind 1998). The growing incongruity between the practice of law and the ideals of justice perhaps only served to increase the emphasis on justice in the rituals of dargah spaces.[10] As Bellamy points out, this ritual vocabulary of justice continues at dargahs despite the colonial and postcolonial disconnect of Sufi circles from the realms of administration and lawgiving. At many Muslim saint shrines, such as the shrine of Bade Sarkar in Budayun, Uttar Pradesh, as documented by Iram Ghufran (2011), there is a culture of petitioning the saints that is very similar to the legal form of the *shikwa*, which was prevalent, as we have seen, in Tughlaq courts. The rituals at Sufi shrines continued the memory of precolonial political forms.

The popularity of petitions began at Firoz Shah Kotla only after the Emergency of 1975–77, a period of brutal autocratic rule. At protests against government actions and policies in Delhi, one can occasionally hear the slogan, *Tughlaqshahi nahin chalegi* (Tughlaq rule will not do). The historical record has not been kind to Muhammad Tughlaq, who has become a byword for arbitrary and tyrannical government. But at the same time, people deposit letters in the ruins of a Tughlaq palace, asking for an intimate justice far beyond the capacities, or the political imagination, of the contemporary state.[11]

Perhaps the history that is remembered through ritual is not about what really was but what *could have been*. If Ibn Batuta is to be believed, it was the very mechanism of justice, the ability of people to deposit letters of complaint to be read solely by the sultan, that led to the depopulation of Delhi. Perhaps in rituals we encounter the past not as a closed chapter but as an open field of potentiality—*what could have been, but wasn't, but could be now, perhaps?*[12]

In a city where, if you're poor, the state of Emergency[13] is not the exception but the rule, in the dark ruins of a Tughlaq palace, the letters come, in multiple photocopies, as if deposited to the various departments of a modern bureaucracy:

> Sarkar[14] I am unemployed and I cannot find work anywhere and if I find work somewhere he doesn't give me money and troubles me instead. Sarkar, I pray to you . . . to turn your generous gaze on me and get rid of my troubles.

> There is a policeman who has been troubling my husband, may he leave Seelampur forever, may he be transferred somewhere else. May Allah grant my husband relief from these policemen. . . . You are a saint and a lover of Allah, please make all our troubles end. . . . If we could get 20,000 rupees from somewhere. Our honour is at stake. It's the matter of our daughter. Please pray to Allah that we get that money from somewhere. . . . I saw you clearly in my dream, so clearly. . . . If you are a jinn, help us in whatever way you can.

> Moin, the son of _____ living in _____ mohalla is locked up in jail in the case of abducting Haji _____'s daughter. Zinda Pir Baba,[15] I have a request for you. That my brother be released from jail at the soonest.

The land of Kam ... s/o _____ is Khata number 1*4, _____

village, _____ Khasra no. 279/#. ... Ya Allah please fulfil the poor man's

wish, may our work be completed without any obstruction or conflict. We are

all your slaves, your children. Please fulfil our desire, and our belief. Let the

documents of our land be released as soon as possible, let the decision be in our

favour, let no one even know about it, and our work be done. Ya Allah, we have

suffered a lot of grief, seen a lot of poverty. If you desire it everything is possible.

Baba sahib *pak*, the plaint is that our niece, whose name is K _____, has

been missing for 21 days. ...

THE ELSEWHEN OF DREAMS

The structure that is known as Pir Ghaib is all that remains of a four-

teenth-century hunting lodge built by Firoz Shah Tughlaq (fig. 5). It stands

on the crest of the hilly Delhi Ridge and would have been northwest of

the city of Firozabad. Today, it stands within the residential quarters of the

FIGURE 5. The Ruins of the Observatory at the Ridge in Delhi: Pir Ghaib
in 1858. *Attributed to Felice Beato, c. 1858–59. Source: The Alkazi Collection of
Photography.*

Hindu Rao Hospital, and despite now being surrounded by buildings on three sides, it still offers commanding views over much of North and West Delhi. The name of this place given in the chronicles becomes immediately understandable from atop the roof of the building—*Kushk-i Jahan Numa*, the Palace of World Viewing. Since at least the early 1820s, when it is mentioned in passing in Mirza Sangin Beg's *Sair al-Manazil* (1982, 191), and possibly long before, it was also the venerated shrine of *Pir Ghaib*, the invisible saint. But Pir Ghaib seems to have become a popular dargah only in the years after 1857, the year of the Great Rebellion, the year that marked the end of Mughal sovereignty and the brutal destruction of the lifeways and physical structures of Mughal Delhi.

An account of a Thursday at the shrine of Pir Ghaib in 1882 was written by the famous Urdu writer Rashid-ul-Khairi (1868–1936) in 1933, based on his childhood memories. Rashid-ul-Khairi was known as *musavvir-e gham*, the painter of sorrow, and his diverse writings—novels, short stories, essays—are marked by a deep nostalgia for and valorization of the precolonial world and its ways of life. Writing fifty years after the events he is describing, in an essay entitled *Jahan abad ka ujra hua saman* (The ravaged picture of a [once] populated world), Rashid-ul-Khairi (2010, 108–10) is already mourning the passing of the *mela* (fair) of Pir Ghaib, its fading away from the calendar of the city: "Among the blossoms of Delhi that were uprooted along with the passing of Delhiwallahs (the old-time inhabitants of Delhi) was the fair of Pir Ghaib, which the people of Delhi celebrated for years *after the Rebellion*. Every Thursday from 4 o clock people would gather and the people of art and skill would show off their wonders and get praises" (my emphasis). Rashid-ul-Khairi then gives a vivid description of the massive crowds that came up from Shahjahanabad to participate in the mela, and the different activities they would be engaged in, from wrestling to grilling kababs. Crucially, Rashid-ul-Khairi relates the mela of Pir Ghaib to the exile and death of the last Mughal emperor of Delhi:

> The Christian year 1882 is close to its end. It's been twenty years since the Emperor died, but time is confronting the emotions of the people of Delhi with its full force. The beauty of their faith has not been annihilated yet, they

remember their emperor in moments of happiness and sadness. And even if the lullabies of eternal separation have patted them to sleep and closed their eyes, the scars scorched on the heart come forth in some fashion or the other. ... From the broken platform of the dargah the call to prayer would echo in the wilderness. ... After the *durud*, there were prayers of forgiveness for the Emperor. At this time, there was nothing in particular to affect hearts, but it would be hard to find a stony hearted one from whose eyes the tears were not streaming.

The particular gathering at Pir Ghaib that Rashid-ul-Khairi describes seems to have commemorated the twentieth anniversary of the death of the last Mughal emperor, Bahadur Shah Zafar. After the rebellion, and the brutal British sacking of Delhi, the emperor was tried and exiled. He died in Rangoon in November 1862, far from his home, and the British promptly acted to erase all traces of his grave (Dalrymple 2006, 3–4). The spot that Bahadur Shah Zafar had selected for his own burial in Delhi remains empty to this day in the courtyard of the shrine of Qutbuddin Bakhtiyar Kaki in the suburb of Mehrauli. One of the couplets attributed to the Emperor, also a well-regarded Urdu poet, achieved great posthumous fame:

Kitna hai badnasib Zafar dafan ke li'e
Do gaz zamin bhi na mili ku-e yar men

How unfortunate is Zafar, that for his burial
He could not even get two yards in the street of the beloved.

In her article on the revolt in Delhi and its afterlife, Nayanjot Lahiri reminds us that "while the British commemoration of their victory was deliberate, creating as it were, a palpable 'landscape of heroism and conquest' that can be archaeologically located, hardly any physical traces of the resistance offered by Delhi's residents exist. A populace that has been brutally suppressed cannot be expected either to commemorate sites of resistance or to set up memorials" (2003, 36). The whole of the northern Ridge was made into hallowed ground for visiting British tourist-pilgrims, full of memorials and inscriptions recounting British actions and sacrifices during the Siege of Delhi. Pir Ghaib, or the "Observatory," had been at the epicenter of the fighting during 1857. It was one of the landmark British positions on the Ridge from which rebel-held Delhi was besieged and bombarded.

In post-1857 Delhi, in a colonized and shattered landscape, the emperor, buried in an unmarked grave in a faraway land, was mourned at the shrine of an invisible saint—one who, according to legend, left no physical trace behind. This act of mourning—and celebration—happened in the very heart of the British "landscape of heroism and conquest." Two significant absences mobilized people to traverse weekly—and reinscribe—a landscape of colonial conquest.[16]

Despite the absence and invisibility of the saint's physical remains, Pir Ghaib continues to be present in the dreams of the community that gathers around his dargah. The formation of the community around his grave can be attributed to dreams. In 2006 I spoke to Rahmat Ali, then the caretaker of Pir Ghaib, and he told me that his great-grandfather had started coming to Pir Ghaib on Thursdays, in the aftermath of 1857. In his story, a group of Muslim men left Delhi for Haj. One of them was a man called Ashraf Ali, from Paharganj. Returning to a city devastated by 1857, one day Ashraf Ali was wandering through what was still largely a wilderness landscape when he came upon Pir Ghaib. Climbing up to one of the inner chambers of the ruin, he fell asleep, and the saint appeared to him in his dream, asking him to take care of his shrine. He came back every week after and lived to be more than a hundred years old.[17] Twenty-five years after 1857, in Rashid-ul-Khairi's account, a massive congregation from the old city was gathering at Pir Ghaib and being moved to tears by the memory of an emperor who had been lost to them after the brutal British crushing of the rebellion. And although the congregation of Pir Ghaib is much smaller today, it has continued, and the major proportion of people who come to Pir Ghaib, and find succour for their problems and ailments, are from a village that was displaced as a direct consequence of 1857.

Chandrawal is a predominantly Gujjar village, now surrounded by the post-Partition expansion of Kamala Nagar and Delhi University. The Gujjars are a pastoralist community who have traditionally had a somewhat antagonistic relationship with the urban settlements of Delhi. In the tumult of 1857 the Gujjars of Chandrawal village, among other things, sacked the estate of Thomas Metcalfe, which was built on their grazing grounds. In retaliation the British confiscated much more of their land after 1857 for the expansion of the European Civil Lines, and the village was relocated from near the river to its present location to make way for the Chandrawal waterworks.[18] The marble plaque outside the village *chaupal* (gathering place) of Chandrawal reads:

> This is the historic chaupal of those who sacrificed their lives and property to help India gain its Independence during the Independence Movement of 1857 and shocked and awed [*chhakke chhuda diye*] the English government and had the name of their village Chandrawal written in gold letters in the history of independence. . . .

In Chandrawal I met Vijindar Khari, the son of the honorary *pradhan* of the village. Khari is active in the real estate business and in state-level politics in Delhi. When I asked him about the history of Pir Ghaib, he seemed perplexed. "The history is written on the board in front of the building," he said.[19] "Have you read it?" he asked me. "What does it say?"

I told him that I knew the history written on the board, that this monument was built by Firoz Shah Tughlaq and that a saint came to inhabit the building and mysteriously vanished while praying so that the building is now known as Pir Ghaib. But, I continued, I wanted to know more about the history of the relationship of the people of Chandrawal to the pir. Khari said that what I was asking was contradictory. "There are two different things," he said. "One is the history of buildings, how they are built and who built them, and the ASI deals with that from a conservation (*sanrakshan*) point of view. Then there is the other thing—people's *manyata*, what they believe in, the things that happen in their own experience that they could write about, but then who would believe them?"

He then told me about his own experience of the pir. He was about to lose a finger that had become infected and had turned black. The doctor had suggested amputation, and Vijindar had agreed. But that night his father had a dream. The baba came in his dream and brought out a finger from his *jhola* (bag), but it was too big to replace the one on Vijindar's hand. The baba addressed Vijindar affectionately in his father's dream and brought out another finger but this one didn't fit either. Then he brought out a third finger and this time it fit perfectly. In the morning his father told Vijindar that he shouldn't get his finger amputated because the baba had come to him in his dream and told him that his son's finger would be saved. The next day, Vijindar went to see a new doctor at a public hospital in Shahdara, in East Delhi across the river, despite his own misgivings about traveling from the relatively posh and upmarket "VIP" North Delhi area to impoverished and dirty Shahdara. When the doctor met him, he kept working on his finger for half an hour and Khari didn't even notice because the doctor kept talking to him. Within three changes of dressings (corresponding to the three fingers in the dream), the doctor cured my finger completely, he said. He held his index finger up. There was not the least sign of scarring or discoloration. "So this is my experience [*tajurba*]," he said, "and everyone in Chandrawal and the surrounding areas has similar experiences, and we believe in the baba, so this is why even the board up there had to include the baba in the history they chose to tell."

.   .   .

Vijindar Khari sees it as exceptional that Pir Ghaib became part of the historical narrative of Firoz Shah Tughlaq's hunting lodge. This is not only because he sees people's experiences as incommensurate with the stuff of history, which he sees as primarily being about how and why monumental buildings were built, and who built them, but also because people's experiences and beliefs linked to these ruins, including his own, are not about history as past but are suffused with the *presence* of the baba with whom they have a deeply personal bond.[20] Dreams, which announce the presence of the saint, make possible the formations of communities around these ruins. And these are communities not just of mourning but also of celebration. We see this in Rashid-ul-Khairi's description of the joyful weekly mela at Pir Ghaib and in the stories Vijindar Khari and his father told me of the exuberant annual processions, with dancing and drumming, that would head up the hill from Chandrawal village to the shrine of Pir Ghaib to celebrate Holi. Saintly dreams, as in Vijindar Khari's story, predict the future. They do not report what has happened but what *could* happen (Koselleck 2004, 210), like the potential cure of Khari's finger or, in other accounts, the winning numbers in informal lotteries (*satta*). But the presence of saints in people's dreams and saintly predictions of future potentials are inextricably tied to medieval ruins, indexing the fourteenth century. As dreams do in contemporary Egypt, in Delhi, too, "they allow for multiple temporalities to coincide, overlap, and at times blend into one another. . . . They enable contacts with the spirits of those who have long been dead . . . indexed . . . by the 'strange clothes' worn by people who seem 'as though they came from another time.' . . . While dream visions often evoke the future, informing or warning the dreamer of what is about to happen, they can thus also let figures of the past enter the present" (Mittermaier 2011, 126). The dreams of the saints in Delhi disrupt the linear, chronological progression of historical time, where the subject of study is irrevocably in the past, but they still significantly index the medieval.

THE OPTICAL (UN)CONSCIOUS: THE ELSEWHEN
OF CINEMA AND OTHER DREAM-IMAGES

Manohar Lal lives in East Delhi, across the river, but was born in a historic suburb of Old Delhi called Paharganj, in the locality of Nabi Karim, very close to the fourteenth-century shrine of Qadam Sharif. His wife's family is from Sitaram Bazar in Old Delhi. Manohar Lal's father-in-law, who believed in the baba, the saint of Firoz Shah Kotla, and had been serving him (*baba ki seva kari*) for seventy years, from the time of his own childhood, used to tell Manohar Lal to pray to the saints, but Manohar never thought that there could be any profit from such things. Around 1990, a decade into his marriage, things started going wrong for him financially, and he went to *mullahs, maulvis, sayanas,* and *bhagats* (various categories of healers, both Hindu and Muslim) for help, but nothing worked for him. This was also the time when his father-in-law died.

One day, shortly after his father-in-law's death, Manohar Lal came to central Delhi to meet a client, but he didn't get the cash advance he had been hoping for. He had no money, not even for the bus ticket back home. Since he was near Old Delhi, he decided to go to his *sasural*, his in-laws' home in Sitaram Bazaar, where he was sure he would get some lunch and some money with which to get home. When he got there, his mother-in-law had gone to the market, and his brothers-in-law, who stayed on the floor above, didn't even ask him if he wanted a glass of water.

As he sat waiting in the front room, he turned toward the niche in the wall dedicated to the *baba*[21] and, for the first time, spoke directly to the saint: "Look Baba, I sit here hungry and thirsty in front of you. I've tried everything I can but I can't even be sure of my children having enough to eat. Do something, please. I am your son-in-law after all. If not for me, do something for your daughter, the one who left from your door. Baba, you are useless and worthless, you don't understand anything." (On Muslim saints as father figures of daughters see Chapter 4.)

After saying these words in anger, Manohar Lal left. A few days later, at a quarter to five on a Thursday morning, just before the *azan* from the nearby mosque, he had a visionary dream in which the saint appeared to him and said, "Son, come to us in the Kotla, we will see about your matter." Some *Mulla Ji* (Muslim preacher, a term often used disparagingly by both Hindus and Muslims) is speaking some nonsense, Manohar Lal thought, and ignored the dream. He ignored the same dream a second time as well. The third time, the saint appeared in his dream, very, very angry. "I have never seen anyone as thick and shameless as you," the baba said to him in his dream. "I've been telling you to come to Kotla, that I will solve your problems, but you don't come." This time Manohar Lal didn't ignore the dream. He woke up and washed his face and when he came back to bed, the dawn *azan* (call to prayer) from the nearby mosque had begun, and his wife was awake. He told his wife about the dreams he had been having, every Thursday morning, in which an old Mulla, wearing a cap and with his back bent with age, kept telling him to come to the Kotla, that he would solve his problems. As soon as she heard this, his wife told him that this was their baba of the Kotla, and he was showing his kindness to Manohar Lal, so why didn't he go? After he started visiting Firoz Shah Kotla regularly, Manohar Lal's fortunes improved.

Amira Mittermaier notes that "visitational dreams" enable a mode of being in the world that disrupts the illusion of the autonomous self-possessed subject, calling attention to in-betweenness and interrelationality instead (2011, 2). Her interlocutors are reminded by their dreams of their connectedness to the living and the dead (171), highlighting their embeddedness in larger realities and larger communities (233). Manohar Lal's dreams of the baba reminded him of his connectedness to his dead father-in-law, who was a devotee of the saint. The obligation placed by the dream connected him to the Muslim saint and the community that gathers at Firoz Shah Kotla, Hindu and Muslim, many of whom have historical links to Old Delhi and its suburbs. The baba appeared to him just before the dawn azan, revealing how the rhythm of Islam, the particular ways in which the day is punctuated by calls for prayers, also informs the dreams and waking lives of non-Muslims.

Manohar Lal told me another story, about the time his youngest son Piyush was five or six years old. As he was very young, he still slept between his parents in their cramped apartment. Very early one morning, before dawn, Manohar Lal's wife shook him awake. Piyush was foaming at the mouth, and his eyes had rolled up into his head. When Manohar Lal picked him up in his arms, he found that the child had emptied his bowels, and he folded like cloth in his father's arms. He was dead, Manohar Lal said, finished. It was very early on Thursday morning, the baba's day.[22] "He died on your day, Baba; you are responsible for this," Manohar Lal screamed and cried. "I will no longer believe in you or serve you." Manohar Lal was in shock and could barely stand anymore. He woke up his younger brother, who lived next door, and the brother took Piyush's body from him to take him to Guru Tegh Bahadur Hospital, the nearest public hospital. They owned no vehicle at the time, so the brother stopped two policemen on patrol on a scooter, and one of them dropped the brother, holding Piyush in his arms, to the gate of the hospital. As they stopped at the gate, the brother saw an angel (*farishta*) descend from the air, hovering atop the gate. The angel wore a black blanket and carried a *fakiri katora* (a faqir's begging bowl) and a stick. The figure extended his hand, and a noose of light came out and caught the boy, and he started breathing. When Manohar Lal got to the hospital, Piyush was sitting up in bed, as if nothing had happened, laughing at his father—"Papa, I am fine, nothing's wrong with me, why did we come to the hospital?" Manohar Lal started crying. His son had died; he had seen and carried his lifeless body, yet here he was, alive again. In the morning the doctor discharged him, and when they were on their way back from the hospital, his brother told Manohar Lal what he had seen at the hospital gate that night. For more than a month after, the young child performed the gestures of *wudu/wuzu*, the ablutions that Muslims perform before prayer. And ever since then, the child, now a young man, has had a preference for eating chicken, traditionally associated with Muslims, rather than goat (sacrificed to the goddess Kali, and traditionally eaten by Hindus).

.   .   .

A ship departs for Jeddah from Bombay, carrying Haj pilgrims. Iqbal, the hero of *Coolie*, a popular Bollywood film from 1983, has a high fever and cannot board. He sends someone else to go on Haj on his behalf. As the ship departs, he stands on the dock singing the song *Madinewale ko mera salaam kehna* (Give my greetings to the one from Medina—i.e., the Prophet Muhammad). The departure of the ship is intercut with scenes of the Haj pilgrimage in the holy sites of Mecca and Medina and a caravan of camel riders crossing the desert. This in turn cuts to Iqbal, now dressed in white robes reminiscent of Sufis from the Mughal era, climbing up the *minar* of a ruined mosque atop a hill, while a storm gathers. As he pleads to the Prophet to save his mother, the scene keeps shifting back and forth between him and his mother, hooked up to a ventilator, battling for her life in a hospital. Finally, the storm breaks, and with a rumble of thunder, a noose of light appears from the sky, and enters the mother's hospital room.

Manohar Lal's brother saw a noose of light emerge from the hand of a black-blanketed figure, a figure recognizable in the Islamic tradition as the Prophet Muhammad, known affectionately as *Kali Kambli Wale* (the one with the black blanket/cloak).[23] The Prophet Muhammad, the noose of light, the hospital, the miraculous return to life—there are many elements in common to the cinematic depiction of a miracle in *Coolie*, and the story of a miracle witnessed and recounted on a dark night in Delhi some years later.

Did the cinematic depiction of the miracle affect the perception and the retelling of Piyush's return to life? Perhaps, though that is not the point I wish to make. Rather, I want to turn to the similarity of the image of the miracle, in both cinematic depiction and waking vision, to rethink the relation of the image to time, as well as to rethink our notions of religious tradition. If a cinematic miracle prefigures a religious experience, then how might that alter our understanding of religious tradition and its modes of transmission?

. . .

The annual Haj pilgrimage commemorates and reenacts the trials and triumphs of the family of Abraham. It was already ancient in the time of the Prophet Muhammad, who died in Medina in 632 CE. The song from *Coolie* brings the time of the Haj and the time of the Prophet together with the time of the ruin and the time of crisis, the mother's life ebbing in the hospital room. The noose of light crosses, in a flash of lightning, all these different planes of time and sears them together.

Many people have argued that Hindi cinema has long been an *Islamicate* cultural form (Kesavan 1994; Bhaskar and Allen 2009). *Islamicate* is a term that Marshall Hodgson first used to distinguish Islam *"in the proper, the religious, sense,"* from the "the social and cultural complex historically associated with Islam and the Muslims, both among the Muslims themselves and even when found among non-Muslims" (Hodgson 1974, 1:59). But the distinction between Islam as religion and Islamicate as culture doesn't hold up for much of Hindi cinema, which is marked by the "pervasiveness of religious imagery" (Dwyer 2006, 9). Kaushik Bhaumik (n.d.) shows how *Coolie* is actually a deeply theological text, an updating of the Sufi ideal of the *Insan-e kamil* (the perfected man), as a man of action. The Islamic miraculous—associated with Sufi saints, the Quran, and the Prophet—constantly intervenes in the film. Early in the narrative, the character of Iqbal, a railway station porter and union leader, is shown in close-up holding a falcon perched on one hand, while wearing the red livery of railway station porters, setting up resonance with the iconography of the renowned Sindhi saint Lal Shahbaz Qalandar. But *Coolie*, despite being a deeply Islamic film, is not entirely a Muslim film. The film was produced and directed by Manmohan Desai, a Gujarati Hindu. The lead role of the film was played by Amitabh Bachchan, one of Bombay cinema's best-known actors, born to Hindu and

FIGURE 6. *Publicity image from* Pakeezah *(1972, directed by Kamal Amrohi).*
Source: Victoria and Albert Museum, London.

Sikh parents, who on many occasions during his long and distinguished career has been cast as Muslim or as closely associated with Muslim characters.

Why was Muslimness such a dominant feature of Hindi cinema, in a Hindu majority country? Why were non-Muslims like Desai and Bachchan so deeply linked with the production of films that can be read as Islamic theological texts? Kaushik Bhaumik (2001), in his history of early Bombay cinema, asserts that "this cinema was directly heir to the courtly grandeur of post-Mughal successor state culture heavily derived from Mughal court practice itself" (198). Bhaumik explains this inheritance, in part, through the location of the cinema, both physically and conceptually, in the *bazar*. The bazar, or urban marketplace, was dominated by Muslim artisans, whose cultural world shared continuities with the Mughal world and with the world of post-Mughal successor states, such as Rampur, Hyderabad, and Awadh, which were very much part of the cultural landscape of early twentieth-century India.

FIGURE 7. *Women walking through the passages beneath the mosque at Firoz Shah Kotla. Photo by author.*

But the historical, market-based explanation for the presence of Islam in early Bombay cinema is insufficient to explain the persistence of Islam in the cinema of post-Partition India, where much of the Muslim elite left for Pakistan, there were massive disruptions of the shared lifeworlds of Hindus and Muslims, and the public culture of the new nation-state was (and is) increasingly pushed toward being more Sanskritized and recognizably "Hindu." It was in overwhelmingly Hindu-majority India, with increasingly restricted access to the Muslim spectators of Pakistan (especially after the war of 1965), that Hindi cinema produced the wildly successful "Muslim socials" of the 1960s, replete with Islamic imagery and a high-Persianate vocabulary and, by the late 1970s and early 1980s, films like *Muqaddar ka Sikandar* and *Coolie*, which, following Bhaumik, we can characterize as Sufi action films.

Crossing the divide of entertainment and piety, the enormously popular and financially successful Islamic films of Bombay cinema brought Islam (in the sense of Islamic theology and ethics) and the images (and linguistic markers) of Islam to Hindu majority audiences (fig. 6). These films, across the various genres of the Islamic film, are replete with what Deleuze would characterize as *crystal images*, images in which we *see time*, images in which the present and the past come together, and are indistinguishable (Deleuze 1989, 81–82). *Coolie*, released in 1983, is in some senses a remarkably "present" film, sympathetically addressing the labor unrest that had gripped Bombay in 1982, the year of the great Bombay textile strike. But despite its contemporaneity, many images in *Coolie* cross, as we have seen, multiple planes of time, bringing the past and present together. Iqbal, the worldly wise trade union leader, climbs the tower of an old, ruined mosque in white robes reminiscent of Mughal-era Sufis. In that moment the film partakes of a long tradition of Bombay Islamic films, across genres. In film after film the characters inhabit and walk through premodern architecture, in cityscapes marked by the arches, minarets, and battlements of precolonial Muslim architecture (Taneja 2009). People still do this today, walking through the ruins and arched corridors of Firoz Shah Kotla, a ruin to which many people, like Manohar Lal, have been brought by their dreams (fig. 7). Firoz Shah Kotla is a ruin that, as a visiting friend from Pakistan once told me, looks like a ruin from a Hindi film.[24]

. . .

A name that is central to popular accounts of Firoz Shah Kotla is that of Laddu Shah. Laddu Shah was at different points of his life a musician, a black marketeer of cinema tickets, and, finally, a healer. The story of his healing powers is always linked to Firoz Shah Kotla, of somehow gaining these powers from the jinns by coming here and then using these powers to heal. People remember him sitting on an elevated spot among the ruins and playing his *been* (a wind instrument with a built-in drone, usually associated with snake charmers). Some accounts say that he so charmed the jinns (*jinnat unke ashiq ho gaye*) with playing his music here that they gave him the gift of healing. It was Laddu Shah's gift of healing, in all accounts, that made people start coming to Firoz Shah Kotla.

Akhtar Ali remembers hearing Laddu Shah playing in Old Delhi many years ago. "It was the year that the movie *Phagun* had released," he said to me (which would make it 1973). It was a Thursday night on Chandni Chowk, the main commercial street of Old Delhi, and Akhtar was selling purses off the pavement, when Laddu Shah, not yet known by that name, came playing his *been* at the head of a procession to publicize the film.[25] He played the *been* so well, Akhtar remembers, that he was handsomely rewarded for it.

Soon after, he became a *blackiya*, a black marketeer of cinema tickets, at Jagat Cinema (a theater associated with a largely male, precariat labor audience in the southern part of Old Delhi). Being a *blackiya* was a lucrative career in 1970s India, in the days before TV and video, when the cinema was the main form of entertainment. Black-marketing was a profession marked by illegality and violence, *gundagardi* in the local parlance. Manohar Lal, who had only heard stories about Laddu Shah, told me *woh ek number ke gunde aur ayyash insan the. Yahan aye to unko gyan prapt ho gaya. Bure aye the, sudhar gaye, Baba ki kirpa se.* (He was a number-one hoodlum and libertine. When he came here, he gained knowledge. He came bad but was reformed by the grace of Baba.)

Jagat cinema closed down in 2006, and my quest to find someone who remembers Laddu Shah's days of black marketeering has so far proved fruitless. But Aarti Sethi's (2009) work around cinema halls in Delhi indicates many facets of black marketeers outside of the utter vilification heaped on them in official and elite discourse. The *gunda*, the tough, was often employed as a gatekeeper by the hall and was the "official" black marketeer of the neighborhood. This "officialness" of the black marketeer indicated the *gunda*'s involvement with and belonging to the neighborhood and the claims the (nonnormative, nonnational) neighborhood made upon the cinema, the space of the normative spectator-citizen. The gunda, often highly performative, was an insurrectionary, disruptive, strangely generous, and charismatic figure, one remembered with a certain fondness, his violent exploits rendered into epic narratives still told to inquisitive researchers. And the very nature of the gunda's work, his deep engagement with human desire (what spectators wanted to see) and his ability to bring desire into effect[26] (by obtaining and selling tickets—at a premium—in a milieu of tight constraint) makes Laddu Shah's evolution from black marketeer of cinema tickets to healer seem not an about-face but rather a smooth teleological continuity.

While he was making his life in the city, Laddu Shah, then known as Naim, visited Firoz Shah Kotla regularly, according to his son Chand. "He kept visiting," Chand told me, "because we were seven brothers and had no sister. So he would go to Firoz Shah Kotla to pray that a girl child may be born in his house. He used to go to a chamber underneath the pillar." Chand also attributes the development of the healing powers of Laddu Shah to Firoz Shah Kotla. "*Jo chiz thi unpe, woh unpe shuru se thi. Khuli yahan a ke, Kotla men. Yun kehte hain na ke achhon ki sangat main baith kar gyan badhta chala jata hai, par thi unpe bachpane se.*" (The thing that was upon him was on him from the beginning, but it became manifest by coming to Kotla. They say that when you are in good company your knowledge increases, but it was on him from childhood.)

He kept going to Kotla to pray for a girl, and slowly changes started happening within him, and his other work slowly stopped altogether. In Chand's account the reestablishment of prayer at the mosque in Firoz Shah Kotla is inextricably linked to Laddu Shah's first miracle, the miracle that definitively marked the end of his old life and the beginning of his new life as a healer. One day Laddu Shah, who by now had a small reputation in the Old City as someone who could foretell people's futures and suggest cures for their ills, looked toward the mosque at Firoz Shah

Kotla and said to himself, "This is Allah's house and it should be inhabited [*abad*]; may it be inhabited by any means." There was a boy in Suiwalan (a locality in Old Delhi) who was paralyzed from the waist down and thus couldn't stand or walk. Even doctors had failed to cure him. In Chand's account various healers had been brought together to see if any of them could cure the child, and a crowd of about two hundred had gathered to watch. The crowd laughed at his father at first; because Laddu Shah had a youthful face, without a beard, he looked too young for serious work like this. When his turn came to look at the child, Laddu Shah asked for two *laddus* (round sweets) and a *pan* (betel leaf) with tobacco. He put the pan in his mouth and took the laddus in his hand and gave the first one to the child, and said, "*Khara ho ja, Allah ke karam se*" (Stand up, by the grace of God). And the child sat up in bed, bolt-upright. Then Laddu Shah gave him the second laddu and told him, "By the grace of God, now run out of the room." And the child stood up and walked to the door. There was complete pandemonium (*hahakar*), especially since there was a prize of five thousand rupees offered for the cure. Laddu Shah said, "I don't want the money; I don't want anything. Tomorrow is Friday, and I want all of you gathered here to promise me that you will offer tomorrow's Friday congregational prayers at the mosque in Firoz Shah Kotla." The first congregational prayer at Firoz Shah Kotla was held the next day and led by Haji Latif, the child's father, a well-known Islamic scholar.

.   .   .

The cinematic *Coolie* doffs his working-class clothes and moves toward the ruin in the garb of a Sufi. Naim the *blackiya* becomes Laddu Shah by moving toward and into the ruins of Firoz Shah Kotla. Laddu Shah's life trajectory from cinema to the sanctified ruin reinforces the connections between the landscapes of Bombay cinema and the religious landscapes and dreamscapes I encountered in Delhi. In bringing together cinema, physical landscapes, and dreamscapes, I am inspired by the texture of conversations and experiences during my fieldwork in Delhi and also by Walter Benjamin's gnomic thoughts on dreams, history, and architecture in *The Arcades Project* (1999). Benjamin believed that although dreams are part of a collective unconscious, this unconscious is historical rather than ahistoric or mythic in the Jungian sense. For Benjamin the unconscious dream life of each generation picks up on the discarded objects of bygone eras, exemplified for him by the architectural form of the Paris arcades of the nineteenth century and the dusty bric-a-brac to be found in the shops still operating there, so significant and full of revolutionary potential for surrealist art in the twentieth century. He saw cinema as a revolutionary medium precisely because of its ability to draw on and to transform the "optical unconscious." Following Benjamin, I believe that Bombay cinema's *Islamicness* originates in its need to conform to the collective dream-life of North India. But why is this dream-life, for both Hindus and Muslims, so suffused with Islam?

Earlier in this chapter I indicated a dialectical relationship between the experience of the postcolonial state and the memory of precolonial political theory. We see this dialectical relationship crystallized in the image of photocopied petitions being deposited in the ruins of a medieval palace. Understanding the persistent linkage of Islam and the precolonial in cinema and dream requires an expansion of this argument and a radically different understanding of Islam and its relation to time. Like the call to prayer from a mosque loudspeaker that pervades the dreams and daily rhythms of both Muslims and non-Muslims, Islam in South Asia spreads far beyond the limitations imposed by our modern conceptions of religion as coterminous with identity. Islam is metonymic of a whole complex of ethical orientations and remembered ways of being linked to the precolonial, not as a bygone era but as a still-present possibility of life or way of being.[27] This metonymic Islam exists in a dialectical relationship with ways of being brought about by colonialism, the postcolonial nation-state, and modern capitalism. The central problematic of the hugely popular "Muslim social" is the ability to live both an ethical life and a life of desire while negotiating both traditional familial codes of honor and a world of bewildering modern changes (Taneja 2010). As I show in the next two chapters, similar ethical dilemmas pervade the waking lives of those who come to Firoz Shah Kotla and are addressed by the medieval saints who appear in their dreams. *The present is the waking world to which the dream we name the past refers in truth.*[28]

The dream we name the past is also a dream of Islam. It is a dream in which the Prophet Muhammad appears to a Hindu and enacts a miraculous cure that is strangely reminiscent of one attributed to him in a blockbuster Hindi film. The Islamic tradition travels strange routes to strange destinations. Non-Muslims at Firoz Shah Kotla, like Manohar Lal, often have very Islamic bodily deportments while praying to the babas,[29] and their speech and letters written to the babas are replete with Islamic theological terms. In his influential essay "The Idea of an Anthropology of Islam," Talal Asad makes the point that anthropologists should understand Islamic practices not as timeless and essential but as part of an evolving debate or discursive tradition, which operates within a field of power and authorization. "A practice is Islamic because it is authorized by the discursive traditions of Islam, and is so taught to Muslims—whether by an 'alim, a *khatib*, a Sufi *shaykh*, or an untutored parent" (Asad 1986, 15). Asad's account of the discursive tradition, while it highlights the dynamism of tradition, is a linear account of transmission, parent to child, *shaykh* to murid. But what do we do with a tradition that is encountered not as authoritative discourse but, as it were, out of the corner of one's eye, in dreams and waking visions, in stories told by neighbors and strangers, in snatches of song playing on the radio? As Veena Das observes, "The heterogeneity of everyday life invites us to think of networks of encounter and exchange instead of bounded civilizational histories of Hinduism, Islam, or Christianity" (2013b, 80).

Asad's emphasis on thinking of orthodoxy as a relation of power has been truly valuable to the anthropology of Islam, but the subsequent emphasis in the anthropology of Islam on studying the life of revivalist, primarily legalist, discourse has, in some senses, served to obscure the ways in which the Islamic tradition travels and has traveled in stories, in gestures, and in cinema in ways that far exceed the ambit of Islamic discourse as produced in seminaries, legal rulings, and reformist tracts and practices. My concern here is not to set up an opposition between authorized discourse and the incoherence, ambiguities, and contradictions of "everyday Islam" (Fadil and Fernando 2015) but rather to broaden our understanding of both authority and tradition as they operate in everyday life. We need to rethink how Islamic authority interacts with, and is affected by, the realm of the popular, a popular that often transcends the bounds of religious identity. We need to rethink what the Islamic tradition is, the ways in which it is transmitted and debated, and who its recipients are.

.   .   .

When I presented the story of Manohar Lal's dreams at a talk at Columbia University in 2012, I was asked a question about conversion. Such a narrative of dream visitation and healing, Amen Jaffer noted, usually ends not just with the dreamer becoming a devotee of the saint but also converting to Islam. Yet despite the dreams making him a devotee of the saint, Manohar Lal did not become a Muslim.

"I have been to Makka-Madina in my dreams," he once told me. "I have been to the dargah of Mustafa Baba, which is just outside Makka-Madina, but I did not go inside. And once," he said, "Baba came into my dreams and said, 'If you start doing namaz in the mosque, then I will get your *nikah* (Muslim marriage) done.'" But Manohar Lal refused the offer. "'What about my wife?' I asked Baba," he said. "You are my *sasusral-wala*, you're from my wife's family, I can't do this."

Mustafa is an epithet for the Prophet Muhammad. With the geographical strangeness characteristic of dreams, Manohar Lal claims to have visited the Prophet's tomb without entering Mecca and Medina, spaces into which only Muslims are legally allowed. In his dreams he pays homage to the founder of the Islamic tradition without entering a space of exclusively Muslim identity. With the temporal strangeness of the dream, the figure of the Prophet Muhammad becomes linked to the saint of Firoz Shah Kotla, who is linked to his deceased father-in-law. He considers the baba so intimate as to be a part of the family, equivalent in some senses to his father-in-law, yet he refuses the baba's offer of becoming Muslim and (hence) marrying again. Becoming Muslim, converting, is a temptation for Manohar Lal, a possibility of selfhood that he ultimately resists.

How do we understand both this temptation and its resistance? I will start by considering the resistance first. One way to understand Manohar Lal's attraction to Islam, as exemplified by the babas, but his reluctance to identify as Muslim is to think of the context of post-Partition India, where a Muslim identity is a huge socioeconomic handicap.[30] In this interpretation Manohar Lal's waking self realizes the potential social, familial, and economic upheavals his decision will cause, and he wisely refrains from becoming Muslim. Another way of interpreting Manohar Lal's dreams is to think of them as staging a criticism of our current understandings of religion and community, where religion is now the dominant mode of one's identity; and the notion of conversion entails a total break from both one's previous interiority and one's previous social identity and intimate relations. *What about my wife?* Manohar Lal asks the baba. In this interpretation, by not letting his intimacy with the Muslim saint and his attraction to Islamic theology determine his social identity, Manohar Lal is following a long Indic tradition exemplified by groups such as the Satpanthis, who despite translating Islamic theology into Indic vernacular languages and forms, did not necessarily identify as either Hindu or Muslim (Sila-Khan 2004; Purohit 2012).

I end by considering a third possibility: perhaps Manohar Lal's continuing intimacy with the figure of the Muslim saint, despite his rejection of a Muslim identity, alerts us to ethical and theological possibilities inherent in Islam, traditions of a cosmopolitan hospitality toward strangers, including those who are strangers to Islam. The next three chapters are concerned primarily with rethinking the role of Islam in the popular religious and ethical life of North India.

CHAPTER 3

STRANGE(R)NESS

Islam began as something strange, and will revert to being strange
as it began, so give glad tidings to the strangers [*ghuraba*].

—Prophetic *Hadith*

Khusrau gharib ast o gada, uftadah dar shahr-e shoma
Bashad ke az behr-e Khuda, sue ghariban bangari

Khusrau is a stranger and a beggar, fallen into your city.
May it be, for God's sake, that you look in the direction of the strangers.

—Amir Khusrau Dehlavi, d. 1325

Sare rind-o bash jahan ke tujh se sujud men rahte hain
Banke terhe tirchhe tikhe sab ka tujhe Imam kiya

All the drunks and vagabonds of the world bow down to thee.
The dandies, the twisted, the bent, the sharp; they all deem you to be their
leader.

—Mir Taqi "Mir," 1723–1810

NAMELESS INTIMACY AND HOSPITALITY TO STRANGERS

It was a Thursday afternoon, and I was at Firoz Shah Kotla, as usual, making desultory conversation, when all of a sudden there was a current of
excitement. A group of twenty Western tourists had walked in and were
looking around. This was a pretty rare event for Kotla, as tourists, especially Western ones, hardly ever come here, unlike at the better-known
historical monuments of Delhi, and certainly not in a group this large.
I was planning to ignore them, but Ajay told me that, as the English
speaker among our group, I should go talk to them. It turned out that
they were a group of art history students from Northwestern University
being led around Delhi by a professor of Tibetan Buddhism, and they'd
come here to look at the Ashokan pillar.

While we were talking, another man who speaks a little English joined us and introduced himself to the art historians: "Myself Ashiq Ali." When the art historians had left for the pillar, Akhtar turned to Ashiq Ali and said, "I've known you for fifteen years now but you never told me your name before!" This was a moment of epiphany for me, when something I had noticed but not yet consciously put my finger on came sharply into focus: people seldom use names at Firoz Shah Kotla. It was the kind of space where it was quite possible to meet someone every week for fifteen or twenty years, have long conversations about politics and theology and personal ailments, pray for relief from each other's sufferings or curse each other out, and never know the other person's name. At most, people use descriptive nicknames—like *Kalakar* (artiste) for a person who likes to sing—or regional epithets—like *Kasabpure Wale* or *Laxminagar Wale* (from Kasabpura or from Laxminagar)—but even those were most often used as references when the person mentioned was not present. Until he introduced himself to the art historians, I had not known what Ashiq Ali's name was, even though we had spoken to each other on several occasions.

About a month after the art historians' visit Manohar Lal (who would have remained Lalaji to me had I not sat down for many interviews with him outside Kotla) told me a story about how, many years ago, when he used to come to Firoz Shah Kotla every day, he and Ashiq Ali (whom he gestured toward rather than naming) had been hanging out at Firoz Shah Kotla when they spontaneously decided to travel together to Sultan Ghari, a thirteenth-century tomb in the far south of the city, a good fifteen miles away. First they took the bus to Mehrauli, ten miles away, and visited the dargah of Ashiq Allah, in the forest outside Mehrauli. Then they walked through what was all still jungle until they reached the tomb of Sultan Ghari, another three or four miles away. They spent a whole day in each other's company, on bus and on foot and at the shrines. "So what's his name?" I asked Manohar Lal. "I don't know," he said; "I've never asked him. You know I never ask anyone's names here."

Two men went off and had a daylong adventure in each other's company, riding buses, walking through forests, eating, visiting shrines, without feeling the need to ask each other their names. People sit together in groups in the lawns here every Thursday and speak sometimes of the most intimate of problems, of disease, of debt, of the death of loved ones, without wishing, or trying, to know each other's names. They speak of their beliefs, their life histories, and their perception of miracles to an ethnographer whose name they never ask.[1]

I began to think of this ethics of nameless intimacy at Firoz Shah Kotla as characteristic of *gharib nawazi*, the culture of hospitality to the stranger, which I believe accounts for the healing and transformative power of dargahs, or Muslim saint shrines.[2] Gharib Nawaz is the popular honorific of the Sufi saint Muin-ud-Din Chishti (d. 1230), whose dargah is the most popular one in the Indian subcontinent. In turning to the title of the saint of Ajmer to think of the ethics of intimacy at Firoz Shah Kotla, I am drawing on Carla Bellamy's (2011, 4) argument that people recognize Muslim shrines as "being of the same fundamental type, and fundamentally connected with one another." I also started thinking about the phrase *Gharib Nawaz* because so many people at Firoz Shah Kotla, across communities, were talking about going to the dargah of Gharib Nawaz in Ajmer that year. At the same time, the song *Khwaja Mere Khwaja*—from the recent movie *Jodhaa Akbar* (dir. Ashutosh Gowariker, 2008), with its opening invocation "*Ya Gharib Nawaz*"—kept playing on the radio and the TV, forming an integral part of the soundscape.

The anonymity of everyday interaction at Firoz Shah Kotla allows for the possibilities of a kinship that transcends the usual boundaries of family and community. Here, people's intimacy is premised on their being strangers to one another. One time when we are all sitting around in the lawns at Firoz Shah Kotla, one of the regulars, who was Hindu, said that 75 percent of people who come to dargahs are Hindus.[3] Everyone nodded in agreement, including the Muslims present. Then he said that the people who go most to dargahs are people from Pehelwan's *qaum* (community or caste). Everyone nodded in agreement again.

It is reflective of the ethics of nameless intimacy that Pehelwan's qaum was never explicitly mentioned. Pehelwan (literally "Wrestler," for he used to be one in his youth—his given name is known but never used) is from the *Balmiki* or *Valmiki* caste. In other words, he is from the Bhangi or sweeper caste, whose traditional work was cleaning the streets and drains and carrying away the shit of the city. This is not something that anyone else at Firoz Shah Kotla ever mentioned to me. Pehelwan told me himself, several months into my research, after we had become good friends. Today, despite affirmative action and education that has benefited their community, a large number of Balmikis are still employed to clean the sewers of the city and perform other kinds of cleaning jobs, still considered to be the lowest class of menial labor (Prashad 2000). Pehelwan himself had cleaned floors, though in the service of a multinational banking corporation. Pehelwan's caste traditionally stayed outside of the main village settlements in the Delhi hinterland, and elsewhere, and weren't allowed to pray in upper-caste Hindu temples, or even formally egalitarian mosques, because they were ritually impure (Lee 2015). But you wouldn't know this from a regular Thursday visiting Firoz Shah Kotla, where you would see Pehelwan as a respected member of our motley congregation of Hindus and Muslims, a man whose friendship and opinion mattered to those who gathered there and whose feet people sometimes touched to ask for his blessings.

I began to understand, through the not-naming of Pehelwan's caste even when it was spoken of, the ethics of *gharib nawazi* as defying communal identification, for names (as opposed to epithets) are easy markers of religious and caste identity.[4] This makes the care that people take to avoid explicit caste and religious identification while interacting with each other in this space quite remarkable. This is a radical suspension of the norms of social interaction in North India, where it is fairly commonplace for people to inquire after the other's caste and religion on first meeting,[5] and where there has been a recent surge in Hindu upper-caste violence against Dalits and Muslims.

In everyday Hindi-Urdu *gharib* means "poor," and *gharib nawaz* usually translates as something like "pro-poor" or "protector of the poor." This translation misses many of the nuances of *gharib* present in Persian and Arabic and literary Urdu.

> In Urdu, "Foreign, alien; strange, wonderful; rare, unusual, extraordinary;— poor, destitute; meek, mild, humble, lowly;—a stranger, foreigner, an alien;— a poor man; a meek or humble person." (Platts 2000, 770)

In Persian, "Uncommon, strange, outlandish, foreign; extraordinary; rare; a foreigner, stranger; poor, needy; humble, gentle, docile." (Steingass 2000, 886)

In Arabic, the gh-r-b root denotes, "to go away, depart, absent, withdraw, leave, to be a stranger; to be strange, odd, queer, obscure, abstruse, difficult to comprehend . . . to say or do a strange and amazing thing; to exceed the proper bounds, overdo, exaggerate . . . to laugh noisily or heartily, guffaw, to go to a foreign country, emigrate; to be (far) away from one's homeland; to become an occidental, become Westernized, be Europeanized; to find strange, odd, queer, unusual; to deem absurd, preposterous, grotesque." (Wehr 1976, 668)

Gharib Nawaz, with all these older valences of the word, means not just one who is kind to the poor but one who is "courteous to strangers; kind to the poor, hospitable." Thinking about gharib nawazi made me think about *gharibi*, poverty. What is the link between poverty and strange(r)ness, both denoted by *gharibi*? Is it that Arabic, Persian, and Urdu hold the potential of imagining being foreign or strange as *a poverty of social relationships*, being estranged (and hence impoverished) by distance or by circumstances? Perhaps these languages hold open the potential of seeing estrangement as a lack, a poorness in the quality of one's social world? The more I thought about *gharibi*, strange(r)ness, the more I realized the multiple valences of the word, as they applied to Firoz Shah Kotla and to other dargahs in India. To be gharib can mean to be mad, to be outcast, to be estranged from family and friends, to be transgressive, to be polluted, to be unable to repay your debts—to be, in some fundamental sense, alone, unable to fit into normative society. In describing the importance of Firoz Shah Kotla in his life, Manohar Lal once said to me, "*Main ganda sanda jaisa bhi aaya hun, unhonen mujhe sambhala hai*" (In whatever condition I've come to him, however dirty and unclean I am, he has taken care of me). The *dar-gah*, the space of the door, the threshold, opens its doors to all strangers. But the *gharibi*, the strange(r)ness encountered here, is not just abject but also productive of new possibilities. Being estranged from one's family and communal identity is often the beginning of the remaking of the self and its relation to the world.[6] This is to say that the dargah is a space for ethical self-fashioning and hence of the practice of human freedom.[7]

I make this assertion while acknowledging that what it means to be human, what it means to be a self, and what it means to be free are certainly not settled questions.[8] The narratives of healing that are told at Firoz Shah Kotla, which I explore later in this chapter, also radically unsettle the idea of a bounded individual self acting on her own free will. Yet these narratives are also narratives of rebellion, of radical self-transformation, of claiming one's desire.

What does it mean to come to the door of those who are *Gharib Nawaz*, hospitable to strangers? Conventional understandings of morality emphasize the adherence to social norms and authoritative rules and traditions as being primarily constitutive of morality. But such understandings of both morality and tradition leave no room for understanding ethical articulations of the self that are opposed to dominant social mores (Laidlaw 2002). At Firoz Shah Kotla I came across countless challenges to the hierarchical order and patriarchal norms that are the dominant understandings of "Indian culture" today, as articulated by Hindu (and Muslim, Sikh, and Christian) upper-caste male speakers, norms that are often enforced both by familial violence and by the violence of the mob. But we see similar challenges to "traditional" values of family and society becoming ethical possibilities in the lives of those who are intimate with Muslim saints and spirits in texts going back at least as far as the eighteenth century.

The saint shrine is the place of nameless hospitality, opening up the possibility of becoming estranged from one's social identity, becoming something other than the role expected of one in a hierarchically ordered society and a patriarchal familial order. In this chapter I highlight some of the myriad potentials that the twinned vectors of hospitality and estrangement open up for the lives of those who come to Firoz Shah Kotla.

A SCENE FROM FIELDWORK,
OR THE OTHER (OF) FAMILY

The aunty with the toffees, an old lady with thinning gray hair and a limp, came from Preet Vihar in East Delhi and spoke only Punjabi. Every week, she distributed sweets among the children at Firoz Shah Kotla and took pride in her self-given label, "Toffee wali Aunty" (the aunt with sweets). Every week, perhaps because she felt some kinship with me because I had responded to her in Punjabi in the past, perhaps because all I seemed to do at Firoz Shah Kotla was sit and listen to people's stories, she would recount to me stories of her children and grandchildren, her travails of getting to Firoz Shah Kotla by public transport, and how dargahs in Punjab were in much better condition than the dilapidated dargah we were in, and she would then complain about Ajay, who would make fun of her every week. One rainy September afternoon, she moved on from her usual diatribes and withdrew from her capacious bag a framed black-and-white photo of a young man who must have been in his early to mid-twenties when the picture was taken. It was a picture of her youngest son, she said. She had been looking for a girl for him. He had gone for a wedding in Old Delhi, and something needed to be fetched. He had told the bride's brother, who was his friend, not to worry, that he would go and get it. He decided to take his scooter because the lanes of the Old City were too narrow for the car he'd been offered to drive. It was New Year's Eve. "The driver of the Blueline Bus must have been drinking to celebrate," she said, "and he killed my son at India Gate. Twenty years later, on New Year's day, I had my accident."[9]

Yunus interrupted her narrative at this point. "You have told us this story twenty times. And shown us this picture twenty times. Now stop it."

Her voice high and close to breaking, she replied, "I've been crazy for the past twenty years. I have to repeat the story."

Yunus continued, less harsh than before:

Everyone here suffers losses. I've been to two funerals in the past two weeks. One was Akhtar's brother, who was old and it didn't matter that much. One was a young man from my neighborhood, who had a brain hemorrhage, and they went to three hospitals that wouldn't admit him because they couldn't pay cash up front. Finally, after many hours they got him into Willingdon (a central government hospital) through someone they knew there who worked in the laundry. They admitted him at 8 pm and he died at midnight. And my brother, younger to me, *jise maine apni god men khilaya hai* (who played in my lap). I taught him to work with my own hands. *Par usne mujh se zyada taraqqi ki, bahut aage nikal gaya, itni taraqqi ki ke duniya se pehle nikal gaya* (But he made more progress than me, he reached far ahead of me, he made so much progress that he left the world before me). He died last year, and left two young children behind. Am I sitting around here crying for him all the time?

Ajay then spoke, forgoing his usual tomfoolery. He told the story of his mother dying of cancer and how he didn't know that she was dying because he was always out of the house. Even on the day that she died, he just came in for some food and left again. When someone finally found him and told him that she had passed away, he remembered her asking him to stay, but he hadn't. After he heard this, he still didn't come home. He then spent the entire night on a borrowed cycle going to tell people about the funeral.

There was a moment of quiet when his story ended, and I used it to say my good-byes for the day and to leave. As soon as I exited the gates of Kotla, I burst into tears. The tears came not just from the conversation but from knowing the things left unsaid in the conversation, a knowledge that came from having become a member of the congregation, a regular, a "participant observer" if you will. Ajay wasn't home when his mother was dying because he is seldom at home. He is the ne'er-do-well, the one who never made much of himself, and has never married or been particularly gainfully employed even though he's in his forties now. He lives at home with his elder brothers and sisters-in-law, and even his nephews, much younger than him, can pick fights with him and boss him around when they get tired of being respectful. Fights at home are pretty common, and when they happen, he leaves home for days on end, spending time hanging out and getting drunk in the park stretching in front of the Jama Masjid, coming back home long after everyone is asleep, sleeping out in the courtyard, and drinking his first cup of morning tea outside the house. He's never said it, but things are probably worse for him since his mother died. His father died when he was very young. But at Firoz Shah Kotla Ajay is always welcome. He has a purpose in life in arranging for and distributing the large *deg*s of sweet rice that Babuji, the hotel-owner and politician, pays for to be distributed every week; and in the community here, he can be generous even with his meager money, buying people rounds of tea and *bidi*s. Here, everyone laughs at his jokes, and he doesn't have to storm off because he has been insulted, as he would with his family.

The aunty with the toffees has grandchildren now from her other son, grandchildren whom she loves and who have developed a taste for the sweet orange rice she brings back from Firoz Shah Kotla, grandchildren whom she spends a lot of time taking care of because she has a daughter-in-law who works at a bank in the prosperous, modern suburb of Noida and takes the brand-new Metro to work. But there is no space in this happy, prosperous family home, looking toward the future being ushered in by the new economy, for voicing the still-present grief at the loss of her youngest, most beloved son who died twenty years ago, before the grandchildren were born. And so she comes here every week, traveling by the Blueline Buses that killed her son and injured her on the anniversary of his death, to this place where she can repeat her grief and loss to the baba, to anyone who will listen, carrying his framed photo and sweets for the children. Though Yunus told her to stop, complaining that he has already heard the story twenty times, he will surely hear it again, for she is mad with grief, as she says, and the mad have their right to be here, more so than anyone else.

And Yunus? Despite outwardly being calm and accepting of death, and lecturing Aunty that death is inevitable and happens to everyone, he has been harder hit by his brother's death than he cares to admit. He spent tens of thousands of rupees on his brother's treatment and is in debt. He doesn't have a steady job anymore, and his drinking has increased to the point where he has passed out on the road a couple of times and is now known in his neighborhood as a drunk. Akhtar lives in the same neighborhood as Yunus in Old Delhi but says, "I don't talk to him in the *mohalla*. I talk to him only here, because otherwise people will say what kind of people do you talk to and how do I explain that we distribute the rice together here at the dargah? So I don't talk to him in the mohalla, but I do talk to him here. In fact, I encouraged him to start coming here so that his drinking goes down a bit."

In his *mohalla* Yunus might be a disreputable drunk, but at Kotla, in the dargah, he is always welcome, and Akhtar feels no hesitation about talking to him. Ajay can transcend his marginal, maligned position in his family and become someone else (or more truly himself), witty and generous. The aunty with the toffees can mourn and vent her grief. These are only three among the hundreds who come to Firoz Shah Kotla to voice their grief and pain. Others write letters that they hang on the walls of dark subterranean chambers so the jinn-saints can read them.

LETTERS AND FAMILY NAMES

Their everyday interactions may be anonymous, but the letters people deposit at Firoz Shah Kotla include names and addresses and photos and identity cards, all methods of identity and enumeration associated with the modern state. Many of these letters are photocopied and deposited in different niches and alcoves all over the ruins. The letters are collected and disposed of at irregular intervals by the ground staff of the ASI. I have picked out some of these letters from the trash; others I photographed in situ with a flash. My sample of letters, collected and photographed over five years (2007–10 and then 2014), numbers about two hundred, a small fraction of the letters deposited here during that time.

At Firoz Shah Kotla an ethics of nameless intimacy among people and a culture of petitioning in which governmental techniques of identification play a dominant role coexist. We cannot understand this seeming paradox without understanding the threats and potentialities that a space like Firoz Shah Kotla opens up for the idea of family and kinship. The anonymity of everyday interaction at Firoz Shah Kotla allows for the possibilities of a kinship that transcends the usual limits of family and community. This alternative family, or rather, this alternative *to* family, becomes the space where one's resentments, frustrations, and problems with one's real family can be safely aired.[10] In the letters written to jinns, the same logic is exemplified. Much of what is written to the baba consists of long litanies against, or concerns about, one's extant family and expressions of feeling alienated from them. The saint, who is addressed in modes strongly reminiscent of one's interactions with government offices, is asked to solve problems that are far more intimate, far beyond the usual scope of what we imagine to be within the government's jurisdiction. Perhaps this is because modern governmentality (Foucault 2007) is increasingly concerned with husbanding the *bios* (Agamben 1998), or bare life, of populations and communities, particularly in postcolonial states (Chatterjee 2004). In contrast, the saint represents a realm of *intimate sovereignty* concerned with the quality of subjects' lives, but the sovereign still needs to recognize the subject who comes before him, and recognition as a subject is inextricably associated here, as I noted in Chapter 1, with the identification techniques of the postcolonial biopolitical state.

Their government is just like our government, I have been told a few times at Firoz Shah Kotla, referring to the jinn-babas. *They have ministries, and parties, and the balance of power shifts.* But the baba represents a conception of government very different from our ideas of modern government. Here, the baba is a kind, loving and accepting father, one to whom you can confess everything, and who, unlike your real family, will not judge you or constrain you. The baba is the ideal of government as a just and benevolent father figure, an antipatriarchal patriarch, *a mai-baap sarkar* (government that is both mother and father, a popular Hindi expression). It is not that "their government is just like our government" but that their government is just like our government *should* be, an uncanny memory of past political theory becoming an ethical desiderata and an alternative (and transgressive) imagination of the family.

Based on an analysis of my small sample of letters collected over the years, there are five kinds of letters written at Firoz Shah Kotla.

One, letters written by men. These letters are usually concerned with paying off debts, getting out of trouble with the law, and receiving better employment opportunities.

Two, letters mostly by married women with children. These ask for the health, safety, and well-being of their husbands and children. A distinct subcategory of these letters asks for the successful marriages of daughters or for solving a daughter's marital problems.

Three, letters by children/teenagers, usually girls, seeking better health for various members of the family and occasionally for success in exams. A distinct subcategory of these letters asks that fathers and elder brothers give up their drinking and drug use and become pious, regularly praying (*namazi*) Muslims.

Four, letters written by women asking for relief from jinns who possess or haunt them. Sometimes these letters also include the wish that their husbands be more loving.

Five, letters that express disaffection with and rebellion against the (extended) family. These are mostly written by young women but sometimes by young men. About half of the writers of these letters are unmarried. These letters are of two kinds. One type, usually written by married women, asks for protection from the jealousy and black magic practiced by the larger extended family, and the other kind (written by both unmarried men and women) is about the desire to marry someone sure to be disapproved of based on familial and societal mores. Often, these two categories overlap.

About half of the letters that I have read fall into the fifth category. These are the letters that I will elaborate upon.

.   .   .

Below is the text (lightly edited) of a letter deposited at Firoz Shah Kotla in the summer of 2007:

> Baba I am very troubled by my family and their behavior. You must know about me, no one understands me at home. Everyone thinks of themselves, why am I the only one who is concerned about this home, and even though I'm the only one who's concerned, I always hear the worse for it. I am always upset by my brother and my mother, these people of my family have made me into what I am today, what I could not even think of being in my dreams. But thanks to the one above that at every turn he has taught me how to walk. I have worked in places ranging from a factory to a mansion, however I have done it, I have seen salaries ranging from 300 to 3000 rupees. I have been working since the age of nine and now I have opened a shop in partnership with my friend B, but my friend is also very sad and troubled. The shop had barely opened when there was a fire at their house and her sister-in-law died. Her family was accused of killing her, and now it's been two months since they have become homeless and here I am running the shop alone. Neither my friend is with me, nor my family. There's not a lot of business coming to my shop. My request to you is that my shop starts doing well, because right now I can't even make the rent for the shop. I am all alone now. Tell me Baba, what should I do? I have put my whole life in front of you. Now you will have to ask Allah for a judgment for me. I am writing this letter with many hopes, you will have to decide my life, whoever is in it.

Baba I had thought if not my family then at least the one I care for, the one I love would be mine. But even in this fate has not supported me. I love that boy so much, I think about him, I want to marry him, but even that boy doesn't understand me. He is worried about me, he takes care of me, but says that I won't be able to marry you. When I asked him the reason he said that my father is no longer in this world and now I am the eldest in the family, I cannot marry like this. I know everything about him but still I cannot leave him because whenever I try to forget him he manages to talk to me somehow, and when he doesn't talk to me I try to talk to him. Somehow we can't leave each other. I don't know if he loves me and why he still talks to me despite all our fighting. . . . I don't know when I started loving him. Now only you can set him right and show him the right way. I have told you everything about myself. I hope you will show me the right way. I will always stay in your shadow. I have seen many sorrows since I was a child. I hope I don't have to see as many in the future, because by this letter you would also know that there is not [just] one sorrow in my life.

Thank you.

I have reproduced this particular letter nearly in full because its eloquence encapsulates the everyday troubles that bring people to Firoz Shah Kotla. This young woman turns to the saint because her family does not support or understand her, and the man she loves cannot marry her because of his obligations to his family. (From the names it is clear that she is Muslim, and he is Hindu, and this may be the reason he does not want to marry her, as it will upset his family.) She turns to the baba for relief from both their families and asks the baba to convince her beloved to marry her, against the (presumed) wishes of his family and against the normative morality of community, where marriages across religious communities are increasingly frowned upon and acted against (Das 2010). Already, this letter seems like a relic from another age in a time when the resurgent Hindu right wing is whipping up hysteria against "Love Jihad"—the covert campaign, in their febrile imaginations, by which Muslim men are seducing Hindu women to increase the Muslim population. I wonder what the Hindu right, with its naked anxieties about maintaining patriarchal control over female bodies and reproduction, will make of the letters written at Firoz Shah Kotla, in which time and time again the wishes made at the dargah challenge the tradition of the "Hindu Undivided Family."

The "Hindu Undivided Family" is a legal term which treats the joint family as a unit for taxation and investment purposes (Birla 2009). The concept of the Hindu Undivided Family is based on the patrilocal joint-family system, prevalent in much of India across religious communities, in which married couples reside with the husband's parents, and daughters go away to stay in their husband's homes, with their *sasural*, the husband's extended family. This patrilocal joint-family system, as both ideal and practice, exerts an enormous amount of hierarchical familial and community control over the lives of individual members, even if this control has shifted and lessened in recent years (Wadley 2002). The Hindu Undivided Family, across religious communities, imagines marriage as a predominantly social as opposed to individual contract.

As the work of Perveez Mody (2002, 2008) shows, the legislative processes of the colonial state empowered communities rather than individuals as the agents in a marriage contract. By being legislated into the laws of the colonial state, the Hindu Undivided Family and its forms of hierarchy and control have become normative through state sanction (Majumdar 2009), displacing and delegitimizing other precolonial forms of family and familiarity, such as the worlds of independent, desiring women we glimpse in rekhti poetry (Vanita 2012). Community now, as Veena Das has noted, "colonizes the life-world of the individual in the same way as the state colonizes the life-world of the community" (1995, 16). So even though the postcolonial Special Marriage Act allows for individuals to contract marriages, under the aegis of the state, outside of the customary laws and strictures of their religious communities, the life of the law, the ways in which it is practiced by members of the police, administration, judges, and lawyers, continues to make such couples vulnerable to the demands of their kin and make "court marriages difficult, dangerous, and shameful affairs" (Mody 2002, 240). Not surprisingly then in contemporary India, couples from different castes or religious groups who have married for love against the wishes of their families, try to conceal the fact of their "love-marriage" through "adjustments" in names, personal dress, and deportment so that an image of social coherence is portrayed to the neighborhood and the world (Mody 2002, 256). In the slums of Delhi, as Claire Snell-Rood found, "nearly every woman had broken ties of marriage or family" (2015, 38). But women either kept these histories secret or "even as they moved away from family, left husbands, [or] scorned bad family members, they still imagined themselves embedded within family. . . . Relationships were not described as broken or ended" (48).

But at Firoz Shah Kotla the letters deposited often articulate not just a great deal of anger against both marital and natal families; they also sometimes imagine and demand a clean break from the family. One woman, for instance, deposited many copies of a letter written in a clear Urdu hand, wishing that her husband would willingly divorce her:

> Ya Allah, A should write and give me a divorce of his own will. I want to marry a second time. Allah T'ala may I find a person who is needy [*zaruratmand*] and constrained [*majbur*], pure of all illness, not suspicious, not miserly, not crafty. He should be straightforward and innocent, good in every way, not a cheater. He shouldn't have a first wife, he should be a person who respects and loves me. He should have his own personal home. He should laugh a lot, he should be very respectable, better in every way. Allah T'ala please give me a home of my own.

In a letter another woman wrote, she first gave an extraordinarily detailed list of her *sasural* and all its inhabitants: her parents-in-law, her two *jeths* (husband's elder brothers), her two *jethanis* (the wives of the elder brothers), her *devranis* (husband's younger brother's wives), and her *devars* (husband's younger brothers):

> Please pray Baba that whoever among them has thought or done ill either about U or U's husband H or about H's work or about U's children and their studies, in whatever way, may the bad thing happen to them instead and may it be so bad that they land up in bed and pass the life of the sick for a year or two, and pray that H's work goes well, and a voice enters his ears and he sells the house in Hapur and buys one in Ghaziabad and starts staying in Ghaziabad forever, just H and U and their children and no one else comes

with them, not sas-sasur, not dev-devrani not jeth-jethani not nand-nandoi [husband's sister and her husband] and if the nand-nandoi do some ill to us may it happen to her instead. . . . What else can I write Baba, nothing is hidden from you. Therefore H's heart should leave Hapur and settle on Ghaziabad instead, and he takes all his stuff from Hapur and starts living in Ghaziabad, please pray Baba.

.   .   .

What is the "self" expressed in these letters? How is this self healed?

Those who have theorized personhood in India have often pointed to how this self is "relational" rather than autonomous or individual, which is taken to be the norm in Western societies (Dumont 1970; Marriott 1976; Sax 2009). As Sarah Lamb points out, "a focus on relationality does not mean that no notion or experience of individuality or individual autonomy exists" (1997, 282). But this understanding of the relational nature of the self has led to an overemphasis on "family values" in the study of ritual healing in South Asia: an overvaluation of the necessity to reintegrate into the hierarchical structures of family and a concomitant lack of attention to the potentials of autonomy, individuality, and estrangement in the processes and outcomes of healing.

Contrasting "Indic" conceptions of being and healing to the individual-centered model of Western psychotherapy, Sudhir Kakar writes, "The underlying values of the traditional temple healing . . . stress that faith and surrender to a power beyond the individual are better than individual effort and struggle, that the source of human strengths lies in a harmonious integration with one's group, in the individual's affirmation of the community's value and its given order, in his obedience to the community's gods and in his cherishing of its traditions" (Kakar 1982, 88). William Sax, writing about possession rituals of the deity Bhairav in the Garwhal Himalayas, largely agrees with Kakar, concluding that "the healing cult of Bhairav works to consolidate the family as a unified, healthy, functioning whole" (Sax 2009, 246). Carla Bellamy, while disagreeing with Kakar on many fundamental points, agrees that the role of healing in dargah spaces "seems not to be conceived of on an individual level; rather, it is conceptualized and experienced through relationships with immediate and extended family members. . . . Social integration seems to be a major measure of one's level of recovery; or, put slightly differently, recovery is only real when it is recognized and accepted by others" (Bellamy 2011, 58).

The letters deposited at Firoz Shah Kotla, however, seem to rebel against the *individual's affirmation of the community's value and its given order*. In many of the letters, the women do not just complain about their families but demand (and hence imagine) a complete break from their marital families: *Just H and U and their children and no one else comes with them, not sas-sasur, not dev-devrani not jeth-jethani not nand-nandoi. . . . He should write and give me a divorce of his own will. . . . Please give me a home of my own.* The extended family, in these letters, is the site of suffering, where the daughter/daughter-in-law/wife is misunderstood and where there is always suspicion of ill-will harbored against her and her husband and children. Rather than seeking a reintegration into the family, as the extant literature on the healing practices of shrines would suggest, these letters suggest a flight from the family—the forming of a romantic couple; a nuclear family; an ideal of love, intimacy, and respect if not necessarily opposed to then certainly separated from the domain and demand of the extended family. At Firoz Shah Kotla we also see the formation of alternative communities, communities of friendship that are explicitly nonhierarchical and nondenominational. The self does not cease to be relational, we could say, but the relations that define the self are radically remade here.

Is it that life in modern Delhi, hypermediated by images from television and Bollywood, has changed people's ideals of the self, and intimacy, and their obligations to the family? I argue the opposite. As the work of Veena Das and Perveez Mody shows, families and caste communities have been empowered in colonial and postcolonial India, at the expense of individual freedom, to regulate the body and sexuality of individuals through the codification of custom. The emergence of community as a political actor in India's political culture, under the regimes of colonial and postcolonial governmentality, has seen an increased concern with controlling female sexuality and often violently patrolling the boundaries of community against "love marriages"—marriages in which individual desire trumps both the wishes of the family and caste principles of endogamy, "widely viewed as a most unholy union" (Mody 2008, 7).

And yet, in Bombay cinema, lovers keep getting together in defiance of parental obligations and societal pressure, triumphing against all odds, to the delight of audiences and cinema cash registers. Is Bombay cinema, as Mody (2008, 8) indicates, offering its spectators a modern "metropolitan" view of love and subjectivity, enlarging the realm of the possible beyond the limitations of communal tradition? Undoubtedly. But Bombay cinema, with its unique relation to the Islamic tradition, and in particular to dargah spaces, is also drawing on a premodern tradition of asserting desire against the dominant morality of family and community. As Veena Das notes, "Individuals need to resist the encompassing claims of even the most vital communities as a condition of their human freedom" (1995, 17). To imagine premodern societies, as has been done in dominant social science paradigms, without the potential for individuals to break through the collective traditions of community and to live on its limits is to reify the uniqueness of the modern, secular, self-reflexive, individual as a way of being unknown and unknowable to traditional societies and to religious communities.

In North India the space of the Muslim dargah has long been the space for the interlinked processes of the articulation of individual desire (against dominant morality) and the unmaking and remaking of the socially constituted self.[11] Katherine Ewing has drawn attention to the figure of the *qalandar* who inhabits dargah spaces, the wandering beggar ascetic who "traditionally" (from at least the tenth century) disrupts all tradition, dramatically drawing people's attention to the arbitrariness of social order and boundaries (Ewing 1997, 21, 201–52). In the rest of this chapter I focus on how the popular veneration of Muslim saint-spirits, going back to at least the eighteenth century, has enabled both the expression of nonnormative desire and the remaking of the self in ways that challenge the dominant moralities of family and community. Both Bombay cinema and contemporary practices at Firoz Shah Kotla draw on these traditions, which, as I will show in Chapter 4, can be traced back to antipatriarchal potentials in the Quran and in the life of the Prophet Muhammad.

INTIMACY WITH THE INVISIBLE

S'adat Yar Khan "Rangin" (1755–1835), true to his *takhallus* (nom-de-plume), was a "colorful" character. "A mercenary, a horse trader, and a poet" (Vanita and Kidwai 2000, 221), he lived and worked and traveled extensively in late Mughal India. He could also be said to be the first ethnographer-poet. He gave the name *rekhti* to a genre of poetry that purports to be "women's speech" and dwells on women's lives and concerns. His introduction (Argali 2006, 30) to his rekhti *Diwan* (collection of poetry) describes a decidedly participant observatory approach. In the days of his youth, he declares, he used to spend a lot of time with *khangis* (married women from respectable households who surreptitiously practiced prostitution), and he used to pay almost voyeuristic attention to them and "pay close attention to every eloquent speech in that community." And in doing this, he got much information about their idioms, language, and phrases (*un ki istilahon, zaban aur muhavaron se bahut si khabar hui*), which he then merely set in verse.

If we take his ethnographic conceit seriously, as I am wont to do, then Rangin's rekhti paints a remarkable picture of precolonial urban life in early modern North India. The poetry of Rangin, and the other early rekhti poets such as Insha and Jan Sahib, depicts a demotic world of urban life and intimacies very different not just from our received image of the poetic worlds of that era, as exemplified by the classical Urdu ghazal, but also from the constrained possibilities of urban life and imagination in the postcolonial present. The social world of these poems is populated with workers, vendors, and servants, both male and female. Ruth Vanita notes that "rekhti for the first time brings into poetry the activities and lives of subordinates—women and men who move between household and marketplace" (2012, 97)—and is characterized by intimacies shared across class, caste, religion, and gender boundaries.

The most striking feature of this poetry is the ways in which it speaks of eroticism, sex, desire, and friendship. There is an expansion in this poetry of the ways in which love and desire can be spoken of and imagined. The unrequited, ideal love of the classical rekhta ghazal is replaced by real love, with all its intimacies, complexities, and vicissitudes, in complex physical and emotional detail. This love exists between women and women, women and men, and men and men. This poetry celebrates consummation with real and attainable beloveds, is frank and celebratory about sensuality and sex, and explores relations that are unconventional in different degrees. Among the unconventional relations portrayed in this poetry were those with male and female spirit intimates—jinns and fairies (or *paris*)—relations that were an essential part of navigating human relations and intimacies.[12] Rangin includes the names of the better-known jinns and paris in the glossary accompanying his *diwan*, indicating that this world was probably little known to elite men:[13]

> Shaikh Saddu, Miyan Zain Khan, Miyan Sadr-e Jahan, Pir Hatile, Nanhe Miyan, Chahaltan, Miyan Shah Dariya, Shah Sikandar, the seven fairies, that is Red Fairy, Green Fairy, Yellow Fairy, Black Fairy, River Fairy, Sky Fairy, Light Fairy: they believe in all of them and know them to be their guides and helpers, but in the case of Miyan Shah Dariya, Shah Sikandar and the seven fairies they say that they are all brothers and sisters and that God sent them from Heaven to be playmates of Fatima [the Prophet's daughter] that they should serve her. They are her slaves and for this reason they consider them pre-eminent—the majority of them even call Miyan Shah Dariya and Shah Sikandar the Princes of Light [*nuri shahzade*], that is to say that they are created from light. (Argali 2006, 45)

Even the unconventional families depicted in premodern rekhti poetry are often shown as sites of tension and strife. For the women who claimed intimacy with them, the male princes of light held open the potential of escape and refuge from the claustrophobic world of the extended family, as is seen in Rangin's "Odes to the Glory of the Prince of Light and in Praise of Miyan Shah Dariya" [*Qaside Nuri Shehzade ki shan men aur miyan shah dariya ki ta'arif men*] (Argali 2006, 146–51):

> *Zaban to ek hai kis kis ka main karun shikwa*
> *Idhar to sas ka dukh hai aur udhar hai nanad ka gham*
>
> I have one tongue, who all should I complain about?
> Here there is the sorrow of my mother-in-law, and there the grief of my
>   sister-in-law.
>
> . . .

Ghazab yeh hai ke meri baith kar kanauti men
Baham yeh mil ke kiya kartiyan hain mujh pe sitam

What really angers [me] is that all of them conspire
Sitting behind my back and heap tortures upon me.

Gharaz ke ghar men mire mach raha hai voh kuhram
Ki jis ke likhne se hoti hai shaq zaban-e qalam

So vexing is the loud lamentation in my home
That the tongue of the pen splits in writing of it.

Nikalun kis ke age tere siva ji ka bukhar?
Mera hai chhut tere hamraz na koi mahram

Apart from you who can I disclose the fever of my soul to?
Apart from you, I have no intimate, no confidant.

. . .

Bulaun sar pe tire aj Shah Darya ko
Ki dur hove mire dil ka sab yeh ranj-o-alam

I call Shah Dariya upon your head [to possess you]
So that my heart's pain and chagrin go away.

Bhadas is ji ki nikalun main kah ke sab dukhra
Javab paun main un se suna ke dil ka gham

I'll get all my frustration out by saying all my sorrows.
I'll get an answer from him by telling him my woes.

.   .   .

Rekhti poetry disappeared from the canon of Urdu, being considered effeminate and degenerate, and as we saw in Chapter 1, the religious world depicted in it was also censured. But remarkable continuities persist between this precolonial poetry and contemporary practices. At Firoz Shah Kotla, as in Rangin's poem, the figure of the jinn-saint serves as the confidant to whom things are said or written that cannot be uttered elsewhere. The jinn/baba, as in the poem, continues to offer a space of refuge and protection from the obligations and claustrophobia, the rivalries and jealousies of family life. Bellamy writes that "the extended family is conceived of as a structure that will ideally preserve and maintain the value of each of its members" (2011, 147). But as rekhti poetry shows, there is also a fairly long tradition of seeing the extended family as a space of abuse and dishonor, a space from which one seeks refuge.

Kakar and Bellamy write about the temple of Mehndipur Balaji and the dargah of Husain Tekri Sharif respectively, both pilgrimage spaces far removed from everyday life, spaces where people go after all the usual, local modes of cure have been exhausted. Kakar, in going through his Balaji case histories, "is struck by their accumulated and repressed rage, the helpless anger of young women at the lack of their social emancipation being the canvas on which the individual picture of hysterical illness is painted" (1982, 76). Bellamy eschews the language and diagnoses of psychotherapy, focusing instead on the violence and the "broken speech" of *haziri*, the utterances seldom remembered by the victim that are slowly and painfully strung into a narrative and a denouement by the victim's relatives or caretakers and other visitors at the shrine. As with the letters, the narratives and judgments generated in haziri often implicate family members as having performed magic or caused magic to be performed on the victim.

Firoz Shah Kotla shares logics and practices of judgment and healing very similar to Mehndipur and Husain Tekri, but it is also significantly different. It is not a distant place of pilgrimage, far removed from the exigencies of everyday life. It is a place located within the city, relatively conveniently accessible by bus (and if you live in Old Delhi, by foot) from places as far away as Ghaziabad and Hapur. It is a place where, as the letters show us, feelings are usually articulated and not repressed (following Kakar's model) and where the same conclusions and narratives of being affected negatively by members of the extended family (that emerge socially, slowly, and painfully through haziri, following Bellamy) are articulated lucidly and forcefully. Perhaps this is why the violent process of haziri on which Bellamy focuses, the full-blown violence that is usually recognized as spirit possession, is a relatively minor part of the practices at Firoz Shah Kotla, where *haziri* usually refers to simply presenting oneself (and, implicitly, one's petition) in front of the saint.

The work and workings of haziri (to paraphrase Bellamy) can follow many different trajectories. Whereas at Husain Tekri the violence of haziri remains confined to the space of the dargah and is not taken back to the family (Bellamy 2011, 148), which is far away, at Firoz Shah Kotla the disaffections and stresses of family life articulated are the same, but *repression* is much less in evidence and social integration (or reintegration with the family) is not the only trajectory of healing. Following the evidence of rekhti poetry, the letters at Firoz Shah Kotla, and my experiences and conversations there, I suggest that the isolation from family and community (dislocation) is not just a part of the process of healing (as highlighted by Bellamy) but also sometimes the desired outcome of healing. Narratives of healing at Firoz Shah Kotla don't quite follow Turner's classic model of liminality and communitas, in which the experience of communitas invariably gives way to the mediacy of structure (Turner 1995, 129). After passing through the liminal stage, Turner's ritual subject is "expected to behave in accordance with certain customary norms and ethical standards binding on incumbents of social position" (95). But the narratives of healing told here are open-ended and ambiguous, telling of radical transformations of the self's relation to the world, transformations that are frightening, unforeseen, and unpredictable.

Anwar Sabri of the dargah of Nanhe Miyan Chishti told me how for the first eight years of serving at the dargah, he was very *jalali* (fierce): "When I went home I would break dishes, I would get angry at the smallest thing, I would get mad. All of this was his [Nanhe Miyan's] miracle. When I became a disciple [*murid*] to my pir, then after my becoming a disciple my anger was taken from me. Now if someone hits me on one cheek, then I turn the other." At Firoz Shah Kotla, too, where haziri is not radically separated from the texture of everyday life, the expression of anger in the space of the family is one of the first effects of visiting the dargah, of becoming intimate with the baba. Manohar Lal told me a story of how serving at Firoz Shah Kotla had given him control of two jinns. He felt the presence of these jinns mostly through an increased sensitivity to slight and insult and a propensity to pick fights: "I had such an ability that if you insulted me say at the electric-pole way over there, I would hear you over here, as if I had a tape recorder [hearing aid] attached to my ear. Every second day I would get into fights, I used to feel a lot of anger."

Manohar Lal then told me a story of how he had beaten up his older brother. One night he had come back late from Firoz Shah Kotla, and his wife told him how his older brother had yelled abuses at his youngest brother's wife earlier that day. Manohar Lal dragged his older brother out into the street and beat him up, despite the fact that the brother was stronger than him. Then, he said, the baba/jinn who had given him the strength and the anger to beat up his brother suddenly left his body: "When the baba left my body suddenly a weakness came upon me and I went and sat down on a scooter parked in the street. Then my brother came and gave me a drink of water, saying brother you must be tired, drink some water. That's when I thought that today I hit my brother. If I had killed him, or if something bad had happened, then my family would have been destroyed. That's when I let go of the two jinns." Since then, Manohar Lal said, his brother hasn't uttered a single word of abuse.

In both Anwar Sabri and Manohar Lal's cases, the anger is associated with the space of the dargah, something they first gain by coming to the dargah and then get rid of after a certain length of time. The anger flies in the face of "harmonious integration with one's group." Manohar Lal beats up his older brother, who, following tradition, is a figure deserving respect, second only to the respect owed to the father. In his account this incident made him give up the jinns that he had acquired and, with them, the propensity to anger he had acquired after he started visiting the dargah but not before changing the dynamics of the family forever by putting an end to the older brother's abuse and bullying.

Lest we think of the anger associated with the dargah as solely a male prerogative, here is Pehelwan's story of how he started coming to Firoz Shah Kotla because of his wife. It was his wife who first started going to Firoz Shah Kotla every day, seven or eight years after their marriage. In the beginning he became jealous and asked her, why do you go to a place where so many Muslim men come every day? She said that she only went to eat the biriyani that was distributed there. Then one day, he saw her slapping her thighs like a wrestler, and she started fighting with him, and she twisted his arm and beat him up. (Pehelwan, as I mentioned earlier, was a wrestler.) Pehelwan saw the baba manifest many forms through his wife, he says, when she was "playing,"[14] sometimes as a eunuch (known for their bawdiness), sometimes as Mastan Baba (a name denoting ecstasy and intoxication), sometimes as Sikandar Baba, all (in his words) "Muhammadan" names. The saint's presence on his wife was often manifested in the uncanny behavior of cats:

> I saw cats walking backwards inside the baoli [stepwell, also a subterranean space inside Firoz Shah Kotla]. Then my wife said, "Let me swim here." I said to them that whoever you are present on her, come upon me. "Come upon me and swim." But my wife didn't listen so I had to forcibly pull her away. . . .
>
> . . . This was the first time I had seen the affairs of the jinns. When my wife was getting better I was lying with her at midnight . . . so as it happened, he [Baba] took on such a form that he spoke in a woman's voice. So I see in my home, this is the absolute truth, a huge fat tomcat [*billa*]. I mean, Baba in the form of a tomcat, and he was walking stiff and haughtily like a very big wrestler . . . and saying, "No one can pick us up, no one can catch us." I said, "Baba we are your children, if we have made any mistake, forgive us." I have done much penance, asked for much forgiveness, then finally my wife got better.

To Pehelwan the baba was indistinguishable from his wife's erratic behavior, manifesting itself as both Muslim and animal. In his own account of these encounters, the Muslim/animal is not a demonic Other that needs to be exorcized, as Sudhir Kakar found in Mehndipur Balaji,[15] but something familial and familiar suddenly turned strange, a speaking cat, a bawdy wife. In his account, to name and recognize this estrangement as Muslim is not to demonize it but to realize the sovereignty of this difference, the need to respect it. It is his encounter with the sovereign untamability of the cat, while lying in his marital bed, that is the turning point in Pehelwan's narrative; this is the point at which he realizes that it is he who needs to change. It was after this encounter, in his narrative, that Pehelwan came to Firoz Shah Kotla, apologized profusely to the baba (*maine bahut mafiyan mangin hain*), and radically changed his own behavior and comportment, after which his wife got better. Ever since then, he has been coming regularly to Firoz Shah Kotla and has become a devotee. He repeatedly says that he has become wiser since he started coming to Firoz Shah Kotla and serving the baba. "I was dirty, unclean before. I used to do bad things."

. . .

In the narratives of healing told at Firoz Shah Kotla the boundary between the self and the world is radically porous; there is no *I* that impresses its will on the world. Rather it is the self that is acted on through dreams, possession, and talking animals. Yet these are also stories of rebellion, of the transgression of dominant social morality, and of radical ethical change. They dramatize actions that, if we were to follow a dominant Western moral epistemology, look remarkably like the exercise of agency and free will. How do we understand rebellion without autonomy, ethical self-formation without a willing *I*? How does modern history understand the agency of the rebel against the colonial order who says, "I did as my God told me to do" (Chakrabarty 2000, 108)? Perhaps this incommensurability comes from a flaw in our conception of agency, understood as the autonomy *to act* of a rational subject who is master of the self—the normative ideal of "Western" (and hence universally desirable) personhood. But perhaps we have never been the "buffered" selves that Taylor (2007) defines us as having become. All along, we have been *acted upon*. We have been porous to the transmission of affect coming at us from outside the individual psyche (Brennan 2004), to the world whooshing up at us in *physis* as in the time of the Greek gods (Dreyfus and Kelly 2011), to the vibrancy of matter (Bennett 2010), to the spirits of history (Lambek 2002). But we (and by *we* I mean the transgeographical community of secular, modern subjects in whose number I count myself) have convinced ourselves, for complex historical reasons (Bilgrami 2006), that we are not so porous after all.[16]

Following Mittermaier (2012), to truly pose a challenge to the liberal model of the autonomous self, we need to recover an ethics of *passion* and not just action, of cultivating the capacity to be acted *upon* rather than acting within and acting against; this is an ethics of humility, relationality, and the contingency of life—an ethics, perhaps, of being "undone by each other" (Butler 2004, 23). Perhaps being receptive to forces outside of us to act even in the remarkably creative, "independent" ways we do—as

Ghalib said, "the scratching of the pen is the voice of an angel"[17]—is a truer analogue of our being in the world than we give it credit for.

Michael Lambek (2003) characterizes spirit possession as inherently ironic because it constantly calls agency into question; who it is that speaks and acts when a person is possessed is never quite a settled question, either phenomenologically or conceptually. Intimacy or kinship with spirits and deities is also ironic in that while it highlights the relationality of the self, the self's embeddedness in and constitution through a network of ties to the world, such intimacy, as we see at Firoz Shah Kotla, also leads to dissolution (Pinto 2014), to the "troubling" of kinship (Ramberg 2014), to the unbinding and unravelling of the self that looks something like freedom.

From rekhti poetry we get a picture of the beginnings of intimacy with the figure of the male jinn/baba leading to a withdrawal from the world and turning against one's intimates:

Phire kyon na ahle gahle banki
Dogana hai haram Nanhe Miyan ki

Why shouldn't she wander here and there without purpose?
My beloved is [now] the sanctuary of Nanhe Miyan.

Mila hai jab se is se Shah Dariya
Woh dushman tab se haigi meri jaan ki

Since Shah Dariya has met her [Since she has found Shah Dariya]
She has been the enemy of my life.

—(Argali 2006, 105)

It is this estrangement from one's society and oneself, the expression rather than repression of anger and discontent, that serves as another trajectory of healing, the often radical reconfiguration of the self's relation to the world. For women, however, this expression of anger is now demonized, whereas men consider it a blessing. "The babas are pure; they wouldn't possess a woman," I've heard repeatedly from men. "*Unpe to sirf gandi cheez aati hai*" (Only unclean things possess them).

CHAPTER 4

DESIRING WOMEN

Pari paikar nigare sarv qade lala rukhsare
Sarapa afat-e dil bud shab jai ke man budam

The form of a fairy, cypress-tall, tulip-cheeked
A scourge of the heart, from head to foot, where I was last night.

—Amir Khusrau (d. 1325)

A SCENE FROM FIELDWORK:
UNUSUAL CONVERSATIONS

On a cold winter night, early in my fieldwork, I sat alone with a woman, listening to her story of desire, love, and loss. She and I had both been speaking with Balon, the unofficial caretaker of the alcove associated with Nanhe Miyan, who usually lingered on at Firoz Shah Kotla for a while after the daytime crowds had dispersed. The woman was a widow; her husband had been dead ten months. She had started coming to Firoz Shah Kotla after his death. The woman asked Balon to make a wish for her, and Balon laughingly said, "You're already much better than you were ten months ago; be happy." Then Balon got up and left, leaving us alone.

Tusi Punjabi ho? She asked me if I was Punjabi in Punjabi, noticing my iron bracelet. When I answered in the affirmative, she showed me her own iron bracelet, nestled among her bangles. Her whole family was in Punjab, she said, and started talking to me about her life. She came from New Seelampur, across the river. She did not have any children; she had been pregnant once but miscarried at five months. "I got late today," she said, "because I always come here after a bath, and I was heating the water today when a friend from the neighborhood came by.

The friend said, 'Why don't you get married again? I have a boy in mind.' But," she said,

> I told my friend that I didn't want to get married. This is the way the world is. If I get married and leave everything, what if he leaves me? If I'm destined to meet someone I will crash into him (*takra jaungi*). If my fate was good, then I wouldn't have lost my husband.
>
> He was a Muhammadan [Muslim], but he never stopped me from doing anything. I would go to the goddess shrine of Vaishno Devi, I had a small *mandir* [temple] in the home, but he never stopped me. Where will I find a man like him? When I was fourteen years old, I came here from Punjab and stayed with my aunt, my mother's sister, and that's when I met him. I told my family I'm not marrying unless I marry him. He was so good looking. I was not any less [*Main bhi koi kam nahin thi*].

She looked directly at me as she spoke, and we weren't that far apart in age—she must have been in her mid-thirties then. The strangest thing about that evening is not her story, which was uncommon enough—a Hindu girl moving from Punjab to Delhi and then marrying a Muslim, cutting off all ties with her family, and integrating into the landscape of New Seelampur, a predominantly Muslim working-class settlement. The strangest thing that evening was the very fact of our conversation. This is not how men and women usually interact with each other in public spaces in Delhi. Outside of zones of relative egalitarianism and the free mingling of the sexes such as college campuses, and modern consumer spaces like shopping malls, Delhi is a hostile place for unaccompanied women in public. The presence of men overwhelmingly dominates the cityscape, including sidewalks and public transport. Women negotiate this landscape at their own peril, constantly facing the threat of sexual harassment, or worse. Outside of fleeting commercial transactions, most women in Delhi are wary of speaking to men they don't know. Yet at Firoz Shah Kotla women talk to men all the time. They talk about lost love and the power of desire. *He was so good looking. I was not any less.* They talk about matters spiritual and theological, and in public debates they have no compunctions about telling men that they are wrong or misguided. They crack jokes with men, and within this space, the men treat them as friends, confidantes, teachers, as equals and even superiors.

The violence directed against women in public spaces in Delhi is violence that does the work of patriarchy—the woman's place is in the home, and if you're out in public unaccompanied, you're "matter out of place,"[1] sexually loose and available, and meant to be treated like dirt. The dislocations wrought by the sweeping changes to the society, economy, and landscape of Delhi in recent years have added a sharper, more brutal edge to a violence stemming from "traditional" patriarchal norms.[2] Encounters like the one I have described above, where women share intimate details of their lives of desire with men who are essentially strangers, are not supposed to happen, certainly not across the boundaries of caste and religion (and occasionally class), as so often occurs at Firoz Shah Kotla. Why is it that a space associated with Islam, a religion associated with a highly patriarchal order (as symbolized by the veiling of women), becomes a space where women can be much freer and more open in interacting with men, and in talking about their desires, than they can be in most public spaces in Delhi?

Is this because dargah spaces, with their tradition of dissent against socially sanctioned morality, are "ambiguously Islamic" (Bellamy 2011)? Or is the ambiguity one encounters in these spaces an inherent part of the Islamic tradition, a tradition that looks far more capacious, and far more capable of including forms of feminine desire and agency that challenge and contradict the patriarchal norms of legalist Islamic consensus once we rethink what constitutes the discursive tradition of Islam and its forms of authority?

GIRL CHILDREN AND OTHER STRANGER WOMEN

Women far outnumber men in the congregation at Firoz Shah Kotla, and the women often express a deep intimacy with the baba, the saint of the pillar. The lady from Laxminagar, a Hindu woman and regular participant in our circle at Firoz Shah Kotla, would sometimes pick up the sweets and flowers left as an offering for the baba, something that she said most others won't dare to do but was fine for her because, she said, *"yeh to hamare baba ki hai, ham kha lenge"* (This is my baba's, I will eat it).

Sometimes the saint spoke as a voice inside her, playfully encouraging her to take the offerings made to him. She prized the things she has collected from his shrine, especially the markedly Islamic ones. Once, she declared during a discussion in the circle of regulars, she had found a silver Saudi Arabian coin at Firoz Shah Kotla, a gift from the baba. When this intimacy with the baba was absent, she felt it keenly. *"Aj interesting nahin aya"* (The interesting[ness] didn't come today), she once told our group at Firoz Shah Kotla, returning from the pillar after an unusually short visit. "I told baba I'll come back again."

Laddu Shah kept visiting Firoz Shah Kotla, his son Chand told me, because they were seven brothers and had no sister. So he would go to Firoz Shah Kotla to pray that a girl child may be born in his house. Laddu Shah was not the only man going to Firoz Shah Kotla to pray for a girl child. A few other men were also praying for girls in a city where many other men (and women) had a very different relation to the possibility of girl children. According to 2011 census data, the child sex ratio in Delhi stood at 866 girls to every 1,000 boys. At least some of this disparity can be attributed to the selective abortion of female fetuses.

Manohar Lal said that his father-in-law used to pray for a girl child at Firoz Shah Kotla as well, and his wife was born as a blessing of the baba. The blessings of the baba are also particularly associated with girl children, as one particular conversation at Firoz Shah Kotla brought home to me:

> Manohar Lal. One time I came here, Brother Salim, and I was late and everyone had gone, but the whole wall over there was full of money stuck to it [as offering]. I said, "Baba, there's no one to take this money off," so I took it all and went and gave it to my daughter. I told her, "I've got this from Baba for you, it's not for me, you should eat [from] it."
>
> Lady from Laxminagar. We do the same thing. If Lal Baba [Balon] is around, we give it to him.
>
> ML. No, I just give it to my children. Not to the boys, only to the girls.
>
> LfL. We do the same, and you know what the young one says, the little mouse? "You only love these two" [the daughters]. And I tell him, "Don't say that, they are daughters."

ML. They're *paraya dhan* [other's wealth].

LfL. Yes, other's wealth.

Neither Manohar Lal nor the lady from Laxminagar were talking to me. They were addressing each other and the others gathered in a circle, about half a dozen people, who gathered together and talked every Thursday. I just happened to be there with my recorder on, listening. I had heard the old adage of daughters being *paraya dhan* (the wealth of others) many a time before, usually in Hindi films. But its being uttered in the context of the dargah struck me with unusual force.

Both Manohar Lal and the lady from Laxminagar give offerings they have picked up from the presence of the baba to their daughters rather than their sons. This is because they understand their daughters as *paraya dhan*, another's wealth and not their own, destined to be given away in marriage to another family, while their sons (and their brides) will stay with them. Even when love and affection is lavished on them, girl children are conceived of as temporary visitors of the natal home, destined to go away. This is why the offerings from the dargah, the space of the strangers and the estranged, are given to daughters and not to sons, to enable them to marry well and hence leave the natal home, *to enable their successful estrangement.*

Babul mora naihar chhuto hi jaye

Char kahar mil mori doliya sajaye

Mora apna begana chhuto jaye

Aangna parbat bhayo aur dehri bhayi bidesh

Le babul ghar aapno, main chali piya ke desh

Babul mora naihar chhuto jaaye

Father, my natal home gets left behind

Four bearers together ready my palanquin

Which will carry me away from everything, known and strange

The courtyard of my home is a mountain now, its threshold is a foreign
   country

I leave my home father, to go to the country of the beloved

Father, my natal home gets left behind.

—Attributed to Nawab Wajid Ali Shah, circa 1856

Wajid Ali Shah is reputed to have composed this *thumri* upon his exile from Lucknow, forced on him by the British East India Company. Looking back from a twenty-first-century perspective, this is already strange and wondrous—a male king using the language and inhabiting the interiority of a young girl, describing her emotions as she leaves her natal home after marriage to express his own feelings as he was exiled from his city. The use of the metaphor of the bride leaving her father's home to express his sorrow at his exile from Lucknow was apt and highly charged: like the bride's departure from her natal home, his exile from his beloved city was final and irrevocable. The bewildering estrangement of moving from a familiar place of paternal love to a place of strange unknowns (including, most of the time, the person you are getting married to) causes the *bidai*, the ceremony of leave-taking from the natal home, to be one of wrenching emotion, especially as depicted in Hindi films.

I believe that Firoz Shah Kotla, and other dargahs, serve as a substitute for the relinquished natal home. For women who come to the dargah, the baba serves as the indulgent, affectionate father of a childhood left behind (as in the lady from Laxminagar's intimacy with the baba and her ease with picking up the offerings left for the baba). And, it is through the women who flock to dargahs that their men first encounter benevolent and loving authority figures in the space of the dargah.

· · ·

In the villages of the Delhi hinterland, such as Chandrawal, new brides coming into the village are first taken to the dargah of the local Muslim saint. I asked Vijindar Khari how the figure of the baba, the saint (of) Pir Ghaib, was different from other village deities. Khari said that the other gods are general, that every village has them, but that the baba is special, unique. He is our *isht-dev*.[3] In Hindu traditions the isht-dev is one's personal deity, freely chosen, to whom one has an abiding attachment and a deeply personal relationship.

The psychologist Sudhir Kakar disputes Freud's assumptions about religion (in *The Future of an Illusion*) through his own psychological and textual investigations of Hinduism. Challenging Freud's notion of the universality of the father-complex, Kakar gives us instead the lack of fathers in contemporary Hinduism: "The only god who is represented with a grey beard and who may be equated with the protective father today, the Creator Brahma, is a forgotten and neglected god who has only one temple in India dedicated to his worship. . . . It would be difficult if not impossible to locate the father in a Hindu's worshipped deity" (Kakar 2009, 142–43). Even paying the scantest attention to the "old fathers," the *pir babas* who are the *isht-dev*, the personal deities and father figures of many Hindus in Delhi would prove that assertion wrong. While Kakar represents a pervasive trend within those who write about and think about Hinduism, one of seeing Hinduism as isolated from all other Indian religions and as understandable only from within its canonical textual traditions, this point is not entirely invalid. The kind of father figure that the *pir babas* represent, the deeply personal, intimate *baba* whom you can curse without consequences, whom you can turn to in times of distress without having to bother about ritual purity, seems very different from the distant, fear-inducing God of the Judeo-Christian tradition with which Freud was primarily concerned.

The graybeard babas encountered at Firoz Shah Kotla are not seen as patriarchs, as stern fathers of sons, but as indulgent fathers of daughters, as can be seen in Manohar Lal's description of the first time he came to Firoz Shah Kotla and his entreaties when he first felt the presence of the baba: "'Baba, if I come to you dirty, however I come to you, you will accept me, you will not punish me, whether I deliberately make a mistake, whether I do so unwittingly, you will not punish me.' So he did not let my *izzat* (honor/respect) get destroyed, after that my work started going well. Even if I don't have a full stomach, I don't go to bed hungry, since I started serving him. My mother and father kicked me out on my backside." Manohar Lal, tellingly, equated and related the baba of Firoz Shah Kotla with his father-in-law, his *sasur*, rather than his father. With his own parents he had a troubled relationship, summed up in the phrase, *mujhe gand pe lat mar ke nikal diya* (they kicked me out on my backside), one of the very few things he ever said to me about them. This is in marked contrast to his reminiscences of his father-in-law, of whom he spoke very fondly and to whose repeated exhortations he connected his discovery of the healing powers of Firoz Shah Kotla. The equivalence for

Manohar Lal of saint and *sasur*, both welcoming and accepting father figures, perhaps points us to the fact that the patrilocal joint family can be as oppressive for the men born into it as it is for the women who marry into it. The wife's natal home, in contrast, free from the expectations of dutiful service, remains, at least notionally, a place of indulgence and affection.[4]

"Don't judge me," Manohar Lal told the baba. "Don't punish me, whatever I may do wrong, whether knowingly or unknowingly." Manohar Lal asks to be returned here to an infantile condition in relation to the baba, a condition where no judgment is passed on him, where no punishment is meted out for his real or imagined misdemeanors, and where he is treated with indulgence and affection. This state of affairs is contrasted, in the very next sentence, by his real relationship with his parents, where he felt betrayed and cheated out of both their affection and his rightful inheritance. At his father's funeral he saw Nanhe Miyan in attendance, wearing an outsized Rajasthani turban.[5]

Once again, Manohar Lal's statements are not exceptional, except in their eloquence, from other acts and utterances at Firoz Shah Kotla. The language of devotees when addressing the babas here is often infantile in relation to the baba, absolving themselves of all responsibility in relation to the baba, who is seen as a nurturing, nonjudgmental father. This first came home to me when I was listening to Vinod, who ran a side business of refurbishing and selling secondhand automobiles, describing the round of propitiation of deities he undertook every time he bought a car, thanks to which, according to him, his vehicles never gave trouble. He always bought cars on a Saturday and first drove to the Old Fort to offer a bottle of alcohol at the Bhairon Temple (Bhairon or Bhairava is a particularly terrifying and transgressive incarnation of the Lord Shiva). The next day, he went to the temple of Hanuman. The third day he drove the car to Ajmer, to get the blessings of Muinuddin Chishti of Ajmer. Before he set out on the journey, he addressed the saint—*Tere pas la raha hun. Aur tere hi dar se ja raha hun. Ab tu dekh le.* (I am bringing it to you. And I am leaving from your door [Firoz Shah Kotla]. Now you watch out for me.)

While his description of the offerings he made at the temples of Bhairon and Hanuman was perfunctory, and seemed purely propitiatory, his account of his address to the baba was far more intimate and personal and was marked by childish insolence and demanding authority: I'm coming to you; now it's your job to take care of me. When he told this story, I realized that much of what we see at Firoz Shah Kotla (and in much more muted ways, at other dargahs) can be understood as infantile acting-out by members of the congregation. A verse from a famous film qawwali from the movie *Garam Hawa* is a good example of the tantrum-like potentiality of popular devotion at dargahs:

> *Jaega kaun ake pyasa tumhare dar se*
> *Kuchh jam se pi'enge kuchh meherban nazar se*
> Ye sang-e dar tumhara torenge apne sar se
> *Ye dil agar dobara tuta Salim Chishti*[6]

> Who will return thirsty from your door?
> Some will drink from the cup, some from a kind gaze
> *We will break this stone of your threshold with our head*
> If this heart breaks again, Salim Chishti.

Much of devotional practice at Firoz Shah Kotla could be understood as "acting-out": the "possession" states manifested by young girls howl-ing and shrieking and violently shaking their hair and their bodies,[7] the letters and prayers that wish harm on those whom you suspect of harm-ing you, the overt and covert sexuality of interactions between men and women. Firoz Shah Kotla is a place of desire and its gratification. The space of justice, as dargahs are conceived to be, is a space where no judg-ment is passed on you, where you are found to be in a state of child-like innocence,[8] and where you have a child's license to indulge in desire, pleasure, and tantrums.

. . .

The structural equivalence of the baba with the father of girls extends to many aspects of devotional life at Firoz Shah Kotla. Laddu Shah's and Manohar Lal's fathers-in-law came here to pray for girl children. Almost all the married men I spoke to started coming to Firoz Shah Kotla be-cause of their wives' or wives' families' connections to this place. Ashiq Ali started coming here after the death of his wife, who was a regular visitor. And unmarried men? They come to check out the women.

Lugaibazi, or the womanizing game, is the foremost activity at Firoz Shah Kotla, judging by the number of times it is spoken of by the men who gather here. Of course, it is always practiced by the other guys, the *lugaibaz*, who only come here to look at and make moves on the women (who are easily a majority among those who come to Firoz Shah Kotla, and most other dargahs, according to the accounts of the self-identified non-lugaibaz). The public persona adopted by most men is that of easily resisting the ample temptation offered by a place like Firoz Shah Kotla, full of strange and often wanton women. So Akhtar once announced that the woman who'd taken him aside in front of all of us had wanted him to give her more of the sweet rice he'd been helping to distribute, and she was, he insinuated, willing to perform some sexual favors in return. But, Akhtar said, *main langot ka pakka hoon* (I tie my loincloth firmly), a saying implying mastery over one's sexual impulses.

In more intimate conversations and extended interviews the temptations of Firoz Shah Kotla are not so easy to resist. Manohar Lal told me once of a stunningly beautiful woman he'd seen at Firoz Shah Kotla, so beautiful that he was overwhelmed by temptation as soon as he set eyes on her, so beautiful that he remembered the moment in crystal-clear detail as he recalled it for me years later, so beautiful that he immediately had to start praying to Baba to save him from the temptation that Baba had placed in his path. "I've never had sex with any other woman except my wife," he felt the need to add. Other, younger, unmarried men and boys feel no such compunctions. They don't resist the temptations offered by a space like Firoz Shah Kotla but actively embrace them. Once when I was sitting with a bunch of (Hindu) teenagers, the conversation turned to the hotness of Muslim girls, which, as they pointed out, was amply in evidence at Firoz Shah Kotla and was one of their prime reasons for coming.

Once, when Ajay and I were supposed to be leaving Firoz Shah Kotla together in the evening to go to Old Delhi, he kept postponing our departure time. Once we left, he told me why. There was a Muslim girl from Seelampur that he was interested in and had talked to briefly before. He was hoping to talk to her that evening and had waited a long time, but she'd already left. While he was waiting (unsuccessfully) for this girl, he said, Vinod came up to him while he was talking to another girl and told him not to tangle with girls with loose morals. But he'd been talking to this particular girl on behalf of one of the guards. He'd arranged a rendezvous for them. She would come at six o'clock on Friday evening, and they'd have until eight o'clock to go off into one of the chambers together before the place was shut for the night.

In a place like Firoz Shah Kotla, where Hindus and Muslims, men and women, high-caste and low come together in ways that disrupt the usual boundaries of family and community, and in the obverse of the ethics of *gharib nawazi*, the dargah opens up the possibilities of temptation, of meeting the gazes (and bodies) of strangers.

In this, Firoz Shah Kotla seems to be drawing on a long tradition linking dargah spaces to the celebration of desire. Consider this extract from the account of a fair at a dargah in eighteenth-century Delhi:

In every corner, lovers embrace their beloveds, and in the streets and markets, the debauched dance with the pleasure of the satisfaction of their carnal desires. Unafraid of the *muhtasib* [supervisor of public morality], drunkards and the lustful stay busy in *shahidparasti* [witnessing beauty]. Such a gathering of beardless boys and prostitutes that it would break the penitent vows of the pious, and with unrivaled fascination those deer[-like] boys would shake the foundation of piety and goodness. Till where the gaze travels once can see beautiful faces and till where one can see there are the entrancing nets of tresses. The equipment of pleasure and companionship is provided on such a large scale that the desires of a whole universe would be satisfied. The causes of vice are available to such a degree that the wicked of the whole world can enjoy bodily pleasures. It is such a condition here that you barely notice when some beardless youth winks at you, and his beauty has just lit up your eyes when the message of some shameless woman reaches you. The markets and streets are full of nobility and the corners resound with the clamor of rich and poor. Musicians and qawwals are thicker than flies and the poor and needy flock thicker than mosquitoes.

In short, this is how the high and low of this city acquire mental and physical pleasures. (Dargah Quli Khan 1993, 123–24)

The above extract is the second half of the description of the 'Urs (or death anniversary celebrations) at the grave of the Mughal emperor Bahadur

Shah I (d. 1712), from the accounts of a Deccani nobleman visiting Delhi for an extended stay between 1739 and 1741. Bahadur Shah's grave is located inside the compound of the dargah of one of the foremost Chishtiya Sufis, Qutbuddin Bakhtiyar Kaki (d. 1235) in Mehrauli.

It would be unusual to come across such scenes of bacchanalia in the better known and more highly regulated dargahs of Delhi today, where the influence of reformist movements has meant an increasing amount of regulation of practices,[9] but in the open lawns and tumbledown ruins of Firoz Shah Kotla, an anarchic space mostly unregulated by any religious authorities (except for the space of the mosque), there is a much more visible continuity in popular practices between the eighteenth century and the twenty-first.

Abhishek Kaicker, in his work on politics and public culture in eighteenth-century Delhi, has shown how by the early eighteenth century, the religious culture around Sufi shrines and tombs was no longer dominated by elite religious practices and idioms of piety. Rather, "it was the teeming populace which inhabited these spaces and shaped their character, their veneration and belief which exalted some and rejected others, their preferences which determined how worship operated outside the narrow confines of the five daily prayers. The mass of the popular, in other words, had come to stand cheek by jowl with the elite in the courtyard of the sepulcher" (Kaicker 2014, 109). It was the behavior and practices of the subaltern classes of Delhi, Hindu and Muslim, Kaicker argues, that brought together pleasure and piety at the site of the saint shrine.

At Firoz Shah Kotla there are remarkable parallels with the eighteenth-century dynamic of the shaping of religious life by subaltern actors. It is said at Firoz Shah Kotla that *yahan har koi baba banta hai* (everyone acts like a baba here). And although this is said derisively, it is also one of the most unique features of religious life at Firoz Shah Kotla. Rather than turning to figures of authority, people turn to each other with their problems and sorrows. This democratization, if we can so characterize it, makes this a space of freewheeling practical advice and theological conversation, with everyone as a participant, irrespective of religion, caste, or gender. Those with reputations of piety and healing powers at Firoz Shah Kotla are not known for their exemplary lives or depth of learning that Bruce Lawrence (1986) characterized as essential for the posthumous fame of saints in Delhi. If anything, the "exemplary lives" here are the very opposite, marked by poverty, illegality, substance abuse, until an about-face usually attributed to the sometimes violent intervention of the jinn-saints. As we saw in Chapter 2, the contemporary popularity of Firoz Shah Kotla is linked in part to a black marketeer of cinema tickets turned healer. Laddu Shah's story, while unique, is not singular. Among those who have gained recognition at Firoz Shah Kotla for serving people, and for healing, are a man who was arrested for allegedly murdering his wife and a man who used to be an alcoholic.

Akhtar of the mosque, a mechanic by trade, gained a reputation as a healer after coming to Firoz Shah Kotla for several years. Then he disappeared for a few years. He was in jail, accused of his wife's murder. But he returned, and his story preceded him, yet rather than any lingering stigma attached to him despite his exoneration by the court, people still came to him to be healed and continued to come to him even when he was in jail.

Balon, until his death in October 2010, used to spend every day at Firoz Shah Kotla, late into the evening, tending to the alcove of the jinn-saint known as Nanhe Miyan (the first sacralized alcove on entering Firoz Shah Kotla), supervising the distribution of *deg*s of rice on Thursdays and Fridays and bestowing advice on the many who sought it from him. Although he never thought of himself, or carried himself, as a holy man, he had a reputation for piety that made people seek his blessings. This reputation of piety never seemed to suffer from the well-known story of Balon having been a raging alcoholic until he was violently cured by the jinns/babas at Firoz Shah Kotla.

By most accounts, before he was cured, Balon was drinking *at* Firoz Shah Kotla.[10] Pehelwan told me of how when he first started going to Firoz Shah Kotla, more than twenty years ago, he would see Balon sitting there, close to the mosque. One day, he went up and asked him about the difference between *paki* and *napaki*, purity and pollution. Balon explained the difference to him, which was ironic, because at this time he was drinking about fifteen *thailis* (pouches) of country liquor a day. When they became friendlier, Pehelwan explained to him that he shouldn't drink and that it was *haram* (forbidden) for Muslims to drink, and that's why the

Mughals lost their empire to the British. Balon agreed with him but said, "I will give up alcohol only when I choose to give up alcohol." And then one day Pehelwan saw Balon with his face bruised and swollen. The story goes that the baba had thrown him around.[11] After this, according to Pehelwan, he just stopped. And from then until the day he died, he went twenty years without touching a drop, twenty years of doing daily "duty" at Firoz Shah Kotla in Pehelwan's words, 8 a.m. to 8 p.m. No one else ever did that or does that, not even the imam of the mosque.

·   ·   ·

Yeh hai maikada, yahan rind hain, yahan sab ka saqi Imam hai
Yeh haram nahin hai shaikh ki, yahan parsai haram hai

This is a wine-house, there are nonconforming libertines here,[12] here the
    pourer of wine is everyone's guide.
This is not the sacred sanctuary of the Sheikh, piety is taboo here.

—Aziz Mian Qawwal

Anwar Sabri, who takes care of the dargah of Nanhe Miyan Chishti at Mandi House Circle, quoted these lines to me, as sung by the popular Pakistani qawwal Aziz Mian, as illustrative of the appeal of the small dargah of Nanhe Miyan Chishti. Wine and intoxication, as celebrated in the poetry and music associated with Sufis and their dargahs, are usually considered metaphorical: the wine is the wine of monotheism (*tawhid ki mai*, to use one particularly memorable phrasing); the intoxication is the intoxication of the remembrance of God. But in historical and contemporary Delhi, as we have seen, the metaphors tend toward the literal, and the above couplet, rather than allegory, could sometimes be read as a straightforward description.

Although Anwar Sabri claimed to belong to the Chishti and Sabri Sufi lineages, or *tariqas*, he chose to explain the appeal of the shrine of Nanhe Miyan not through the discourse of the Sufi masters of these lineages but through the words of a *fauji* (military) qawwal, renowned for his appeal to soldiers and other subalterns, his words and music circulating widely on cassette tape. Here we see the popular transmutation of the elite traditions of Sufism. In Aziz Mian Qawwal's words, spiritual intoxication does not remain the domain only of the spiritual elite but is an experience open to the collective, *all* the nonconforming libertines for whom the imam pours the wine. Anwar Sabri's deployment of Aziz Mian to explain the popularity of the shrine of Nanhe Miyan reasserts the ways in which the realm of the popular dynamically interacts with and transforms the discursive tradition of Islam. This leads us to two questions. First, what is the relationship of the "impossible desire" of the Sufi for God, so central to the discourse and practices of mysticism, and the expression and consummation of earthly desires, often transgressive and illicit, which characterizes the public culture of shrines such as Firoz Shah Kotla? And second, what is the nature of the *authority* of the popular that enables it to reshape these discourses? I take up each of these questions in turn.

DESIRE, LOVE, AND OTHER TRANSGRESSIONS

Actively seeking possession by (and other forms and degrees of intimacy with) the fairies and "princes of light" seems to have been an important ritual in the lives of women in late eighteenth- and early nineteenth-century Delhi and Lucknow. Many of Rangin's poems deal with the desirability and transformative effects of such possession:

Go mere sar par nahin Lal Pari ki baithak
Bandi par degi yaqin Lal Pari ki baithak

Even if the Red Fairy is not upon my head [yet]
This slave [girl] is certain she will give me a sitting.

Kokh aur mang donon se thandi hai jo deti hai
Jhar balon se zamin Lal Pari ki baithak

She is cold both of womb and the parting of her hair [has children and is
     married]
Who possessed by Lal Pari sweeps the ground with her hair.

Hai Jummerat ghar ko apne dogana mat ja
Aj de dal yahin Lal Pari ki baithak

It's Thursday, don't go back to your home, lover
Today let the Red Fairy possess you right here.

—(Argali 2006, 74–75)

In another ghazal:

> *Hai Zanakhi meri woh Lal Pari*
> *Ho jise dekh kar nidhal pari*
>
> My partner is [beautiful like] the Red Fairy.
> Even a fairy would be knocked over looking at her.
>
> *Woh chadhi gaat wah ji kya sakhti*
> *Woh parizad chhab jamal pari*
>
> That high bosom, oh what firmness
> That fairy-born one, that picture of beauty fairy.

—(Argali 2006, 96)[13]

As we have seen, the figure of the male jinn/baba is one of estrangement, sending one on a sometimes difficult path of separation from family and community. To be intimate with the feminine fairies, it would seem from the above, is different; it is to open oneself to both desire and its fulfillment. The desire celebrated in rekhti poetry is also far from heteronormative; much of rekhti poetry celebrates love and desire between women, as in the extracts I have translated above, and the vocabulary of rekhti is replete with words for romantic relations and sexual acts between women (Vanita 2012, 115–44). Rekhta poetry, it should be noted, was deeply influenced by the discourses of mysticism, where the Sufi's desire for God remains unconsummated. In the consummation of desire in rekhti poetry, we have an example of how the emergent popular of the eighteenth-century world interacted with and reshaped elite discourse, including elite religious discourse.

The fairies' presence continued in the lives of men and women in Delhi into the 1970s. A historian recounts how when he visited the *baoli* (stepwell) at Firoz Shah Kotla on May 17, 1976, an old Muslim lady told him that the baoli was a *hammam* (bathhouse) of the fairies (Mishra 1982, 57–58). The ASI report from 1977 also reports women speaking of fairies: "Similar homage was being paid at one of the mihrab recesses of the adjacent mosque. A lady . . . informed me that these offerings are in honour of the fairies who come to the mosque every night" (ASI, f24/76/77-M [T]).

But hardly anyone speaks of the fairies at Firoz Shah Kotla anymore, at least not the men, with whom I had the most interactions. The left-most mihrab recess of the western wall of the mosque, once associated with fairies, is now associated with male jinns/babas. All the letters I have seen at Firoz Shah Kotla are addressed to the male saints. On one of our times wandering together through Firoz Shah Kotla, I asked Pehelwan about the paris at the baoli. "Of course there used to be fairies there," he said. "This is where the *sakhis* [female companions] used to bathe the queens." He went on to say that earlier there were both paris and babas at Firoz Shah Kotla, but now it's only the babas; the paris are gone. When I asked him why, he said, "*Pariyan pare hain, Khuda se age hain, jaise jaise unka raz khulta gaya, unhon ne parda kar liya.*" (The paris are from beyond, from beyond God, as their secrets became known, they retreated behind the veil.)

Pehelwan's elegant explanation for the disappearance of the fairies was one of homonymy and puns. He linked the Persian *pari* to *pare*, Hindi for beyond, apart. As their secrets became known, they have once again moved beyond the veil. Though Pehelwan did not say it, the vanishing of the paris is not hard to understand. The jinns/babas are male and have Quranic sanction. The paris are feminine and are not mentioned in the Quran. Islamic (and Hindu) reform continues to be increasingly uncomfortable with sexuality, especially female sexuality in the realm of religion (Ramberg 2014). At least in the vocabulary of the men, the fairies, whom both men and women once loved and desired, have been replaced by *gandi chiz* (dirty things), which only possess women.

Though the paris seem to have disappeared from Firoz Shah Kotla, their effect lingers. As Pehelwan explained, they are *veiled*, a term that merely highlights their invisibility, not their inefficacy. Firoz Shah Kotla is still a place where desire is fulfilled, even when it disrupts normative boundaries of family and propriety.

One day, as we were sitting around at Firoz Shah Kotla, Pehelwan told a story about Indira Gandhi, who according to him was the best prime minister India ever had. The story concerned Imam Bukhari, the hereditary leader of the congregation of the Jama Masjid, calling Indira Gandhi a *randi* (whore), in a public speech. She was the prime minister,

and she could have bombed the Jama Masjid to smithereens. But instead, she just laughed and said, "*Yeh to mera prachar kar rahe hain*" (He is
doing good publicity for me). Turning to the man wearing a skullcap (and
hence obviously Muslim), whom I hadn't seen before, and who had just
come and joined us, Pehelwan said, "Don't take me amiss, but what the
Imam Sahib did was wrong."

The man showed no signs of taking things amiss and readily agreed
with Pehelwan. "You're absolutely right," he said. "I heard the speech with
my own ears. And he was wrong to say that. After all, Indira Gandhi was
married to a Muslim. His name was Firoz Khan, [and] he was a Farsi.[14]
How could he be a Gandhi? Do Hindus marry in the same *gotra*?[15] They
gave him the name Gandhi after. . . . She was married to a Muslim; she
was a bahu [bride] of the *qaum*. It was wrong of the Imam to call his own
bahu a *randi*."

The man with the skullcap then proceeded to trash the imam of the
Jama Masjid and his ethics and politics and claimed that he never prayed
behind him despite living right next to the Jama Masjid. What stuck
in my mind was that the popular perception of Indira Gandhi being
married to a Muslim didn't change people's notion of her being the best
prime minister the country ever had.

It was Pehelwan who first told me, a few months before this conversation at Firoz Shah Kotla, about Indira Gandhi being married to
a Muslim. "*Ab 'ishq ho gaya to ho gaya.*" (If love happens, it happens.) It
was not love between a Muslim man and a Hindu woman that was the
problem.[16] It was the imam's calling a bride who had come to his community a whore.

. . .

In these times of the waging of "Love-Jihad," how do we understand the
ways in which love across the boundaries of religion (and caste, and class)
is taken to be so unproblematic in popular discourse at Firoz Shah Kotla?
In the popular affirmation of desire we see in everyday conversation at
Firoz Shah Kotla, and in the praise of desirable fairies in rekhti poetry, we
see a long tradition of the reshaping of the "desiring subject," so central to
Sufism, to more popular, earthly ends.

In her book on modernity, psychoanalysis, and Islam, Katherine Ewing argues that Western psychoanalysis, by reducing desire to the biological, obscures its significance as a force "that constitutes the subject within a political order. Desire has been privatized and located within the apolitical sphere of the medicalized psyche" (Ewing 1997, 253).

In contrast, Ewing reads the Sufi understanding of desire as profoundly political in that it radically destabilizes social and epistemological certainties. In classical Sufi discourse the subject is constituted by an overwhelming desire, the desire for God. This overwhelming desire of the Sufi for God is presented in Sufi poetry by the imagery of the moth whose desire for the flame is so strong it ultimately enters the flame and, in dying, becomes one with it. This obliteration of the self, the *fana* so highly valued as a goal in Sufi mystical literature, is in Ewing's Lacanian reading of Al-Ghazzali an obliteration of cultural traditions, the symbolic order through which the ego-self is constituted. In Sufi tradition, as represented by Al-Ghazzali and Rumi, rational thought processes and language by themselves are unable to lead us to "truth," to knowing God. Access to truth requires a prophetic irruption, "a disruption of the imaginary, of the ideologies, including the ideology of the 'self' that places a screen or 'veil' between us and truth" (Ewing 1997, 259). The Sufi's quest for God is thus a movement away from the symbolic and imaginary orders, a movement away from "the illusory ego, the series of illusory self-representations that we cling to to avoid having to face exposure as a fluid, changeable subject. Paradoxically, it is a position of owning one's desire, and not renouncing it, because to be in this state is also to be in a state of recognition that the 'self' is nothing, that it is an illusory construction, an imaginary fantasy" (262–63).

The desiring Sufi is thus fundamentally subversive of the social order, but most Sufis remain faithful to the tenets of the sharia. But the potential subversion of all order by the Sufi, a potential glimpsed even by a pillar of orthodoxy like Al-Ghazzali, is embodied in the antinomian, insurrectionary figure of the *qalandar*, who lives beyond all law and who, as Ewing notes, has been a part of the rhetorical tropes and lived traditions of Islam for more than a thousand years.

Classical Sufism recognizes the love for an earthly beloved as *'ishq majazi*, a love that is metaphorical for the real love, *'ishq haqiqi*, that is the soul's desire for God. What happens, as it does in the popular reshaping of tradition, when divine desire turns to an earthly beloved? We could say that the socially constituted self, the self that follows the patriarchal and hierarchical norms of family and community, melts away before the flame of desire. In the popular culture of North India the esoteric understandings of desire in Sufism (Kugle 2007, 210–11)—the valuation of desire for an earthly beloved as an aspect of worshipping the beauty of God—find expression in the trope of the Sufi dargah as the space where desire is invariably blessed—even desire that transgresses and queers boundaries of family, of religion, of nation, and of gender.

A man crosses the border from India to Pakistan to meet the woman he loves. He is Indian; she is Pakistani. He is Hindu; she is Muslim. She loves him but is engaged to someone else. That evening, a Thursday, her family and the family of her fiancé go together to a dargah in Lahore to pray for the marriage to be successful. She accompanies them to the dargah, her face stricken with grief and despair. She prays at the grave of the pir. All this transpires while the qawwals sing, "*Aya tere dar par diwana*" (The crazy one has come to your door). It starts raining. When she turns from the grave, she sees her Indian lover standing, framed by the entrance arch of the dargah. She runs to him in the rain and embraces him. Both families look on aghast.

Two women come to the dargah of the saint Chiragh Dilli in Delhi. They are sisters-in-law, both married to brothers who live together in a joint family, both suffering from spousal neglect. They find companionship, love, and sexual fulfillment with each other, but secretly, within the confines of their marriages and their marital home. It is only at the shrine of the Sufi that a more radical wish can be uttered. "Let's leave [the family]," says the younger woman to the older, after making a wish that they can be together forever.

The former was a scene from *Veer Zaara* (dir. Yash Chopra, 2004), the story of a cross-border romance between an Indian man and a Pakistani woman, which was a blockbuster hit. The latter was a scene from *Fire* (dir. Deepa Mehta, 1996), the 1998 Indian release of which generated an immense amount of controversy and violence by Hindu right-wing activists. In the reasons given by the leadership of the Hindu right-wing party, the Shiv Sena, members of which spearheaded the violent protests and attacks against the film, it was the film's threat to the patriarchal family order that justified their attacks and a call for a ban on the film. The fear was expressed that films like this would "spoil women" and encourage them to leave their husbands and families.

What remained virtually unaddressed in all the controversy, political and academic, that followed the release of *Fire* and its violent reception in India was the small but crucial role that the dargah played in the film. Perhaps it passed unheeded because the dargah as a site of the blessing of transgressive desire is so ubiquitous in Indian film and television, as it is in quotidian life, that it doesn't merit comment. But the paradox that this ubiquity raises is a profound one. If Islam, as represented by its normative jurisprudential traditions, is overwhelmingly patriarchal, why do spaces identified as Muslim become the places where wishes can be uttered by women that upset patriarchal orders of family and community?

AMBIGUOUSLY ISLAMIC,
OR THE AMBIGUITY OF ISLAM?

What is the genealogy of Bombay cinema's portrayal of dargah spaces as spaces of licensed transgression? A possible link is suggested by Bombay cinema's connection to the Punjabi cultural religion. The two films I mentioned in the last section were both made by filmmakers of Punjabi origin, Yash Chopra and Deepa Mehta. This is not merely a coincidence, for as Kaushik Bhaumik's (2001) work has shown, actors and filmmakers from the Punjab region have long had a dominant role in the Bombay film industry. And they come from a region where, as Farina Mir's (2010) work shows, a shared sense of piety, across religious identities, was anchored in the veneration of Muslim saint shrines.

Mir finds this shared sense of piety articulated in the *qissa* or epic-romance storytelling tradition of Punjab, which flourished from the seventeenth century onward, in which the story of the lovers Hir and Ranjha is told and retold again by Hindu, Muslim, and Sikh authors and storytellers. The bare bones of the story, which "has been circulating in northwest India for at least the past four hundred years" (Mir 2010, 1), go something like this:

> A young man named Dhido sets out from his village Takht Hazara on an epic journey in search of the renowned beauty named Hir. Through trials and tribulations, he makes his way to Hir's hometown of Jhang, where the two fall in love at first sight. Their love blossoms on the banks of the Chenab River, where Ranjha (as Dhido is always called) takes cattle to pasture each day, Hir's father having hired him—at her suggestion—as a cowherd. Hir and Ranjha's idyll is soon interrupted, however, when Hir's family learns of her liaison. Her parents reject Ranjha as a suitor for their daughter because of his low-status occupation and they betroth Hir to Seido Khera, a bridegroom Hir's father considers more appropriate to his family's landlord status. Hir is forcibly married to Khera, but refuses to consummate her marriage, and Ranjha makes his way, disguised as a yogi, to her married home. In this disguise, Ranjha is able to contact Hir and the two elope. The Kheras pursue the lovers and in most renditions of this tale commonly known as *Hir-Ranjha*, or simply as *Hir*, the two die for their love. (Mir 2010, 1)

Muslim saint-figures play a crucial role in many parts of the narrative. The *panj-pir*, the five iconic saints of the Punjab, comfort Ranjha at the beginning of his quest and sanction his search for Hir (Mir 2010, 124). And it is the *panj-pir* that Hir calls on to sanctify her union with Ranjha, in front of the religious scholars called on to judge their case (145). Hir uses the authority of the saint shrine to articulate her love for Ranjha as a form of piety.

Against both her mother, representing the familial order, and the figure of the *qazi*, representing the "nexus between *sharia* and social power" (Mir 2010, 140), Hir constantly emphasizes that her love for Ranjha is sacred, thus articulating this love as a form of piety, in tension with norms of Indic and Islamic pious behavior, which emphasize the performance of one's duty to parents and elders. In all versions of this epic romance, whether told by Hindu, Muslim, or Sikh authors, Hir subverts and challenges this latter notion of piety. "Instead of adhering to an order of behavior as sanctioned or forbidden under Islamic law and social custom, she defines a code of behavior, anchored in her devotion to her lover, which has its own set of principles" (Mir 2010, 178). This set of principles, anchored in the veneration of saint shrines, opened up another ethical possibility for the lives of Punjabis, across confessional divides, in tension with the morality of family and community. This tension, often dramatized by filmmakers from the Punjab, plays out again and again as the central theme in the plot of Bombay films, maintaining a fidelity to the epic-romance tradition.

Despite the shared norms of piety espoused by the Hir-Ranjha texts being inextricably linked with Muslim saint shrines, Mir does not see this piety as having any direct relation to Islam or to any of the major religious traditions of the Punjab. "Characters' participation in this world of devotion and devotional practice bears no direct relation to Islam, Hinduism, Sikhism, or any other religion. The way saint veneration is presented in these texts points to *an independent set of beliefs* that are neither in direct conflict nor coterminous with Punjab's major religious traditions" (Mir 2010, 181–82, my emphasis). In arguing for the independence of the piety connected with saint shrines from any of the major religious traditions of the Punjab, Mir makes an argument similar to Carla Bellamy's, who, based on her ethnographic work on the shrine of Husain Tekri, asserts that "dargah culture is properly understood as a (religious) culture in and of itself, rather than a culture that draws its forms of authority and practice from Hinduism, Islam, or a syncretic combination of the two. Rather than 'Hindu' or 'Muslim,' dargah culture is South Asian" (Bellamy 2011, 6).

Why the discomfort, despite the explicitly Muslim identity of these shrines, with thinking of the culture around these shrines as (unproblematically) Islamic? I think that the discomfort stems from a complex array of factors that inform not just these two works but dominant academic paradigms for the study of religion in general and Islam in particular. The participation of a large number of non-Muslims in dargah culture, both in terms of literary production and ritual practice, makes it hard to think of these sites as authentically "Islamic." As Bellamy puts it, "The [dargah] culture's creators, many of whom are non-Muslim, do not seek to define 'an islam as Islam'" (2011, 6). But to understand a discourse as Islamic only when it is addressed to and attested as such by Muslims is to per-form a very (epistemologically) modern conflation of religion and iden-tity, which may not be relevant to those who participated and continue to participate in the culture of Muslim saint shrines. As Shahab Ahmed (2016, 444–52) shows, if we put aside the category of "religion" and focus instead on *meaning*, the idea of non-Muslims making meanings in terms of Islam, or Islamic discourse, becomes unproblematic. Many Hindus at Firoz Shah Kotla have a very keen understanding of Islamic theological debates and vocabularies, as I show in the next chapter.

The analytic discomfort also arises from two interlinked sets of prob-lems, both related to the emphasis on authority in the constitution of the discursive tradition of Islam, following Talal Asad. One is the empha-sis on the Islamic tradition as being primarily constituted by *protocols of prescription.*

In using the phrase *protocols of prescription,* I am drawing explicitly on the distinction Shahab Ahmed makes between prescriptive and ex-ploratory authority in the construction and transmission of (the Islamic) tradition. The Islamic discursive tradition is shaped by both prescriptive and exploratory forms of authority, Ahmed argues, but the dominant aca-demic understanding of the Islamic tradition focuses exclusively on the prescriptive, as being primarily and even solely constitutive of the Islamic tradition (2016, 270–95). The paradigms of prescriptive authority are based largely on "the mimesis of a pristine time of the earliest genera-tions of the community (the *salaf*)" (S. Ahmed 2016, 81). For instance, one of Carla Bellamy's reasons for arguing that the forms of piety and devotion encountered at Muslim saint shrines in South Asia are "am-biguously Islamic" at best is because she finds that the culture at these shrines fits uneasily with the discursive tradition of Islam, because its cre-ators and participants "do [not] regularly or explicitly relate the shrine to the founding texts of the Islamic tradition, or consistently use historically Islamic means of introducing and maintaining relations between dargah culture and the founding texts and major concepts of the Islamic tradition" (Bellamy 2011, 14). Bellamy finds the culture of dargahs to be not quite Islamic not just because of the participation of non-Muslims but also be-cause she does not encounter the authoritative protocols of *prescriptive* discourse in the space of the dargah, the ways in which the practices and narratives of dargah culture can be connected to authoritative Prophetic precedent through authenticated chains of hadith transmission. So according to Bellamy, pilgrims' stories about magic being performed on the Prophet Muhammad cannot be recognized as unambiguously Islamic because while "stories about magic being performed on Muhammad are preserved in the hadith collections . . . none of the pilgrims who related this anecdote to me knew the specifics of the hadith, or even felt it necessary to legitimate the story with a *sahih* (sound) pedigree" (Bellamy 2011, 14).

But this invites the question, What are the *historically Islamic means* of maintaining relations between contemporary practice and foundational texts and contexts? The popular, as opposed to exclusive (legal-scholarly), knowledge of the protocols of hadith soundness is a relatively recent phenomenon even in the Arabic speaking world, linked to the spread of print culture and the growth of mass literacy in the postcolonial era. Dreams, however, have a far longer history of connecting individuals and their practices to foundational figures like the Prophet Muhammad and Imam Ali and calling people to the dargahs of saints (Moin 2012).

What gives certain kinds of dreams their authority in the Islamic tradition? Shahab Ahmed sees the authoritative nature of dreams in the Islamic tradition—as exemplified by the hadith, "the good dream of a faithful person is one forty-sixth of prophecy"[17]—as illustrating the value of the self and the agency of the self in the ascertaining of Truth in Islamic discourse, "whether by methods philosophical or Sufi or some admixture of both" (2016, 339). For Ahmed the idea embodied in this hadith—that even the quotidian experience of dreaming while asleep allows any individual Muslim to participate, even if fractionally, in the process of revelation—powerfully illustrates how the self has been the locus of authoritatively *Islamic* meaning making in the Islamic tradition.

In the dreams of Egyptian women, as Amira Mittermaier's work shows, the appearance of the Prophet as a figure of mercy often sanctions deviations from sharia obligations (Mittermaier 2011, 164–69). Dreams are now considered disruptive because they evade and exceed prescriptive legal discourse, but they are very much part of the Islamic tradition, going back to the Prophet, to the Quran, and to the authoritative texts of Sufis such as Ibn ʿArabi (Mittermaier 2011). This is not a conundrum once we realize that "orthodoxy—the insistence on adherence to singular truth on pain of sanction (often, legal sanction)—was not only *not* definitive of a prevalent Muslim notion of Islam [historically speaking], but where the prevalent Muslim notion of Islam was a discursive tendency that was simply not oriented to orthodoxy" (S. Ahmed 2016, 276). What, then, was this tradition oriented toward? In Ahmed's masterful and pathbreaking account, "the historical *bulk* of the normative discursive tradition of Muslims is non-prescriptive and non-orthodoxizing—instead it is *explorative* of a multiplicity of truths and values—at least, this is how it forcefully appears when we do not pre-emptively exclude from that discursive tradition those texts that are, historically, the most read, recited and invoked texts of Muslim self-expression, exemplified in the literary canon of the Balkans-to-Bengal complex" (285–86).

The idea of dreams as giving every believer access to, and the authority of, prophecy, Ahmed finds, is also operative in the idea of the inspiration of the poet as the simulacrum of Divine Revelation—a logic that underlies the authoritative nature of the poetic works of Hafez, Rumi, and Bullhe Shah. These are just a few "canonized" poets (in the double sense of being considered saints or exemplary humans and being widely read) whose works were central to the everyday religious experience of Muslims in the vast geographical area stretching from the western fringes of the Ottoman Empire to the eastern fringes of the Mughal world. The exploratory and experimental works of these widely read, recited, and emulated poets opened up *"possibilities of meaning* beyond those produced within the four walls of the methods and norms of the academy of *tafsir."* This epitomizes "the dislocations and relocations and circulations of the Quranic text into an economy of meaning-making by Muslims comprising the imagining, reading, performing, audition of, investment in and affiliation with fictional narratives and forms and figures. . . . Muslims' reading and conceptualization of Divine truth was informed by a range of inter-textualities of fiction, and by dynamics of self-consciously explorative and creative meaning- and truth-making" (S. Ahmed 2016, 310).

But these works have been excluded from the contemporary academic understanding of the discursive tradition of Islam, with the analytical consequence of "over-emphasize[ing] prescription and orthodoxy in the conceptualization of Islam" (S. Ahmed 2016, 281). So, for example, in Farina Mir's reading of Waris Shah's *Hir*—an outstanding example of Muslim meaning making through fiction and poetry and a work given a status equivalent to scripture by Punjabis across religious denominations (Mir 2010, 3, 150–83)—it is only the qazi, or Islamic judge, who represents the authorized discourse of Islam. Hir's discourse of piety, which opposes that of the qazi by drawing on the authority of Sufi saints, is seen as illustrating *an independent set of beliefs* not coterminous with Islam or any of Punjab's other major religious traditions. Here Islam is recognized only in the patriarchal vision espoused by the law schools and increasingly propagated by revivalists as "true" Islam. This recognition of the Islamic tradition only in its legalist and now revivalist iterations, as it were, not only narrows the breadth of the tradition but also fundamentally misrecognizes the transmission of tradition as strictly linear when it is in fact rhizomatic and dialogic. Alternative visions and understandings of Islam have always challenged and coexisted with prescriptive legal norms. In other words, the dispute between the qazi and Hir is fundamentally constitutive of the Islamic tradition rather than outside of it.[18]

By identifying the ethical possibilities that the figure of Hir opens up for the lives of Punjabis across confessional boundaries as *independent of Islam*, we can recognize only forms of feminine agency that conform to the patriarchal jurisprudential order as Islamic, as in Saba Mahmood's work (2005). This leaves no room to understand other modes of agency, if they explicitly challenge this order, as anything other than un-Islamic, thus reifying (rather than complicating) the differences between Islamic and Western-feminist modes of women's agency. The emphasis, in the social sciences, on the prescriptive nature of the discursive tradition of Islam narrows the possibilities of "human freedom" for women within the tradition. Yet Hir expresses her defiance of the patriarchal norms of family and community by invoking the authority of Muslim saints, as do the women who come to Firoz Shah Kotla (metonymic for the millions of women who visit Muslim saint shrines throughout the Islamic world), who express their longings, their desires, and their defiance of the patriarchal norms of family and community in a space sanctified by the presence of Muslim saints. Is this because Sufi shrines, with their traditions of hospitality to non-Muslim others, and their traditions of the celebration of earthly desire, are at best "ambiguously" Islamic? Rather, following Leila Ahmed (1992), I would assert that what is encountered at saint shrines is an ambiguity inherent to Islam, the antipatriarchal potential that is as much part of the Islamic tradition as patriarchal jurisprudential traditions.

.   .   .

In Joyce Flueckiger's intimate portrait of Amma, a prominent female Sufi healer in the city of Hyderabad, the problem of authority remains: "Amma's life narratives and informal conversations suggest that she, too, lacks a safety net, a previously articulated story or model for female religious authority and action in the public domain upon which she can base or to which she can connect her own *innovative* position and life story. . . . Her only models of public spiritual authority within the Sufi contexts she lives in are male" (2006, 141, my emphasis). But despite the overwhelming absence of normative traditions to guide her, Amma successfully negotiated a position for herself as a female healer, with innovative spiritual, ethical, and healing practices. Using Shahab Ahmed's paradigm, we can say that Amma displayed surpassing exploratory authority, making meaning of Islam for herself, meanings that were recognized as authoritative by those who came to be healed by her. Her husband, Abba, also a Sufi *murshid*, explained the difference between his spiritual authority and Amma's with the phrase, *"Khilafat* is a man's; *vilayat* is a woman's." *Khilafat* means succession, authority; *vilayat* or *walayat* refers to closeness, proximity; and the term *wali* is used to denote a saint, one who is close to God.[19] Working with the semantic ranges of the two terms, Flueckiger interprets the phrase as saying, "External, institutional religious authority belongs to men, but proximity to God [spiritual authority, wisdom] belongs to women" (2006, 151). Using Abba's terms, what have we lost and ignored in the Islamic tradition by focusing only on (patriarchal/prescriptive) *khilafat* and not on (exploratory) *vilayat*?

The figure of the Prophet Muhammad, as he comes down in popular traditions, embodies many, many traditionally "feminine" qualities, such as modesty, humility, and gentleness, so much so that even an influential "reformist" text such as Maulana Ashraf Ali Thanvi's *Bihishti Zevar*, concerned with disciplining women's characters, ritual lives, and sexuality, holds the Prophet up as a model of pious imitation for women (Metcalf 1992, 253–58). He is a figure whose popular *bios* are marked by his love, affection, and respect for the women in his life, as Fatima Mernissi recounts in telling of her grandmother's, and her own, affective relations with the beloved Prophet (Mernissi 1991, 62–65). And as the work of Asma Barlas (2002) has shown us, the Quran itself can be read as an antipatriarchal text.[20] In her analysis of the Quran's antipatriarchal potential, Barlas points out that in the Quranic narrative the Prophet Muhammad himself is never the symbolic father of the Muslim community. "From the denial of symbolic fatherhood to the Prophet [Quran 33:40], which exegetes pass over in silence, I derive the lesson that in Islam, God's Rule displaces *rule* by the father. . . . The Quran views fathers in a fundamentally different way than patriarchies do" (Barlas 2002, 121). Barlas also connects the antipatriarchal potential of the Quran to the bios of the Prophet: "Given that the Prophet is not sacralized as a father, is it also a mere coincidence that he loses his father, Abdullah, in his own infancy, and all his sons in theirs; that only his daughters survive, at a time and in a place when people viewed girls as a curse?" (Barlas 2002, 121).

The Prophet is remembered as a loving father of a daughter (Fatima) and not of sons; he is remembered as a man who embodied feminine qualities and loved and respected women and often preferred them to men (Mernissi 1991, 65). Yet he is also remembered as making misogynistic statements, which come down to us in corpora of sound hadith that form the basis for the dominant patriarchal readings of the sharia. This is the ambiguity inherent in Islam, both the patriarchal readings of the law, and the antipatriarchal potential of the Quran and the *bios* of the Prophet. The dominant academic understanding of the discursive tradition of Islam has focused on the former but not the latter. How does the antipatriarchal potential of Islam get transmitted, elaborated, and understood down the centuries?

To understand this, we need to turn to the realm of the popular, to the ways in which stories, dreams, images, and songs make Islamic meanings in ways that surpass and evade the prescriptive discourses of Islam and are yet also in constant conversations with them, like Hir and the qazi. The sanctified jinns and fairies of rekhti poetry, spirits that allowed women to *experiment* with the dynamics of estrangement and desire, were connected, in popular tradition, to the memory of the Prophet's daughter, Fatima: "In the case of Miyan Shah Dariya, Shah Sikandar and the seven fairies they say that they are all brothers and sisters and that God sent them from Heaven to be playmates of Fatima" (Argali 2006, 45). At Muslim saint shrines, shrines dedicated to figures mimetic of the Prophet (in that they try to emulate the revelatory states and ethical stances of the Prophet), women outnumber men, recalling the Prophet's preference for women over men. The men who come to Firoz Shah Kotla come through their women, and like Manohar Lal in his dreams, they associate the saints not with their fathers but with their fathers-in-law. Like the Prophet, the saints are seen as antipatriarchal father figures, considered the fathers of daughters and not of sons. And so the food offered to the saints is given not to sons but to daughters. The Muslim saint shrine, given the resonant presence of the Prophetic image and Quranic ethics, seems to be unambiguously Islamic.

.   .   .

What is at stake in claiming that the culture of Muslim saint shrines like Firoz Shah Kotla is Islamic? There is certainly a political stake here, given that words published in 1991 still hold true today, perhaps more than ever: "Islam alone is condemned by many Westerners as blocking the way to women's rights" (Mernissi 1991, vi). Given the blinkered views of Islam dominant in almost all forums in the West, and the equation, in both academia and media, of patriarchal readings of Islam with all of Islam, it seems vital to assert that "human freedom"—the potentialities of ethical self-fashioning, exploring religious meanings, and owning one's desire—remains open for women within living Islamic traditions, and not just as hermeneutic exercises returning to the Quranic text.[21] Equally, if not more, important is simply to do justice to the world that my interlocutors at Firoz Shah Kotla so generously let me into. In this world relations between religions were not characterized only by competition (winning converts) or syncretism (doctrinal dilution and mixing). In an idea that seems radical from Western academic perspectives, but commonsensical and ordinary to people at Firoz Shah Kotla, one religious tradition opens up ethical possibilities in the lives of those who identify with another. Islam opens up a set of ethical possibilities for the lives of those who come to Muslim saint shrines, irrespective of their religious affiliation. And this traffic does not go just one way. To take one example, Maulana Hasrat Mohani, the well-known Urdu poet, freedom-fighter, and devout Muslim, wrote several poems dedicated to the Hindu deity Krishna (Naim 2013). Reading those poems, we can see that perhaps his attraction for Krishna, renowned for his eroticism and divine love-play (*Ras Lila*), deepened and broadened the potentialities of love (*'ishq*) for Hasrat, an affect central to his devotional life *as a Muslim*:

> *Hasrat ki bhi qubul ho Mathura men haziri*
> *Sunte hain 'ashiqon pe tumhara karam hai khas*
>
> May you accept Hasrat's attendance at Mathura.
> I hear you are especially kind to lovers.
> —Hasrat Mohani quoted in Naim (2013, 39)

To conclude, not only do we have an incomplete picture of the ethical potentials *within* Islamic traditions by leaving dargah culture out of our accounts, but we also can't understand the life of contemporary Hinduism without understanding the potentialities for healing and self-fashioning that Muslim shrines open up for the everyday lives of Hindus. In the next chapter I will look at the processes of translation, and what I call *translation as a mode of being*, to understand the ways in which Islamic spaces, such as the dargah, become an integral part of the ethical landscape of India.

CHAPTER 5

TRANSLATION

Jahanon ka bikhrav simta hai mujh men
Teri sans ka tarjuma karte karte

The scatter of the worlds has gathered into me
In the process of translating your breath.

—Riyaz Latif

SAT YUG = IRAQ?

One Thursday afternoon I found myself walking around Firoz Shah
Kotla with Pehelwan and Pandeyji, one of the ASI-appointed guards.
Pandeyji, as the name suggests, was a Brahmin from eastern Uttar
Pradesh who took his Brahmin heritage very seriously. He never ate any
of the offerings distributed at Firoz Shah Kotla because they would com-
promise his dietary purity, and he was prone to quoting Sanskrit *shlokas*
and verses from Tulsidas's *Ramcharitmanas* in his conversations with me.
As the three of us walked around the grounds of Firoz Shah Kotla, I
was highly aware of the slightly absurd and surreal quality of the scene:
an anthropologist (usually understood to be Punjabi) walking between a
Brahmin and a Balmiki, situated on the very opposite ends of the spec-
trum of caste. Pandeyji was, perhaps more so than usual, waxing Sanskritic. At one point the conversation turned to *Gandharva Vidya*. The
Gandharvas, in archaic Hindu and Buddhist mythology, are male nature
spirits, renowned for their musical skills. *Gandharva Vidya* (Gandharva
knowledge) now refers to music and dance. Pandeyji was in full flow,
telling a story that involved Arjun of the Mahabharata being one of the
prime practitioners of Gandharva Vidya, when Pehelwan said, "It was
Amir Khusrau who brought *gandharva vidya* [to India]."[1] Amir Khusrau
was a fourteenth-century Muslim, a disciple of the famous Chishti saint

149

Nizamuddin Auliya, renowned for his (legendary) invention of both instruments (the sitar) and modes of singing (qaul, qawwali), but he would, by most modern ways of reckoning, be considered far outside the Hindu Sanskritic world that Pandeyji was evoking.

My notes from that evening contain a boxed off section that says simply Khusrau = Gandharva, and then Sat Yug = Iraq, for, later that evening, as we were drinking tea outside Firoz Shah Kotla, Pehelwan started talking about Valmiki/Balmiki, the sage who is said to have written the Sanskrit Ramayana and whom his community claims descent from. "They say Balmiki was a thief," Pehelwan said. "But the Ramayana is set in the Sat Yug [the true, the right, the beneficent age]," he continued, "and if Balmiki was around in Sat Yug, then how could he be a thief? There was no crime in Sat Yug. Like in Iraq they still leave their doors unlocked."

. . .

I found a strange and compelling parallel to Pehelwan's worldview in the writings of Dara Shukoh, the seventeenth-century Mughal prince. In his best known work Dara Shukoh writes:

> After knowing the Truth of truths and ascertaining the secrets and subtleties of the true religion of the Sufis . . . he thirsted to know the tenets of the India monotheists [*muwahhidan*]; and having had repeated discussion with the doctors and perfect divines of this [i.e., Indian] religion who had attained the highest pitch of perfection . . . he did not find any difference, except verbal, in the way in which they sought and comprehended Truth. Consequently, having collected the views of the two parties and having brought together the points . . . he has compiled a tract and entitled it Majma'-ul-Bahrain or the "Mingling of the Two Oceans," as it [is] a collection of the truth and wisdom of two Truth-knowing (*Haq-shinas*) groups. (Dara Shikoh [i.e., Shukoh] 2006, 66)

"The extraordinary idea that Sufi and Hindu thought differ only terminologically determines the structure of the whole work, which seeks to establish notational isomorphisms in the philosophical vocabulary of the two disciplines" (Ganeri 2011, 26). Jonardon Ganeri is here describing the Mughal prince Dara Shukoh's (1615–49) extraordinary work *Majma ul bahrain* (The meeting of the two oceans), which as Ganeri says, seeks to find notational isomorphisms, or equivalences, between the theologies of Sufi Islam and Vedantic "Hindu" thought and practice.

For Dara Shukoh, reading and understanding the Upanishads was essential to understanding the Quran because they were part of the same series of divine revelations, the Upanishads being the first of the books of divine revelation from God (*asmani kitab*) and the Quran being the last. "Dara Shukoh viewed the Upanishads as hermeneutically continuous with the Qur'an, providing an extended exposition of the divine unity that was only briefly indicated in the Arabic scripture" (Ernst 2003, 186).

"How, though, can an imported text from an alien tradition be thought of as in this way 'hermeneutically continuous' with Islamic scripture?" (Ganeri 2011, 24). The question of the how indicates our distance from the world and the worldview of Dara Shukoh, for whom the Upanishads and the Quran were part of the same tradition of Prophetic revelation from God. For him, the logical and expostulatory clarity of the Upanishads would make it easier to understand the allegorical and poetical nature of the truths in the Quran. Ganeri understands the worldview of Dara Shukoh, the worldview that undergirded his projects of translation, as one of "religious cosmopolitanism" and hospitality: "As a devout Muslim and an adept Sufi practitioner, he was already firm in his convictions. He had no expectation of learning something *fundamentally* new from the Upanishads and the other Hindu texts, nor indeed any real openness to the possibility of doing so. Dara Shukoh's hospitality had its roots in a different idea altogether, that the stranger, if welcomed and understood, would turn out to be no stranger at all" (Ganeri 2011, 23).

While Dara Shukoh's elevated position seems to make him an exceptional figure of rapprochement between the faiths in India, and his death is often seen as "a kind of civilizational tipping point away from Mughal policies of religious tolerance" (Kinra 2009, 166), he was part of a much longer tradition of translation and of finding equivalences between Islam and Indic faiths that was centuries old before his death (Behl 2012) and continues long after it (Alam 2004). I bring up Dara Shukoh here not to highlight his singularity but because his mode of thinking—one that found "notational isomorphisms" between Sufi and Vedantic terminology, one that used the Upanishads to understand the Quran, one that welcomed and understood the stranger as intimate and familiar—is the closest thing I know to the mode of thinking I encountered repeatedly at Firoz Shah Kotla, particularly when talking to Pehelwan.

The first time I noticed this mode of thinking—which made equivalent the seemingly disparate, which welcomed the stranger—was when I was borrowing a fieldwork technique from Vijay Prashad (2000), who did extensive work on the formerly "untouchable" communities of Delhi, particularly the Balmikis (Pehelwan's *qaum*), in the early 1990s. Prashad noted the modern silence in these communities about the figure of Lal Beg, while the colonial ethnographic record of a hundred years ago was full of descriptions of the "religion" of Lal Beg, the god of the "sweeper" community, and many of the Balmikis were identified as Lal Begis. So he decided to bring up Lal Beg in a conversation, and he found that Lal Beg and the worship of Lal Beg had not entirely vanished in these communities. There were still those who remembered Lal Beg, and the rituals and songs of the veneration of Lal Beg, despite the increasing Hinduization of these communities (see also Lee 2014).

I decided to emulate Vijay Prashad and bring up Lal Beg the next time I talked to Pehelwan at his small shop in the Balmiki settlement close to Firoz Shah Kotla. He immediately looked serious and said, "Yes we believe in Lal Beg. He is a *Sayyid*; the Punjabis call him *Panj Pir* [the five saints], [but] in our community he is called Lal Beg. These Sayyids are things of *hava*, of the air and the wind; they are storms; they can move to and dwell wherever they want to. They have come from Iraq and settled in Firoz Shah Kotla."

I don't quite know what I was expecting. Perhaps I anticipated that Lal Beg, or Pehelwan's conception of Lal Beg, would be somehow unique, certainly distinct from the jinns/babas of Firoz Shah Kotla. But that turned out not to be the case. Instead, there was a constant process of translation, of finding equivalences: *Lal Beg = Sayyid (from Iraq) = Panj Pir = Hava = Jinn/Baba at Firoz Shah Kotla*. Once I noticed it, I saw this mode of thinking surface again and again when I heard Pehelwan talk. And each time, he would bring together elements that, for most people, are widely separated by chronology and religious and cultural divisions. For Pehelwan, Iraq was still the place, despite all the war and bloodshed of recent years, where the saints came from. For him, the long-gone Sat Yug of the Indian past was present in the faraway and mythic, yet contemporary and quite real, country of Iraq. Khusrau brought *Gandharva Vidya* to India. The Upanishads make clear the mystical allegories of the Quran. In Pehelwan and Dara Shukoh's mode of thinking, the usual distinctions between religious and cultural traditions disappear, as do the spatial and temporal boundaries between India and elsewhere, past and present.

This translatory mode of thought does two things: it makes Islam, as embodied by Muslim saints, an integral part of Indic ethical life, popular cosmology, and local landscapes, without any exotic particularity left over in the process; and it makes it possible for Hindus and Muslims, despite their obvious and fundamental theological and ritual differences, to act as a "single moral community" (Durkheim 1995) in the space of the Muslim saint shrine. I draw on Jan Assmann's (2006) work to propose that what we see articulated at these shrines is the Invisible Religion of North India, the historically constructed and contingent—rather than perennial—world of shared ethics and cosmology that transcends the visible religious differences of Hindu and Muslim. The historical presence of Islam, as exemplified by the Muslim saints, may not have fundamentally changed the ways in which a hypothetical Hindu interacts ritually with gods and goddesses, or what Assmann characterizes as visible religion, but Islam's presence has had a far greater impact on her ethical life: the potentialities of relating to self and other, to family and world.

TRANSLATION AS A MODE OF BEING

It would be hard, if not impossible, to construct a textual genealogy that links Dara Shukoh's translatory thought to that of Pehelwan's.[2] But there is a kinship that links the thought of a seventeenth-century Mughal crown prince and a twenty-first-century Dalit shopkeeper, and to explore this kinship is, as I see it, an ennobling move. This ennobling move is necessary to move away from the colonial derision heaped on the subaltern mode of translatory thinking, which we see, for example, in Richard Carnac Temple's "The Genealogies of Lal Beg" in his *Legends of the Panjab*:

> It is well known that the scavengers, or at any rate a large proportion of them in Northern India, are Lalbegis or followers of Lal Beg, and that they have a religion of their own, neither Hindu or Musalman, but with a priesthood and a ritual peculiar to itself. This religion may be best styled hagiolatory pure and simple, as it consists merely of confused veneration for anything and everything its followers, or rather their teachers, may have found to be considered by their neighbors, whatever be its origin. Thus we find in the Panjab that in the religion of the scavenger castes the tenets of the Hindus, the Musalmans and the Sikhs are thrown together in the most hopeless confusion, and that the monotheism taught by the medieval reformers underlies all their superstitions. (Temple 1884, 1:529)

The dismissive adjectives used by Temple to describe Lal Begi beliefs are metonymic of a whole history of colonial knowledge creation about India and its traditions (Cohn 1987). There is the dismissal of the "scavengers" as being unable to formulate a coherent religious tradition, a dismissal for which the extremely class-conscious British officialdom of high empire found easy equivalents in Brahminical texts. Added to this was the British incomprehension that "religion" could exist outside of their understanding of canonical religious traditions and oppositional identities. Fueled by these colonial epistemologies, and the enumerative imperatives of colonial rule that brought in a system of separate electorates based on the numerical strength of religious communities, there were massive campaigns throughout the late nineteenth and early twentieth centuries to "convert" the Lal Begis, so they could be counted as Hindus or Muslims. This is a story much better told elsewhere, particularly by Vijay Prashad (2000). Here, I am interested in the kinship of Pehelwan's thinking—heir to the religious tradition classified as "hopeless confusion" by Richard Temple—to that of Dara Shukoh's and Dara Shukoh's own investment in *'irfan* (gnosis or mystical knowledge) with which his translatory thinking was intrinsically linked, and how this gives us a different insight into "hopeless confusion."

Dara Shukoh *did not find any difference, except verbal, in the way in which they sought and comprehended Truth.* If he did not find any difference, except linguistic, in the way that Sufis and Hindus (for lack of a better word) comprehended the Truth, then why the need to translate at all? How does positing equivalences between seemingly unrelated things, or "welcoming the stranger," as Ganeri characterizes the translations of the Upanishads into the intellectual and spiritual world of Islam, "increase esoteric knowledge"? This was, after all, Dara Shukoh's stated goal for this exercise in translation (Ernst 2003, 186).

Shankar Nair offers us an important insight into the above question. Moving away from the extant body of work on the "translation movement" of the seventeenth century, when a large number of Sanskrit texts were translated into Persian, Nair urges us to look beyond "imperial political motives, pragmatic considerations for successful ruler-ship in a religiously and ethnically diverse empire, and natural processes of linguistic expression and accommodation" (Nair 2014, 393). Rather, he asks us to pay attention to the theological worldview underlying Sufi attempts at translation, independent of social and political considerations. Focusing on the seventeenth-century translation into Persian of the *Laghu-Yoga-Vasishta* by the Persian émigré Mir Findiriski, Nair argues that the work of seeking equivalences, even if imperfect and imprecise, between the metaphysical Arabo-Persian vocabulary of Sufism and Sanskrit, "can give way to another kind of transcendent perfection" (Nair 2014, 402), which is the transcendence of language and symbolism itself. Nair sees the translation project as inseparable from the intellectual and spiritual project of Sufi thought to break through language to reach the level of universal reality. "What is at one level, the use of an ostensibly Hindu vocabulary to express substantially Sufi ideas is, at the same time, an attempt to express, as far as language will allow, what is universal and shared between both communities, precisely because Sufi thought contains within itself the insistence that it should transcend its own concepts and formulations" (Nair 2014, 402). A widely known instance of this insistence on the transcen-

dence of difference is found in the poetry of Ibn 'Arabi,[3] from his volume
Tarjuman al-Ashwaq or *The Translator of Desires*:

> My heart can take on
> any form:
> a meadow for gazelles,
> a cloister for monks,
>
> For the idols, sacred ground,
> Ka'ba for the circling pilgrim,
> the tables of the Torah,
> the scrolls of the Qur'an.
>
> —(trans. Sells 1991)

. . .

In his understanding of translation as not an instrumental use of language but as a potential transcendence of language, Nair's understanding
of translation is remarkably similar to that of Walter Benjamin, who in
his difficult and allusive essay "The Task of the Translator" insists that one
needs to translate because only in translating can we get a glimpse of the
truth beyond (and behind) all languages.

In Benjamin's thought the task of the translator is to go beyond "the-
penny-in-the-slot called 'meaning'" (Benjamin 1986b, 179), the arbitrary
linkage of signifier and signified presumed by Saussurean linguistics.
In his thoughts on the translatability of language Benjamin introduces
a crucial distinction between authorial intention and the way in which
language connotes meaning. We could understand this as a difference
between the denotative (precise, literal) and connotative (wide variety of
associations) meanings of words: "Fidelity in the translation of individual
words can almost never fully reproduce the meaning they have in the
original. *For sense in its poetic significance is not limited to meaning, but de-
rives from the connotations conveyed by the word chosen to express it. We say
of words that they have emotional connotations*" (1969a, 78, my emphasis).

Paul de Man, in his exegetical reading of Benjamin's essay, expands
on the difference between the French *pain* and German *Brot* to illustrate
the difference between "das Gemeinte," what is meant, and the "Art des

Meinens," the way in which language means (de Man 1985, 39), which depends far more on the connotative dimensions of meaning.[4]

> The translation will reveal a fundamental discrepancy between the intent to name *Brot* and the word *Brot* itself, in its materiality, as a device of meaning. If you hear *Brot* in this context of Holderlin, who is so often mentioned in this text, I hear *Brot und Wein* necessarily, which is the great Holderlin text that is very much present in this—which in French becomes *Pain et vin.* "Pain et vin" is what you get for free in a restaurant, in a cheap restaurant where it is still included, so *pain et vin* has very different connotations than *Brot und Wein.* It brings to mind the *pain français, baguette, ficelle, batard*, all those things—I now hear in *Brot* "bastard." This upsets the stability of the quotidian. . . . The stability of my quotidian, of my daily bread, the reassuring quotidian aspects of the word *bread*, daily bread, is upset by the French word *pain.* What I mean is upset by the way in which I mean—the way in which it is *pain*, the phoneme, the term *pain*, which has its set of connotations that take you in a completely different direction. (de Man 1985, 40)

In de Man's example we see translation as an act that profoundly unsettles the everyday, including the everyday uses and meanings of language. Neither *pain* nor *Brot* remain the same in the process of translation, their connotative domains changed and enlarged by the task of the translator yet exceeding and evading the intention of both the author and the translator. It is in this unsettling, paradoxically, that we get a glimpse of what Benjamin calls "pure language" (Benjamin 1969a, 74) and through which the Sufis, in Nair's reading, attempted to transcend language. Pure language, if we are to follow de Man's exegesis of Benjamin, is to be glimpsed in translation not as unity but as an unsettling polyphony of the ways in which languages mean. What might it mean to glimpse such polyphony in the field of religion?

.   .   .

Tony Stewart critically engages with Saiyad Sultan's *Nabi Vamsa*, his Bengali hagiography of the Prophet Muhammad emerging from the Middle Period of Bengali language and literature, in which the Prophet is referred to as *avatar*, the Sanskritic term for the gods who are incarnations of Vishnu. Writing against earlier scholarship that saw in this text a syncretism that mixes aspects of Hinduism and Islam, Stewart thinks of this and other similar texts as expressing a "thoroughly Islamic worldview" through "an ostensibly Hindu vocabulary" (Stewart 2001, 286). Stewart sees, in the translation of the *nabi* (prophet) as an *avatar* (incarnation of the deity) not theological confusion and dilution but what we could call "a harmony of connotations." Saiyad Sultan's equivalence of *nabi and avatara* drew not on their denotative equivalence (as they denote radically different theological concepts) but on their connotative equivalence, as both terms connote "inspired guidance."

As Stewart and de Man show us, the very act of translation expands the semantic domains of the concepts that are twinned in the process, be it *Brot/pain* or *nabi/avatara*. We could say, following Nair, that the Sufi's desire to transcend language through the act of translation has an expansive and unsettling effect on the way languages work in the world. Paying attention to the connotative (rather than the merely denotative) equivalences allows us to encounter and track the possibilities such translation opens up for the creative application of "doctrine to real life" (Stewart 2001, 263): how Sufi saints, men whose reputations are linked to their piety and their knowledge of Islamic scripture (Lawrence 1986, 42), become father figures and *isht-dev* for Hindu men and women or, for that matter, how jinns, a separate race of beings, translate into intimate, indulgent father figures for so many people in contemporary Delhi.

.   .   .

Pehelwan told me once about the time when he went to Amarnath, a high-altitude pilgrimage in Kashmir, where people go to worship an ice-stalagmite as a *svayambhu* or naturally occurring *Shiv-Ling* (Shiva symbolized as a sacred phallus). But the low oxygen made him uncomfortable, and he broke out into a rash, and even there *"mera man inhin pe lag raha tha, jabki voh inse bade Baba hain ... woh Triloki nath baba hain jinhen Baba Adam bhi kehte hain."* (Even there I was thinking only of the baba [of Firoz Shah Kotla], though the baba [at Amarnath] is an even bigger baba than him. He is Triloki Nath Baba [The baba who is lord of the three worlds], also known as [the biblical] Adam.)[5] *"Sab jagah ka apna nizam hota hai, apna tariqa hota hai, par baba to ek hain.*" (Every place has its own order/arrangement, its own way of doing things, but the Baba is one.) "When I came back to Delhi," Pehelwan went on to say, "the first thing I did was bow my head [*matha teka*] at his court."

A few days later, when I recounted this snippet of conversation to my friend Kaushik Bhaumik, he asked me, "Why were the Chishtis the most successful Sufi order in India?" Then he provided the answer: "because they were ascetics that danced in ecstasy." "Like Shiva?" I responded. "Exactly," he said.

Kaushik's answer is not a non sequitur, because the Chishtis are the best-known of the Sufi orders in India. The image and name of the unknown Sufi saint in India is often that of a Chishti (for example, the grave of Nanhe Miyan Chishti we encountered in Chapter 1), and the ethics articulated by both Hindus and Muslims at Firoz Shah Kotla are remarkably similar to those expressed by saints of the Chishtiya order. The reason that Shiva and the Sufis can be translated, can be understood as similar despite their obvious differences, is because they are both figures that hold open similar potentialities for life, in this case a dyadic tension between asceticism and ecstasy.

In expanding the idea of translation from language and literature to potentialities of life, I am also inspired by Barry Flood (2009), who extends the idea of translation from its usual linguistic realm to the realm of material culture. His argument is that "translation" between medieval Indic and Islamic cultures was not just linguistic. It was not just texts and languages that were being translated across what have conventionally been held to be distinct cultures and regions but styles of coinage, clothing, and architecture. The implication of his work is that these modes of translation, which directly impacted the habitus of those who lived with this material culture, were as important as linguistic and textual translations. Following Flood's work, one can argue for translations that move beyond text and language to encompass the realms of gesture, bodily discipline, and ways of being. Such translations can have a far longer duration and become far more widespread than the elite and somewhat fragile world of textual circulation and translation, especially in the years before print.

One of Flood's examples of material translation is the pillar at Firoz Shah Kotla (see also Flood 2003). Flood sees its installation inside Firoz Shah's palace complex as a link to legendary Indian traditions of kingship associated with the pillar. This was Firoz Shah's attempt, as it were, to translate his rule into an Indic *style* of sovereignty.[6] Today, over 650 years later, in a world where translators between [certain] texts and languages (Persian and Sanskrit, for example) are a dim and distant memory, those who come to touch the pillar and to pray in the chamber beneath it, both Hindu and Muslim, view it as a marker of sovereignty, a court, a space of justice.

Following Stewart's insight into the expansion of the semantic domains of theological terms through the act of translation, and de Man's reinforcement of Benjamin's distinction between what is meant and the way in which languages mean, I ask several questions: In what ways are the potentialities for life expressed by both Shiva and the Sufis transformed and expanded by the act of translating between them? Does the equivalence of Sufi and Shiva make either of them dance differently or hold open differing *mudras* for the lives of their translator-devotees?[7] What is the pure language released for Pehelwan by the work of positing the notational isomorphism *Lal Beg = Sayyid (from Iraq) = Panj Pir = Hava = Jinn/Baba at Firoz Shah Kotla*? What are the potentialities of being and selfhood, ethical orientations and affective states opened up by this act of translation? In what ways does this translation unsettle Pehelwan's quotidian and provide new possibilities of being?

LOCAL COSMOPOLITANISMS

Translation as a mode of being opens up two distinct possibilities for the lives of the congregation at Firoz Shah Kotla: one, a resolutely local geography that is simultaneously cosmopolitan and, two, a shared ethical world that brings together Hindus and Muslims and others, across the boundaries of religion and caste.

Even though Pehelwan insisted that the baba is one, whether encountered at Amarnath or at Firoz Shah Kotla, he was quite uncomfortable and distressed on his pilgrimage to Amarnath and was only happy when he returned home to the baba at Firoz Shah Kotla. Pehelwan identifies as Hindu, so by conventional ways of understanding things, he should have been more comfortable with Shiva. And in any case, in Pehelwan's account, Shiva was the same as Adam, the first of the prophets in Islamic tradition. The difference between the two babas lay not in their religious identity, in Pehelwan's account, but in geography. One baba resided in the high, distant mountains of Kashmir, and the other was close to home. And it was the local baba that Pehelwan returned to from his pilgrimage, with a great deal of relief.

But the resolute localism of Pehelwan's religious psyche is also deeply cosmopolitan. In June of 2010 I took a break from fieldwork and the relentless heat of Delhi and went to Iran for a short holiday. When I came back, I brought small Turkish-style charms against the evil eye, made of blue glass, for my friends at Firoz Shah Kotla. Everyone was pleased with the gifts, but Pehelwan was especially moved. He held the charm reverentially to his eyes and said, "You brought these from Iraq? That's where all the *walis*, the saints, come from."

I was startled by this, for Pehelwan is not one to mishear things. But every time I said "Iran," he would mention Iraq. It wasn't a simple mishearing. For despite seven years of the ongoing Iraq War, he wasn't thinking of the modern nation-state of Iraq but rather the obsolete, almost forgotten term for the central and western parts of greater Iran (which included large parts of central Asia and present-day Iraq), an area that included what are now central Iranian cities such as Isfahan, Kerman, and Qom, from where many of the Sufi saints now buried in India originally came. Despite the Iraq War, and all the discourse of terrorism and weapons of mass destruction (which he was aware of), for him Iraq remained the place where the saints came from.

A few weeks later, I was sitting at Pehelwan's small grocery shop in the Balmiki colony. He proudly showed me where he had hung the little bauble that I had got from "Iraq." He said a lot of people had asked him to get the same thing for them since they'd seen it in the shop. But he told them that it was a special gift from Iraq and that I would get more from Iraq the next time I went. "People from my *biradari* [brotherhood] don't get to go there," he told me. We made some more small talk and then he asked me if I'd seen the place where the *jind-shaitan* (jinns and Satan) are stoned. I was surprised, because this was obviously a reference to the ritual stoning of the Devil, which happens at Mina in Saudi Arabia as part of the annual Haj rituals. "No," I said. "That's in Saudi Arabia, and I haven't been there. And besides, they only let Muslims go there."

Pehelwan got visibly upset at this. "Really? That's very wrong," he said. "Everyone should be allowed to go according to their faith [*shraddha ke anusar*]. We let the Muslims come to Hindu holy places, like in the Amarnath Yatra,[8] where so many Muslim brothers participate." Then he grumbled something about *kattar* (strict) Muslims in Saudi Arabia. But the grumbling aside, what was remarkable to me was Pehelwan's complete disassociation of the idea of faith (*shraddha*) from religious identity and his shock at the notion of a religious pilgrimage exclusive to one community.

How do we understand Pehelwan's disassociation of faith and identity? This disassociation does not appear so singular if we see Pehelwan as the inheritor of a long tradition of translation that has made Muslim saints—from Iraq and other points west—an integral part of the sacred geography of local Indic landscapes, a geography shared by all, irrespective of their confessional identity. This tradition of translation has meant that a deeply local geography of sainthood could simultaneously be cosmopolitan, encompassing both the saints' origins and their ends without any contradiction.

.   .   .

Here is a quote from an eighteenth-century account of an annual fair associated with the tomb of the saint Nasiruddin Mahmud "Chiragh-e Dehli" (the Lamp of Delhi), a disciple of and spiritual successor to Nizamuddin Auliya, who died circa 1356 and whose grave became one of the major pilgrimage centers of Delhi: "In truth you are the lamp of Delhi, rather you are the lamp and the eyes [*chashm o chiragh*, dearly beloved] of all Hindustan. The pilgrimage to your tomb is on Sundays. In the month of Diwali the crowds are especially impressive. In this month the people of Delhi come on every Sunday to gain the bliss of pilgrimage [*ziyarat*]" (Dargah Quli Khan 1993, 120).

The eighteenth- and nineteenth-century accounts of the fair associated with his grave, such as the one above, mention that the fair happens in the month of Diwali, a festival month in the Indic calendar, which does not necessarily coincide with the 'urs of the saint, which is calculated by the Islamic calendar. It was only when I was at the shrine of Chiragh-e Dehli and saw the clay lamps lit in offering there, the same clay lamps traditionally lit during Diwali, that I made the connection. In the festival calendar of Delhi, every year, the festival of lamps (Diwali) was celebrated at the shrine of the lamp of Delhi (Chiragh-e Dehli), a festival at which the chroniclers note that both Hindus and Muslims came together. A lamp may be just a lamp, but the connotative equivalence of *chiragh* and *diya*, across different mythologies, histories, and religious identities, had created the possibility of a shared lifeworld.

Diana Eck has asserted that the "common cosmos" that underlies the sacred geographies of India is dominantly "Sanskritic." "Within India, there is implicit a kind of geographical 'Sanskritization' that has constructed a common cosmos by the local adaptation of names and qualities of India's renowned rivers, mountains and *tirthas*" (Eck 2012, 55). The presence of Chiragh-e Dehli in the Indic festival calendar of the city, and the prominence of his shrine in the sacred geography of the city, indicates not just a process of Sanskritization but acts of translation that made the landscape as Persianate as it was Sanskritic, embedding the distant indistinguishably into the local.

Compared with the subtlety of this local cosmopolitanism, it is modern nationalist thought, as exemplified by Vinayak Damodar Savarkar's limited and limiting ideas of sacred and nationalist geographies, which seem boorish and parochial. Savarkar (1883–1966), the originator of the Hindu right-wing ideology of *Hindutva* (Hinduness), argued that Muslims and Christians could never be patriotic enough because their sacred spaces lay outside India—in Mecca, Jerusalem, and the Vatican (Menon and Nigam 2007, 37). But in the landscapes of Delhi we see local geographies sanctified by the presence of saints from Iraq, even for non-Muslims, and a shared moral world in which it is hard to distinguish Hindus from Muslims.

A SINGLE MORAL COMMUNITY?

Balon was a taciturn man, and it was hard to get him to talk sometimes. But the one thing he could always be trusted to wax eloquent about was his dislike of Taslimuddin, the Waqf Board–appointed imam of the mosque at Firoz Shah Kotla. One of the first things Balon ever said to me was "*Mera uthna baithna tumhare logon men zyada hota hai. Main in masjid walon se dur bhagta hun.*" (I spend most of my time with your people [i.e., Hindus]. I run far away from these people of the mosque.")

The antipathy between them was so great that the imam stopped talking to me after he had seen me talking to Balon, whereas he had been quite welcoming before. Balon had predicted that this would happen. Balon saw himself as opposed to the imam, though this was not an opposition between the dargah and the mosque. Balon's critique of the imam was never about his conduct of prayers or anything straightforwardly theological. His critique was always personal, about the imam's character, about his (alleged) financial greed and lack of humility.

> *Namaz padhane ka ilm hota hai. Allah ne fazal diya hai. Yeh apne pet ko hi ilm deta hai.*
>
> It is a knowledge, given by Allah, to lead people in congregational prayer.
> He only gives knowledge to his own stomach.

> *Woh apni baglen chauri kar ke chalta hai. Imam ko aise chalna chahiye?*
>
> He walks with his arms wide [arrogantly]. Should an Imam walk like this?

Balon found a lack of humility even in his gait, which he felt was contrary to how the imam, the leader of prayer in a mosque, should behave. He linked the lack of humility to Taslimuddin's involvement in business and moneymaking. He also did "computer work"[9] and his wife put up a stall selling flowers and incense outside Firoz Shah Kotla on Thursdays. In Balon's worldview the money that Taslimuddin made out of his businesses outside the mosque was antithetical to the humility necessary for the position of an imam.

The imam was the target of criticism for many of those to whom I spoke at Firoz Shah Kotla. These criticisms were articulated by those who worshipped regularly at the mosque at Firoz Shah Kotla and by those who didn't, like Balon, as well as by the non-Muslims who regularly visited Firoz Shah Kotla. Through these criticisms of the imam, ostensibly a man of piety, I got a sense of the contours of a shared piety, common to the congregants at Firoz Shah Kotla.

"*Imam ne qaum parasti kar di hai,*" Pehelwan complained about him. (The Imam has sowed communal discord.) "*Use pir paighambaron ke bare men batana chahiye ke unhon kitni 'ibadat ki, kitne balidan kiye, tabhi to ja kar unka naam Hazrat Jalaluddin hua, par woh batata hai—Hindu Muslalman ka fark, kis ko masjid men aana chahiye, kisko nahin.*" (He should tell us about the pirs and the prophets, how much they prayed, what sacrifices they made, that's how his name came to be Hazrat Jalaluddin[10]—but instead he tells us the difference of Hindu and Muslim, who should come into the mosque and who shouldn't.)

Manohar Lal had a story similar to Pehelwan's. They both used to sit in the mosque at Firoz Shah Kotla and found a great deal of peace there. But when the new imam was appointed, he made them leave the mosque, saying it was open only to Muslims for prayer. The Laxminagar couple didn't approve of the imam because they found him selfish and ungenerous, unwilling to enter into reciprocal relations of gifting, while readily accepting gifts from them. They used to offer him sweets on Diwali and even Eid, and he never reciprocated by giving them anything on any of the Muslim festivals, so they stopped giving him anything.

Akhtar, who spent many hours Monday and Thursday mornings praying in the mosque and had some renown as a healer, was also bitter about the imam. He told me that the imam had tried to stop him from praying in the mosque, saying that he's a criminal, even though he had been found not guilty by the court. Akhtar said that all those who prayed at the mosque were turning against the imam and had stopped giving him the skins from the animals slaughtered at Baqrid, like they used to. In Akhtar's account, they also found him too crafty, too involved in money and business deals, and contemptuous of the people from Delhi who made up most of the congregation at the mosque. (Taslimuddin was from Bihar, and both Akhtar and Balon, who belonged to Old Delhi, had also voiced their contempt for him in regional terms, as an outsider prospering on the earnings of the hard-working people of Delhi.)

Raju, who occasionally sat as a healer under the pillar at Firoz Shah Kotla, and prayed at the mosque, and was planning to go on *tabligh*[11] when I spoke to him, said to me, gesturing to the imam, "There are some people who laugh at other's *ibadat*, at other's ways of worshipping. There are those who believe in *niyaz* [*jo niyaz ko mante hain*] [and] those who don't." According to Raju, the imam was very much in the second camp. But, he said, I can't really say bad things about him because people have to pray behind him. Chand, Laddu Shah's son, articulated a similar dislike of the imam but refused to elaborate because, after all, people had to pray behind him in the mosque.

. . .

Niyaz, a term I encountered quite often in conversations at Firoz Shah Kotla, was often used by Muslims to explain their differences with other Muslims. Those who came to Firoz Shah Kotla and other dargahs were those who believed in niyaz. The other kind, and this was usually in reference to the imam, were the ones who didn't. *Niyaz*, as the dictionary definition (Platts 2000, 1164) shows us, is a multivalent word from Persian. Its many meanings involve a position of humility, of need, of supplication in relation to someone who is the bestower of gifts. In the case of those who came to Firoz Shah Kotla, and other dargahs in Delhi, to believe in niyaz is to place oneself in a position of indebtedness and gratitude to the jinn/saint. It implies a belief in the saints and their efficacy in interceding with God and hence solving problems and bestowing good fortune. The imam, in contrast, did not believe in the efficacy of the jinns/saints at Firoz Shah Kotla. In the few times that he spoke to me before I incurred his displeasure, he always dismissed people's petitioning of the jinns as the *andh-vishvas* (blind belief) of ignorant people. He did not deny that there were jinns at Firoz Shah Kotla. He said they prayed in the mosque, because Shah Waliullah used to pray here, and he attributed any benefit people got from praying in the mosque to the fact of Shah Waliullah's praying there. As for the business of petitioning the jinns in other parts of the ruins, he saw it as completely pointless.

The division between those who believe in niyaz and those who don't was a difference articulated by Manohar Lal as a difference between Hindus and "Muhammadans."

> ML. Our Hindu brothers come here more. Here there's 75 percent of us Hindus and 25 percent Muhammadans.
>
> AVT. Why is this?
>
> ML. It's because our people [Hindus] believe in the *buzurgan e-din* (the elders of the faith), they believe in the *buzurg* (elders), they believe in *kudrat* (nature). These Muhammadans say that there is Allah, and no one but Allah. Now tell me, hasn't Allah also made ladders, ways for us to reach him? Those that he has sent, these angels (*farishte*), aren't they made by him? We'll climb one ladder at a time to get to him, or will we reach there directly? So who are those rungs in the ladder between us and God—it's them [the saints].

What Manohar Lal attributed to "Muhammadans" is actually a pretty neat encapsulation of the Muslim revivalist position, that there should be no intermediary between God and man. What is interesting is that Manohar Lal sees Hindus as the opposing party in a debate that is usually thought of as a debate between two factions of Muslims, the more mystically in-clined and the revivalist (or the Barelvi *maslak* versus the Deobandi and/ or the Ahl-e Hadith). Manohar Lal's articulation of difference between Hindus and Muslims being very similar to the articulation by Muslims of the differences *between* Muslims indicates that the realm of shared piety, of those who come to Firoz Shah Kotla and other dargahs, is not co-extensive with religious identity. Aspects of this piety are highlighted for us by people's criticisms, across confessional divides, of the imam's conduct.

The imam was disliked by people for being proud and money-minded, for being intolerant and dismissive of the beliefs of others, for being over-conscious of communal identity, for being greedy and selfish, and for not participating in rituals of reciprocal gifting. Significantly, none of these criticisms were ever directed at his conduct of rituals. No one criticized him on how he led the prayers or on the sermons he gave or on any of the recognizable, ritual forms of Islamic piety. The reason for people's dislike of the imam was never articulated as a difference between the mosque and the dargah. It was articulated in terms of the imam's shortcoming in qualities far broader than ritual observance—his perceived lack of humility, lack of tolerance, and greed.

TRANSLATION AND INVISIBLE RELIGION

> All translation is only a somewhat provisional way of coming to terms with the foreignness of languages. An instant and final, rather than a temporary and provisional solution of this foreignness remains out of the reach of mankind; at any rate, it eludes any direct attempt. Indirectly, however, the growth of religions ripens the hidden seed into a higher development of language.
>
> —Walter Benjamin

> Invisible religion relates to individual religions much as "language" relates to particular languages.
>
> —Jan Assmann

Based on his work on ancient Egyptian religion, Jan Assmann suggests a distinction between what he calls Invisible Religion (IR) and Visible Religion (VR). Invisible religion consists of a culture's underlying notions of cosmological order, justice, and ethics, while visible religion consists of one's ritual relationship to the deity. Assmann illustrates the principle of invisible religion through the ancient Egyptian concept of *maat*, which "signifies the principle of a universal harmony that manifests itself in the cosmos as order and in the world of human beings as justice" (Assmann 2006, 33). The realm of invisible religion, of cosmology and law, is far broader than visible religion, one's mode of relating to the deity, which, while important, is merely a subset of the larger realm of invisible religion. "On this plane religion can be equated with order as such. Here sacred order is not opposed to profane order, but order is sacred as such, in contrast to disorder" (Assmann 2006, 34). Assmann illustrates the relation of IR to VR through a diagram, which he calls the "Egyptian triangle" (2006, 35). The problem, Assmann says, is that the failure to make a "distinction between IR and VR leads to an ethnocentric narrowing of our concept of religion, since we tacitly base our definition of religion on the familiar characteristics of VR and thereby mistakenly 'identify religion with one of its particular forms'" (2006, 32). If commonplace ideas of justice and ethics are shared across religious divides in India, as we have seen, then we can think of the Muslim saint shrines and their shared understanding of justice and ethics as being the recognized loci of North India's historically evolved invisible religion, of which Hinduism and Islam as religious identities are merely the visible subsets.

In the *Fawa'id al Fu'ad*, the famous collection of the discourses of Nizamuddin Auliya compiled by his disciple Amir Hasan Sijzi, Nizamuddin Auliya articulated the difference between two distinct, if related, kinds of piety:

> "There are two forms of devotion," he explained; "One is mandatory [*lazim*], the other is supererogatory [*muta'addi*]. Mandatory devotion is that from which the benefit is limited to one person, that is, to the performer of that devotion, whether it be canonical prayer, fasting, pilgrimage to Arabia, invocations, repetitions of the rosary, or the like. But supererogatory devotion is that which brings benefit and comfort to others, whether through the expenditure of money or demonstration or compassion or other ways of helping one's fellow man. Such actions are called supererogatory devotion. Their reward is incalculable; it is limitless. In mandatory devotion one must be sincere to merit divine acceptance, but in supererogatory devotion even one's sins become a source of reward." (Lawrence 1992, 95)

The differences in piety articulated by those who believe in niyaz as opposed to those who don't map on to the differences between mandatory and supererogatory forms of devotion articulated by Nizamuddin Auliya. The mandatory forms of the faith were the ritual subset (or, if you will, core) of a much larger world of piety and devotion to God, which was not based on ritual but on bringing "benefit and comfort of others." Similarly, the imam was never criticized or opposed because of his ritual devotion. He was criticized for not participating in, and being dismissive of, the larger realm of piety that everyone at Firoz Shah Kotla could participate in, irrespective of their ritual allegiances. Nizamuddin Auliya's distinction between two forms of devotion, which we could also understand as the difference between ethics and ritual practice, is also analogous to Assmann's distinction between invisible and visible religion.

Nizamuddin Auliya's ideas of supererogatory piety were reflected in his personal conduct and in the institutions of his *khanqah*, which became foundational for Sufi ideas of pious conduct and the functioning of dargahs all over the subcontinent. Humility, the openness to people of all religious and social backgrounds, the emphasis on personal poverty and the regular redistribution of gifts and food among the poor (*langar*), an empathy and openness toward women, a compassion toward those considered "sinners," all of which are found both in Nizamuddin's discourse and his conduct (see Nizami 1992), are the very same elements of piety that are celebrated at Firoz Shah Kotla in particular, and dargahs in general. Even though many of those who come to Firoz Shah Kotla seldom make the journey to Nizamuddin Auliya's shrine, the figure of Nizamuddin Auliya is still very much part of the mythos of those who come to Firoz Shah Kotla. Pehelwan told me that Firoz Shah Kotla is the space where all the saints from all the different dargahs of Delhi come for "meetings." The first saint he named was Nizamuddin Auliya. Raju told me that Nizamuddin Auliya is the other dargah he visits and that "he wears the crown of Delhi" (*unhonne Dilli ka taj pehna hai*).

The ethics of *gharib nawazi*, so central to the life of Muslim shrines, are deeply connected, as we have seen, to the history, politics, and theology of Islamic sovereignty in India. This history of the presence of Islam has had a huge impact on conceptions of justice and ethical life. These ethics permeate not just North India's most visible cultural form, Bollywood films, but also everyday life across communities. *The historical presence of Islam*, as exemplified by the Muslim saints, may not have fundamentally changed the ways in which a hypothetical Hindu interacts with gods and goddesses, or what Assmann characterizes as visible religion, but has had a far greater impact on her ethical life, the potentialities of relating to the self and other, to family and world. Islam is not external to Hinduism; rather, the ethical and cosmological world of North India, its invisible religion, is impossible to imagine now without the presence of Islam.

As an example of the way the presence of Islam has affected the ethical world of North India, I cite here a couplet from the most canonical of

Hindu texts, the *Ramcharitmanas*, the life of Lord Rama, written during
the reign of Emperor Akbar.[12]

> *Jehi jan par mamata ati chhohu. Jenhi karuna kari vinh na vohu.*
> *Gai bahor garib nevaju. Saral sabal sahib Raghuraju.*
> —(Goswami Tulsidas, *Ramacharitmanas*, Balakand 1.13.)

> All gracious and compassionate to the humble: who in his mercy ever re-
> frains from anger against those whom he loves and knows to be his own:
> protector of the poor;[13] all good, all powerful, the lord Raghuraj.
> —(Growse 1887, 10)

Garib nevaju is an immediately recognizable vernacularization of *Gharib
Nawaz*. It is significant for the first Persian loan word in the most ca-
nonically "Hindu" of North Indian texts to be *garib nevaju*—a term for
which Tulsidas could not, or did not think to, find an Indic equivalent
when retelling the story of the god-king Rama out of Sanskrit and into
the Avadhi vernacular. *Ram-Rajya*, the reign of Rama, is a byword for
the utopian ideal of good government, including for no less a figure than
Mahatma Gandhi. What does it tell us if the Persian phrase for one who
is hospitable to strangers is an integral part of the political theology of
the kingdom of Rama?

Shahid Amin's work on the memory of the popular warrior-saint of
eastern Uttar Pradesh, Ghazi Miyan, shows how the connotative domain
of *Jihad*, paradigmatic in the West of Islamic "holy war," expands in the
process of telling the warrior's tale in an Indic landscape, where the fight
against infidelity/oppression becomes simultaneously a fight to save cows,
which are sacred to Hindus:

> There is little doubt that the narrative of Ghazi Miyan is about the Sword of
> Islam. But its denouement—the Ghazi's martyrdom is played out in terms of
> an enduring and non-exploitative relationship between Hindu herdsmen and
> women and the Muslim protector of their cows. . . . Protected by a *ghazi* in
> the wilds of the Nepal foothills, herdsmen do not become converts to Islam or
> even subjects to a new "Islamic state": they become ardent follower devotees.
> In effect, they give assent to a *life which has been well lived on two different regis-
> ters*: the call of Islam and the call to save cows. (Amin 2005, 291, my emphasis)

Amin reads the story of Ghazi Miyan as a "popular history" of the "Muslim conquest" of North India. In his retelling we see something of the historical process of translation through which the ethical world, the invisible religion of North India, has been created. It is a translation without any "exotic particularity left over in the process." The exemplary life of the Islamic warrior-saint blends seamlessly into the Indic landscape and its ethical world while at the same time transforming both of them. For Benjamin, true language "is concealed in concentrated fashion in translations" (1969a, 77). Similarly, it is only through translation of that we see, concealed in concentrated fashion, something of (the) invisible religion (of North India).

I borrow the idea of "translation without any exotic particularity left over in the process" from Faisal Devji's essay on Iqbal's thought and the centrality of translation to his modes of engagement with the other, including both poetic and political engagement: "More interesting . . . are those poems in which Iqbal performs what I want to call a complete transformation of difference, which is thus apprehended as such without representation, and without any exotic particularity being left over in the process" (Devji 2009, 251).

Such translation, I have attempted to show, is not just unique to Iqbal's poetic oeuvre but is also (a now vanishing?) part of the texture of everyday life and thought in South Asia. The esoteric ideas of Sufism have become so invisible, so much a part of everyday life, without any exotic particularity left over in the process, that they are hard to recognize, as it was hard for me to recognize the translation implicit in the month of Diwali being especially auspicious to visit the shrine of Chiragh-e Dehli. Why do so many petitioners come to Sufi dargahs asking for help with the marriage of daughters? Might this have something to do with the idea of the Sufi saint as the "bride of Allah," and the celebrations related to their death anniversary being known as 'urs, signifying their marriage to Allah?[14] Why do lovers come to Sufi shrines to seek blessings? Might it have something to do with the centrality of love, 'ishq, to Sufi thought and practice, with the Sufi understanding of human love ('ishq majazi) being figurative, metaphorical and allusive of (or in other words a *translation* into human terms of) the true love (*'ishq haqiqi*) that is humankind's love for God?

· · ·

The idea of actively seeking and finding kinship (and hence hospitality), and translating between things seemingly unrelated and even opposed, lives on in Delhi at the space of the *dargah*, most apparently within the medieval walls of Firoz Shah Kotla and its congregation. Here non-Muslims translate themselves as Muslims in their bodily deportments during prayer and in their language of address. Here non-Muslims can understand Muslim spirits as loving, benign father figures. The ethics of anonymity at Firoz Shah Kotla seem to be completely in line with this translatory mode of being, for to be burdened with a name is to be burdened with an identity and a history, a given place in the world. It precludes the possibility of transcending that given identity, of "passing" for something or someone else.[15] And what is passing except a kind of translation of the self, making yourself more familiar, more understandable to your audience? During conversations at Firoz Shah Kotla, which often turn to matters of religion and philosophy (the very bases, in the modern world, of communal identity), it is not easy to distinguish who is Hindu and who is Muslim. In an India where the polarizing rhetoric of the Hindu right wing has entered the rhythms of everyday life, Firoz Shah Kotla, contained within medieval walls, seems like a remnant from an older world.

But those walls have long been breached.

LOST IN TRANSLATION—
ANOTHER VIEW OF MODERNITY
I asked Pehelwan once about people's beliefs about Lal Beg in his community, and he said that "these days people in my community don't really believe in this [the veneration of Lal Beg]; they believe in and worship Shiv and Bhairon; they worship Kali; they worship Sai Baba." "Why have they stopped believing in Lal Beg?" I asked. "Because," he said, "since people have become educated, foolishness has increased." (*Jab se log padhe likhe hue hain, murakhta badhi hai.*)

I understand Pehelwan's counterintuitive equation of education and foolishness as an indictment of the modern. *Padha likha hona* (to be educated) is his way of saying "to be modern." Modernity, then, is not just the loss of the tradition of Lal Beg but the inability to see that when you are worshipping Sai Baba, you are in a sense still worshipping an aspect of the old god you no longer remember, because Sai Baba, like Lal Beg, is a *sayyid*. Modernity is not just the loss of tradition but the loss of the mode of translatory thought, which can see the underlying (connotative) kinship between seeming (denotative) contradictions. Somewhat idiosyncratically, I define the modern, rather than a discrete and inevitable time period, as a tendency, a style of thinking and being in the world, that gains dominance at different times among different places and communities.[16] The modern, as we know it, is opposed to the translatory mode of thinking, the mode that strives beyond language toward "pure language."

How can the translatory mode of thinking be opposed to the modern, one might be tempted to ask, when the modern world is marked by an ever-increasing number of translations? Translation facilitates the increasingly global reach of capital as contracts, documents, and speech acts are constantly being translated from and into English, Arabic, Chinese, and Korean, to name just a few. Appliance instructions now come in half a dozen languages, and many children on New York's Upper East Side now grow up learning Mandarin in order to be competitive in the world to come. Here, Ronit Ricci's (2011) insight that the idea of translation itself is not universally translatable, being a cultural practice that varies widely in different times and places, is valuable. The mode of translation I have been alluding to throughout this chapter—let us call it "medieval," in distinction from the modern, though similarly unconstrained by chronology—is very different from modern practices of translation, which are deeply entwined with the hegemonizing tendencies of global capitalism.

This difference is perhaps best captured by Benjamin's citation of an aphorism from Rudolf Pannwitz: "Our translations, even the best ones, proceed from a wrong premise. They want to turn Hindi, Greek, English into German instead of turning German into Hindi, Greek, English. . . . The basic error of our translator is that he preserves the state in which his own language happens to be instead of allowing his language to be powerfully affected by the foreign tongue" (quoted in Benjamin 1969a, 80–81). In an earlier, "medieval," mode of translation, as practiced in South and Southeast Asia, this was certainly the case, as Arabic deeply influenced the vocabularies and even grammar and syntax of the languages into which its literature was translated, such as Tamil, Javanese, and Malay (Ricci 2011, 158–65). Javanese, Malay, and Tamil, in the process of translation, became somewhat Arabic. These languages were "so powerfully affected by the foreign tongue" because the very act of translation proceeded, as it did for Dara Shukoh, from the idea that the stranger, if welcomed and understood, would turn out to be no stranger at all.

While the processes of translation deeply affected and transformed the target languages, at the same time they deeply indigenized the content of the original literature. If we can follow Pannwitz's metaphor further, it is as if German became Hindi in the process of translation, while what was originally written in Hindi became *heimlich* (homelike) in Germany, without any exotic particularity. Ricci, in her study of the movement of the Arabic *Book of One Thousand Questions* into Javanese, Malay, and Tamil, highlights how the dominant idea in these translations "seemed to be that to 'translate'—or as we have seen in the case of Javanese, to 'Javanize' (J. *njawakaken*)—meant to retell or rewrite the texts in ways that were both culturally appropriate and impressively creative. Using one's imaginative powers and literary skills in making a story Javanese was considered the appropriate thing to do" (Ricci 2011, 57). Similarly, in the *Cirappuranam*, the seventeenth-century Tamil telling of the life of the Prophet, the Prophet's Arabia is described as "the Tamil land, with its monsoon clouds, flora and fauna, mountains and waterfalls" (Ricci 2011, 57). Translation, in these instances, meant indigenizing what was foreign, not in the sense of erasing or eliding difference but in making that difference into an intimate and integral part of one's imaginative, moral, and physical landscapes.

Ricci contrasts this mode of translation to the moods and motivations that accompanied the translation of the *Book of One Thousand Questions* from Arabic into Latin in twelfth- and thirteenth-century Spain, a project inextricably tied up with the Crusades and the Reconquista, in which fidelity to the source text was viewed as an important principle:

"the stress on accuracy and translation was explicitly employed as part of an effort to undermine and discredit the teachings offered in the Arabic text" (Ricci 2011, 65). The act of translation in this context was an act of distancing, meant to ensure that the stranger remained estranged and unwelcome. The emphasis on fidelity in these estranging translations noted by Ricci is crucial, then, as fidelity in the translation of individual words, as Benjamin reminds us, can almost never fully reproduce the meaning they have in the original. To emphasize denotative fidelity is to miss the connotations, to deliberately miss the ways in which both the "original and the translation are recognizable as fragment[s] of a greater language, just as fragments are part of a vessel" (Benjamin 1969a, 78). Seven hundred years after the Toledo translations, we see the same estrangement and discrediting accompanying colonial translations of native religious material, such as Richard Carnac Temple's translations of the genealogies of Lal Beg. This is the kind of translation in which the poetry is lost. Modern translations of religious material, with their emphasis on fidelity, become tools of power and domination and reinforce incommensurability rather than reconciliation between religious traditions. The legacies of these translations live on at Firoz Shah Kotla along with the other, "medieval" modes of translation and translatability explored in this chapter. At Firoz Shah Kotla, "medieval" and "modern" worldviews can exist within the same person and be deployed at different moments. This presence of the modern within the medieval space—both architecturally and conceptually—of Firoz Shah Kotla is the story I turn to now. This is a story of the emergence of the modern as a loss and diminishment of the world and its possibilities.

.   .   .

Manohar Lal had been keeping away from our usual gathering at Firoz Shah Kotla for a while. He'd come in at odd times, go straight to the *laat*, and leave without stopping to talk to anyone. It emerged slowly that he was upset with Balon, who had said something rude to him. Balon was quite an irascible character, especially on Thursdays, when he had to handle both the offerings to Nanhe Miyan and the distribution of the degs of sweet rice.[17] Finally, everyone else intervened to bring Manohar

Lal back to the fold and to patch things up between the two. Manohar Lal recommenced hanging out with everyone, but his anger with Balon lingered. "I'll get you picked up by the cops," he said to Balon, only half-jokingly. *Daadhi waale* (Bearded one). *Osama!*

In his anger Manohar Lal did a complete about-face from his stated policy of not caring for anyone's identity at Firoz Shah Kotla (see Chapter 3). Suddenly, Manohar Lal was threatening to do the very thing that the modern excels at—using identity as a weapon. Balon fit into a typology, that of the bearded Muslim as terrorist suspect, and in his anger, a man who never asked anyone's name at Firoz Shah Kotla was willing to use Balon's identity against him.

Balon's long, hennaed beard, skullcap, and traditional salwar kameez visibly marked him as a Muslim and as a pious Muslim of a certain kind, one easily identified as "fundamentalist" and hence "terrorist" in the logic of the post-9/11 world. But Balon was pretty equal-opportunity in both his anger and his affection. In speaking of him after his death, Pehelwan repeatedly said of him, "*Woh Hindu Musalman ka farak nahin karte the.*" (He did not differentiate between Hindus and Muslims.) His best friends among the congregation at Firoz Shah Kotla were the Lady from Laxminagar and her husband. He shared with them things about his life that he did not share with other people at Firoz Shah Kotla. When one of his daughters had to have a hurried hush-hush marriage with the boy that had made her pregnant, it was only the Laxminagar family, among the people from Firoz Shah Kotla, who knew of and attended the wedding.

This fact came up in a conversation shortly after Balon's death. He died suddenly in October 2010, in the midst of my fieldwork. One week he had been there, active as usual, but looking a little pale and tired, coughing at frequent intervals. For years everyone had been warning him to stop eating *gutkha*, chewing tobacco laced with lime, so no one thought much of his cough. The next week, for the first time in as long as anyone could remember, Balon did not show up at Firoz Shah Kotla. The week after, news came that he was dead.

As we gathered in our usual circle, mourning Balon's absence, the Lady from Laxminagar bravely said, "*Ek aadmi chala gaya par hamara samaj to chalta rehna chahiye.*" (One man is gone but our society should keep going on.) But though the degs kept getting distributed, and people kept coming to Firoz Shah Kotla in growing numbers, our own small society rapidly fell apart.

Two weeks after we learned of Balon's death, I came to Firoz Shah Kotla as the degs were being distributed. I found Ajay sitting separately while a young man I didn't recognize was part of the distribution. Ajay was angry. It turned out that Nawab, an entrepreneur from Nizamuddin who financed five degs at Firoz Shah Kotla every Thursday, had started making a fuss about Ajay distributing the degs after Balon's death—*"chamar bhangi ke hath se bata hua ham kaise kha sakte hain?"* (How can we eat what's distributed by the hand of an untouchable?) In reporting Nawab's words to me, Ajay acknowledged his caste for the first time. Usually he shied away from this, and even when I had asked him before, he would never tell me his surname.

"So," he said, "I stopped distributing the deg. But I also stopped getting tea for everyone like I used to. I told him, *'chamar bhangi ke paise ki chai pi rahe the itne din.'"* (You were drinking tea from an untouchable's money all these days.)

Balon's death brought home to me how so much of what I valued about the place was embodied in his person. The ethics of nameless intimacy that I had wondered at had disappeared, at least in our small corner of Firoz Shah Kotla, with the vacuum created by his death, and with it the easy camaraderie and joking that I eagerly looked forward to every week. Bhrigupati Singh (2011), in his work in rural Rajasthan, has characterized the relations among different castes and communities there as "agonistic intimacy." From my experience, Singh's characterization holds true in Delhi, as well, especially among those who live in Old Delhi, belonging to communities that have centuries of intimate knowledge of each other. This made Firoz Shah Kotla even more interesting, because it served as a space where the *agon* was, even if temporarily, suspended or, rather, manifested in highly personalized, individualized ribbing (like the references to Balon's *lugaibazi*) that never resorted to communal insult or stereotype. Of course, the communal mode of agonistic intimacy could and did surface outside Firoz Shah Kotla, outside the space of the dargah, when people had my ear alone. But caste-based insults and discrimination being publicly deployed inside Firoz Shah Kotla was, after all my years of visiting and hanging out there, a shocking and grievous thing.

The couple from Laxminagar was seen less and less often. If I wanted to meet with Manohar Lal, I had to call him on his cellphone. Pehelwan started to appear later and would seldom hang around with the others. I started meeting him more often at his shop. In the months after Balon's passing he remembered him many times during our conversations at the shop and always called him Abba (Father). He also reiterated many times that he thought of him as his own father. "*Jab se Abba chale gaye hain, dua salam to sab se hai par ab man nahin lagta,*" he told me. (Since Abba is gone, I still get along with everybody, but now my heart isn't in it.)

CHAPTER 6

STONES, SNAKES, AND SAINTS
Remembering the Vanished Sacred Geographies of Delhi

Qafas men mujh se rudad-e chaman kehte na dar hamdam
Giri hai jis pe kal bijli woh mera ashiyan kyon ho?

In the cage, don't be afraid of telling me the events of the garden, friend
The one on which lightning fell yesterday, why would it be my nest?
—Mirza Asadullah Khan Ghalib

THE SHRINE OF THE STONE SAINT

One day, following in the footsteps of Ashiq Ali and Manohar Lal, a friend and I went to the dargah of Ashiq Allah, in the protected forest north of Mehrauli. On our way back to Mehrauli, we came across a large outcropping of rock, just outside the circuit of the ruined, overgrown walls of Qila Rai Pithora. A large boulder, some of it daubed with green paint, was balanced naturally on this outcropping, and with some effort the boulder could be rocked to and fro by one person, without being displaced from its position. Here we met a man from Gaya district in Bihar, who lived near the Auliya Masjid in Mehrauli, and he told us that this outcropping was the mazar of *Patthar Baba* (the Stone Saint), and being able to rock the boulder was the sign of his blessing. Further in the forest, he told us, back the way we came, there is the mazar of Bela Rani (Jasmine Queen). As the setting sun colored the scattered monsoon clouds delicate shades of pink and orange, and the birds in the trees and bushes hailed the coming of dusk, he told us how coming here gave him a lot of *sukun* (tranquility). *"Yahan main gham se bahar ho jata hun."* (Here, I come outside of sorrow.)

. . .

How can a stone be a (Muslim) saint? This seems like a theological impossibility, unless we consider the literature on Islam and deep ecology

181

(Ammar 2001) or the elevated moral status given to plants and animals in the Quran (Tlili 2012) and to stars and planets in medieval Muslim mystical and philosophical literature (Goodman 2009). Though there is a long, if minor, tradition of venerating animals as Muslim saints in South Asia and other parts of the Muslim world (Taneja 2015), here I am concerned with the phenomenological rather than theological aspect of the question of how a stone can be a saint. If we take the recognition of sainthood to be a marker of sacrality, then what was the experiential dimension of the sacred for our man from Gaya that made him recognize this place as a mazar, as the grave of a saint? From our brief interaction and experience of the space, his sacred seemed to be an immersion in the ecological surround: the world of birdsong, greenery, sunset, and stone. Following the philosopher Akeel Bilgrami (2006, 2014), we could say that the man from Gaya had an "enchanted" worldview, a worldview in which the natural world is seen as intrinsically imbued with values rather than being brute and inert.

Such an enchanted worldview was once common in Delhi, where one of the primary experiences of the sacred, for both Hindus and Muslims, was ecological: based on greenery, flowing water, the scent of flowers, and the potentialities of affective transformation and healing that result from opening our sensate selves to nature. In premodern Delhi the sanctity and blessing of Muslim saints was integrally linked to local ecology and topography. We see this in the accounts of Dargah Quli Khan, a young nobleman from the Deccan who visited Delhi in 1739 and described a city bustling with fairs and festivals, trade and pilgrimage. One of the many pilgrimages he described as part of the city's regular calendar was the weekly ten-mile pilgrimage from the city of Shahjahanabad (now Old Delhi) to the dargah of the saint Hazrat Qutbuddin Bakhtiyar Kaki (d. 1235) in Mehrauli, a *qasba* or small township famed for both its greenery and the presence of saints: "People . . . leave Delhi at night [for Mehrauli]. First they make the pilgrimage [to the grave of Hazrat Qutbuddin Bakhtiyar Kaki] and then they ramble amongst the springs and the abundant greenery that are everywhere here due to the blessings of your [Qutbuddin's] feet, and especially they go to see the Hauz-e Shamsi, which is among the blessed springs, and gain many kinds of benefits from their wandering. All around your light bestowing tomb there are the tombs of many men of God" (Dargah Quli Khan 1993, 118).

Many things are notable about this account from Dargah Quli Khan. First, the greenery of Mehrauli is directly connected to the saint, literally to the blessings (*barakat*) of his feet. Second, rambling among the greenery (*sair*) is not differentiated from the pilgrimage to see the tombs but is narratively placed in the midst of visits to the saints' tombs, and its benefits are both similar and intrinsically linked to those received from visiting the saints. But rather than following this precedent, and considering his tranquility when being among greenery as being associated with the blessing of the nearby dargah of Ashiq Allah, or of the even more renowned dargah of Qutbuddin Bakhtiyar Kaki in Mehrauli, our friend from Gaya understood the rock outcropping, and its effect on him, as a mazar in its own right, without knowing any details of the saint buried there, except that he was somehow a part of this massive outcrop of living rock.

Within minutes of leaving the man from Gaya, my friend and I walked into the urbanized village of Mehrauli, now densely built up and clogged with traffic. The dargah of Hazrat Qutbuddin Bakhtiyar Kaki now lies in the midst of this urban chaos, separated from what remains of the green of Mehrauli by acres of brick and concrete and the constant din of buses leaving from the Mehrauli bus depot. The tomb of Qutub Sahib is now literally disconnected from what little remains of the greenery of Mehrauli by the massive postcolonial growth of urban Delhi. We could say perhaps that this disconnect gives an autonomous sanctity to ecological elements: no longer connected to the *walaya* or sanctity of Qutub Sahib, the stone outcropping becomes a saint in its own right.[1]

But Patthar Baba is not a saint for everyone. As we sat at, or rather on, the shrine of the stone saint with the man from Gaya, no one else came to join us, though many people traversed the path just to the west of the outcropping, a path connecting Mehrauli to the dargah of Ashiq Allah. For a while a group of middle-aged Hindu women from Mehrauli sat and chatted nearby, but no one came to pay their respects to the shrine of the stone saint. Apparently, the saintliness of the stone was obvious only to the Muslim migrant from Bihar.

While his experience of sacrality at the rock outcropping recapitulates an older idea of sacrality in the city, this experience is no longer comprehensible as sacred to most "natives" of the city because they live in an increasingly disenchanted Delhi, where the natural world has been devalued. The experience of the sacred in Delhi, once intimately tied to local ecology and topography, has been drastically transformed in colonial and postcolonial Delhi, a transformation of the city's spiritual landscapes that is intimately tied to the transformations of the city's physical landscapes.

In this chapter I trace the processes of erasure and remaking that have led to a drastic transformation in the experience of enchantment and the ontology of the sacred in the modern city. I will also look at the emergence of new religious forms, which recapture an older sense of the sacred in the contemporary city, though in radically reconfigured ways—for example, the veneration of snakes and cats as saints at Firoz Shah Kotla. Like the man from Gaya's singular veneration of the stone saint, this is a minor tradition, but it is one that holds open potentialities for a radical reworking of ecological thought and its relation to urban life.

THREE VISITS TO A SACRED DAM

To illustrate the ways in which the experience of the sacred in Delhi has transformed from the precolonial to the postcolonial, I present three accounts, separated in time, of the same sacred place, a spring and pool just downstream from a massive fourteenth-century masonry dam known as the Satpula (fig. 8), once part of the southern boundary of the Tughlaq city of Jahanpanah. The first account is from approximately 1739, the second from 1847, and the third from field notes written in 2010.

The Satpula in the Muraqqa-e Dehli

One of the places that Dargah Quli Khan wrote about on his visit to Delhi was what he called a *chashma* (spring) near the dargah of the fourteenth-century saint Hazrat Nasiruddin Mahmud "Chiragh-e Dehli" (d. 1356), colloquially known as Chirag Dilli.

> In truth you are the lamp of Delhi, rather you are the lamp and the eyes [*chashm o chiragh*, dearly beloved] of all Hindustan. The pilgrimage to your

FIGURE 8. *Satpula seen from the north. Photo by author.*

tomb is on Sundays. In the month of Diwali the crowds are especially impressive. In this month the people of Delhi come on every Sunday to gain
the bliss of pilgrimage. There is a spring near the dargah, here they pitch
tents and enclosures and bathe in the spring and often people find complete
cures from their old diseases. Muslims and Hindus both make the pilgrimage in the same fashion. From morning to evening the caravans of pilgrims
keep coming regularly. In the shade of every wall and every tree they spread
out carpets and give due praise to luxury and the happiness of hearts. It is
a strange and wondrous excursion and amusement and an extraordinary
spectacle. Everywhere there is color and music and in every nook and corner there is the sound of the *pakhawaj* and *morchang* (drum and jews harp).
(Dargah Quli Khan 1993, 120)

The dargah of Chiragh-e Dehli, located in the midst of the Tughlaq city
of Jahanpanah, was built on the banks of a stream known as the Naulakha
nala. The stream's entry into Jahanpanah was regulated by a large dam
with seven sluice gates known as the Satpula, located about half a mile
south of the dargah. The water that collected downstream from the dam
(supplemented by the groundwater that bubbled up here in a spring) was
renowned for its healing properties, and these healing powers were connected to the blessing of the saint. Once again, we see the connection,

in popular religion and in Dargah Quli's narrative, between the *barakat* (blessings) of the saint and the local ecology.

Dargah Quli Khan was writing from a world in which the natural and moral orders were deeply intertwined and indistinguishable. It was a world of *natural supernaturalism* (Bilgrami 2014, 182–83), in which the natural world was not (just) an object of scientific study and manipulation but also enchanted, in that it was filled with value and meaning. There is a long Islamic tradition of seeing the ecology as full of the signs (*ayat*) of the work and presence of God. For example, *sabza* (greenery) was traditionally seen as a "veil of mercy" and a "comfort to the eye" (*qurrat al-'ain*) (Husain 2000, 76). There is also a long tradition of linkage between the sanctity of saints and the "order of nature" (Nasr 1996, 281). It is no surprise then that in Dargah Quli Khan's narrative the ecology of Delhi is invariably linked to the sanctity of the saints, and his accounts of the dargahs of Delhi are filled with descriptions of springs and wells, tanks and streams, gardens and trees and flowers. But the blessing of the saints, as bestowed through local ecology, was not merely passively viewed and contemplated. The water, the trees, the air, and the scent of flowers all had active physiological and psychological effects that directly impacted one's body and sense of self. The environment, we could say, had a moral impact. In his description of the gardens that were a part of the tomb-complex of a Mughal general, Mir Musharraf, Dargah Quli Khan writes:

> Even if an abstemious one with a dry intellect [*khushk dimagh*] comes here then by the freshening of his brain [lit., moistening, *tar-dimaghi*] he will be held in a state of intoxication and go mad. If a heedless and unintelligent enforcer of morals [*muhtasib*] reaches there, then by the intoxication and climate of the place he will be intoxicated and ennobled [*mast o sarshar*]. The freshness of the air there makes one want to drink wine. And the colorfulness of the place makes [one] want to listen to music and lose one's senses. (Dargah Quli Khan 1993, 124–25)

Dargah Quli Khan's description of the garden, and the effects it had (or could potentially have) on even the driest, most abstemious and pleasure-denying person (the stock characters of the *zahid* and the *muhtasib*), is best understood through the canonical medical texts of Ibn Sina (Avicenna), which were (and are) widely acclaimed in the Indo-Pakistan subcontinent (Husain 2000, 124). As Faisal Devji points out, the humoral theory of the body and healing, central to the Avicennan tradition (known in the subcontinent as Unani [Ionian/Greek] medicine), implies that the body is not autonomous but tied to the world, implying a porosity of what we could consider the body's subjective interiority to the exteriority of nature.[2] Yunani treatments did not conceive of, or try to treat, the body exclusively: "it dealt not with a specialized truth but with a more general sensuousness, with bodily behavior and pleasure, in other words with the vast field of ethics" (Devji 1993, 192). The vast field of ethics, tied inextricably to the environment, also linked the body to the *topos* of the city and its surrounds. By the late Mughal period, when Dargah Quli Khan visited the city, the gardens were sacralized as the abode of the saints and pitted against the vain agitation of the city (Wescoat 1996). The space of the garden both expanded and contradicted the usual morality of the city. The shrines of saints and the gardens and springs associated with them were, as we have seen, sites where pleasure, sanctity, and the play of desire came together, as at the spring associated with the shrine of Chiragh-e Dehli. In the landscape of precolonial Delhi, in the green of garden and forest, it was hard to make a distinction between beneficial medicine, sensual pleasure, sanctity, and the overwhelming of the senses.

The Satpula in the Asar us-Sanadid

More than a century later, in 1847, we get an account of the same spring, and the Tughlaq era dam behind it, in the first edition of Syed Ahmad Khan's *Asar us-Sanadid*:

> This Satpula is near the Dargah of Roshan Chiragh Dehli. In truth this is the hunting lodge of Sultan Firoz Shah Tughlaq. . . . In the middle of this wall is a very big stream. . . . To let the stream flow, they made arches and a bridge over them. For this reason it is famous as the Sat-Pula (seven span bridge). . . . May God will that the English administrators get this dam repaired and make it as strong and well made as it once was.
>
> At this place the *khadims* [servers/administrators] of the Dargah have spread a strange kind of net to trap people and make money. They say that

Hazrat Roshan Chiragh Dehli once came by the arches of this dam at a time when the time for the 'Asr prayers was growing short, and there was no water to be found. At that place he scraped the ground with his hands and immediately water came forth, and he did his ritual ablutions with that water, and he gave this blessing that whoever bathed with this water would be cured of all sickness. And stating this to be a miracle (*karamat*), they have dug a small well in front of the arches, whose water is certainly not pure according to the dictates of religion. They do not give this water to anyone without taking an offering or gift from them. Firstly this tale is not proven by any books, and even if it was proved, then this tale is not counted as a miracle. Because a stream has been flowing at this place for hundreds and thousands of years and it is the rule of the bed of rivers and streams that if you dig just a handful, water will come out. In short, Muslims have against their religion (*din*), given this small, unclean hole in the ground glorification like the water of the Ganga and established it as a *tirt* [tirtha; Hindu place of pilgrimage], and they bathe the sick with its water. In the month of Katik [Kartik, usually mid-October–mid-November] and near Diwali, on Saturdays, Sundays and Mondays there is such a crowd that it is beyond description. Women come bringing their children and bathe them with this water, and in small earthen pots they keep the water with lotus leaves (*saras ke patte*) and take it away as *tabarruk* (blessed offering). The unique thing is that some ignorant men also believe in this and they also come and bathe here and they say that if anyone had done some magic, even that would be washed off. In these days, the Khadims make a killing. They don't give a jar full of water for less than six *takas*. When I went to draw a picture of this dam it was coincidentally a Sunday. And many Hindus and Muslims had come for *tirt* [pilgrimage], and the crowd was such that it became difficult for me to draw. May Allah save all Muslims from unbelief and idolatry (*kufr o shirk*) and relieve them of corrupt beliefs. Amen, o Lord of both worlds. Whoever worshipped (*puja*) any except Allah he lost his religion by his own hands. (S. A. Khan 2007, 46–48)

In 1847, when Syed Ahmad Khan first published this account of the Satpula as part of his book on the historical remains of Delhi, much had changed since Dargah Quli Khan's visit, over a century ago. While Delhi was still nominally the seat of Mughal sovereignty, the British now controlled much of India, including the administration of Delhi, which they had been in effective control of since 1803. Syed Ahmad Khan, born into a noble family with intimate connections to the Mughal court, exemplifies how deeply pervasive British influence was, despite the ostensible continuity of Mughal rule in Delhi. As a young man, Syed Ahmad Khan worked as an administrator of the North West Provinces of the British Bengal Presidency, south and east of Delhi. He was also deeply influenced by Western ideas of science and nature.[3]

By the mid-seventeenth century, a new view of nature and its relation to both God and man had arisen in England, a view promoted by an alliance of scientists affiliated with the Royal Society, expanding merchant capital, and the Church of England. In this view Nature emerged as a new category, as a material world divorced from man, morality, and divinity. God was now conceived of as a watchmaker who had set the mechanism of the world in motion but existed outside of it. Nature was (now) brute and inert, an object world to be scientifically observed and materially exploited. Divinity, in this new view, was utterly transcendent and removed from the material world (Bilgrami 2014, 279–327). To believe otherwise was to indulge in "fetishism," which was a new definitional category also emerging at this moment (Pietz 1987). Syed Ahmad Khan was deeply influenced by this view of nature and, concomitantly, an utterly transcendent divinity, as we see in his account of the Satpula. He found the belief in the sanctity of the spring and the custom of bathing in its water so offensive that he used the Indic/"Hindu" word *tirt/tirtha* to describe it rather than the word *ziyarat*, the standard Persian/"Islamic" word for pilgrimage to saint's tombs. He constantly reiterates the un-Islamic nature of the practices at this spring, equating the association of Islamic sacrality with nature as the equivalent of unbelief and idolatry. Later in his life, Sir Syed Ahmad Khan (Companion of the Order of the Star of India), keen to bring Islamic theology in line with this particular genealogy of English scientific rationality, was called (often derogatorily) *"nechari"* (naturalist) (M. Hasan 1998). The term *nature* was borrowed virtually unchanged into Urdu because there was no Indic or Persian word then that could signify a material world utterly devoid of morality and divinity.

Satpula, Monsoon 2010

The third account of visiting the Satpula is my own.

The Satpula is no longer a sacred site. In July 2010, when I visited, there was no sign of a spring or well in front of the dam, and the ground did not seem any more moist than the monsoon slush in the streets of the villages of Chiragh Delhi and Khirki I had walked through to get here. The stream that once came to the Satpula has now been diverted and flows about fifty meters to the east. It is black and fetid, carrying the sewage of South Delhi toward the Yamuna. The only people to visit Satpula on any regular basis are young men looking for a place to play cards who find the secluded arches ideal for this purpose. Asked if they know about the history or sanctity of the place, they shrug their shoulders. There is no sign of the many varieties of trees that Syed Ahmad Khan had written about that made this place *dilkusha* (heart-attracting). Across from the Satpula there are now five massive shopping malls.

Trying to find out how things had come to this pass, I went to the dargah of Chiragh-e Dehli and spoke to Pirzada Zameer Ahmed, the hereditary caretaker of the dargah, descendant of the *khadims* whom Syed Ahmad Khan had excoriated in his prose for making a profit from the waters of the Satpula. The pirzada said that yes, there used to be a *mela* at the 'urs of Chiragh-e Dehli, and on the occasion of the 'urs people would go from the dargah to the Satpula. This, he said, stopped twenty-five or thirty years ago when the slum settlements of Khanpur and Madangir came up and their sewage lines came into the water here. Before that you could drink this water straight from the stream flowing past; it was that clear. Earlier, when people went to Satpula, they would bathe with their clothes on and then leave the clothes they bathed in there. Once they bathed at the Satpula and then came to and did *haziri* at Chiragh-e Dehli's dargah, they were sure to have a child. Whether the child would be a boy or a girl was, of course, a matter of luck and fate. "I have sent people there myself," he said, and he also claimed that he had been in charge of the dargah since 1983. "But I don't send people anymore," he said, "because of the dirtiness." Then he said something that sounded highly ironic to me. Gesturing to the tomb of the saint, he said, "*Duniya ka nizam to inhin ne sambhala hai. Agar abhi barish ki jagah ole paren, to yahin ham bebaq ho jaenge.*" (He controls the organization of the world. If right now there was hail instead of rain, we would be finished right here.)

The pirzada seemed unperturbed as he spoke of the fouling of the stream that flowed past the dargah, a destruction that had occurred in his lifetime and mine. In his words the order of nature was still unperturbed, and still connected to the blessing of the saint. For me, however, the fouling and abandonment of a water body whose sacrality was specifically connected to the memory of the saint seemed to be an irrevocable loss. Hoping to elicit a different response, I went to Khirki Village, which is across the stream from Chiragh Dehli and within the traditional boundaries of which the Satpula lies.

Khirki, like Chiragh Delhi, is a village mostly only in name now. The agricultural land of the village was bought by the government in the 1960s, and the former fields of the village have made way for middle-class residential colonies and, most recently, the massive malls of the Saket City Center, now right across the road from the village. The village has changed from an agrarian economy to one based on real estate. Using the money from the sale of their lands, the traditional *zamindars* (landholders) of the village built up their houses and invested in property, both in Khirki Village and all over the city of Delhi. Khirki, like many of the other "urban villages" of Delhi, now plays host to a substantial migrant population who rent rooms and apartments from the village zamindars.

A friend who works with an artist collective based in Khirki, one of the many migrants now at home here, took me to meet some of the old zamindars of Khirki. It was early in the evening, about five o'clock, and there were about five or six of them in a small park in the middle of the village, playing cards. I asked them about the Satpula. Many of them answered, though barely looking up from their game of cards. One of them said that Satpula was a dam, "part of the fortification wall of the Hindu king Prithviraj Chauhan's fort, and this dam was built to regulate the flow of water in and out of the fort, and it was used for bathing and water for horses and things like that. The Muslims destroyed everything else, and only this was left. This was built in 1100. That's all there is to it." Another old man said that the dam/bandh was built much later. They disagreed, but both disparaged Muslims. Another man, on my prompting, volunteered that "there used to be a spring here, in front of the dam. The water was absolutely blue, till twenty-five to thirty years ago. People used to come to bathe here. Muslims used to come; the Punjabis used to come from Malviya Nagar. We used to go and bathe a lot, too. Our buffaloes used to bathe as well and would spend the whole day wallowing in the water." Another man interjected, "Women who didn't have children would also come to bathe here."

Apart from the notable anti-Muslim slant, the stories the card-playing zamindars told about Satpula were not different from the story of the dam told to me by the pirzada at the dargah. The chronology of the fouling and abandonment of the Satpula was also the same; once the sewage from Madangir overflowed into the stream, that was the end of that. My field notes from that evening sum up my frustrations and my questions rather angrily: "But what I don't understand in all of this—either in their accounts or in the account at the Dargah of CD [Chiragh Delhi] is just this—how can you be so apathetic to all of this? How can the destruction of something that was once—in your own lifetime—considered sacred elicit so little response that you're barely distracted from your card game while talking about it?"

THE SKY HAS CHANGED, THE EARTH HAS CHANGED; OR, FORGETTING A SACRED GEOGRAPHY

How do we understand the ways in which the sacred geography of Delhi, as exemplified by the Satpula, has passed almost entirely unmourned?[4] If the sanctity of the saint was still connected to the environment, as in the account of the pirzada, then surely the fouling of the stream by sewage should have elicited some mourning?[5] Here I find Akeel Bilgrami's distinction between two levels of epistemological relation to the world quite useful. Bilgrami distinguishes between a *collective, public* epistemology of disenchantment and a *quotidian* responsive relation to the world filled with value properties:

> The conceptual transformation by which nature came to be conceived as natural resources is one that occurs at a level of *collective, public* understanding, a form of understanding generated by alliances made between powerful forces

in society that control governance, political economy, and a slowly emerging and increasingly consciously determined public opinion on these large collective and public matters.

...By contrast, there is a level of understanding in these very same people that is and remains *quotidian* in its responses to the world. (Bilgrami 2014, 206)

By *quotidian* Bilgrami here alludes to the ways in which "ordinary people everywhere still see the world, including nature, as making normative demands on them" and "perceive the world to be shot through with value properties, that is to be enchanted" (2014, 205). Because of this coexistence of the *collective, public* knowledge (disenchantment) and *quotidian* response (enchantment), individual mentality finds itself existing in two quite different frames—or, metaphorically speaking, falling between two stools—and hence prone to inconsistencies in its judgments and responses. So the pirzada, while committed to a traditional (or to use Bilgrami's term, quotidian) theology in which the saint still controls the inherently moral order of the weather, does not see the contradiction inherent in disassociating the polluted flow of the stream from the sanctity of the saint. This is because the pollution of the stream belongs to the collective, public form of life in the city, in which the decisions that led to the sewer lines being led into the stream were made by government bureaucracies that, while consisting of individuals who believe in the sanctity of (some) rivers, were collectively firmly committed to a disenchanted worldview, in which there is no sanctity inherent to water channels, which are to be used instrumentally for the disposal of sewage.

Syed Ahmad Khan's *nechari* outlook might have had very little impact on traditional Islamic theology (Faruqi 2006). But if we take him to be representative of the colonial and postcolonial elites who fully embraced the ideology of disenchanted nature, an elite that encompasses, across the usual divides of religion and race, figures as diverse as Khan, Jawaharlal Nehru, and the British administrator GF de Montmorency (who makes an appearance later in this chapter), then the impact these elites had on religious life, through their profound reshaping of both sacred geography and public opinion, is as yet completely unstudied. In the next section I focus on the ways in which the policies of the colonial and postcolonial state profoundly changed the relation of Delhi's populace to one of the most sacred elements of Delhi's precolonial landscape—water.

. . .

In some of the remaining protected greenery of the Delhi Ridge, atop the massive masonry wall of a fourteenth-century embankment dam, is the small dargah of Moluddin Chishti. According to the gravestone, the saint was buried here on 11 Rajab 1300 Hijri, which corresponds to May 18, 1883. According to Ali Khan, the current caretaker, the saint was buried at the site where he lived, prayed, and meditated for many years.

The saint's living and praying atop the wall of a Tughlaq era dam as late as the late nineteenth century points us to a long-standing trend in the history of Delhi in which sites where water was abundant were associated with the sanctity of Muslim saints and with the Prophet. Shaikh Yusuf Qattal (d. 1526) is remembered as living and praying among the arches of the Satpula and being buried there. Nizamuddin Auliya (d. 1325) is remembered as having spent time meditating and praying at the Hauz Rani reservoir. Nasiruddin Mahmud Chiragh-e Dehli's memory is associated not just with the healing powers of the Satpula but also with the miracle of lighting lamps with the water of the baoli (stepwell) adjacent to the dargah of Nizamuddin. In later memory the construction of the Hauz-e Shamsi reservoir by the Sultan Iltutmish (d. 1230) was ascribed to the inspiration of a Prophetic dream in which the site of the reservoir was marked by the hoofprint of Buraq, the winged steed on which the Prophet ascended to heaven. What is remarkable is that none of these sites can be classified as "pristine" nature; they are sites of hydrological engineering, where a plenitude of water is created through the careful interaction of human technology with the environment. Dams, Prime Minister Jawaharlal Nehru famously said, are the temples of modern India. The insinuation was that technology, rather than antiquated religious traditions, was the faith that independent India would follow. But the narratives associated with dams and saints in Delhi indicate that traditional dams were sacred spaces long before Nehru introduced "modern" into the equation and that the divides between nature and culture,

and between "Hindu" sacrality and "Muslim" history, are far more complicated than received wisdom would have us believe.[6]

Water was important to Ali Khan's narrative of the history of the
dargah of Moluddin Chishti as well. "There was so much water collected behind this dam," he said, "that it was a *jhil* (a lake), stretching
from Dhaula Kuan to Rajinder Nagar" (populated areas at two ends of
the protected Delhi Ridge, separated by about five miles). Ali Khan had
not seen the water gathered. These were stories he had heard from his
father and grandfather. Here we see, coming down in family lore, the
memory of the vast and intricate systems of water management built in
the time of Firoz Shah Tughlaq (1350–88). The embankment on which
Moluddin Chishti's dargah was built may not have stretched all the way
from Dhaula Kuan to Rajinder Nagar, but there were many dams, em-
bankments, and reservoirs built along the Delhi Ridge during that time
to collect, preserve, and control rainwater. At a time when the vast majority of Delhi's population deals with chronic water shortage, and the water
table has sunk to mine-deep levels, the remembered plenitude of water
beckons like a mirage—a vast, glimmering sheet of water.

According to Ali Khan, the water from the dam was used to irrigate
the fields of Malcha Village. In 1911 the British attacked the village,
scaring away the villagers by firing their cannons. The village emptied out.
"Where the mansions are today," he said, indicating the posh diplomatic
enclave of Chanakyapuri to our east, "is where the village used to be." At
first I thought that his account was merely telescoping history, conflating
the violence of 1857, when the countryside around Delhi was convulsed
with violence, with 1911, the year when New Delhi was declared the
capital of British India. But his insistence on associating violence with
1911 points us to a largely unreported aspect of the history of Delhi;
there may not have been any cannons fired, but the making of Delhi as
the new capital of the British Indian Empire was experienced as an act of
enormously disruptive violence by those who lived through it.

The declaration of the capital was followed by a massive land-acquisition
drive to make space for the new planned city. But the new city was not
being built on a *tabula rasa* but on land that for centuries had been witness to dense interconnections between sacrality and ecology. The process

of land acquisition was challenged by hundreds of petitions that articulated the sacredness of the sites that were being acquired and explained how their acquisition and destruction would hurt the "religious sentiments" of the petitioners. What is most interesting about these religious sentiments is how closely they are tied to the texture of ecology and everyday life. Extracts from a file titled "Applications Regarding the Preservation of Temples, Mosques etc. Within the Terminal Station Area (Orders Regarding . . .)" (CCO, f68/1915/Revenue and Agriculture) are illuminating:

> . . . a Hindu deputation of certain Mohallas in the matter of the preservation of certain Hindu shrines and their belongings . . .
>
> They represent upwards of ten thousand inhabitants and about two thousand daily wayfarers.
>
> There are three distinct places to which their representations relate and the objects which they desire to safeguard range from actual necessities of existence to social amenities and sacred buildings and their belongings.
>
> 1) Gupeshur Mahadeo Temple including well, chabutra and Baghichi etc. at Teliwara.
>
> The well is the sole means of supply of water to the Hindus of these mohallas, is itself one of the best wells and there is a great demand for water.
>
> The temple is very old, has a public fair of its own on Chait Badi Chaudas and two fairs of these Mohallas at Shivratri. . . .
>
> A piao [drinking station for wayfarers] is also maintained there which gives relief to thousands of wayfarers daily all the year round.
>
> 2) Mangladevi group of shrines and well at Pul Mithai.
>
> The well is in much daily demand being regarded by three mohallas—
>
> Pul Mithai
>
> Tokriwalan
>
> Kalikar
>
> —as their sole means of drawing water and being resorted to also by the distant mohallas of
>
> Teliwara
>
> Rui ki Gali
>
> Jatwara

both for its better water and for the crowd at Teliwara well. The water of this well is regarded as better in some respects than that of [the] Teliwara well.

It is a fact that other spots which were tried in Teliwara yielded brackish water confirming a traditional faith in the efficiency of the temple wells. (my emphasis)

Another petition from the same file related to the issue, one accompanied by thousands of signatures, was much more succinct:

The petitioners have been greatly horrified and their religious feelings have been injured to a great extent since they have heard that both these places are being acquired for the Railway purposes. Whereby these said places where the petitioners worship always will be destroyed and that the petitioners will be deprived of drinking water as well at these places.

Therefore the petitioners humbly pray that both of these places may not be acquired and destroyed, because on account of want of good drinking water and for removal of sacred buildings the petitioners will not only badly suffer but their souls will also suffer.

Temple wells are the ones where sweet water is found. Other wells dug in the neighborhoods, probably as a reaction to news of the temple wells being acquired, are found to be brackish. The presence of sweet water probably determined the location of the temples to begin with, as well as dargahs and mosques, which in Delhi are/were located on the banks of streams or rivers or were built with accompanying wells and tanks. The petitions against the acquisition and future destruction of these temples are conscious of this link between ecology, everyday life, and sacrality, and they articulate it as such: *on account of want of good drinking water and for removal of sacred buildings the petitioners will not only badly suffer but their souls will also suffer.*

The colonial government of Delhi eventually decided to let the "sacred buildings" stand but with some caveats, as we see in the note of GF de Montmorency, the assistant to the chief commissioner of Delhi: "It might be true that mohala [*sic*] festivals take place at the temple, which is private property. But I don't think that we can allow any large gathering at it. *I don't think we can give any promise to preserve the well. These mohallas are to get a filtered water supply*" (my emphasis).

The British government decided to preserve the religious structures, for the time being, but even then, they weren't sure about the wells and wanted to replace them with filtered, piped water (see also Sharan 2011, 2014). The bringing of piped water would delink the sacred from the everyday ecology of the city. Although this delinking was occasionally resisted in the beginning, in the long run (extending into the postcolonial era) it proved to be a remarkably successful strategy, instrumental in changing not just the ecology of Delhi but the very experience of sacredness.

. . .

I spoke to Bhagwati Prasad, a researcher and artist who had been researching water problems in Delhi. He had worked extensively on people's relationship to water and their memory of water sources. His research, which he has presented graphically in *The Water Cookbook* (2011), shows how the coming of piped-water supplies to villages drastically changed their relationship to local water bodies. When we spoke, he explained some of these changes:

> Till [the coming of centralized piped water] you had two sources of water, the river and wells, to which you were deeply connected. And the third was the rainwater collected in *jhors* (overground rainwater trenches), which you had to maintain. The jhors were always on the land of the village commons, controlled by the *panchayat* (the village's autonomous governing body), who were responsible for maintaining it, seeing that the water wasn't dirtied. There are still some villages that we saw where the *jhors* are maintained from which they [the villages] can get a year's worth of water for agriculture. . . . But in villages that have come within the perimeter of Delhi's urbanization, things have changed, and these old ways are going. Till now they were limited to the jhor and the wells, but then the government made promises of a centralized system of water: there will be taps and running water in your homes and you will drink straight from them. People were very happy then; they said who will go [to] the well now, who will go to the jhor, or to the river? They were happy to begin with, but over the last twenty years—the lines are still the same, there is no system of cleaning, [and] no one knows what's going

on inside the pipes, unlike with the visible water sources, where you can tell whether the water is dirtied or not. So there's a situation now where when people open their taps, water comes out black, and people thought that this is dirty water that we're drinking. So people have now turned to groundwater. They say, this [the municipal water supply] is now destroyed, let's get water out of the ground, maybe that will be cleaner. But when we asked about the three traditional water sources, when we said, didn't you ever think that you used to have wells, etc., then they would say as soon as the pipeline entered their villages, everyone stopped sharing the wells.

The panchayat's relationship with the wells also slowly finished. When the wells started drying up, which happened because people started pumping the groundwater and hence water levels went down, the panchayats didn't try to dig the wells deeper. And the wells died. People slowly started occupying the land of the jhors, incorporating them into their individual fields till there was nothing left. Today in a village no one knows on what land the jhor was, how big it was . . . so the river is destroyed and the jhors are finished, so now, we asked them, because of the one source of [piped] water you left all these other sources of water, and that one source is also now polluted, so what do you do? They say now we draw water from the ground, we go down to 400 feet, some say 200, some say 150, and that's how we get clean water. . . .

. . . When you ask people how this has happened, how everything has been destroyed in the last ten or fifteen years, then people give very strange answers. People from villages by and large say that the polluted water comes from upstream, it's not polluted here. Most people blame industries. There are people who take industrial waste, which it is illegal to dump into rivers, and bring it to water bodies close to the villages and dump it in the dead of night. But there's been no attempt to stop that. There's no protest from the villages to stop the dumping. There's a complete disconnect between the villagers now and their old sources of water. The dumping is happening in front of their eyes, on their own land. The dumping happens into a stream that runs through their fields into the river. They know it, they see it, they talk about it, but they've never protested it.

They know it, they see it, they talk about it, but they've never protested it. They don't even look up from their card game when speaking of the destruction of a neighborhood spring in their own lifetime. (But *they* are not separable from *we*, all of us who live *within* the impact of modern urbanization on the natural world from which we are increasingly conceptually and experientially distanced.) Bhagwati attributes this apathy, similar to the apathy I encountered concerning the Satpula, to the coming of piped water and to its fundamental redefinition of people's relationship to water.[7] Piped water, while it never quite lived up to the promises of a centralized clean, uninterrupted water supply (see Sharan 2014), did drastically alter how people conceived of their relationship to water. By the time the taps, which is to say piped water, proved to be both erratic in supply and increasingly polluted, people's relationship to local water bodies had already changed. The communally managed wells and jhors had dried up or been filled up and incorporated into farmland, and the local rivers and streams had been polluted by sewage and industrial effluent. The changes in the nature of the water bodies were mirrored by changes in the communal life of the village. There was no longer cooperation of the sort that had marked the communal husbanding of shared water bodies. Now it was every family for itself, and those who could afford to drill deep to get groundwater were doing so. Infrastructure changes sociality. Infrastructure changes us.

"The Land Reforms Act and the Panchayat Act of 1954 were enacted by the Government of Delhi which opened access to the common lands of rural Delhi and so started a process of free riding on the common lands" (Chakravarty-Kaul 2011, 74). From the accounts I heard in Begampur village, the private takeover of lands formerly held in common and the filling of the village jhors also dates back to the 1950s. To Bhagwati's account I could add the many stories I heard of traditional water bodies, many of them connected to the ritual life of the city, being filled up to make way for residential and commercial space for migrants in post-Partition Delhi. The famous *hauz* of Qadam Sharif dargah? Gone after partition, according to the *khadim* of the dargah, filled up to make space for refugee houses. The Lal Diggi tank in the Ramlila Grounds south of Old Delhi, where water chestnuts grew and where Ram and Sita used to be rowed across in a boat every Dussehra? Filled up to make way for Kamala Market and its shops allotted to refugees, according to Nasim Changezi.

.   .   .

A letter addressed to the Director General, Department of Archaeology, in June 1966:

> I beg to draw your kind attention that a historical culvert constructed dur-
> ing the regime of Mohammad Tughlak has been demolished by Shri S. P.
> Kapoor, a resident of 74, Govind Puri, Kalkaji, New Delhi, inspite [*sic*] of
> objections raised by his neighbors and people of the locality. He has also
> taken help from the Chairman of the South Zone, Municipal Corporation,
> Chaudhry Dilip Singh and Councillor of the said area Mr. Narain Singh in
> the abovesaid [*sic*] demolition which in the public interest cannot be good.[8]

The ASI took no action because the culvert, not being a "protected" monument, was outside its jurisdiction. The letter gives us a brief illumination of the ways in which the landscape of Delhi was rapidly transformed in the years after 1947. The old village landscapes of Delhi were transformed into housing estates, like Govind Puri, for the Punjabi refugees who flooded into the city in the aftermath of Partition violence. The Punjabis, like S. P. Kapoor, had no attachment to the remnants of the past, whether human or ecological, which they now found themselves living amidst. Neither did members of the Delhi administration, committed to building a modern city, not one whose growth was stymied by the remnants of the past. So the culvert, and the paths it carried over the flow of water, and the channel through which the water flowed all vanished from the landscape of Delhi, like hundreds of other "unprotected" premodern structures. The cumulative effects of the changes of land tenure and subsequent erasure of natural and manmade features radically transformed the landscape of Delhi and deeply affected the *collective, public* life of the city, not just in the intellectual sense that Bilgrami means by the term but at the level of concrete, everyday reality, at the level of the *quotidian*. How did these cumulative transformations of the landscape affect people's experience of the sacred, which, as we have seen, was deeply anchored in the landscape?

A conversation in Khirki Village illuminated the ways in which the transformation of the landscape brought with it entirely new senses of the sacred and entirely new forms of religious life. The card players of Khirki, while they didn't have very much to say to me, directed me to meet

Nathu Master. Nathu Master was a retired schoolteacher or "Master," widely recognized as an authority on the village and its history. We had a long and wide-ranging conversation in which he spoke about the ways in which the village had changed in the course of his lifetime, the way village lands had been acquired by the government, and the way fertile fields and orchards, crops and trees, had disappeared, virtually overnight. We also discussed the demographic shifts that happened as a result of Partition, when the Muslims of the village left and Punjabi refugees were settled in the village instead. When I asked Nathu Master what the sacred places in the village used to be before Partition, he said there were no such places:

> What can I tell you? All this increased business of worship (*puja path*), this came with the Punjabis, because they were depressed [he used the English word] by the Muslims. Two days ago I was reading the report of Cliff [Radcliffe] who did the Partition, that in the Punjab the population was 55 percent Muslim, and 45 percent Hindu and Sikh . . . so those who are depressed, they remember God [*Bhagvan*] more. . . . Now I tell you, no one here used to understand about temples and things like this . . . so those people had more religious faith, you could say, or were closer to God, or to rituals of worship, or to religious books, compared to us . . . and when they came, we people were greatly influenced by them. . . . These people, in these circumstances, being oppressed by the Muslims, kept remembering God. . . . Were we dead that despite remaining independent [he used the English word] forever, we didn't? So that's why now temples etcetera . . . now there are lots of them here. . . . There are three temples all built together. There is a temple of the *Devi* [Great Goddess] which my brother built. Someone built a temple to Sai Baba, and one of my friends built the temple of the family of Shiva. . . . There is so much faith [*astha*] now. Back then, there was a boy from Chiragh Dilli who used to study with us called Kalu Ram. His mother was a widow and she had built a temple to Shiva in her house. So the women from our village used to go there on *Shivratri* and offer water there, and as little kids, we used to go along with our mothers and aunts. . . . So there was nothing really religious here.

AVT. And did you also go to the dargah in Chiragh Dilli?

Nathu Master. Yes, we used to go to the Chiragh Dilli dargah. . . . We used
to go a lot. . . . We had deep relations, we had very deep relations [*gehre
sambandh*] with the Muslims of Chiragh Dilli. We used to study together. . . . My father was a Master [schoolteacher], and in that time
most of the schoolteachers were Muslim, as were the officers.

When I first heard Nathu Master use the word *depression*, I thought he
meant oppression, and was merely mistaken in his choice of word. But
Nathu Master, an educator and a PhD whose fieldwork was on vocabulary acquisition among schoolchildren, chose all his words with care. His
use of *depression* to characterize the state of the Punjabi refugees was very
precise. We know now that those who have suffered violent trauma and
displacement suffer from depression. And even if his transhistorical account of Muslim majoritarian oppression in the Punjab was inaccurate,
it certainly captured the psyche of the refugees who had come to India,
deeply affected by violence inflicted on them by Muslims in the name of
a new Muslim state. And it is to the memory of this violence, and its affective aftermath, that Nathu Master connected the coming of new gods
and new beliefs to the village.

Bhrigupati Singh (2011, 443), in his thought-provoking work on
poverty, religion, and everyday life in rural Rajasthan, argues that modes
of impermanence are internal to forms of religious life. Deities are associated with forms of life and aspiration, he argues, and the waxing and
waning of gods and their popularity is linked to the waxing and waning of
forms of life. "An ascendant deity has a particular rhythm, musical, moral
and temporal. . . . A deity must add something 'new' to an ongoing movement of life" (B. Singh 2011, 441). What is the newness that these newly
waxing deities brought to the landscapes of Khirki after 1947? Nathu
Master remembered the time before 1947 as one of deep and peaceful
relations with the Muslims of Khirki and of Chiragh Dilli. After 1947,
local Muslims disappeared and the specter of Muslim violence became
ensconced in the mythology of Khirki, coming east with the refugees created by Partition violence. Devi, the goddess whose temple in Khirki was
financed by Nathu Master's brother, is known and depicted in Delhi and
post-Partition eastern Punjab as *Sheranvali* (Erndl 1996), the one who

FIGURE 9. *The goddess Durga riding a tiger while fighting a demon. Artist unknown, eighteenth century, Guler School. Public domain image. Source: Wikimedia Commons.*

rides a lion, a form of the goddess long associated with martial mythology. This form of life, fighting against implacable demon(ized) enemies, found a renewed home in post-Partition Delhi in the aftermath of 1947, as Hindu and Sikh refugees from the Punjab streamed into the capital in their millions and as the new nation-state was increasingly identified with the image of the martial goddess Durga (fig. 9), seated astride a lion (McKean 1996). Millions had sacrificed themselves to Bharat Mata, Mother India, the goddess whose lion-riding iconography was similar to that of *Sheranvali*, with the addition of the outlined boundaries of the new nation.

The image of the goddess superimposed on the image of the nation-state is significant. The new deities of postcolonial Delhi were no longer rooted to locality but linked to the abstract space of the nation-state. As Punjabi refugees, disconnected from their own lands and their own sacred geographies, became almost overnight the majority population of the territory of Delhi, the autochthonous population, as in the village of Khirki, was rapidly disconnected from its agricultural land and sacred geographies by government fiat—often in order to provide land and housing to the refugees streaming in.

BHULI BHATIYARI AND JHANDEWALAN: WHO FORGETS, WHO REMEMBERS?

The genealogy of one of the most popular temples in Delhi, the Jhandewalan Mandir, the Temple with the Flags, bears witness to the growing disconnect between ecology, the everyday, and the sacred. I became curious about the temple while reading Syed Ahmad Khan's account of a structure now altogether disconnected from the history of the temple, a fourteenth-century structure known as the Bhuli Bhatiyari ka Mahal, which could be translated as the Palace of the Forgotten (female) Brewer, an apt name, as we will see. Of the Mahal, Khan wrote:

This building has been built atop a high hill from which the natural scenery can be seen far and wide and especially in the rainy season the water flowing everywhere and the waving of the greenery in the wind all around gives wondrous pleasure. . . . Here there is a very big fair of Pavan Parichha (testing the wind) in which all the city's Brahmins, [Hindu] astrologers (*jotishi*), fortune tellers and [Muslim] astrologers (*najumi*) gather to test the air and test it by planting a small flag (*jhandi*) and thousands of Hindu and Muslim spectators gather to watch. (S. A. Khan 2007, 267)

In the second edition of the Asar, Syed Ahmad Khan tells us that this building is built atop a Tughlaq-era dam that is still in good condition and that the Fair of Wind Testing takes place atop the dam on the full moon of the month of Ashad,[9] traditionally the beginning of the monsoon. It was the reference to the flag, the *jhandi*, that caught my attention. Surely, I thought to myself, there must be some connection between the flags mentioned in Khan's account and the name of the Jhandewalan Temple, especially as they are both relatively close to each other (to get to Bhuli Bhatiyari ka Mahal, you get off at the Jhandewalan stop on the Delhi Metro).

Today, while Bhuli Bhatiyari ka Mahal still stands among greenery in the reserved forest of the Delhi Ridge, the Jhandewalan Temple, about a kilometer to the northeast, is situated amid a dense agglomeration of buildings atop high ground, with the city stretching out on all sides. The official history of the temple, as seen in extracts from an English-language pamphlet produced by the Badri Bhagat Temple Society, however, remembers the original landscape of the temple as very similar to the one described by Syed Ahmad Khan in relation to the Bhuli Bhatiyari ka Mahal:

> Now, at that time, there was only a quiet, green wooded hill where the Temple now stands. Fruit, flowers and trees grew in abundance. The only sounds were of birds, peacocks and deer. Also, the soft splash of the sparkling spring waters. This peaceful environment drew people seeking peace and tranquility. It was soon discovered that the plants and springs had healing powers. So they flocked to this enchanted place, seeking cures.
>
> Badri Bhagat's [the founder of the temple, a nineteenth-century Delhi cloth merchant and philanthropist] favorite spot for meditation was the same peaceful green hill. One evening, while meditating, he dreamed that somewhere on that quiet hill, near a healing spring, an ancient temple with

a powerful Deity lay buried. He determined to try to find it to re-establish a
place of worship on that blessed spot.

From then on, Badri Bhagat devoted his energy, time and wealth to locate the lost Temple. . . . He created his new Temple and installed a new deity
above the old one. Then, he hoisted a flag [*jhanda*] above his temple to attract
worshippers. So it came to be known as the Jhandewalan Deviji Temple.

The deity that is worshipped aboveground now is, of course, Sheranvali,
Durga astride a lion. What, then, was the old idol, the one that lies buried
in the origin myth of the temple but whose aura permeates the new one?
Perhaps what lies buried are the greenery and flowing water eulogized in
the description of the temple's past, now vanished under tons of concrete.

The official history of the temple had nothing to do with the Bhuli
Bhatiyari ka Mahal, though the narrative of greenery and flowing water
linking both places was similar. But when I asked the manager of the
Jhandewalan Temple, Surendra Pandey, if he knew anything about
the Pavan Pariksha ka Mela, and started describing it to him, it rang
a bell with him. "You mean Pavan ka Mela," he said, "the Wind Fair."
He'd been associated with the temple from 1979, and although it had
never happened during his time at the temple, he remembered one of the
old temple priests telling him about it. The priest, Pandit Kamal Nayan,
had told him that people from Delhi and nearby villages used to come
to the temple for the Pavan ka Mela the way they now come for the
Navratras.[10] My question about the temple's past made Surendra Pandey
reminisce about the stories he'd heard of what the temple and this area
used to be like. There was a well here that people would come to bathe
in because it had healing properties. It closed down a long time ago because it got dirty. Speaking about the greenery that once surrounded the
temple, he said that this temple is a counterpart (*pratirup*) of the temple
of Vindhyavasini Devi.

The temple of Vindhyavasini Devi, in Mirzapur, in eastern Uttar
Pradesh (close to Surendra Pandey's hometown of Ayodhya), is named
for the Vindhya hills, where it is situated. *Vindhyavasini Devi* literally
translates to "the goddess who dwells in the Vindhyas." Vindhyavasini
is both a local goddess, deeply tied to and immanent in the landscape of

the Vindhyaksetra, a lush landscape of forested hills and waterfalls, and also a great goddess, *Mahadevi*, who is the primal energy underlying the whole universe (Humes 1996). Vindhyavasini is also a different kind of goddess from Sheranvali. Traditionally, she was considered a benevolent, nonascetic goddess, one who had given up her *ugraswarupa* (fiery manifestation) (Humes 1996, 70). Pandey's positing, then, of the temple of Vindhyavasini as a counterpart of the temple of Jhandewalan was telling. For at the temple of Vindhyavasini there has been a concerted effort by the Brahmin priests to "universalize the Goddess, uprooting her from a proximate, immediate, and localized immanence and supplying her with a more lofty and dislocated transcendence" (Humes 1996, 71). This theological shift is also manifested in the landscape of the Vindhya area, "where there has been a gradual disintegration of the vivid sacred reality that was once considered to be the direct transformation of the goddess herself into phenomenal *Vindhyaksetra* [the land of the Vindhyas]" (Humes 1996, 72).

. . .

The priest Pandit Kamal Nayan was long retired and now well into his nineties. He was in ill health, as well, so our meeting lasted only a few minutes. He told me he remembered the rituals of Pavan Pariksha very well, from his childhood in the 1930s, when he was a student-priest at the Pathshala (school) associated with the Jhandewalan Temple. At 6:30 on the morning of Ashad Shukla Purnima (the full moon of the month of Ashad), the learned men of Delhi would come and test the wind (Pavan Pariksha). Among them were the astrologer (*jyotishi*) Jamna Dhar *ji* and the principal of the Jhandewalan pathshala, and under their supervision the wind would be tested. If the wind blows from the east (*purv*), then the clouds give excessive rain. If the wind blows from the northwest (*paschim-uttar*), then the rain is satisfactory (*santoshjanak*). So the learned ones (*vidvan*) used to say. Asked why the ritual of testing the wind had stopped, Pandit Kamal Nayan blamed the Hindu right-wing political party, the Jan Sangh, which was formed in Delhi in 1951: "If these Jan Sanghis won't do it, then what can I do? They just want a foolish Pandit who will agree with everything they say."

He refused to elaborate further, but then he started reminiscing about what Jhandewalan was like in his day:

> There was a beautiful sweet watered well. People would come from far to bathe in its water. A pot of the water from the well used to sell in Khari Baoli [a major commercial area of Old Delhi] for 2 *annas*, because the *Seths* [merchants] there demanded it. Where all the offices and other buildings are now, there were *Ber* trees there, *Jamun* trees. We used to play there, and eat the fruits of those trees. But now the world has changed. There used to be many Banyan Trees near the temple. Jhandewalan was a garden then. It used to be called Ram Bagh. It used to belong to some Muslim. He went into debt and sold it off to Badri Bhagat and told him to do something *dharmik* [religious] with the land, and Badri Bhagat built a temple.

I asked him about Bhuli Bhatiyari ka Mahal. He said, that was very far, and it was all jungle. "We used to go there to shit. And there was no one there but us students." Perhaps reminded of the "Islamic" nature of the building by my question, he started talking of incidents he remembered from his childhood and youth, of Hindus and Muslims throwing stones at each other. Hindus and Muslims would stay on opposite sides of the crossroads, and neither would cross the road toward the other. "*Musalmanon ka aur Hinduon ka hamesha hi bair raha hai.*" (There's always been enmity between Hindus and Muslims.)

Shortly after he said this, I was dismissed. Even talking to me for a few minutes had taxed Pandit Kamal Nayan's strength. A while before talking to Pandit Kamal Nayan, I had asked Nasim Changezi if he remembered anything of Bhuli Bhatiyari ka Mahal from his childhood. He remembered nothing either, except that he and his friends sometimes used to go there to eat *ber* (jujubes). So somewhere between 1854, when Syed Ahmad Khan wrote the second edition of the Asar, and the 1930s, Bhuli Bhatiyari ka Mahal had ceased being a place of ritual importance to the city.[11] In the middle of that time period, in the 1880s, Badri Bhagat had built the Jhandewalan Temple.[12] Perhaps as a consequence of the building of the temple, perhaps owing to the growing animosity between Hindus and Muslims (as remembered by Pandit Kamal Nayan), somewhere in this time the festival of testing the wind moved a kilometer north to the Jhandewalan Temple and became an exclusively Hindu festival rather than one celebrated (or at least observed) by both Hindus and Muslims.

Or perhaps there is a more straightforward explanation. The fair moved because by the 1920s, the Public Works Department had built a large reservoir immediately north of the Bhuli Bhatiyari ka Mahal known as the Jhandewalan Reservoir (Sharan 2011), in almost exactly the same place as the Tughlaq-era dam that the Bhuli Bhatiyari ka Mahal once stood at the southern end of. The Tughlaq dam was built to control the runoff of the monsoon rains from the Ridge and to channel it to the gardens and orchards and farms of the city immediately to its east. Five hundred years later, building their city in the footprint of the Tughlaq city, the British engineers constructed their reservoir on the high ground of the Ridge, in exactly the same place, to use the gravity of water flowing down from the height of the Ridge to pump water to the thirsty new city they had built below it.[13] Of course, the water now ran through subsurface pipes, and the flow was both invisible and highly controlled.

Even Pandit Kamal Nayan did not remember any connection between the *jhandis* once used to test the wind and the name of the Jhandewalan Temple. In his time a *yantra*, some kind of circular metallic weather vane, had been used to test the wind. And then the festival itself disappeared from the calendar of the city. Only the name of the flags remained attached to the temple. A newspaper profile of the temple, written in 1992, calls the temple a "Vaishno Temple" located on Jhandewalan Pahadi—the hill of the flags. It would seem, from the newspaper story, that it is the hill that is remembered for the flags, independently of the temple. The newspaper profile of the temple in the *Hindustan*, dated September 7, 1992, linked the end of the festival to Partition:

> In old times there used to be two fairs here. The first one was on the day of the full moon of Ashad. It was called the Wind Testing Fair (Pavan Pariksha Mela). In this there was special testing of how the rains were going to fall. The second fair was that of Shravan Shukla Teej [the third day of the month of Shravan/Sawan, waxing moon], which was known as Teejon ka Mela. This was mainly a fair for girls. On these days girls would hang swings and swing

on them. After Pakistan was made these fairs stopped being held here. After Independence, for a little while, these fairs were held in the Ram Lila ground [south of Old Delhi], and after a while they stopped being held there too. (Gaur 1992)

What does the making of Pakistan have to do with the stopping of the festivals of Pavan Pariksha and Teejon ka Mela, both linked to the monsoon? The Teejon ka Mela, or Hariyali Teej, coming in the midst of the monsoon month of Sawan, has long been associated with fertility and consummation. The swings were set up to enjoy the cool monsoon breezes and the showers of rain not just at Jhandewalan but all over or-chards and gardens in Delhi and North India, swings set up in trees by Hindu and Muslim women, a sacralization of fertility and feminine play. But the playful, fecund, seductive aspect of the goddess seems to have disappeared from Jhandewalan after the Partition. Perhaps this has some-thing to do with the enormous amount of violence inflicted on women's bodies during those times.

Pandit Kamal Nayan linked the end of the Pavan Pariksha Mela to the interference of the Jan Sangh, ascendant in the new nation-state of India. Perhaps the Hindutva ascendant in the capital of the new nation-state, committed to a uniform and masculine Hinduism, found the mela to be too feminine, too committed to a specific geography, too connected, perhaps, to Muslim presence. The national headquarters of the Hindu nationalist Rashtriya Swayamsevak Sangh or RSS, of which the Jan Sangh was the political wing, lie only a short walk down the hill from the Jhandewalan Temple. In any case, the radically changed religious land-scape of Delhi, the move of the Wind Testing Fair from Bhuli Bhatiyari ka Mahal to the Jhandewalan Temple, and then its complete excision from the calendar of the city seem to indicate complete amnesia with regard to the city's past, an amnesia inaugurated and amplified by the upheavals of Partition. But there are strange survivals.

. . .

What does it mean to forget gods and rivers and festivals? Bhrigupati Singh ascribes a positive affective and intellectual valence to the forgetting of gods. Here, he is writing about the waning intensity of the deity Tejaji in district Shahbad, in rural Rajasthan:

> Was it misguided of Tejaji (through the medium of Mathura) to request a longer life in Casba Nonera? Why should anyone be disappointed with the declining intensity around Tejaji? Do they not know that deities have ascending and descending rhythms, that they are "guests"? The deity Karas receded making space for Tejaji, and one day Tejaji will have to make space for another, as yet unknown. In some ways, to retain an investment in the present and in the future, it is crucial not to know, not to expect religious life to have a stable unifying function. There is, we might say, a process of "forgetting" necessary and internal to Hinduism that leaves an opening for the futurity of aspiration, the not-yet that might take different forms of intimacy and agonistics. (B. Singh 2011, 443; see also B. Singh 2015, 190)

"With Tejaji, I undertook a genealogy of morals," Singh says (2015, 286). Singh's work is in an extended conversation with Nietzsche, and in his positive appraisal of "forgetting" he echoes Nietzsche, in whose *Genealogy of Morals* forgetting is an active force and a positive virtue: "there could be no happiness, no cheerfulness, no hope, no pride, no *present*, without forgetfulness" (Nietzsche 1989, 58). Memory for Nietzsche is linked to *unnatural* habit instilled through punishment, which inhibits and distorts the will, and to the cultivation of *ressentiment*.[14] Many in postcolonial Delhi would agree with the Nietzschean valorization of forgetting as making way for the new: *Maulana, half of Delhi is graveyards and mosques. Our schemes will fail if we don't have room to build.* But as I found when I went looking for traces of what was remembered of the sacrality of Bhuli Bhatiyari ka Mahal, the question of who remembered and who forgot was deeply tied to issues of power, class, and access to the benefits of state power.

I visited Bhuli Bhatiyari ka Mahal twice during my fieldwork. Both times, the building stood completely empty and overgrown with weeds. There was no one there for either of my visits, and from the undisturbed growth of weeds inside, it seemed like no one had been there at all for many months. But there seemed to be no dearth of sanctity all around the Mahal. Immediately to the south of the Mahal, I found a small makeshift shrine at the base of a young Pipal tree and a few painted clay statues of the gods Lakshmi and Ganesh, freshly garlanded with flowers. Immediately east of the Mahal was a wall with a gate, leading to the Delhi Development Authority's Bhuli Bhatiyari Park. Here there was seed scattered for birds and an earthenware bowl of water. I walked through the gate and went about a hundred feet into the park when I saw something to my left that made me stop short. A little bit to the left of the park was a small, slender tree whose branches were draped with many kinds of clothes in various states of disarray (fig. 10). It was astonishing to see a tree growing clothes in the midst of the forest. What was even stranger was that the tree, apart from the clothes, was not particularly striking. It blended in with the other trees and, being of slender girth, couldn't possibly be very old. When I later checked the species of the tree, I found that it was a yellow oleander, a "small evergreen tree from Mexico and the West Indies with narrow, shiny leaves and bright-yellow trumpet-flowers. . . . It has become popular with civic agencies in India at least partly because not even goats will touch it owing to the poisonous principle of its milky sap" (Krishen 2006, 174).

I walked further into the forest, hoping to find someone who would explain the tree and the clothes to me. In a few minutes I came upon

FIGURE 10. *Strange fruit. Yellow oleander tree, Central Delhi Ridge. Photo by author.*

a small horticultural office of the DDA, tasked with taking care of the greenery in this part of the Ridge. I first spoke to Rajbir Singh, a section officer in charge of this part of the Ridge. He said that the tree was known to cure skin diseases. If you bathe under the tree, people believe, and then pour water on the tree, and leave your clothes where you bathed, then you will be healed. But he believed that this was all superstition (*andhvishvas*). He said that no locals come here, only people from far away like Gurgaon and Faridabad. "Where do they get the water to bathe?" I asked Rajbir. "People bring the water with themselves," he told me.

The yellow oleander tree, one among many hundreds growing in the Ridge, is a native of the New World. It was introduced into Delhi only with the colonial afforestation of the Ridge and propagated by post-colonial government horticulture. It is not a tree with any long-standing tradition of sanctity or healing; it is known for its poisonous sap, not for any medicinal properties. How, then, did this tree gain the reputation that it has, attested to by the discarded clothes draped all over it? Being healed by bathing, and then leaving one's clothes, is traditionally associated, as it once was at the Satpula, with bodies of water considered sacred. In the healing powers attributed to this tree, perhaps we see the ghost of the water that once flowed abundantly here. And the ghost of the fame of Bhuli Bhatiyari, once known as the place where astrologers tested the wind to find out how much rain Delhi would receive.

I asked Rajbir about Bhuli Bhatiyari ka Mahal, and he didn't remember seeing anyone celebrating any festival there or praying or living there. "There is some celebration close to it," he told me, "but it's not what you're saying." (I was talking about the testing of the wind in Ashad.) To give me further details, he called one of the gardeners, Muhammad, who had been working in the park since 1984.

Muhammad told me that the Pipal tree I had seen south of the Mahal with the statues under it was planted by a government official who comes in every Sunday to make offerings, and he's the one who put the statues under the tree as well. There was a spot on the other side of the Mahal where people used to bring a goat to sacrifice in the month of *Chait* (mid-March). He says they were Kanjars from Nabi Karim (an area north of Pahar Ganj). They had colored a stone with geru (ocher) and would sacrifice a goat on it as an offering to the Ban Devta (the God of the Forest). This stopped four or five years ago, Muhammad said, when laws toughened on the Ridge. But even before that it was illegal, and they were ordered to stop it, but they did it anyway by bribing the police. I asked Muhammad why people come all the way here from Nabi Karim. His answer: because there's no open space there.

After I spoke to Rajbir and Muhammad, I went back to the Mahal. About a hundred feet to the west of the Mahal, I found a flattish, ocher-colored stone propped up against a *kikar* tree (fig. 11). The stone had the faint, rough carving of a face on the top and a much-decayed flower garland draped around it. The tree had three bright red ribbons tied to it. It seemed like the Kanjars were still making their annual pilgrimage.

Kanjar in everyday speech means "pimp." Kanjars, who were declared a criminal tribe by the colonial government, were associated with prostitution, thievery, kidnapping, and poaching. Traditionally, they were nomadic and lived by hunting and gathering and trading forest produce (as well as by performing music and dancing). But the provisions of the colonial Criminal Tribes Act, which implemented the imposition of a constant regime of surveillance and restrictions of movement on the members of any group declared "criminal," essentially sedentarized them.

FIGURE 11. *"Ban Devta"/Forest God? Central Delhi Ridge. Photo by author.*

In 1915 the Kanjars were declared a Criminal Tribe in the province of Delhi.[15] In 1922 a letter from the deputy commissioner of the province to the chief commissioner discusses proposed restrictions on their movements:

> In view of the extraordinarily bad record (of Kanjars), the Senior Superintendent of Police has suggested that it should be restricted under section 111(a) of the Act, to Bagh Karaul, where the majority live at present, but that to enable the members of it to earn a living within a restricted area, they should be allowed to wander within the jurisdictions of the Police Stations of Paharganj and Raisina [New Delhi] between sunrise and sunset, to work as labourers and punkah coolies. He adds that their women have a bad reputation and are generally believed to be members of the oldest profession in the world. (CCO, f101/1922/Home/CCO, "Proposed Restrictions on the Movements of the Criminal Tribe of Kanjars")

Bagh Karaul, now known as Karol Bagh, is west of Bhuli Bhatiyari ka Mahal and the forested ridge it stands within. Surely their wanderings would have taken them through this, the only patch of forest now accessible to them by colonial law, as they "wandered" toward menial labor in the new boomtown capital the British were building to its east. More than ninety years later, their descendants, who call themselves the Gihara community, remember their ancestors working on the construction of the New Delhi Railway Station and working for British "messes" as stewards, room boys, and occasional hunters of game.

I found a community of the Giharas in Paharganj, who remember settling there in 1947, after the Muslims who used to live in that area left. They directed me to speak to Rajkumar Gihara, who, along with his day job in real estate, was a passionate community historian. It was not a *devta* (male deity) they sacrificed to at Bhuli Bhatiyari, he said, but a goddess, the *kul-devi*, the goddess of the community, Mari Mata, also known as Bhadava Mata. Mari Mata is a traveler, like her people. Rajkumar and others used a stock phrase in introducing her: *voh Neemach se aayi hain* (she has come from Neemach [a town in the Malwa region, now on the border of Madhya Paradesh and Rajasthan]). The ritual sacrifice made to her is known as the Bharvasi Puja. In this puja, Rajkumar Gihara explained, people sacrifice a goat for the sake of their children (*apne bach-chon ke sadke ke upar vahan bali di jati hai*). The whole of our community puts its money together, and once a year we come together in the way our ancestors used to live in the forests (*pura samaj paise milakar usi rup men ata hai jaise unke purvaj janglon men rehte the*). This involves not only ritual sacrifice, and the consumption of meat, but also the imbibing of alcohol, which has led to the disapproval of the authorities and the restrictions on the annual gathering at Bhuli Bhatiyari, which the Giharas still regularly try to circumvent. "But why Bhuli Bhatiyari?" I asked Rajkumar Gihara. "Because," he said, "we want a forest place, and in Bhuli Bhatiyari you still get the atmosphere [*mahaul*] of a forest."

Apart from their annual visit to this piece of forest, the Kanjars have no more connection to forest produce than the former agriculturalists of Delhi have to farming. They have become completely urbanized over the past three or four generations, working in sedentarized urban professions. Yet they return to Bhuli Bhatiyari every year, remembering "the way our ancestors used to live in the forest." How, then, has this tradition continued, so close to Bhuli Bhatiyari ka Mahal, when the Fair of Testing the Wind has, for all practical purposes, long been forgotten? In what ways might such remembrance make us think of questions of power, forgetting, and memory?

The postcolonial state wishes to forget all forms of life and sovereignty that came before its own existence (see Chapter 1). For those who would also benefit from the largesse of the state, it is beneficial to forget. So the former zamindars of Khirki, men who have become wealthy as a result of the monetary compensation they received from the government for their lands, barely get distracted from their card games when asked about the former sacrality of Satpula. In the scale of *value* (the enormous monetary gains they have made), how can the *values* that this land once held match up? But what about those who have never benefited from the state's benevolence? What about the landless artisans and laborers who were and are an integral part of the landscape of urban and rural Delhi but who were never compensated by the government because they were never counted as landowners? What about people like the Kanjar/Giharas, people whose affective connections to geography would never translate into monetary value? Bhagwati Prasad, working on the memories of water in Delhi, connected memory and forgetting to the "angle of class": "People of very low social standing who live in slums and villages, who had a direct relation to water, they will tell you they have always had a direct hand in the pollution of streams. But if you shift just a little, to where you have apartments and such like, then it's very strange there. They know that water goes out of their homes. Where it goes, they don't know. They have no memories of the water or any understanding of the role they have in polluting it."

.   .   .

The forgetting that Nietzsche eulogizes as necessary to a life-affirming vitality seems slightly darker when we think of the *Übermensch* as a class position. Memory gives us not just *ressentiment* but an engagement with possibilities of life, of connections to the land that are lost to those living in the concrete towers bestowed on them by the state and by capitalist modernity. Remembering can be joyful, too, like the Kanjars drinking in the forest at their annual Dionysian festival. For memory is not just an evocation of what once was but what may yet be. At Firoz Shah Kotla the remembrance of older relations to nonhumans take particularly joyous forms, a critique of the anthropocentric biases of reformist Islamic piety that choose to forget these potentialities for life.

SAINTLY ANIMALS AND ECOLOGICAL THOUGHT AT FIROZ SHAH KOTLA

One time, as I sat chatting in our usual circle at Firoz Shah Kotla, a large centipede emerged from the grass near my feet. I pointed to it in mild alarm because I was barefoot, and in the fading light the centipede seemed huge. Everyone else's reaction was entirely different. He is giving us *darshan*, I was told, the term used for the auspicious sight of a deity. I was congratulated for being lucky enough to see the *baba*, or saint, appear before my eyes. Then the centipede-saint disappeared into the earth again.

In the subterranean spaces of Firoz Shah Kotla people also encounter the saints as snakes and cats (Taneja 2015). And in contrast to the densely human streets of Old Delhi and working-class East Delhi, home to the majority of people who come here, Firoz Shah Kotla is now a zone of zoological density and diversity in the life of the city. Cats used to be plentiful here, prospering on the milk offered by devotees. Newcomers to the site often asked if this is where they could find the *Billiyon ka Mazar*, the mazar of the cats.[16] Now there are a lot of dogs. There are many, many colonies of black ants here, prospering on the flour offered outside their burrows and the sweets offered to the saints in subterranean chambers. Pigeons flock to the grain scattered for them every day, and kites gather to feast on the meat thrown to them. In the dark passages and chambers under the mosque, dense clusters of bats hang from the ceilings, chittering and squeaking over the heads of pilgrims as they fly through clouds of smoke and incense. Firoz Shah Kotla was a little-known and rarely frequented site until the late 1970s, when its popularity increased dramatically. Why did this strange dargah, unusual in its plentitude of animal life and animal sacrality, become popular at that moment in the life of the city?

I have connected the unusual presence and veneration of jinn-saints at this dargah to the experience of everyday life in post-Partition Delhi, where state institutions actively work to forget everything that precedes the inception of the state in 1947. The other-temporality of the jinn-saints, much longer lived than humans, challenges this magical amnesia of the state by positing the remembrance of times beyond human memory, in a city where violence and the post-Partition state have actively worked to erase Muslim memories. The sacredness of animal life at Firoz Shah Kotla performs a similar subjunctive nostalgia, both remembering and performing a time when human and animal worlds could be in much closer communion than they are now. The veneration of animals as saints in this space is not merely a vestigial survival of premodern attitudes toward animals but an active critique of the anthropocentric nature of reformist Islamic piety.[17]

In Chapter 1, I recalled the story, popular at Firoz Shah Kotla, of Shah Waliullah's encounter with the jinn. Shah Waliullah is claimed as a founding figure by all the different *maslaks* (sects) of Indian Sunni Islam. On first encountering this story, I read it as a story legitimizing, through the figure of Shah Waliullah, the theologically unusual veneration of jinn-saints at Firoz Shah Kotla. But the story can be read rather differently, too, a reading supported by the presence and veneration of animals in the contemporary practices at Firoz Shah Kotla. We can instead read this story as a popular critique of the anthropocentric emphasis of much of modern Islam. After all, Shah Waliullah, claimed as a founding father by adherents of the Dar-ul-'Ulum Deoband, among others, is brought to trial for killing an animal.

The hadith record that Waliullah invokes in the story to justify his killing of the snake is quite ambiguous. In the canonical collections of Bukhari and Muslim there are clear exhortations to kill snakes, but there are also prohibitions. Interestingly, the hadith that narratively most resembles the popular story of Shah Waliullah is one that advises restraint and the avoidance of killing snakes, if possible. This hadith tells us that when the pious Muslim Abu Sa'id Khudri was praying, his companion heard a rustle in a woodpile and, finding a snake inside, jumped up to kill it. Abu Sa'id Khudri told him to sit down. He finished praying and then narrated the story about why snakes in the home were not to be harmed for three days, as according to the Prophet, in Medina, they were jinns who had become Muslims.[18] By contrast, Shah Waliullah shows unseemly haste in killing the snake in the story told at Firoz Shah Kotla, and he ignores prophetic authority, which associates snakes with Muslim jinns.

The trial of Shah Waliullah by the jinns resonates with another narrative of a dispute adjudicated by the jinn, the Ikhwan al-Safa's famous *Case of the Animals versus Man Before the King of the Jinn*. The Ikhwan, the anonymous members of a tenth-century esoteric fraternity based in the southern Iraqi city of Basra, were inspired to write this fable by the talking animals in the *Kalila wa Dimna*, the Arabic fables translated (via Pahlavi) from the Indian *Panchatantra* fables, which share many parallels and stories with the Buddhist Jatakas. In the fable, when humans are shipwrecked on an island previously uninhabited by humans, they start hunting, trapping, enslaving, and maltreating the animals they find there. The animals complain to the king of the jinn, and both parties, humans and animals, are asked to present their cases before the king.

Through most of the text of the epistle the case does not go well for the humans. The animals-given-voice complain eloquently about human failings, most of all their mistreatment of and cruelty toward animals they have domesticated. So humans, on the one hand, are unflatteringly portrayed as cruel, dishonest, cunning, proud, and, ultimately, utterly helpless without animals. The animals, on the other hand, are consistently praised for their selflessness, their industry, and their unfailing ethical service toward other creatures and toward the glory of God. It is only at the very end of the fable, in what comes as a surprise twist, that the superiority of men over the animals is acknowledged. Men are superior to animals because they have prophets and saints among them "who are like the angels on high!" (Ikhwan al-Safa 2009, 313). It is because of the saints, who potentially have the same status in the hierarchy of creation as the angels, that the humans are superior to animals. But at Firoz Shah Kotla we could say that the trial concludes somewhat differently. It is not just any ordinary human that is tried for killing an animal at Firoz Shah Kotla. It is a human saint, one of the most revered figures of modern Indian Islam. And it is not human saints that are venerated at Firoz Shah Kotla but jinns, often in the form of snakes and cats and centipedes. If the only thing that separates animals from humans in *The Case of the Animals versus Man* is the human potentiality to acquire sainthood, then that final frontier, as it were, is crossed at Firoz Shah Kotla.

I am not trying to posit a direct textual connection here between the Ikhwan al-Safa and contemporary jinn and animal veneration at Firoz Shah Kotla. Rather, I am intrigued by the way that certain themes—the trial by jinn of an injustice perpetrated by humans on animals, the seeming human victory—resonate through time and space and continue to have a popular life. This, too, is the transmission of tradition, even if not authorized by *isnads*. In the differing conclusion of the trial, as it were, in contemporary Delhi, we see a much more satisfying ending to *The Case of the Animals versus Man*, one much more in line with Richard McGregor's sensitive and nuanced reading of the Ikhwan's epistle (McGregor 2015). Drawing on the attribution of religion to animals in the Quran, in early modern Muslim travelogues and in *The Case of the Animals versus Man*, McGregor argues that the "religion of animals demonstrates the ready capacity of Islamic discourse to creatively trouble the anthropocentric boundaries that constitute it" (McGregor 2015, 223). Rather than pointing toward inequality and hierarchy, for McGregor the conclusion of *The Case* points us toward the overlap and shared sensibilities of animals and humans.

Mohammad Soualaheen, a member of the organizing committee of the Masjid at Firoz Shah Kotla, remembers that when the first *namazis* (worshippers) would come to offer prayers at Firoz Shah Kotla in the late 1970s, there would be snakes lying on the steps of the mosque, which would slither away to make room for the congregants. Back then, there were no floodlights on the Ring Road (which runs just to the east of the mosque), and on winter nights during Ramzan, it would be so dark that people couldn't see their hands in front of their faces when they raised them for worship. In his nostalgic retelling of what Firoz Shah Kotla used to be like in the "good old days," the spiritual charge of the place came from it being a space of the ecological sublime, a space where humans walked among snakes without fear, and where the darkness that enveloped worshippers was primordial and pure, a thing of awe and wonder, unlike the light-polluted nights of contemporary Delhi.

Bashir Bhai remembers the good old days of Firoz Shah Kotla as a time when the bats in the subterranean chambers under the mosque, in the passages known as the *Sat Dar* (seven doors), were more plentiful than they are now: "Now the affects [*asarat*] [of Firoz Shah Kotla] are less than they were before. . . . The bats are gone. . . . They are in the shade of the jinns. We say they are bats. But we don't know who was [really] there. They are much less now. . . . When we first used to come here inside [the Sat Dar] it seemed like we were walking on velvet, so dense were their droppings on the floor." Bashir Bhai's nostalgic account of walking on the velvet of bat droppings, as the bats hung in thick masses overhead, insists that this place and its weekly gathering, which seems so ordinary now, so habitual, was once a site of wonder. It was a site where humans walked among bats and jinns, not separated from the natural world but part of the continuum of being.

In the gardens of Firoz Shah Kotla, in its plenitude of animal life, I see a reflection of the vanished sacred landscapes of Delhi, now lost to sewage and concrete. In the long-established dargahs of Delhi, such as Nizamuddin, Chiragh Dehli, and Qutub Sahib, the distance between the local ecology and the human experience of these dargahs has grown exponentially in the last few decades. In Intizar Hussain's evocative prose, the coming together of the tall grass of the monsoon and the call of the peacock with the words of Amir Khusrau are replaced, thirty years later, by concrete, marble, and a landscape all too human, shoulder scraping against shoulder. The very nature of religious life in Delhi—its profound connection to *life*, animal and vegetal—has been profoundly altered in Delhi over the last few decades, and this has passed almost completely unnoticed in the scholarly literature on the city and its religions.[19]

Yet one of the most surprising aspects of my fieldwork was how frequently the working-class populace that came to Firoz Shah Kotla—from some of the most densely human parts of the city—referred to animal lore in their conversations. Their familial history was rooted in the urban; their families had belonged to Old Delhi for at least three or four generations. But they knew the names and kinds of grasses that grew in the lawns of Firoz Shah Kotla, which of those were good for buffaloes to eat, and what kinds of parrots nested in which trees, to summarize just one conversation. They remember a city that the state and the city's elites have forgotten, a city whose communal life extended far beyond the human. And as the number of people coming to this shrine increases every year, so does the number of animals.

In September and October of 2014, when I returned after a three-year absence, while the cat population had decreased (and some of the humans I knew were no longer there), there were many more dogs and a population of kites that now ran into the hundreds. The dramatic increase in the number of kites was directly linked to a new ritual that had come to Firoz Shah Kotla since my last visit, that of flinging "raw meat skyward."[20] It was a thrilling sight, to see tens of kites swoop and dive at close quarters to get at the pieces of meat flung upward by humans standing in a ruined courtyard, below the steps of the mosque, and then sail out of the melee, meat triumphantly caught in their claws (fig. 12). When I asked why people were flinging meat to the kites, I got two kinds of answers. One was that these were God's creation (*makhluq*), and it was a religious duty and an obligation to feed all of God's creatures. The other answer was that this was *jan ka sadqa* (the charity/donation of life). When one had severe problems and difficulties (*pareshaniyan*)—*ke jan pe*

FIGURE 12. *Kites circling above the ruins of Firoz Shah Kotla. Photo by author.*

a ke ban baithi thi (when one's life itself was in question)—one touched the meat (in a bag), prayed over it, and then flung it to the birds. By consuming the meat, the kites also consumed the humans' troubles. One man told me that after throwing the meat to the birds, *sab halka ho jata hai* (everything becomes lighter).

Rather than thinking of this as sympathetic magic, what if we thought of this as sympathy, the establishment of common feeling, and hence of kinship? For in Urdu and Persian a close companion is called a *ghamkhwar*—one who eats your sorrow. At Firoz Shah Kotla the birds are now ghamkhwar for the humans who feed them, the companions who consume their sorrows. Why is this important? In the words of Donna Haraway (2016, 2), "Making kin as oddkin rather than, or at least in addition to, godkin and genealogical and biogenetic family troubles important matters, like to whom one is actually responsible... What must be cut and what must be tied if multispecies flourishing on earth, including human and other-than-human beings in kinship, are to have a chance?" In her latest book, *Staying with the Trouble*, Haraway sees an ethical imperative in the forming of nonnormative, nonreproductive multispecies kinship. "Make kin not babies!" in her memorable formulation (2016, 102). "If there is to be multispecies ecojustice, which can also embrace diverse human people," Haraway (102) says, "it is high time that feminists exercise leadership in imagination, theory and action to unravel the ties of both genealogy and kin, and kin and species." If everyday religion as seen at Firoz Shah Kotla is already troubling the boundaries of kinship—in ways that couldn't be adduced just from paying attention to the corpus of Indic and Islamic "religious texts"—then what I hope to show here is that feminists and other thinkers situated within secular academia can learn a lot from paying attention to religion as a way of critically thinking and being in the world.

Are local, religious forms of knowing and acting adequate to hyperobjects, such as global warming (Morton 2013), which are profoundly nonlocal and massively distributed in time and space? I do not know. But I do know that the presence of animals as saints at Firoz Shah Kotla radically decenters the anthropocentrism that, in no small measure, has got us to the age of planetary instability that we now know as the Anthropocene. It opens up affective and intellectual possibilities of connecting to the world not as God's deputies (as modern translations of the Quran would have it), or as errant and concerned managers of the world we have transcended, but as animals once again in kinship with our fellow creatures, with the snakes and bats that make space for us to walk among them.

CHAPTER 7

THE SHIFTING ENCHANTMENTS
OF RUINS AND LAWS IN DELHI

Pa'e fatiha koi a'e kyun? Koi char phul charha'e kyun?
Koi ake sham'a jala'e kyun? Main woh bekasi ka mazar hun.

Why should anyone come and read the *fatiha*?
Why should anyone offer four flowers?
Why should anyone light a lamp?
I am that shrine of destitution.

—Attributed to Bahadur Shah "Zafar,"
last Mughal emperor (d. 1862)

A GARDEN NOW DESTROYED

In September 1857 the last Mughal emperor, Bahadur Shah "Zafar," was taken prisoner at Humayun's Tomb, the vast red sandstone and white marble mausoleum built in the reign of the emperor Akbar (r. 1556–1605), close to the dargah of the Sufi Nizamuddin Auliya.[1] He had come to take refuge at the tomb of his ancestor once the besieging British forces broke through, and he was taken back to Shahjahanabad, to the Red Fort, which he had fled less than three days before. He was imprisoned in the Red Fort to await trial, after which he was deported to Rangoon, where he died in exile. On the road north, back from Humayun's Tomb to the city, two of the emperor's sons were killed by a vengeful British officer. It is an irony rarely noted that the last Mughal emperor was captured, an act that was effectively the *coup de grâce* for the Mughal dynasty, from the first Mughal tomb in India, built between 1565 and 1572.[2]

Humayun's Tomb is also known as the "dormitory of the house of Timur." Many of the later Mughal emperors and princes are buried in the immense crypts that form the base of the massive building, including Dara Shukoh. It is no longer possible, however, to tell who is buried where. Many of the graves are now inaccessible, as entrances to the crypts are kept locked up. And even on the few marble cenotaphs that are visible on the high platform of the building, there are no names or dates of death, only beautifully incised Quranic verses.

Humayun's Tomb, and the identities of the royals buried there, came up in a conversation with Nasim Changezi. "Do you know," I asked him, "which grave is whose?" "Bahadur Shah Zafar knew," he said and chuckled. And he would have told his sons, when they went on pilgrimage to Nizamuddin and stopped at Humayun's Tomb, to read the *fatiha* at the graves of their ancestors.

The disconnect between the memory of people and the materiality of the graves that happened with the exile of the emperor and the destruction of the royal family is metonymic of the ways in which lived connections to the remains of the past were severed by the destructions of 1857 and subsequent colonial rule. The extensive buildings and ruins of Mughal and pre-Mughal Delhi south of Shahjahanabad were deeply connected to the life of the city through rituals of remembrance, stories, and regular excursions. The built structures of precolonial Delhi were, as we saw in the previous chapter, intricately tied to the local ecology. This whole world was blown apart in 1857. Muhammad Hussain "Azad," one of the littérateurs who survived that calamity, bore witness to this destruction.[3] Writing a scholarly essay on the history of Delhi in 1864, while in exile in Lahore, he began with lines of a distinctly apocalyptic cast: "Delhi's traces of the ancients [*asar-e qadima*] . . . are an awful scene of the destruction of the world [*haibatnak nazara barbadi-e duniya ka hai*]. Ruin piled upon ruin, and every grave a desolation. The rubble of brick buildings, and broken slabs of red sandstone and white marble are scattered on deserted land, stony and barren. There is no cultivation except at a few small locations, and no trace of trees or orchards [*sardarakhti*]. These desolate ruins spread south from Shahjahanabad" (Azad 1978, 2:221).

The British, as is the wont of conquerors, also saw much of this landscape as desolate and rendered meaningless. In 1911, Delhi was declared the new capital of British India, and the hunt began for a suitable site for a new imperial city. The architects soon settled on the plain to the south of Shahjahanabad, or Mughal Delhi. In 1912, Herbert Baker, one of the architects, stood on top of Raisina Hill looking east toward the plain on which the new city of Delhi was to be built. The plain was dotted with villages and fields and, among those villages and fields, old mosques and tombs and temples and fortifications built before British rule, spanning centuries. But looking down on this landscape, soon to be radically transformed by the new city that so far existed only in the plans of its architects, Baker saw only, in his own words, "the deserted cities of drear and disconsolate tombs" (Singh and Rai 1984, 40). Reading these cities as deserted allowed the British to unleash an unprecedented wave of land acquisition and destruction on the landscapes of Delhi to create *terra nullius* for the new city to be built upon.

But it was this wave of destruction that, paradoxically, made the landscape of premodern Delhi come alive. The ruinscapes of the premodern past became animated with an unprecedented agency. The ruins of the premodern past now became embodiments of the lost lifeworld of Muslim rule, sites at which this lifeworld became *present*, and which had to be saved at all costs. The jinns of Firoz Shah Kotla were not exceptional in this ruinscape, as the mystically tinged prose of Rashid-ul-Khairi so powerfully illustrates:

> When finding some free time from the apparent dignity of the Abode of Government [British New Delhi] the traveler enters these ruins where he is greeted as a guest by the cooing of the dove and the silence of the fruitless trees, then first of all the grief of the ruin shakes hands with him, gusts of sorrow-fated wind embrace him. And those few scattered and broken bricks that still identify the graves of the praise-worthy dead call out their welcome at his reception. There is nothing here to relieve the eye that sees appearances. Those eyes are needed here which see with contemplation and read with silence. Every leaf of this jungle, every brick of these graves, every atom of this dust is a book, a history, a lesson. (Rashid-ul-Khairi 2010, 62–63)

Every brick of these graves, every atom of this dust. Rashid-ul-Khairi's evocation of the materiality of the ruin, rather than the agency of the saintly dead,[4] making the Muslim past alive and present was not just a literary trope in the decades after 1911 but a huge factor in the politics of the city as well, where the acquisition of every brick and every atom of dust was furiously contested. In the two decades that it took to build British New

Delhi, the dead and deserted landscape of Baker's prose kept coming alive in a flurry of protests and petitions, forcing the plans of the new city to change, diverting roads and railway tracks from their originally intended courses, forcing the new city to treat the remains of the old cities it was built among as more than merely background.[5] The enchanted politics of the city that came to the fore in the years after 1911, with the complete identification of the ruins of Delhi with the lifeworld of Muslim rule, continued to be an important part of the city's life for more than a century to come (Kavuri-Bauer 2011; H. Ahmed 2014; Rajagopalan 2016).

In 1947 this identification led to enormous violence against Delhi's Muslim monuments under the protection of the ASI, as I showed in Chapter 1. In the postcolonial post-Partition city this violence led to a paradoxical politics of *disenchantment* around these ruins (in Bilgrami's sense of the term) through legal magic (in Das's sense of the term)—the selective reading and application of the laws regarding the preservation of historic buildings—to ensure that these sites stayed "dead." Conflicts and riots spread into the city from the struggles around these monuments, including Firoz Shah Kotla, and legal magic, radiating outward from the ruins, had a devastating effect on the life of modern New Delhi a century after the inauguration of the imperial city. I will conclude this chapter by thinking about how color became a deeply emotive issue as new paradigms of conservation restored the original look of these monuments at the beginning of the second decade of the twenty-first century and attempted to reconnect them to the life of the city.

MAGICAL DISENCHANTMENT: 1947–1992

> I went and met this fellow, the Secretary of the Jamiat Ulema-e Hind, Mehrauli Block. . . . He was leading this whole thing [campaign for Muslims to pray in the protected Quwwat-ul-Islam mosque]. I tried to argue with him, I said, do you not know what you're doing? You've broken the locks of the mosque and gone in. Tomorrow, two hundred *knicker-wallahs* [members of the RSS] will come here and they'll say this is not a mosque, this is a temple. And in India they've made a list of six thousand, which they say are mosques made after breaking temples. Right now there's no puja, no *ibadat* in any of them, all

of them are locked up. You've broken four locks here, they're going to occupy all six thousand. What will you do after that? . . . It's a mosque, mosques are where prayers are read, once a mosque always a mosque. . . . Idiotic arguments.

—Sohail Hashmi

Many of the members of the Indian National Congress, which came to power in India after 1947, were also members of the Hindu-majoritarian Hindu Mahasabha and believed, implicitly or explicitly, that a Hindu-dominated independent India would be a place where the historical wrongs perpetrated over the centuries of Muslim domination would be avenged and erased.[6] Perhaps the most telling moment of the dominance of this Hindu-majoritarian thinking in the life of the new state was President Rajendra Prasad's consecration of the restored Somnath Temple against the express wishes of Prime Minister Jawaharlal Nehru (Thapar 2005, 192–93).

The Hindu majoritarian dominance of much of public life in the new state, and the impunity of Hindu violence directed against Muslim spaces of worship and "Muslim" monuments, created a huge problem for the (ostensibly) secular state—as Nayanjot Lahiri points out, "An extraordinary irony must have stared everyone in the face. As the two nations came to be divided along religious lines, India became the inheritor of a rich Islamic heritage. . . . 'Almost all the Mohammadan monuments of the first importance' remained in India" (Lahiri 2012, 295–96). How was the state to preserve these monuments "of the first importance," while avoiding the Hindu violence that, as we have seen, aggressively targeted these monuments in the years after Partition? The state's answer was to "kill" these monuments: to aggressively police their usage, to "museumize" them, to make sure no religious conflicts erupted at these sites by effectively stifling all traditional religious usage. These were to be monuments of national importance by becoming completely secular sites of tourism, where *national* heritage was to be consumed as *secular* spectacle, and no religious usage was permitted. The ASI's policy and philosophy of preferring "dead" to "living" monuments, already well-developed in colonial India, now had hitherto unmatched government support. The recalcitrant medieval Muslim landscape of Delhi, which refused to stay dead under British rule, was finally to be laid to rest in independent India.

Perhaps the most surreal story of this "killing" of the landscape is the one recounted by Ata-ur-Rahman Qasimi, in which Maulana Azad insisted on the Tughlaq mosque at Mandi House Circle being saved by burying it. The story of the mosque's burial, in order to preserve it, resonates with larger policy decisions taken by the government in the years after Partition and Independence, which increasingly entombed monuments and removed them from the world of the living. In 1952 the Ministry of Education issued a notification:

> In exercise of the powers conferred by sections 15 and 23 of the Ancient Monuments Act, 1904 . . . the Central Government hereby makes the following rules. . . .
>
> No conferences, meetings, receptions, poetical symposia, wrestling bouts, physical culture feats and other functions of like nature shall be held in any monument maintained by the Central Government except where such conferences, meetings, receptions, poetical symposia, wrestling bouts, physical culture feats and other functions are held under the terms of a subsisting agreement under section 5 of the said Act or are held as a matter of religious convention or usage or by virtue of any special rules framed in respect of any particular monument or monuments under section 15 thereof.
>
> Any persons guilty of breach of the foregoing rules shall be punishable with a fine which may extend to twenty rupees.[7]

The government now wished to avoid occasions for the gathering of people within the space of protected monuments, being afraid of the consequences of a crowd. The "physical culture feats" seems to be a pointed reference to the Rashtriya Swayamsevak Sangh (RSS), the right-wing organization that modeled itself on the Nazis and on the Hitler Youth and emphasized early morning drills for its volunteers. The more immediate cause for the proclamation of the new rules was most probably because of the Bhojshala and Kamal Maula Mosque, a protected mosque in Dhar, Madhya Pradesh, built with temple remains, which the Hindu right wing claimed was built on the location of a school and temple to Saraswati (the goddess of learning) built by the semilegendary Hindu king Raja

Bhoj.[8] "In 1952, tensions between the two communities surfaced when Hindus planned to celebrate Bhoj Diwas (Bhoj Day) at the structure. The sanction to hold the function was given" (Kaur 2003). (The reconstructed Somnath Temple had been inaugurated just a year before, in 1951.)

·   ·   ·

In 1966 a group of Muslim transporters and bus operators wrote to the ASI. Long-distance bus services had just been shifted from near the Old Delhi Railway Station to the new Inter State Bus Terminal, just outside the Kashmiri Gate of the Old City. The shift had deprived the transporters and their Muslim passengers of a mosque to pray in. The applicants wished to be granted permission to use the Qudsia Bagh mosque, which was near the new bus station, "lying vacant and not being used so far. . . . It is, therefore, prayed that your honour will look into the matter and favour us with the necessary permission to use the mosque for the purposes of saying prayers. . . . The act of kindness will be a boon to the entire Muslim community, visiting the capital daily" (ASI, f3/2/D2/7/66 M). While the mosque was lying derelict for a long time, worship was revived in 1929, and presumably continued till 1947, when Partition violence caused the congregation to scatter, and the mosque fell into disuse again.[9]

In response to this request the language of an internal memo from the superintendent of the North Western Circle to the director general of Archaeology is telling: "*This is a dead mosque and is not in religious use.* Built by Nawab Qudsia Begam, mother of the late Mughal Emperor, Ahmad Shah, in AD 1748. This building is of considerable historical and archaeological importance, and is in a fair state of preservation. . . . *As the mosque has been long dead the revival of worship may not be permitted*" (my emphasis). The transporters persevered and kept writing letters, and some Muslim politicians took up their cause as well. In 1969 Fakhruddin Ali Ahmed, minister of industrial development and company affairs (under whose jurisdiction the administration of Waqfs fell), wrote to V.K.R.V. Rao, minister for education and youth services:[10]

> The Highway Transport Association and the Delhi Waqf Board have been making persistent representations to the Central authorities, including the

President and Prime Minister, for permission to say prayers at the Qudsia Mosque. . . . In fact we have been receiving similar representations about some other mosques. . . .

It, however, appears that as a matter of policy the Central Govt. in the Ministry of Education has not been permitting revival of prayers in the mosques declared as protected monuments . . . and they have also not been inclined to consider the release of these mosques by declaring them "deprotected" under the provisions of the said Act.

I would like to draw your attention to Section 16(1) of the AMAS&R Act, 1958, which lays down that a protected monument which is a place of worship shall not be used for a purpose inconsistent with its character. Rule 7(2) of the rules made under the Act permits even the holding of a meeting, reception, conference etc., in the premises of the monuments if it is held in a pursuance of a recognized religious usage or custom. *Offering of prayers happened to have been broken by such unfortunate and unavoidable circumstances of partition turmoil*, in the country, [but] is certainly a purpose most consistent with the objects with which a mosque came into being. I, therefore, feel that the existing policy at least to the extent of the ancient monuments of the nature of mosques does call for a review so that in appropriate cases . . . permission is granted for saying prayers or that the mosque itself is released in favour of the people concerned. (my emphasis)

This is the only time, in all the correspondence I have managed to look at concerning the revival of prayers in mosques, that the Partition of the country and its effect on the Muslim congregations of now deserted mosques is ever mentioned, rather than the generic *very long time* preferred by the Archaeological Survey. Finally, eight years after the initial application, permission was granted to individuals to worship in the mosque in 1974, a permission conveyed by the Waqf Board, with many caveats:

It has been agreed now by the Education Ministry that individuals wanting to offer prayers in Qudsia Mosque, Delhi may be allowed to do so and in case of groups of persons there would be no objection to one of them acting as Pesh Imam [the leader of prayer]. No "Azan," however would be permissible. The contention of the Education Ministry in this regard is that since no customary evidence for the prevalence of the (Friday) prayers with Azan at the time this mosque was declared a protected monument by the government is available, it would not be proper to resume this practice.

As the availability of water for "Wuzu" (Ablution) the Education Ministry feels that no accretions or alterations would be permissible within the protected limits. On spot inspection, a suitable place can be indicated where such arrangements may be made by the waqf. The actual spot, however, will be outside the protected limits.[11]

It took twenty-seven years in the life of the new nation-state before one "protected mosque" could be used for worship in a way that had been largely unproblematic for all protected structures in the time of the colonial government. The conditions of worship, however, were still far more restrictive under postcolonial rule than under the colonial government. In the colonial period, for example, all protected monuments were open to the public till 10 p.m. Under the new rules formalized under the 1958 Act, which superseded the 1904 Ancient Monuments Act, monuments were only accessible between sunrise and sunset. But the enforcement of the much stricter rules, at least in the case of the Qudsia Bagh Mosque, also seems to have become much more lax. The mosque acquired a regular imam who started living in the premises of the mosque sometime between 1974 and 1983, in direct contravention of the terms of the 1974 agreement, as well as a muezzin, who gave the call to prayer, again in contravention of the agreement. In 1983 officials of the ASI came to inspect the mosque and threatened to take police action to evict the imam. This led to the filing of a suit by the Muntazima (Organizing) Committee, Qudsia Bagh Masjid, against the Ministry of Education and the ASI.

The court's decision, in the matter of the Muntazima Committee, Qudsia Bagh Masjid versus the Government of India is also instructive, for it equates the "protection" of the mosque by the Government with the voiding of all customary rights of worship:

The offering of prayers in the Mosque in question in pursuance of the permission granted by the Government is an ante-thesis of any vested right of the plaintiff or of the Muslims in the matter of offering prayers in this mosque which has been declared a "Protected Monument" [a] long time back by the Government in the year 1913 after inviting objections against the proposed declaration and the aforesaid permission also appears to negative any contention of the existence of any recognized religious usage or custom in the matter of offering prayers in this mosque. It thus appears to be made out that the plaintiff or the Muslims have no right to offer prayers in the protected monument in question at any time. . . .

. . . This provision of law [Section 16 (1) of the 1958 Act] casts a duty upon the Central Government maintaining the protected monument for using it for purposes inconsistent with its character of being a place of worship or shrine. *This provision of law cannot be construed to mean that the public or any member thereof shall thereby get a right to offer prayers in such a protected monument.*[12] (my emphases)

.   .   .

Excerpts from an Interview with Jayant Tripathi, Standing Counsel, ASI (2010)—

Jayant Tripathi. ASI does not, except for a few temples, like to maintain monuments which are living monuments, where there is any human habitation, I mean, Jaisalmer Fort being one exception, and some temples in Orissa, and the Madurai Temple or wherever. There was a very strong move, in fact I think it was initiated by the High Court itself in Delhi, that the Jama Masjid should be declared a protected monument, and the ASI took a very tough stand on that and said, we will not, come what may.

Anand Vivek Taneja. Is that ASI policy or ASI law? Because as far as my reading of the 1958 Act goes, there's nothing against customary usage, right?

JT. There's nothing against customary usage, and a living monument, a living structure can be a Centrally protected monument, there's no dichotomy over there—the Act actually specifically provides for that. If you're the owner of a property, you're living on the property, it can still be declared to be a protected monument, and some restrictions will be placed on you.

AVT. Then why is the ASI so against the idea of living monuments? . . . If the law does not actually have a problem, why the restrictions?

JT. Yeah, I don't know.

AVT. Do you have theories?

JT. Not really.

. . .

JT. Invariably what happens is that if there is a dispute about a particular monument—now what is happening in a lot of mosques or tombs— there are encroachments within the protected area itself, and those people say we're staying here with the authority of the Waqf Board, and we say, well, you can't. In the protected area we won't allow you to stay. Which is also perhaps incorrect, because the Act does permit, in terms of Section 6, if it is a living monument, so it could be permitted, but I suppose for some policy reason, ASI has not been permitting it. . . .

. . .

JT. What's happened is that invariably, the courts do tend to side with the ASI, because the dominant objective over here is for a "greater public good."

. . .

How do the courts assume that control of a place by a particular community or person is somehow antithetical to the "greater common good"? The question is perhaps too easily answered: the equation of religion (particularly Islam) with backwardness and irrationality, and the allowing of religious practice hence being seen as inherently dangerous to the "heritage" of the building, reduced in the secular imagination to its physical structure, made available for the scopic pleasure and consumption of scholars, scientists, and cultural tourists, the *exemplary* citizens of modern India. More tragic, in the language of these assumptions, is the inability to imagine the coexistence of the "benefit of all" or the "greater common good" and the "worship of a particular community." The "particular community," of course, is Muslim, for as my interview with Jayant Tripathi— and many Muslim petitions related to praying in mosques—shows, there is no fundamental problem with the coexistence of continuing Hindu religious practice and ASI protection at historical Hindu temples, such as the Meenakshi Temple in Madurai. In other words there is no conflict or contradiction, when it comes to the Hindu temple, between the "benefit of all" and the "worship of a particular community." This only makes sense if Hindus are seen as not "particular," one of many religious communities in India, but "all," entirely constitutive of the public.

. . .

> Jayant Tripathi. The ASI does not own probably 90 percent of the monuments around the country. . . . In 90 percent of the cases the ownership vests with some government department, invariably with the municipality, but not with the ASI. In quite a few cases, it may be with the Waqf Board.
>
>   . . . What the ASI does is, when the monument is declared as protected, a gazette notification comes out. In some of those the ownership of the land is given. In most of them the ownership is not given. The ASI has just assumed that if it is notified as a Protected Monument it belongs to the ASI—*hamara ho gaya hai* [it belongs to us]. But *hamara nahin hua hai* [it does not belong to us]. Because the Act actually specifically provides that if the monument is not owned by the ASI, then what is the procedure to bring it under the ASI? . . . You have to acquire it. You have to pay compensation for it. That's never been done. [In] 75 percent of the cases it's government land, so government-to-government transfer is really not going to cost anything. But still it's a formality that needs to be completed. And it certainly needs to be carried out in the case of the Waqf Board or other private owners.

Two things stand out for me in Jayant Tripathi's narrative: first, the common sense of the Waqf Boards being separate from government, despite being bodies constituted by the Delhi (and other state) governments. Second, if the ASI ever tried to acquire Waqf properties through the proper procedure, as described by Tripathi, it would run into the same trouble that the colonial government faced in the 1910s and 1920s—namely, that Waqf land cannot be bought and sold, and hence the question of accepting compensation, and of the ASI becoming proprietors of a mosque, would not arise.[13] But the ASI, in the words of its own lawyer, acts in utter disregard of the laws that govern its own functioning. It assumes that protection is equal to proprietorship, and it assumes that protection equals a negation of customary usage, neither of which can be assumed from a reading of the law. And yet, as Jayant Tripathi told me, if and when disputes arise and matters come to court involving the ASI and the Waqf Board, *the courts do tend to side with the ASI, because the dominant objective over here is for a "greater public good."*

The Indian state, as Veena Das (2007, 162–83) has observed, oscillates between a rational mode and a magical mode. The magical mode seems to turn on with alarming frequency when the courts and their procedures for verifying truth and establishing justice encounter any questions that have to do with Muslim claims to custody and ownership of property that run counter to the state's amnesia with regard to the states of affairs that preceded it. The Waqf Board is antinational because it remembers (and unfortunately, wishes to revive) forms of property and customary usage far older than the nation-state and its ideal secular-scopic citizens. Santhi Kavuri-Bauer contends that in the postcolonial dispensation, the government set up an "imaginary identification . . . between Indian citizenship and its mirror, the national monument" (2011, 146). The Waqf Board's claims to the ownership and usage of national monuments, as in the case of the Waqf registration of the Taj Mahal in 2005, which Kavuri-Bauer writes about, falls foul of this because it exposes "the misrecognition that underlies the identification of a national 'I' in the mirror of the monument. To maintain the fantasy and wholeness of national unity, the monument must be rendered a space limited to representing Indian national heritage, and any act that alters this illusion is viewed as illegitimate and pernicious" (160). Muslim prayer alters the illusion of national heritage because Muslim presence still fits uneasily with the idea of the Hindu-secular nation. When I spoke to Faizi Hashmi, a senior officer in the Delhi Administration and former CEO of the Delhi Waqf Board, about the question of praying in protected mosques, he prefaced his (very careful) response with the statement, "I'll respond as a citizen of the country, with a deep interest in heritage." Prayers in protected mosques, it seems, cast doubts on his loyalty both to the country and to the idea of heritage.

. . .

The movement to pray in protected mosques that began in Delhi at around the same time as the Qudsia Bagh case did not demand the handover of centrally protected mosques to Muslim authorities or wished to deprotect these monuments. The movement's main aim was to be able to use these mosques for prayers, particularly the Friday congregational prayers, without fundamentally changing the nature of these spaces as monuments open to all. The movement could be said to be, then, demanding the coexistence of "benefit of all" and the "worship of a particular community" or the inclusion of Muslim prayer into the idea of national heritage.

The much-publicized campaign to pray in "protected" mosques primarily targeted the mosque at Safdarjung's Tomb, the ASI-protected mosque closest to Prime Minister Indira Gandhi's residence. Though there seems to be no direct relationship, at least in the newspaper reportage of the time that I have access to, between the Qudsia Bagh case and the Safdarjung agitation, the timing of the case and the agitation suggests more than mere coincidence. Justice Chandra's adverse judgment in the Qudsia Bagh case was pronounced on June 30, 1983. The movement to pray in protected mosques began shortly after and had made it to the newspapers by August:

> The Muslim Muttahida Mahaz has, in a memorandum to the Lok Sabha Speaker, Mr Balram Jakhar, demanded that Muslims should be allowed to offer prayers in old mosques located inside protected monuments.
>
> The memorandum described as "unconstitutional and undemocratic" the restrictions imposed by the Archaeological Survey of India on the use of such mosques. It demanded that among other things, representatives of Muslim organizations should be associated with the maintenance of these mosques.
>
> For several months, various Muslim organizations have been demanding freedom to offer prayers in protected mosques, and every Friday members of these organizations offer namaaz outside such mosques to press their demand.[14]

Section 144, the provision inherited from colonial law against unlawful assembly that prohibits a gathering of more than ten people at a time in public space, was imposed on the area around Safdarjung's Tomb for several months at a stretch, from June 1983 to sometime in March 1984. Those who came to pray were often arrested for violating prohibitory orders. And still they came, every Friday afternoon, for the weekly congregational prayers, which were usually conducted on the roads outside the monument, as the worshippers were denied entry to the mosque by heavily armed police. Through looking at newspaper clippings from more than thirty years ago, the method of the protesters sounds very much like the Gandhian method of *satyagraha*, the nonviolent mode of protest so celebrated in the narrative of Indian nationalism. Writing about these events, the English and Hindi press of the time saw these protests as irrational and avoidable and always potentially violent. Nothing sums this up better than the headline used by the *Hindustan Times*, when first writing about the Safdarjung protests, which used the headline—"Mosque Gatecrash Averted."[15] The Safdarjung protests continued for nine months. In August questions were raised by Muslim MPs in Parliament about the situation arising out of the refusal of the ASI to allow Muslims to pray in protected mosques.[16] In February 1984 Muslim politicians declared that they would be joining the protestors in praying outside the Safdarjung mosque and thus courting arrest by violating Section 144.[17] Following this declaration, Section 144 was lifted from around Safdarjung's Tomb, and Friday prayers were allowed in the mosque there. At a meeting between senior government ministers and Muslim Members of Parliament it was decided that prayers would be allowed in many mosques in monuments all over India.[18] This agreement was never formalized, however, and the issue remained contentious.[19]

In September 1986 a Hindu-Muslim riot broke out in the Old City. The riot originated with a scuffle at the mosque at Firoz Shah Kotla.[20] About fifty men, some of them wielding *trishuls* (tridents), attempted to walk into the mosque at Firoz Shah Kotla with their shoes on, after many speeches (of unspecified, but presumably inflammatory content) over a loudspeaker (in obvious contravention, it might be added, of the Ancient Monument Rules) in the lawns of the monument. When an old lady and some Muslim youngsters present in the mosque tried to prevent them from entering the mosque with their shoes on, a scuffle ensued. One of the Muslim boys was wounded in the scuffle, by what is reported to have been a *trishul* (traditionally, the weapon of Shiva, its public deployment is now usually associated with Hindu mob-violence). The perpetrators of the violence were not caught. Following this incident, the imam of the Jama Masjid in Old Delhi gave a speech against the police and the authorities for failing to apprehend those who had begun the scuffle and deliberately disrespected the mosque. Four hours later, the riot began.[21]

In the aftermath of the riot the English (and Hindi) press wrote mainly negative articles about the movement to pray in protected mosques in Delhi:

> The Masjid Basao Committee [The Committee to Settle/Populate Mosques], which seeks restoration of mosques to the people, has laid claim to all these buildings. A fairly powerful movement exists, with the tacit support of several important politicians, seeking use of these monuments as places of worship.
>
> Some religious enthusiasts have even moved courts to get possession of these monuments.
>
> The ASI has a very clear-cut policy on this matter, a survey spokesman said. These monuments come under the Ancient Monuments and Archaeological Sites Act, 1968 [*sic*]. Under the Act, no one is allowed to use these places for any purpose other than archaeological and historical research.[22]

> Yet, strangely enough, as ASI sources reveal, the Prime Minister's office despite repeated representations by the ASI and regular intelligence reports has yet to take a decision regarding those monuments where groups of Muslim fundamentalists have been regularly "invading" for the past five years. . . .
>
> Even as the Jami Masjid issue hangs in the balance, there are several other equally sensitive sites that have been causing much tension to ASI officials, who do not even have proper security set-up to face religious fanatics and also "goondas."[23]

> The latest mosque-grabbing wave, mainly by self-appointed imams and individuals who floated organizations, began in 1982–83.
>
> In fact, many lives could have been lost last year in a communal flare-up regarding the Moth ki Masjid [a fifteenth-century mosque of the Lodi era near South Extension, South Delhi] but for the prompt action by the ASI officials who got a stay from the additional sessions judge, Tees Hazari, on July 3 on an order that had been passed the same day by a sub-judge handing over the monument to the Muslim Samaj Sudhar Samiti [Muslim Social

Improvement Committee]. This was done minutes before the courts would have closed for the Id festival! . . .

Tensions had mounted as the neighbouring villages were inhabited by Jats and Gujjars and the entire agitated population was ready to react.[24]

The Muslim organization had approached a court of law for permission to use the Moth ki Masjid mosque for prayers. The judge granted the permission for offering prayers through his reading of the 1958 Act (Qasimi 2001, 27). Everything, in short, was done peacefully, legally, through due procedure. But somehow, in the narrative of the article, the threat of communal violence becomes a Muslim responsibility. The attribution of all violence and fanaticism to Muslims, while ignoring and glossing over growing Hindu violence and fanaticism, shows how remarkably close the worldview of the secular, English-speaking press was to that of the Hindu majoritarian movement, gaining remarkable strength in those days. The Hindu right wing, it should be remembered, is not at all averse to a secular state. As Partha Chatterjee reminds us, "In its most sophisticated form, the campaign of the Hindu right often seeks to mobilize on its behalf the will of an interventionist modernizing state in order to erase the presence of ethnic or religious particularisms from the domain of law or public life, and to supply . . . a homogenized content of the notion of citizenship. . . . The Hindu right in fact seems to project itself as a principled modern critic of Islamic or Sikh fundamentalism, and to accuse 'the pseudo-secularists' of preaching tolerance for religious obscurantism and bigotry" (Chatterjee 2010c, 205).

It is widely held that in order to deflect criticism from the growing charges of pandering to Muslim obscurantism in the aftermath of the Shah Bano Case[25] (and perhaps, though this is not often spoken of, the charge of letting too many dead mosques come alive), the Congress government, in order to retain the Hindu vote that it saw as being lost to the resurgent Hindu right, brought another "dead" monument back to life.[26] In 1986 the locks of the Babri Masjid were opened, allowing Hindu visitors unrestricted access to worship the idols that had been installed there in 1949.

Six years later, on December 6, 1992, a mob demolished the Babri Masjid.

SECULAR NECROMANCY IN THE LIFE OF THE CITY:
1992–2010
On June 16, 1992, the Archaeological Survey of India issued a notification:

> S.O. 1764—Whereas by the notification of the Government of India in the
> Department of Culture Archaeological Survey of India no. S.O. 1447 dated
> the 15th May 1991, published in the Gazette of India . . . the Central Gov-
> ernment gave one month's notice of its intention to declare areas up to 100
> meters from the protected limits and further beyond it up to 200 meters
> near or adjoining protected monuments to be prohibited and regulated areas
> respectively for both mining operation and construction. . . . Now, therefore,
> in exercise of the powers conferred by rule 32 of the Ancient Monuments
> and Archaeological Sites and Remains Rules, 1959, the Central Government
> hereby declares the said areas to be prohibited and regulated areas.

The timing of the notification, in the months before the destruction of
the Babri Masjid, makes me suspect that this notification was also targeted at the right-wing campaign to build a temple at the very site of the
Babri Masjid. Even though the Babri Masjid was not a protected site,
one of the many solutions offered to the growing dispute, one around
which a certain consensus built up in the late 1980s, was to declare the
Babri Masjid a protected monument of national importance (H. Ahmed
2014, 238). The Indian Parliament, pressed by Muslim politicians, had
already passed the Places of Worship (Special Provisions) Bill in 1991,
"specifically An Act to prohibit conversion of any place of worship and
to provide for the maintenance of the religious character of any place of
worship as it existed on the 15th day of August, 1947." Of course, for
the four decades or so before the crisis, the state (as exemplified by the
ASI) had chosen to forget the religious status of mosques in Delhi (and
elsewhere) before 1947. The Babri Masjid was specifically omitted from
this act, but the intention of the act was clear: to prevent further con-
troversies about the religious status of historic places of worship and to
prevent the destruction and occupation of mosques and Muslim places
of worship of the kind that had occurred in the wake of Partition. The
government chose to counter the growing threat of Hindutva violence by
legislating memory.

The 1992 notification, though its antecedents are unclear, also potentially allowed the government to control possible strife related to historic Muslim religious structures. Through this notification, the government could legally prohibit construction anywhere within a one-hundred-meter radius of any protected monument and regulate (which is to say prevent) any construction within a further two hundred meters, hence theoretically keeping any potentially inflammatory construction at least three hundred meters (984 ft.) away from any protected mosque. But this is all conjecture. I asked Jayant Tripathi what he knew of the reasons for the 1992 notification. His answer neither confirms nor denies my suspicions:

> Jayant Tripathi. When the act is enacted in 1904, there is no concept of prohibited area, regulated area. . . . In 1958 they put the provision in the Act, that you can by rules prohibit or regulate construction and mining operations. From '58 to 1992, nothing happens. In 1992 something happened, [but] no one is very forthcoming as to what exactly.
>
> Anand Vivek Taneja. So in 1992 when exactly does this happen? It's curious because it's the year of the Babri Masjid demolition.
>
> JT. It could perhaps have something to do with the situation in Ayodhya, to preempt it, but I don't know. That's just a guess. . . . We asked the ASI many, many times, *ke sau meter kyon tha* [why was it a one hundred meters]? *Nahin us time pe koi problem thi, isliye sau meter bol diya tha* [There was some problem at the time, hence we said a one hundred meters]. . . . There was some political reason behind it, something to do with some specific monument, somewhere, which was then foisted on all the monuments.

The vagueness within the ASI about what exactly happens perhaps indicates that the order was hush-hush, came from above, and was not generally known about, even among the officials of the ASI. In any case, whether the notification has anything to do with the Babri Masjid or not (though I strongly suspect it does), it is a fairly drastic piece of legislation. Visualize, if you will, a medieval mosque, falling apart, dark with age and disuse. Imagine it located in the midst of a bustling city, full of houses and shops. Now imagine an invisible force field radiating from this disused mosque, a hundred meters in every direction. As far as the force field goes, the landscape is permanently frozen; everything about it will now remain exactly as it was on June 16, 1992, from now to the end of time.[27] Not only can contentious temples not be built, but houses cannot add new rooms, shops cannot add new awnings, power lines cannot be laid, and new buildings cannot be built. The dark monument at the center is now a Medusa, petrifying everything that falls within its gaze.

The law creates strange monsters. This particular monster was actually ignored for much of the first decade of its existence; perhaps the destruction of the Babri Masjid made its implementation academic, and no one in the ASI paid the new rule and its potential consequences very much attention. It was when the BJP (the party at the forefront of the Ram Temple agitation) came into power in 1999 that the new rule started being implemented. The ASI, by this time, was under the Ministry of Tourism and Culture, which was under the charge of Jagmohan (famous for bulldozing slums during the Emergency), who was also later in charge of the Ministry of Urban Development. Under his tenure the force field was activated, and it became a new and terrifying thing in the life of the city, leading to many demolitions of shops and homes.[28] Jayant Tripathi summarizes the life of the new rules:

> The notification says one hundred meters, and then beyond the one hundred meters another two hundred meters, so up to three hundred meters. Within the one hundred meters is a prohibited area. The rule says that if it's a prohibited area, you cannot construct. And in the regulated area, one hundred to three hundred meters, you can only construct with the authority of a license which is to be issued by the DG [Director General] of the ASI. Very well. Now, the rule has been made, the notification has been issued, it's not implemented, as is the case with most things in India. . . .
>
> Even the ASI is not aware of quite what the implications are. Slowly, the realization dawns on them, and somewhere from 1999 to 2000, somewhere around that time they start enforcing this rule. And I think in 2002 they wrote to the MCD [Municipal Corporation of Delhi], at

least in Delhi, and said you cannot give construction permissions within one hundred meters, end of the story. Now obviously in a place like Delhi that's going to cause a lot of hardship because the rule as it was being enforced is that you cannot do squat to premises within a one hundred meters. You have a house within one hundred meters, it's derelict, it's falling down, you cannot reconstruct.

Anand Vivek Taneja. That's . . . crazy.

Jayant Tripathi. Completely crazy. . . . So, there are a lot of protests. ASI has no idea what to do. ASI in its attempt to be people friendly decides that it will give permissions from 2002 onwards or so. And those were completely discretionary. And wherever there is going to be discretion, there is going to be corruption, or misuse, or allegations of corruption and misuse. Because that was happening, in 2006, the Ministry and the DG decided that they would formalize this system.[29] So an expert advisory committee was constituted, which had a former DG ASI, some conservation architects, some historians, along with the DG. The function of this committee was to aid and advise the Director General. . . . All the cases of permission within one hundred meters were being referred to the committee, and the committee used to call for further information, or reject, or grant permissions.[30]

Now, that system was in place until 2010. In 2010 a lawyer called Gaurang Kanth filed a case—he stays in Nizamuddin East [way too close to way too many protected monuments, particularly Humayun's Tomb]—against his neighbor. Now his neighbor was one of those cases which had applied for permission to the committee, had been granted permission, and had thereafter started construction. Now *prima facie* the court felt that, no, you can't carry on construction, there is a blanket ban, and prohibited means prohibited. So the neighbor went and appealed within the High Court, and eventually the judges said, ASI, you're completely in the wrong. You had no power to grant permission within the prohibited area because the rule says that it is prohibited for construction. So, kindly, all the permissions that you have given in the last so many years, kindly withdraw them, and carry out the relevant demolitions.[31]

Now, what had happened was that this was the eve of the Commonwealth Games. So your stadium projects, Delhi Metro, Barahpulla Nalla, all these projects within one hundred meters which had applied to the advisory committee and had been granted permission, they were all going to be jeopardized. So the government had no option but to amend the Act in order to save these constructions. . . . What this Act does is create the fiction that with effect from 1992, with retrospective effect, the Director General ASI has the power to grant permission in the prohibited areas. And then with prospective effect from 2010 that power is taken away. . . . Now, in the prohibited area, no one has the power to grant permissions. And the prohibited area, which was earlier under the rules, is now brought in under the Act. So the legislation itself, instead of the subordinate legislation earlier, saying what the prohibited area was, now the legislation itself says what the prohibited area is.

AVT. Which is? . . .

JT. One hundred meters. And the regulated area is three hundred meters. In fact, while the act was being drafted, there was a proposal that the prohibited area be three hundred meters. . . . Now, take any monument as a point in space. Draw a one-hundred-meter circle around it. . . . 31,600 square meters per point in space. There are four thousand monuments. Multiply that by say half of that, two thousand. You get some enormous number. Now you are saying that in this area you cannot construct even if the land is yours. Now the AMASR Act has the provision that if I am the owner of some land, and on account of some rule, some law, some direction of the ASI, I am unable to enjoy that land, the ASI has to take over my land in the same manner as the Land Acquisition Proceedings. That means I have to be paid compensation.

AVT. At market rate?

JT. At market rate, naturally. Now I will be a fool and I will assume that the market rate is a uniform one lakh [one hundred thousand rupees/about fifteen hundred dollars] per acre. We are talking about close to India's GDP for a year. . . . Just at one lakh an acre.

I want to return now to the image of the dark mosque in the middle of the bustling city. This is not entirely a hypothetical image, for many of the medieval buildings of Delhi (and elsewhere) are finished with lime-plaster, which is a shining, glowing white when freshly applied but darkens fairly rapidly with oxidation. As long as these buildings were in regular use and repair, they would have been white. In charge of the ASI, with its hands-off conservation policy, these buildings have turned almost black. In other words, they are now photonegatives of themselves. Imagine one of these dark negatives-of-itself glowering within the technicolor landscape it inhabits. Once people perhaps lived inside this mosque, as they did in the Khirki and Begampuri mosques. Even when people stopped living in them, some of them surely came to pray or to watch wrestling matches or to hang out. The mosque, even as it darkened and fell apart, remained a part of people's lives and stories, their sense of themselves and their place in the world. All this started changing after independence, as, owing to government legislation and policy, people became more and more estranged from these monuments. But rather than becoming irrelevant to their lives, these monuments took on a new and malevolent importance, thanks to the 1992 rules, which continue with greater force in the 2010 act. Living next to this dark, brooding pile of masonry, alien now to your life and your world in every way you can think of, is now a curse. Conservationist Ratish Nanda, to whom I spoke in July 2011, sums it up quite eloquently:

> This attitude is made worse by government. For example, the Gymkhana Club, it's a notified building. Portions of the ceiling collapsed. They're not being given permission to rebuild the ceiling. You know, and that makes people anti-heritage. . . . When you say shut down Mathura refinery, without really analyzing that the Taj is not getting affected by the Mathura refinery, it's getting affected by the fucking acid that the ASI is putting on it. . . . Then people lose jobs, then you have slogans like *Agra Bachao, Taj Hatao* [Save Agra, Remove the Taj]. So we have not done anything to make people realize that heritage is an asset. We have done everything to make people realize that it's a burden. We have built fences, we have stopped entry, we have stopped people building legally within zones as a blanket rule. We have done almost everything to say, "If you touch it, we'll send seven generations of your family to prison!"

WHAT COLOR IS THE SECULAR?

On August 6, 2010, *The Indian Express* carried a story about the "flawed" nature of restoration efforts at many of New Delhi's medieval monuments:

> With monuments getting a facelift before the Commonwealth Games, heritage enthusiasts and conservationists are questioning the process adopted to make the ruins appear new. As part of the makeover, the monuments are being coated in lime plaster.
>
> Heritage enthusiasts have regularly raised the issue with conservation bodies like the Indian National Trust for Art and Cultural Heritage (INTACH), the Department of Archaeology and the Archaeological Survey of India (ASI), complaining the monuments are losing their charm.
>
> ... Recently, residents and enthusiasts near Gulmohar Park have been in talks with the INTACH and other officials over the conservation of Darvesh Shah's mosque, a Lodhi-period monument. The monument, according to INTACH officials, was in ruins and needed intensive intervention to reconstruct portions that had collapsed.
>
> Artist Arpana Caur and architect Gautam Bhatia, who go for regular morning walks in the park, took note of the changing look and colour of the monument and raised the issue with INTACH and the state department of archaeology. "Along with structural reinforcement, retaining the look of the monument during conservation is also important. The colour of the monument is so white that it has a completely different look from what it earlier used to be. We have voiced our concerns but officials working on the project have refused to see reason," Caur told Newsline.[32]

The bringing of bright colors back to medieval buildings makes a lot of people in Delhi very unhappy. This is not a new thing. The preference for ruins decolored and dilapidated, very much part of the English conservation aesthetic imported to India (Guha-Thakurta 2010), has continued in the postcolonial era as well. In 1966 prominent littérateur Mulk Raj Anand wrote to the minister of education, suggesting new rules for the preservation and use of monuments because "many temples and Mosques which are actually in worship, though protected by the Archaeological Survey of India, are *fouled by improper use and also sometimes painted in the most garish colours* (as in the case of several South Indian shrines)."[33]

Sohail Hashmi, writing on the popular left-liberal website Kafila.org in 2009, remarks ruefully about one of the great Tughlaq mosques in Delhi:

> The mosque is currently managed by the Waqf Board and the present management seems to have gone overboard in restoring and maintaining this 622 year mosque. The mosque is no longer black; it has now been painted over in shades of green blue and pink. The Kaali Masjid (Black Mosque) is now a white, pink, blue and green mosque. (Hashmi 2009)

In an interview with *Open* magazine, he unfavorably contrasts the upkeep of mosques that are under the control of the Waqf Board with that of "protected" mosques:

> The problem, says Hashmi, has to do with the mosques' upkeep. "Take the case of four mosques built by Juna Shah Telangani, a noble in the court of Firoz Shah Tughlaq (1309–1388)," he says, "two of them are protected and two are not. You can see the difference." . . . The domes of Kali Masjid have been painted green, and several families live in the basement. "Who will recognize it today as the finest example of Tughlaq architecture?" asks Hashmi. (Vij 2009)

The protected mosques he is referring to are the vast Begampuri and Khirki mosques. Unlike their unprotected counterparts, these mosques are completely empty of worshippers and have had no structural modifications. But they are also falling apart, covered with graffiti, full of bats and bat droppings, and dark. Their makers never intended them to be dark. The Kali Masjid, the black mosque, was not black by human design but by the effects of moss and oxidation. I had once suggested to Sohail, who is a major figure in promoting heritage walks in contemporary Delhi, that structural modifications apart, whitened, colorful mosques full of worshippers are perhaps closer to the spirit (and the look) of what they would have been like in the fourteenth century. He was not very happy with this suggestion.

But he is not the only one. Jayant Tripathi told me that "one judge who is quite active and supportive of the ASI is very fond of using the term, 'Restore the monument to its pristine glory.'" But the restoration to pristine glory, getting as close to the original intended look of the monument as possible, often makes the city's intellectual and cultural elite break out in hives. Ask Ratish Nanda.

Ratish Nanda is currently the projects director for the Aga Khan Trust for Culture, India. The Aga Khan Development Network's Urban Renewal Initiative is simultaneously working in Nizamuddin Basti, Humayun's Tomb, and Sundar Nursery, north of Humayun's Tomb. The project aims not just at restoring heritage buildings and landscapes in this area but also at improving the quality of life of the people of Nizamuddin Basti, who live amid one of the densest extant ensembles of medieval architecture in the country (and possibly the world).

I was in Ratish Nanda's office in July 2011 when, to illustrate a point he was making, he pulled out a report with some photographs. The first photograph was that of a weathered, mostly dull-gray, domed building, not particularly interesting. The second photograph was of an utterly beautiful building, one with a shining white dome set on a striking base, with tall arches containing elaborate red-sandstone lattice screens, framed by facades of elaborate red and white arabesques. It was the same building, six months later, transformed by restoration. I kept saying "Wow" as I looked at the picture of the restored, recolored building (the Sundarwala Burj in Sundar Nursery), its unexpected beauty leaving me at a loss for more words. Ratish picked up on this.

> That is it, you see. That is the problem. The problem in our whole Indian conservation scene can be summed up in one word. And that one word is, Wow. We have lost the wow factor. Our buildings are no longer wow. And that is why people are no longer interested. Who will be interested in that (pointing to the photo of the tomb before). It's some silly domed structure that some one or two fanatics like you and I will go and see. . . .
>
> . . . Doing this building took a lot of balls, man. Because every Mary, Susan and Jane in Delhi is going to say, "What is this garish paint you're putting on?" People actually came to me, people I know well, saying, "Oh you know ASI is destroying something in Sundar Nursery, putting garish paint" and all that. . . . "Yeah, right."

The work Ratish and INTACH are doing is a radical departure from how conservation has been done by the ASI for at least a century. This model of conservation has meant leaving buildings untouched as far as possible, and if this means that the building, as a result, looks weathered and ruined, then so much the better.[34] So despite (or rather, because of) the "wow" factor, INTACH and Ratish are still quite defensive and even apologetic when they speak of the brightness they have restored to these buildings, justifying their interventions on structural grounds, as the spokesman for INTACH did in the news article I cited in the beginning of this section or as Ratish did, initially, in his interview with me:

> Ratish Nanda. See the point is that when you get to a monument, to that scale, you've got nothing left to work with! You've got gray cement, you've got yellow cement, you've got no *jalis* [filigree screens]. . . . You've got birds going in. What is its significance? The significance is its ceiling. I can't fix the ceiling and leave the outdoor like that. I had to get rid of all the cement. If I get rid of all the cement then what do I do? Should I not put the final layer? Why not?
>
> Anand Vivek Taneja. So what you've done is restore the building to what it would have looked like in the seventeenth century.
>
> RN. Yeah.
>
> AVT. So why do you think that's a problem for people?
>
> RN. Because it's all elitist. If I do this work in Nizamuddin [in the Muslim settlement around the dargah], they'll all praise me. I've done work on the baoli, put red sandstone, painted it white, they're all worshipping. . . . I've had four families come, say we're living in this tomb, can you fix it? We want to continue living there but [only] if you can make it like that. . . . This is this city, you know. The Hindi press is going to celebrate, the English press is going to criticize. . . . See this has all come from this English landscape follies, this ruin in an English landscape. These are important buildings, these aren't ruins for fuck's sake!. . . . I was taking some photographs yesterday . . . [of] this most beautiful tile-work. These buildings were covered with tile-work![35]

Ratish makes a clear distinction between the elite English speakers on one side and the Hindi-speaking people from poor and crowded Nizamuddin Basti on the other. The former don't like the color and brightness he is restoring to these monuments. The latter love it. This is a distinction as sharp, and as arresting, as the one Goethe made more than two centuries ago, between "people of refinement" on one side and "Men in a state of nature, uncivilized nations, and children" on the other. The latter "have a great fondness for colors in their utmost brightness." The former "seem to be inclined to banish color from their presence altogether." "It is as if there are two presences glowering at each other, shifting uncomfortably from one foot to the other. It is as much a body thing, a presence thing, as conscious intellection. One 'presence' is people of refinement. The other is vivid color" (Taussig 2009, 3–4).

Michael Taussig (2009) sees this distinction between *chromophiles* and *chromophobes*, as he terms them, stubbornly persisting into our present moment, a history so deeply ingrained that it is unconscious, bodily habit or, as he terms it, the *bodily unconscious*. Think of the artist and the architect out on their *habitual* morning walk, jarred so badly by the whitening of a wall that it caused them to make enough of a fuss for it to make the newspapers. And so it persists, even in India, in the difference between the Westernized, aesthetically European-ized elite of Delhi, and the color-loving *hoi-polloi*. It is no wonder that INTACH is so defensive about what it's doing. It's structural necessity, they say. The patina will return in a few monsoons. The building will no longer be so *offensive*, the apologetic subtext says.

So what is it that color does that makes people have such visceral reactions to it, reactions of such intense distaste (or attraction)? Color, Taussig insists, is not, as is often thought in the West (a term that we can extend perhaps to Delhi's Anglicized elites), merely subsidiary to form. Color is something alive, unmanageable, something "that we need to fence in with lines and marks, the boundary riders of thought" (Taussig 2009, 17). Color makes it far more difficult to remain a detached observer, an outsider looking in. Color pulls one *into the image*. Color then spells trouble for those accustomed to looking at *the world as exhibition* (Mitchell 1989), to those accustomed to standing *outside* the landscape and looking in as detached observers. The sudden bright whiteness returned to the mosque makes it impossible to treat as the picturesque ruin you are habituated to as part of the landscape you look on daily. The ruin is no longer comforting background, and a position of detached observation becomes impossible—cause enough to put any *person of refinement* off their morning walk (fig. 13).

But the people of refinement in Delhi don't have the same completely adversarial reaction to color in the rest of their lives. One look at an elite Delhi wedding, all the brightly colored silks and jewelry that the women, and even some of the men, are wearing, is enough to tell you that these people don't have the same generalized aversion to color that Goethe observed. So what is it about the ruins that turns on the chromophobia? In other words, what might be the politics (and the history) behind such a marked aesthetic aversion?

Perhaps, given the rhetoric of "living" and "dead" buildings, the twinned concern for inappropriate religious practice and inappropriate color being added to monuments—*many temples and Mosques which are actually in worship . . . are fouled by improper use and also sometimes painted in the most garish colours*—we could say that colors bring the ruin to life. If the bright vividness of color is returned to a dark mosque, as it has been in Gulmohar Park, the next thing you know, it will be positively spilling over with skullcapped worshippers as it is the unfortunate habit of "living" mosques to do.

FIGURE 13. *The whitening of Darvesh Shah's mosque. Photo by author.*

I am not trying to be facetious here. Rather, I am trying to point toward the deep-seated anxieties that both colored and "living" monuments
provoke among the secular elite of modern Delhi. For the most part this
elite lives in modern housing estates located in the midst of the medieval
ruins strewn over all of South Delhi. As long as the ruins are dead, it is
lovely to have them around, as signs of times gone by. As elements of the
landscape they are delightful in the same way that, as Ratish points out,
follies were delightful in the parkland of an English manor. Follies, of
course, are *faux* ruins, without any of the intricate connections to human
life that remain as the residue of a "real" ruin. But the ruins of Delhi are
not yet follies, despite all the colonial and postcolonial effort expended
into disconnecting them from the fabric of everyday life. As we have seen,
these ruins were, and are, part of an intricately connected landscape of
property, religious ritual, and customary usage. Let's call it medieval. This
medieval Muslim landscape, as in the case of the Waqf Board's claims
on various mosques and tombs in Delhi, while radically transformed and
worked upon, has not been entirely erased. Rather, it is as if it has moved
into a parallel universe, ceding this one to the postcolonial developers of
the city, leaving the ruins of mosques and tombs as the only points of connection between the two universes. I deliberately use the metaphor of parallel universes here to underline the fact that this medieval landscape is
in no sense past. It still has its claims on the modern city, claims that are
denied and forgotten but still exist, and not without some legal plausibil-
ity. As long as the ruins are dark and unused, "dead" to use the parlance
of the Archaeological Survey, the illusion of the *pastness* of the medieval,
its lack of relevance to the present landscape of Delhi can be maintained.
The ruins can be follies. But color the ruin, restore its brightness, and the
medieval is no longer past but present; the mosque becomes a portal to
that parallel universe, through which all kinds of medieval claims and
lifeways can reassert themselves on the landscape of contemporary Delhi.
The tenuousness of the modern landscape's hold on the city is revealed,
as is its uneasy coexistence with an Islamic landscape that post-Partition
violence was meant to take care of but didn't quite.[36]

I remember an incident from 2005, at hole 17 of the Qutub golf
course, built by the Delhi Development Authority on what used to be the

agricultural land of the village of Lado Sarai. I was photographing a large fourteenth-century wall mosque next to where players tee off, which was recorded in the "Zafar Hasan List" back in 1915, but which did not appear in INTACH's guide to Delhi's built heritage (Nanda et al. 1999). One of the two golfers playing the hole turned and asked me what I was doing. I told him that I was a researcher and was photographing this structure because it wasn't in the records. "Just don't put us into any history books," he laughed. I asked him if he knew anything about the structure. He turned serious at that and gave me a little lecture: "Friend, I've been playing golf here for ten years, but I don't know anything about this. It is much cleaner now than it used to be. But so far no one has come and occupied it, or made a nuisance and disturbed our game" (Taneja 2008).

The nervousness of the man's laugh at the idea of being in "history books" has stayed with me. What was it about this ruin that he didn't want to know? Why was the idea of "knowing anything" about the place connected with occupation, nuisance, and disturbing his game? Is it that if he acknowledged the history of the place, he would have to acknowledge the theoretical right that Muslims have to pray in that mosque at the tee-off point of hole number 17? I imagine that this was the nightmare he was keeping at bay with his wish not to know—Muslim men dressed in their best Friday white, walking across the billiard green of the fairway to come pray in the mosque, disrupting the smooth undulating carpet of manicured grass that the Delhi Development Authority had spread for the recreational benefit of government officers, sweeping god knows how many histories and other claims on the land under it.[37] The erasure of the Muslim city of memory (Sundaram 2010, 179) is the very condition for the possibility of modern Delhi. *Maulana, half of Delhi is graveyards and mosques. Our schemes will fail if we don't have room to build.* The "coming alive" of this city of memory, through color or through prayer, cannot but be a problem.

CONCLUSION

REMNANTS OF DESPAIR, TRACES OF HOPE

DESPAIR: AN AUTOBIOGRAPHICAL STATEMENT

Mil hi ja'ega raftagan ka suragh
Aur kuchh din phiro udas udas

You are bound to find a trace of the departed;
Keep up this melancholy wandering for a few more days.

—Nasir Kazmi[1]

I did not understand my motivations behind this study until a particular moment in a city far away from Delhi. It was in June 2010. I was in Isfahan, Iran, on a short break from fieldwork and the scorching heat of the Delhi summer, visiting my friend and colleague Seema Golestaneh. It was my first evening in Isfahan, and Seema's uncle Ahmad Tabaizadeh took me to the Pul-i Khaju, a bridge across the River Zayandeh, which flows through Isfahan.

The Pul-i Khaju is an elegant and complex structure, built in the mid-seventeenth century, a two-level combination of bridge and dam with sluice gates. Every evening, Isfahanis gather around the arches on the lower course of the bridge to socialize, dip their feet in the water, watch the sunset, and sing and listen to song. The vaulted arches under the bridge have marvelous acoustics, and every evening these arches resonate with the melodic verses of Hafez. Walking up to the bridge with Agha Tabaizadeh, I was struck by the singing emanating from under the bridge and began to weep.

259

I wept in that moment because, in viewing the celebration of life and beauty and music that occurs nightly at this bridge, I was reminded of another. The Satpula in Delhi, like the Pul-i Khaju, is a combination bridge and dam with marvelous vaulted arches. But where the Pul-i Khaju bustles with life and laughter and song, the Satpula lies dark and abandoned. The stream that used to run through its sluices has been diverted around it and is also dark and fetid, full of untreated sewage. In Dargah Quli Khan's account, and even in Sir Syed Ahmad's, the Satpula is described as one of the most sacred sites of Delhi, bustling with people and music, renowned for its healing properties. But before I came to Isfahan, *I could not imagine what the Satpula had once been.* In that moment in Isfahan, as I stood by one old bridge and remembered another, I realized what I'd been searching for in Delhi, and why.

When I applied to graduate school in the winter of 2005, I opened my statement of academic purpose with these lines: *I came to Delhi when I was eighteen years old. I fell in love with this modern city full of broken walls and derelict domes. I knew, I know the sadness it takes to resuscitate Carthage.*[2] At that point I had spent seven years wandering among the ruins of premodern Delhi, seemingly scattered haphazardly among modern shopping complexes and housing estates. Why did I love these ruins so much? A great deal of my wandering among them was solitary and melancholy. The buildings were mostly dark and silent, their interiors often smelling of bat shit and human piss. If, by their very presence, the ruins indicated other times and other possibilities for life, by their very darkness and solitude they indicated that these times were irretrievably in the past. In that moment at the Pul-i Khaju in Isfahan, I realized that what I was searching for among the ruins of Delhi was not a knowledge of the past as past but the possibility that the past held open for my own life, for my present.

People have been coming to the Pul-i Khaju for centuries, dipping their feet in the river for centuries, singing the poetry of Hafez for centuries. Tradition is often imagined and spoken of as a stream. In that continuity of the contemporary quotidian with the past, the stream of tradition coming together with the flowing waters of the Zayandeh, I saw for the first time an image of what Delhi's past could have been, and also what it could be again, in a city where all streams have been defiled and diverted by the violent remaking of its landscapes and lifeways by colonial and postcolonial regimes.

In speaking of minority histories and subaltern pasts, Dipesh Chakrabarty turns to the figure of the Santal rebel, who so troubled the historian Ranajit Guha by attributing agency not to himself for his rebellion but to the god Thakur. Chakrabarty suggests another gesture available to the historian apart from "historicizing the Santal in the interest of a history of social justice and democracy; . . . that of seeing the Santal as a figure illuminating a life possibility for the present" (2000, 108). Chakrabarty suggests an ethical imperative for not thinking of the past as past (an imperative I consistently *failed* to live up to until that evening in Isfahan).

Mil hi jayega raftagan ka suragh. You *will* find some trace of the departed. Why the imperative to keep searching for these traces? Perhaps because from those traces (left in the archive, or in the ruins) we can reconstruct and retell the past, make it possible for those in the present to reimagine and thus reinhabit it. Carlo Ginzburg, the master practitioner of the craft of microhistory, of imaginatively recreating lifeworlds out of archival traces, has famously compared the method of the historian to that of the hunter who creates an intimate, detailed portrait of his prey from the barest signs of the animal's passing:

> Three brothers (runs a story from the Middle East . . .) meet a man who has lost a camel. . . . At once they describe it to him: it's white, and blind in one eye; under the saddle it carries two skins, one full of oil, the other of wine. They must have seen it? No, they haven't seen it. So they're accused of theft and brought to be judged. There follows the triumph of the brothers: they immediately show how from the barest traces they were able to reconstruct the appearance of an animal they had never set eyes on. (Ginzburg 1980, 13)

This story is central to Ginzburg's account of the development of a new epistemological paradigm in the social sciences at the end of the nineteenth century. This is what he calls the semiotic paradigm, common to disciplines as diverse as archaeology and psychology and the genre of the detective novel. From the faintest material traces left behind, a whole narrative world can be reconstructed. The story of the three brothers is central to this paradigm, both as exemplary illustration and as genealogical link.

In the original story, of course, the brothers are not hunters. Ginzburg makes light of this and moves on to the points he wishes to make. But based on the details that he passes over, we could tell an entirely different story of the relation of the modern semiotic paradigm to older forms of knowing. What if we thought of these brothers as *qasida* writers rather than hunters? One of the central themes of the *qasida*, the classical Arabic ode that continues to inform the Arabic literary tradition as well as other non-Arabic literatures within the world of Islam (Sells 1989), is that of the remembrance of the beloved and the journey of the beloved away from the lover. Qasidas open in the beloved's abandoned desert camp-site, where the only evidence that remains of her passing is tent marks and torrent beds in the sand. These silent traces are invocations for the remembrance of the beloved, and from the abandoned campsite, the rest of the poem, an imaginative remembering of the beloved, springs forth.

The poet and his ode are always haunted by the loss of the unattainable beloved. The worlds the historian can recreate in painstaking detail are worlds now otherwise lost to us, except through the imagination. To relate the genealogy of the modern social sciences to the Arabic qasida is also to acknowledge the sentiment, the never quite entirely instrumental emotions, that lies at the heart of both academic and everyday engagement with the past.[3]

You will find some trace of the departed. Nasir Kazmi wrote these lines on the other side of the unspeakable violence and continuous destruction of the Partition of India, which, among its myriad effects, turned many mosques in Delhi into dark, abandoned ruins. But Kazmi's mid-twentieth-century Urdu ghazal, written centuries after the classical qasida, seems to point us back to the campsite abandoned at the beginning of the classical ode. One day, these lines seem to suggest, you will find the traces of the beloved's passing. One day you will be able to begin a qasida anew. *One day, perhaps, you will be able to imagine what you have lost.*

In Delhi, sometimes, even the imagination of what the past could have been seems well-nigh impossible, so thorough and widespread and far-reaching have been the destructive effects of colonialism, Partition violence, and the postcolonial remaking of the city. We have lost so much that we are largely unaware that we have lost anything, even though we are surrounded, in Delhi, by the traces of the departed. The traces are fetishized, and the departed are forgotten. If the imagination is the only way we can know the past, then the imperative on imagining the past as a possibility for the present takes on an even stranger and stronger urgency in Delhi: we must be able to imagine the lost past in order to realize that we have lost it. But the imagination is a language, too—one that needs to be learned. To make the mute remains of the desert campsite speak, one must know a whole grammar of trace and gesture, an entire language of longing, a way of inhabiting the traces of the beloved. Meanwhile, the hot winds of the desert have been blowing for decades, attempting to obscure all traces of the passing.

HOPE? OR THE JOYFUL POTENTIALS OF ETHNOGRAPHY

> What ails me? For Hafiz Mian such questions cannot be answered
> without taking into account the history of the country, the
> proximity of Hindus and Muslims, the deep ambiguity of kinship,
> the presence of evil spirits, and the whisperings of the devil.
>
> —Veena Das

What, then, can heal me?

. . .

In the summer of 2016 a friend sent me a news article from Lahore. "This might interest you!" The article was about the Mughal-era Lahore Fort and how concerns for security have increasingly cut the fort off from the everyday life of the city. But at the same time as the seventeenth-century fort has been barricaded with armed rangers and barbed wire, one part of the fort has become increasingly sacred and has seen an upsurge in *life*, both human and nonhuman. The Moti Masjid, the small "pearl-like" royal mosque within the fort, has become renowned in the last couple of years as a place inhabited by "favorable jinns":

> Some other guides join Qayum and animatedly explain how people have
> started arriving in flocks at the mosque to light candles and oil lamps. Two
> small cloisters inside the mosque are gaudily carpeted and colourful plastic
> pegs for hanging rosaries dot the walls.

> Visitors have covered these walls with messages addressed to the jinns of Moti Masjid; each visitor asking the jinns to petition to God on their behalf. Each wall also bears a sign proclaiming that graffiti in the mosque is *sakht gunah* [a grave sin]. A group of women sit fanning themselves and discuss theological matters and local gossip. (Majoka 2016)

The parallels with Firoz Shah Kotla are striking, including the petitions addressed to the jinns and the women discussing theological matters. Why did this site become recognized as particularly sanctified by the presence of jinns in the past couple of years? What might this have to do with the political geography of post-9/11 Lahore, where suicide bombings and counterterrorism precautions have altered and unsettled the sacred landscapes of the city, particularly Sufi shrines? Are the jinns of Lahore, like the jinns of Delhi, spirits that allow their human followers to reclaim spaces, and times, that new political orders would take away from them?

Unlike the jinns who fly across the borders between India and Pakistan every ten minutes in the stories I heard at Firoz Shah Kotla, unlike the stories of the subterranean tunnels that connect Lahore to the other Mughal centers of Delhi and Lahore, indexes of longing for an unpartitioned world (Zaman 2015), it is much harder for me, as a citizen of the Republic of India, to cross that particular border. So I turned to Google instead and typed in "moti masjid lahore jinnat." Among the many videos and articles I found, one in particular stands out, which connects the presence and continuing worship of the jinns in the mosque to the time of the sixteenth-century emperor Akbar: "Then the Jinns told that afterward old Jinn undertook the responsibility of serving the Moti Mosque and now 40 Jinns are continuously serving this mosque. This service is continued for the last many centuries and never diminishes. If human beings are not serving, the Jinns are definitely serving" ("Natal Friend of the Jinns"). As in Delhi, so in Lahore, the jinns allow for an unbroken continuity with the past in a human landscape that is incredibly fractured and discontinuous.

. . .

Bajrangi Bhaijaan (dir. Kabir Khan, 2015) is also a story about that fractured landscape, fissured, like a splitting iceberg, by the India-Pakistan border. A mute little Muslim girl from Pakistan finds herself stranded alone on the wrong side of the border. Her savior turns out to be a staunch Hindu devotee of the monkey-god Hanuman, a high-caste Brahmin, with a past career (albeit brief) in the RSS. He develops a great deal of love for this little girl, much before he discovers she is Muslim and Pakistani, and this love leads him into a series of "transgressive acceptances," transgressive, at least, from the North Indian Brahmin standard that the eponymous protagonist espouses: of "non-veg" food, of Muslim shrine spaces, of the land and people of Pakistan. Defeated by the impossible bureaucracy of traveling legally between the two countries (the girl can't even speak her own name), he smuggles her and himself across the desert border between the two countries.

The love that develops between the two is named, by a witness and chronicler in the film, as *muhabbat*. Muhabbat is love, of course, but it is a term that has dominantly and increasingly been used, in Bombay cinema, to speak of adult heterosexual coupledom. *Bajrangi Bhaijaan* is a radical film, even by the standards of Bombay cinema, because the central *muhabbat* of this film is not between Bajrangi and his fiancée but the deep filial love that develops between a young Pakistani Muslim girl and an Indian Hindu Brahmin man, who at the end of the film she names as her *mama*. It is significant that when their relationship is finally named—by the child, who regains her speech at the very end of the film, as they stand in the snowy no-man's-land between the opposing barbed wire fences of the border—she identifies him as her mother's brother. For as Victor Turner tells us, in patriarchal societies, where paternal descent is the "'structural' link par excellence," maternal kinship, as epitomized by the mother's brother, "in the domain of kinship, represents communitas" (Turner 1995, 114). Matrilineality in patriarchal societies, in Turner's analysis, opens up the individual to a morality beyond the segmentary, status-oriented obligations of kinship, attached to hierarchy. Rather, the matrilineal relation connects the individual to a wider, more egalitarian ethics beyond the patriarchal lineage and allows for the "assertion of individuality as against status incumbency" (117). But the kinship between Munni/Shahida and Bajrangi is not only not a biological given (Carsten 2000); it is doubly transgressive of the logics of both nation and community.[4] The kinship that muhabbat forges in this film is a kinship that sanctifies the sheer contingency of being brought together (Das 2013a), a kinship that "troubles" the biologic of both kinship and nationalism. And this "troubling" kinship (Ramberg 2014), which blesses a love at odds with the logics of community and nation, is blessed by the dargahs of Muslim saints in both India and Pakistan.

Dargahs like Firoz Shah Kotla are sites of what I have called "anti-patriarchal" kinship, sites where the saints are seen as the loving fathers of daughters. It is the affect of loving acceptance embodied by this "anti-structural" relationship (in Turner's terms) that makes these shrines sites of radical ethical self-fashioning, of the owning of one's desires, of the unmaking and remaking of the socially constituted self, especially for women. The affective inheritance of these sites is, as this book shows, also a part of the Islamic tradition, but to understand the ethical potentialities that this shrine opens up for both Muslims and non-Muslims as Islamic, we need to understand the tradition as not simply discursive but also visual, imaginal, bodily, affective, olfactory, cinematic, and we also need to rethink the nature of "authority" in the constitution of tradition (S. Ahmed 2016). Like kinship, tradition is not only patriarchal.

And like kinship, (the Islamic) tradition is not only bound to family and community but is an ethical *inheritance* that is open to members of all religious groups, irrespective of religious *identity*. In *Bajrangi Bhaijaan* the protagonist, with his Brahminical upbringing, is shown as being viscerally repulsed by the Muslim shrines and mosques he has to enter as part of his relationship of love and guardianship of the Pakistani girl. But as he continues to encounter the Muslim/Pakistani "other," he is surprised by how easily he embodies the gestures of Islamic *adab*. These gestures, it turns out, are not foreign at all, but a deeply embedded part of himself. The non-Muslims who come to Firoz Shah Kotla easily slip into Islamic gestures of prayer and salutation; Perso-Arabic theological and ethical terminology comes easily to their lips. The shared "Muslimness" and more-than-Muslim audience of both Bollywood and the dargah, of Indian popular culture and Indian popular religion, point us to how Islam, and its ethical potentials, is an integral part of the North Indian self, across religious identities.

·   ·   ·

On one of my last visits to Firoz Shah Kotla, in August 2016, I came across a group of men having a vigorous debate. True to the ethics of nameless intimacy at this place, they did not ask me my name as I joined their small and intimate circle. The two leading conversationalists were Muslims but of different theological orientations. One was an ardent follower of Sufis and Sufi shrines; the other was of a more modern revivalist orientation.[5] They came from different parts of the city, one from the far south and one from the east, across the river. Somehow, they had found themselves at this shrine, where they had been coming since "the year of the Commonwealth Games," 2010. And every Thursday they made a point to come together at Firoz Shah Kotla to vigorously debate matters of religion.

In the year that Balon's death had made the small community that I had become part of in Firoz Shah Kotla break apart, another intimate community had formed in another part of this vast space. And like the community that had formed around Balon, this was not a community of any theological or social homogeneity but of enormous differences and endless debate. If there was a commonality, it was of class: they were all from the working class, and they all had limited formal education. Yet their consciousness of their own lack of education, posed in the question asked to me when I first came and sat among them, did not stop them from *authoritatively* discussing Islam:

Q. *Ap jaise padhe likhe ham jahilon ke bich kaise a baithe?* [How did an educated person like you come and sit among us ignorant ones?]
A. *Apki taqrir sunke a gaya.* [After listening to your speech.]

The speeches of the uneducated were elegant and fiery and funny, and moved easily between the contemporary and early Islamic history. When I dropped in on their conversation, they were talking about sectarianism in Islam, or *firqaparasti* (literally, sect-worship):

N (the revivalist). I know someone who went to Madina, but wouldn't pray
   behind the imam there. That's not right.
A (the Sufi). You know that both sides prayed [*namaz padhi*] at the battle
   of Karbala, but they didn't pray together, because it was a battle of al-
   legiance [*baiat ka jhagda*].

N. But that's not right!

A. *Par agar man nahin kiya kise ke piche namaz padhne ka to kyon padhun?* [If I
   don't feel like praying behind someone, why should I?]

To explain his support for the idea of not praying behind someone with
whom he disagrees, the working-class Sufi then brought forth the idea of
ashiq ka mizaj (the humor/temperament of the lover), or Sufi seeker, and
the ways in which the seeker responds spiritually only to his chosen Sufi
master. He illustrated his point by telling a canonical story about Amir
Khusrau and his love for Nizamuddin Auliya. But what was striking to
me was his insistence that the individual believer, and *what he felt*, was
authoritatively Islamic enough for the believer to not follow, in prayer or
in ethical example, the imams or authoritative knowers and interpret-
ers of Islam. At Firoz Shah Kotla, exploratory authority, to use Shahab
Ahmed's phrase, is alive and well in the constitution, transmission, and
continual questioning that forms the "discursive tradition" (Asad 1986)
that continually asks, *What is Islam?*

· · ·

One evening, as we walked around Firoz Shah Kotla, Santosh Mishra
said to me, "This must have been built by the jinns. Otherwise how would
it have survived so long? Even things built with modern machinery fall
apart so quickly, and this has survived more than six hundred years." This
was one of many conversations at Firoz Shah Kotla where the material
remnants of the past were seen as enchanted by the very fact of their survival and by their difference from the contemporary.

"Buildings speak to me," Ratish Nanda said to me the first time I had
an extended conversation with him, in the summer of 2008, when I was
doing preliminary fieldwork. At that point Nanda had been involved in
heritage conservation in Delhi for more than a decade, and his comment
was in response to my query about why he did the work he did. Buildings speak to him, he said, and he felt the need to restore them to their
past glory, to save them from being swallowed by the ugliness of modern
urban sprawl that often threatened to overwhelm them.

There is a long genealogy of such unmediated access to the past in architectural history and archaeology, going back, in the Indian case, to James Fergusson in the early nineteenth century. "I could read in the chisel marks on the stone the idea that had guided the artist in his design, till I could put myself by his side" (Fergusson, quoted in Guha-Thakurta 2004, 21). As the work of Yannis Hamilakis (2007) and Nadia Abu El-Haj (2001) shows, the construction of the practice of unmediated access to a (necessarily) lost past was integral to the archaeological project of constructing (exclusionary) ethnonational pasts. But I cannot simply be critical about Ratish's practice because I feel a deep kinship with him. Buildings speak to me, too, the ruins of Delhi's past, so different from everything that comes after, the boxy ugliness of modern(ist) brick and cement that surrounds them. Ruins have invoked longings in me that I still cannot completely comprehend. It is this affective relationship with the ruins of Delhi, which began when I first started wandering through these ruins as a college student in 1998, that has also constructed my intellectual landscape. "There were no ugly buildings built two hundred years ago," Ratish said, and I had to nod my head in agreement. There were no ugly buildings built two hundred years ago, at least none that have survived. The premodern past built beautifully, and it spoke directly to Ratish, conveying an aesthetic universe—a culture lost to and lost by modernity—which he tries to preserve for an uncaring city.

In that conversation during the summer of 2008 I tried to tell Ratish that the people who wrote to jinns, or the people who wanted to pray in protected mosques, were in a sense akin to him, to us; for they, too, were moved by the ruins of the past and were trying to make that past present, alive. He vehemently disagreed: "These people have no respect for the past; they would cover it with cement if they got a chance." He went on about the ignorance of Muslims, the cynical land grabs by Muslim organizations of heritage buildings, the terrible sin of whitewashing these ruins of the past, their (Muslim) inability to appreciate the past that they claimed as their own. While Ratish disagreed with the ASI on most things, on this they seemed to agree—that "living" monuments, in which people pray, and live, and make modifications, are not the way to make the past come alive.

When I spoke to Ratish in the spring of 2010 and again in the summer of 2011, his approach to conservation had shifted considerably. He attributed this to the work he had been involved with in Nizamuddin, where it was not only the conservation of buildings on the agenda but also, linked to that, the improvement of the quality of life for people of the basti:

> Ratish Nanda. A lot has changed over the last four-five years when we've been engaged with this. See, working in Mehrauli Archaeological Park was a ball. I mean you've got monuments, you're given money, you fix them . . . even then, we could have been much more ambitious . . . in terms of treatment of monuments.
>
> Anand Vivek Taneja. In what ways?
>
> RN. We were focused on simple preservation. . . . We could have been more focused on actual restoration, to put back a lot more significance. Working in Nizamuddin is a different ball game altogether. I mean, you have human beings.

It is interesting that in his narrative of how his thinking has transformed, working with human beings shares space with the restoration of monuments to "significance." By significance, of course, he means the restoration of medieval mosques and tombs, as much as possible, to their original state, which includes the restoration of their vivid color schemes. Is there a connection, then, between human life and the "life" of these monuments, restored through color? Ratish now thinks of these buildings as not just conveying an aesthetic universe, as he earlier did, but of also now being important for influencing the moral universe of the people of Delhi: "I think it also leads to communal harmony. Hindus hate Muslims because they're suspicious of each other. You go to pray in a temple you go to pray in a mosque and you pray to idols. . . . If people understood each other's religion better, there would be not so much stress, and you can do it through buildings."

. . .

How do you do develop communal harmony through buildings? Ratish didn't elaborate, so I will hazard my own guess. In my interpretation I move entirely away from the theological and political complications of the Ismaili-funded Aga Khan Development Network's intervention in the life of the city, to make a somewhat phenomenological point.

Akeel Bilgrami (2006, 2014) alerts us to the dichotomy within the Enlightenment, the difference between a vision of the world that saw nature as brute and inert (and hence a God entirely transcendent) and a nature imbued with value, a more immanent view. Particularly in its post-colonial career, the ASI has in a sense recapitulated this difference in material form. It wishes the monuments under its control to be entirely free of any trace of divinity—hence "dead." But there are others who believe that these buildings are imbued with value; whether this value is interpreted as divine or worldly is a matter we will leave aside for the moment. Ratish wants to restore these monuments to both their aesthetic and ecological value. For him this means restoring them, as far as possible, to all their multicolored glory, standing amid gardens also restored as much as possible to what they would have been like. Ratish's ultimate ambition is to transform the area stretching north of Humayun's Tomb, dotted with medieval buildings, into the biggest urban open space in the world, bigger than Central Park. When I asked him if he saw this as somehow reviving the old sense of Delhi as a sacred landscape, he replied, "We're more keen to revive bird habitats and things like that." In recent years, as the plans to make this park (now called the Dinpanah Archaeological Park) have come closer to fruition,[6] Ratish's Facebook timeline has increasingly filled with pictures of birds, many species of which flock to the renewed gardens around the ruins. When I talked to him about these birds in August of 2016, in his office in the Sundar Nursery complex just north of Humayun's Tomb, he said that the conservation project has evolved into creating bird habitats as part of conservation. "I've documented seventy-eight bird species sitting right here. Once we're done, there will be a 150 bird species. . . . We're trying to get every kind of protection, from wildlife to heritage [for the Archaeological Park]."

When I asked Ratish about the birds on his timeline, he said that he had started photographing the birds as a form of relief from the pressures of conservation work and that "they keep me sane." That comment stuck with me. When he first spoke about bird habitats, he spoke as a manager husbanding the landscapes and creatures at his command. It is only years later that he acknowledged that it was not just him creating habitats for the birds but that the birds were also making the city more habitable for him. "Humans become," to cite Anna Tsing (2015, 263) in the context of Matsutake mushrooms, "only one of many participants in making livability." Those who come to Firoz Shah Kotla, in their myriad encounters with jinns as snakes and cats and birds, have known this all along.

How different are the birds on Ratish's secular Facebook timeline from the birds that are fed for religious reasons at Firoz Shah Kotla? Not very, I would wager. If we think of enchantment in the way Akeel Bilgrami does, as a view of the world that sees the natural world as imbued with value, and not brute and inert, then I believe that the intervention that Ratish is making in the landscape of Delhi is a *reenchantment*, which his own secular language is sometimes inadequate to articulate. He is restoring an older mode of enchantment to the city. In this mode buildings do not need to be ruined and tumbledown for the work of human beings and ecology to come together (Simmel 1965). Humayun's Tomb, after all, is situated in a simulation, in a making immanent, of the garden of paradise.[7]

The idiom of the architectural and ecological restoration that Ratish and the Aga Khan Trust for Culture are bringing back to the city might be Islamic, but the enchantment they are returning to the city's landscapes is one that crosses the boundaries of the religious and the secular. My conviction of this comes from one time I was hanging out at Pehelwan's shop in the summer of 2011.

Pehelwan's shop is small and cramped, six feet by four feet, in a narrow alley in the Balmiki colony south of Firoz Shah Kotla. Of dubious legality like all structures in the colony, the shop is made of cobbled-together brick and tin and plastic sheeting, and, like almost all structures in this cramped settlement, it gets very little direct sunlight. That evening, as I sat with him, the setting sun found its way through a narrow crack between buildings and cast a golden patch of light on the far wall of Pehelwan's shop, illuminating a framed picture of the goddess Kali and the amulet I had brought from Iran. This seemed to transport Pehelwan almost to ecstasy. Look, he said, *Surya Dev* (the sun god) is saluting the mother goddess (*mai ko haziri de rahe hain*) in my shop before he sinks. *Hai na kudrat ka kamal?* (Is this not the miracle of nature?)

If Pehelwan's consciousness can find such *naturally supernatural* enchantment in the cramped, dark confines of his grocery shop in the heart of a slum, where the rays of the sun make the briefest of entrances, how might it react to a Mughal tomb-garden at the height of its glory? What would happen to a man of such exquisitely permeable sensibilities in such a place? Where the dazzling white tomb at the center pulls the eye in, covered with red polychromy to match the flowers all around, and the flash of color from the underside of birds' wings, where the carpets inside the tomb chamber match the patterns of the lawns and flowers outside, where the work of nature and the work of culture come together not in a ruin but in the perfection, the completion, of the building's design?

I don't know about communal harmony, but if Hindus and Muslims, if all of us, could, in this place, share some sense of enchantment, perhaps it could be the beginning of a conversation.

POSTSCRIPT

On May 17, 2017, the Union Cabinet of India, dominated by the Hindu nationalist BJP, approved an amendment to the Ancient Monuments Act discussed in this book. "The amended Act gives the Centre the power to begin construction work in the "prohibited" area—a 100-metre radius—around the monuments."[1] Given the BJP's history with medieval Islamic monuments—especially the destruction of the Babri Masjid in 1992—this has led to much consternation among historians and conservationists.

"To justify this [the amendment], we are offered a note for the Cabinet prepared by the Ministry of Culture. Significantly, the ministry . . . pleads the cause of roadways, railway tracks, and unknown private landed interests. . . . The note claims that lives would be endangered if an elevated highway is not allowed to pass within 100 meters of Akbar's tomb in Agra . . . The third and final instance is that of an unnamed hospital (private?) which cannot supposedly expand except by intruding within 100 meters of Tipu Sultan's palace in Bengaluru . . . The . . . two are interesting instances since they do not only concern "Muslim" monuments, but are associated with two men in the Rashtriya Swayamsevak Sangh's [the ideological body of the BJP] cross hairs, namely, Akbar and Tipu Sultan" (Moosvi 2017).

The amendment passed by the cabinet has short-circuited a debate that had been unfolding in India over the "prohibited areas" and building restrictions, including "site specific" rules being drafted by the National Monuments Authority, rather than a blanket ban. As Saptarshi Sanyal notes, "The blanket rule on the 'prohibited areas' should, and has, been debated at various professional and academic fora. Certainly a law originating from a colonial outlook needs review, given our current depth of knowledge on heritage. However, doing away with protection without survey and documentation can be catastrophic" (2017).

Rather than giving local communities a say in how they are to live with the remains of the past, it is the central government—dominated by an ideology that perceives India's Islamic past as problematic and shameful—that wishes to arrogate to itself the power to choose the relation of the material remains of the past to infrastructural visions of the future. As violence and bigotry against Muslims has grown exponentially under the current dispensation, in parallel with the growing rhetoric of infrastructural modernity, the resonances with immediately post-Partition India seem clear: *Maulana, half of Delhi is graveyards and mosques. Our schemes will fail if we don't have room to build.*

NOTES

INTRODUCTION

1. This is a reference to Ranajit Guha's famous essay (1996), which asks us to move beyond statist paradigms in the writing of history.

2. On critiques of Western historiography and its insistence on banishing "temporal pollution," see Palmie and Stewart (2016).

3. In arguing for the past as holding open potentialities for life, I am drawing on both Nietzsche's ([1874] 1980) thoughts on the relation of history to life and Koselleck's (2002) thoughts on conceptual history. Linked closely to Koselleck's idea of concepts—which transcend political events and periodization—is his idea of the "simultaneity of the non-simultaneous," the co-occurrence of forms of life usually divided by discrete periods, such as "medieval" and "modern." For parallel ethnographic examples see Lambek (2002, 2016) and Wirtz (2016).

4. For a broad overview of the political theologies of Indo-Islamic kingship see Alam (2004). For the (normative) duty of the king to accept petitions from all subjects, see Nizam al-Mulk ([c. 1090] 1960).

5. I use "in a sense" here to indicate that the work of Partition has not concluded but remains an ongoing process of dispossession and disruption, especially for religious minorities in India and Pakistan, as Vazira Zamindar's (2007) work shows.

6. CCO here refers to the Chief Commissioner's Office Records in the Delhi State Archives. Archival material is referenced throughout this book by abbreviations for the collection, file number, and year of origin.

CHAPTER 1

1. Shab-e Qadr (Urdu/Persian) or Lailat al Qadr (Arabic), "The Night of Power," marks the night on which the Quran was first revealed to the Prophet Muhammad. By South Asian convention, Shab-e Qadr is generally held to be the twenty-seventh night of the sacred month of Ramzan/Ramadan.

2. See also Rajagopalan (2016, 14–17).

3. Graves are usual but not necessary for spaces to be identified and treated as Muslim saint shrines. What matters is saintly presence. A well-known example of a dargah not centered on a grave is Hussain Tekri Sharif. See Bellamy (2011).

4. When William Dalrymple, a young British writer, stumbled upon Firoz Shah Kotla in the mid-1980s, his interlocutor told him about jinns and how Delhi was full of them. From this encounter he got the name of his famous book, and now a popular descriptor for the city, *City of Djinns* (Dalrymple 1993).

5. On *sahaba* jinn in contemporary Lahore see N. Khan (2006, 240–42; and 2012, 131).

6. These interactions happen in the realm of the *barzakh* (intermediate realm), associated with dreams and visions, between the incorporeal realm of spirits and the physical world of bodies. On graves and the *barzakh* see also Ho (2006) and Mittermaier (2011).

7. A profound paradox confronts those who work with the state and its documents in South Asia. Official records are deeply entrenched in all aspects of everyday life—birth certificates, building permissions, property records—yet the state works, both actively and entropically, to deny access to its own documentary records (see also Das and Poole 2004). Even Matthew Hull, who has done pathbreaking work with the documents of the Pakistani bureaucracy, recounts that it was much easier for him to find and read "current files" rather than documents from the archives, which he found only through serendipity (Hull 2012, 28). Aradhana Sharma (2013) characterizes this, in the context of bureaucratic subversion of the spirit of "transparency" of the Right to Information Act, as the state's "mode of erasure."

8. The surprise is not altogether misplaced because oral accounts also indicate that the popularity of Firoz Shah Kotla increased dramatically in 1977.

9. ASI, f24/76/77-M(T), "Closing of Mausoleum in Kotla Ferozshah, New Delhi, to Visitors."

10. ASI, f33/10/83-M, "Suit Filed by the Muntazima Committee Masjid Qudsia Bagh Delhi in the Court of Distt. Judge Delhi Regarding the Claims for Offering Prayers."

11. For the agreement between the Anjuman and the Delhi government see CCO, f56/1926/Education, "Correspondence Relating to the Rangrez Mosque." For issues specific to the Qudsia Mosque see CCO, f1(13)/1929/Education, "Correspondence Relating to Mosque at Qudsia Gardens, Delhi."

12. At that time the ASI was under the jurisdiction of the Ministry of Education.

13. Most of the spaces of veneration scattered throughout Firoz Shah Kotla are unregulated, without any officially appointed figure to lead ritual activity. However, the mosque has an imam, or prayer-leader, appointed by the Delhi Waqf Board. The imam is trained in a Deobandi madarsa and actively discourages and disparages the practices of jinn veneration at Firoz Shah Kotla, deeming these practices to be superstitions. The conflict with those who insist on the presence and sanctity of jinns seems like a classic conflict between those belonging to the Deobandi and Barelwi *maslaks* of Sunni Islam. But the difference is expressed, by those who insist on the presence of jinns, as a difference between local Delhi people and outsiders (the imam is from Bihar).

14. Wrestlers traditionally oil themselves and slap their thighs to warm themselves up and also at the beginning of a bout before they clinch with their opponent, so it can be construed as an aggressive move.

15. While Nasim Changezi was speaking mostly in Urdu, he used the English word here.

16. The second time we talked, Nasim Changezi used both criticize and the Urdu *nuqtachini*, which best translates into English as "punctiliousness," and here it indicates his family's scrupulousness in matters of faith and, hence, their criticism of any perceived deviation.

17. The copy of the book I own gives no mention of a first publication date or any publication date at all. I did interview Waseem Sahab, however, the current proprietor of Astana Book Depot, who told me that the book had first been published in the 1950s, when his father ran the publishing house.

18. Satan [Iblis] is a jinn rather than a fallen angel in most Islamic traditions.

19. I am deeply indebted to Pasha Mohamed Khan for bringing Ibn Kathir's narrative to my notice.

20. See Foucault (1977, 139).

21. In recent years the government of India has launched a program to develop a Unique Identification Document, or *Aadhar* card, a unitary form of identification with biometric data that will eliminate the various diverse kinds of government-issued IDs and collate all the data of citizens in one centralized database. Under the current government an Aadhar card is becoming mandatory for accessing various state welfare services.

22. We could say, following the work of Bhrigupati Singh (2012; 2015, 33–102), that in the movement from fear to intimacy people are moving from the fearful to the friendly pole of sovereignty. Singh argues that sovereignty is bipolar, including elements of both coercion and contract.

23. On messianic time and the abolition of (Jewish) law see Agamben (2005). *Secularized* messianic time, I would argue, concerned with the relatively mundane future of the nation rather than the eschatological arrival of the Messiah, encompasses radically different ethical potentialities, as we see in the ways in which Partition violence played out.

24. The correspondence that follows is from ASI, f15B/10/55-G, "Preservation of Monuments in Delhi–Request from Jamiat-E-Ulema New Delhi."

CHAPTER 2

1. Janamashtami is the festival celebrating the birth of Lord Krishna, traditionally associated with the heavy rains of the monsoon month of Sawan.

2. In the stage setting of the Baroque play, Walter Benjamin saw the spatialization of time—"history merges into the setting"—which he perceived as bringing together the time of history and the time of nature (Hannsen 1998, 41–57).

3. In using the metaphor of the cessation of the flow of time, I am drawing on Merleau-Ponty's critique of the pervasive metaphor of time flowing and passing. Time is not an objective datum of consciousness, but rather, consciousness deploys or constitutes time, and through the "ideal" nature of time, it ceases to be imprisoned in the present (2002, 476–81).

4. Here I am drawing on Deleuze's interpretations of Bergson's idea of "time as duration," in thinking about the "time-image" (not only) in cinema, the ways in which the image can give us a direct experience of the Bergsonian "depth" of time (Deleuze 1989).

5. Admittedly, men rather than women are much more likely to be urinating in public spaces in India. And accidentally inciting wrath and vengeance through careless urination is usually associated with the jinn.

6. Ashis Nandy argues that millions of people in the world still live outside history: "They do have theories of the past; they do believe that the past is important and shapes

the present and the future, but they also recognize, confront, and live with a past different from that constructed by historians and historical consciousness" (Nandy 1995, 44).

7. In ideal terms the shikwa was oral, but in practice, as Brinkley Messick's work on shikwas in Yemen shows, the shikwas were virtually always written (Messick 1993, 173).

8. "To articulate the past historically does not mean to recognize it 'the way it really was.' It means to seize hold of a memory as it flashes up at a moment of danger" (Benjamin 1969b, 255).

9. Even so, normative Mughal political theory heavily emphasized the primarily kingly duty of dispensing justice to the populace. See Darling (2002).

10. "Rituals gain force where incongruence is perceived and thought about" (Smith 1982, 63). Muslim theologians and Sufis felt so alienated from British legal procedures that they actively spoke and worked against the colonial court system. "Rashid Ahmed Gangohi of Deoband was of the opinion that British law did not reach the standard of justice of the ulama. He therefore allowed a follower of his to lie to the court of law 'in order to conform to [a] standard of truth above that of British law.' In another case, he condoned the escape from jail of a man wrongly imprisoned by the government" (Liebeskind 1998, 233).

11. There are close parallels between the practices of petitioning at Firoz Shah Kotla and at the shrines of Golu Devta in the Kumaon region of the Himalayan state of Uttarakhand. As Aditya Malik (2016) shows, many of the legends and stories of Golu Devta show precolonial justice (as embodied by Golu Devta) as being superior to the forms of power wielded by the colonial and postcolonial state, while yet encompassing colonial and postcolonial legal forms, such as judicial stamp papers, within the ritual vocabulary and material culture of the shrines, in remarkable parallels with Firoz Shah Kotla.

12. See also Naveeda Khan (2012, 55–77) on the past as a field of potentiality in Iqbal and Bergson's thought.

13. Here I bring together Emma Tarlo's (2003) observation that the actions taken by the government against Delhi's poor during the Emergency were not exceptional but merely an intensification of business as usual, with Benjamin's famous statement that "the tradition of the oppressed teaches us that the 'state of emergency' in which we live is not the exception but the rule" (1969b, 257).

14. *Sarkar* means both "Lord" and the more common "Government," as in Bharat Sarkar, the Government of India.

15. *Zinda Pir* means "Living saint."

16. See also Scott (1990).

17. There is a 1915 file of annoyed British responses to popular veneration at Pir Ghaib in the Delhi State Archives. Bisharat Ali, the man named in the ASI report as the *mujawar* (caretaker), hailed from Sada Sohag ka Takya in Paharganj and claimed to be the hereditary mujawar of the shrine. This would imply that his family had been taking care of the shrine for at least one generation previously, taking the family's relation to the shrine back to the late nineteenth century, if not all the way to 1857 (CCO, f211/1915/Education).

18. For more details on the British remaking of the landscapes north of Delhi after 1857, see Amin (2001) and Lahiri (2003).

19. There are sandstone informational slabs erected by the Archaeological Survey close to all the major "protected" monuments in Delhi. The slabs are inscribed primarily in English and usually are full of mind-numbing architectural detail rather than local stories or beliefs about the structures. In the slab at Pir Ghaib the legend of the saint and his disappearance is also briefly narrated.

20. Similarly, Nosheen Ali (2016) writes about poetic culture and a different experience of time in South Asia, through her interviews with poets in northwest Pakistan, who refer to long-dead Sufi poet-saints as their contemporaries.

21. The niche, or *taq*, inside the home is a fairly common phenomenon for the veneration of the saints and jinns in Delhi, across communities. In premodern buildings, of which Old Delhi still has a substantial number, this seems to be a lingering continuation of older practices of illumination, pre-electricity, when lamps and candles were placed in the niche. There seems to be a strong reference here also to the 'Verse of Light' (Ayat an-Nur) from the Quran (24:35), which is a verse central to Sufi mystical thought: "God is the light of the heavens and the earth. The light like the light of a lamp in a niche." In modern houses lacking niches, a kind of wooden projecting niche, or *ala*, is constructed, with a mirrored rear-surface to reflect the light of the lamp.

22. *Jummerat*, Thursday evening, the eve of the *Jummah*, the day of congregational midday prayers, is traditionally the day to visit the graves of saints.

23. Muhammad is referred to as the *Kali Kambli Wale* (the one with the black blanket) in Indian Muslim devotional poetry and songs. The Prophet's cloak is also celebrated in the famous "Qasida al-Burda," in which the thirteenth-century Egyptian Sufi Al-Busiri praises the Prophet, who had revealed himself to him in a dream.

24. I would like to thank Ali Sethi for this perceptive observation.

25. A procession with musicians was a common method of film publicity in Delhi till the 1970s (Sethi 2009, 67).

26. On the ethics of efficacy see Piliavsky and Sbriccoli (2016). The term *amil*, often used for Muslim healers, indicates action, *amal*. An amil, like a *gunda*, is efficacious; he acts in and on the world.

27. In this my argument follows Aamir Mufti's (2007) reading of "Muslimness" (as sign and culture) as signaling ambivalence toward the project of colonial and postcolonial modernity, an ambivalence that is recognized by secular nationalism only as temporal backwardness, or "lag."

28. "The new, dialectical method of doing history presents itself as the art of experiencing the present as the waking world, a world to which that dream we name the past refers in truth" (Benjamin 1999, 389 [K1, 3]).

29. Most characteristically, in the way people bring their hands together, cupped along the edges, like Muslims do for *du'a* rather than the way one would join hands with both palms together in front of the image of a Hindu deity.

30. This finding is highlighted in the Prime Minister's High Level Committee report, *Social, Economic and Educational Status of the Muslim Community in India* (2006)—popularly known as the Sachar Committee Report. See also Gayer and Jaffrelot (2012).

CHAPTER 3

1. Only one person ever asked me my name at Firoz Shah Kotla, someone with whom I was quite familiar at the site and had been talking to since 2007, and this was in late 2010. Someone had told him I was Christian, and he was convinced I was not, and he wanted to confirm this. So even asking the name, four years into our knowing each other, was to identify what I was *not* rather than what I was. No one ever addressed me by my name, though I have spent hundreds of hours at Firoz Shah Kotla over the years. People did ask me, on a fairly regular basis, about my parents and my siblings and their professions, my financial situation, and about life in America. The ethics of namelessness is changing somewhat, however, with the ubiquity of cellphones.

2. On the culture of hospitality in Egyptian saint shrines, and the alternative forms of community and political imagination they make possible, see Mittermaier (2014).

3. The term *Hindu* is very much part of people's self- and community identity today. However, the use of the term elides the variety of *qaums* (*qaum/kaum* or community being the term used in Delhi for what sociologists would recognize as *jati* or caste) by which people traditionally classified themselves and recognized their differences, and, as conversations at Firoz Shah Kotla and other shrines indicate, continue to do so.

4. On names in South Asia see Copeman and Das (2015).

5. See, e.g., Shahid Amin (2004, 96).

6. As Veena Das (2015) shows, the experience and narratives of illness and suffering in Delhi are not just biomedical but also absorb and embody ideas of social failing and familial betrayal. Narratives of healing, similarly, are not just bodily but also simultaneously stories of the remaking of the self's relations to the social world.

7. On ethics and freedom see Laidlaw (2002, 2013).

8. Like Al-Mohammad (2010, 426), I believe that persons are constituted in relation to other persons, animals, objects, landscapes, and the world, and these relations *are* ethics. Laidlaw (2013) also asks us to seriously consider cosmologies that expand the ideas of the ethical subject far beyond the lifetime of an individual. For critiques of virtue ethics, and the emphasis on self-fashioning in anthropology, see Mittermaier (2012) and Piliavsky and Sbriccoli (2016).

9. Blueline Buses were private buses that operated in Delhi between 1992 and 2010. Their drivers very quickly became notorious for rash and irresponsible driving and for hundreds of deaths on Delhi roads. See Sundaram (2010, 139–71).

10. On rethinking kinship beyond the biological, see Carsten (2000). On kinship extending beyond humans to gods and spirits, and the ways that such extended kinship "troubles" normative ideas of kinship, gender, and the relational self, see Ramberg (2014).

11. Dargahs are often, to borrow the words of Sarah Pinto from the parallel but related context of women's psychiatric wards, "spaces of dissolution": "An ethical perspective attentive to dissolution addresses selfhood and relations as matters of movement, condensation, and dissipation rather than points of arrival" (Pinto 2014, 260).

12. See also Janice Boddy's (1989) work on the *Zar* cult in northern Sudan. Boddy found that by accommodating the spirits that possessed them, women could expand and

regenerate their sense of self, recontextualize their experiences, and reformulate everyday discourse to portray consciousness of their own subordination.

13. The conjuration of jinns through spices and smells was, however, very much a part of the high court culture of the sixteenth-century Deccan (Flatt 2016) and, more proximately, the royal court of early nineteenth-century Lucknow (Vanita 2012, 70). Flatt also draws connections between the cult of fairies and long-standing traditions of the veneration of *yoginis* (feminine goddesses and their human embodiments, associated with female sexuality and fertility) in the Deccan.

14. *Khel* or *khela* (play) is another word for the phenomenon usually translated as "possession."

15. In the ritual transgressions demanded by Muslim spirits possessing Hindus at the shrine of Mehndipur Balaji, Kakar reads the "psychological depth of the antipathy between Hindu and Muslim" (1982, 63).

16. And in the disconnect between our autonomous self-conception and our experience lies the feeling of the uncanny (Hanna 2016).

17. *Ate hain ghaib se yih mazamin khayal men / Ghalib sarir-e khamah nava-e sarosh hai* (They come into the mind, these themes, from the invisible [*ghaib*] / Ghalib, the scratching of the pen is the voice of an angel). See Ghalib, *ghazal* 169, verse 13 (www.columbia .edu/itc/mealac/pritchett/00ghalib/169/169_13.html).

CHAPTER 4

1. See Mary Douglas, *Collected Works*, vol. 2, *Purity and Danger: An Analysis of Concepts of Pollution and Taboo* (1966; New York: Routledge, 2003), 36.

2. As the work of Chatterjee (2010b) and Das (2007) shows, "traditional" patriarchy is bound up with more proximate histories, including responses to colonialism (Chatterjee) and the effects of Partition violence (Das).

3. Vijindar Khari is not the only Hindu I have encountered using the term *isht-dev* to describe their relationship to an identifiably Muslim saint. In a much more fleeting encounter at Sultan Ghari, the venerated tomb of a thirteenth-century prince in southern Delhi, a young woman from the village of Rangpuri also described Sultan Ghari as "our isht-dev." At Firoz Shah Kotla the term *isht-dev* is not used, presumably because the Hindus here are more fluent in Islamicate vocabulary as a result of their continuing links to Old Delhi and its traditions of Urdu speech.

4. If, however, the husband happens to be from a different religious community than the wife, or from a lower class/caste status, then things are decidedly more complicated (see Mody 2008).

5. Manohar Lal's family hails from Rajasthan, four generations ago.

6. These lines are from the song "Maula Salim Chishti," from the film *Garam Hawa* (dir. M. S. Sathyu, 1973). The lyrics are by Kaifi Azmi and Aziz Ahmed Khan Warsi Qawwal.

7. Bellamy prefers to use the term *haziri*, also used at Firoz Shah Kotla, rather than "spirit possession." Violent haziri of the kind that is central to Bellamy's work in Husain Tekri is relatively rare at Firoz Shah Kotla and is understood even by the healers present at Firoz Shah Kotla to be purely performative most of the time. On "possessions," hys-

teria, and performance see Pinto (2014, 196–98). On the parallels between psychodrama therapy and spirit possession discourses see Bonilla (1969); and Schmidt and Huskinson (2011).

8. Bellamy (2011, 16) also writes of those afflicted who come to Husain Tekri conceiving of themselves as *ma'sum* (innocent) as an integral part of their healing.

9. For the evolving restrictions on devotional expression in the dargahs of Delhi see Kumar (2010).

10. I saw others take surreptitious swigs out of *pavva* (quarter) bottles on Thursdays at Firoz Shah Kotla, and there were often scenes where those who had landed up at Kotla drunk and disorderly had to be pacified by their sober friends.

11. *Patki*, violent throwing and falling, is one of the ways in which a body is rid of possessing spirits in the vocabulary of Firoz Shah Kotla.

12. Shahab Ahmed (2016, 37n94) translates *rindi* as "nonconforming libertinage."

13. I am grateful to Ruth Vanita for her help with clarifying and more accurately translating these poems.

14. Parsis, like Indira Gandhi's husband Firoz Gandhi, are normatively Zoroastrians. But their Persianate names seem to lead to some semantic confusion with Muslims, who often have Persian names as well. Feroz Khan, for example, is the name of a well-known Muslim movie star. While *Parsi* now denotes the Zoroastrian community in India, *Farsi* usually refers to the Persian language.

15. A *gotra* is an exogamous clan group.

16. For a possible Sufi genealogy of such thinking see the episode of the Shaykh Sanan, who becomes a swineherd because of his love for a Christian girl, in Attar's *Conference of the Birds*, and Abul Kalam Azad's (1991) defense of the Sufi Sarmad's love for the Hindu boy Abhay Chand.

17. "Versions of this Hadith appear in all the canonical collections of hadith, including *Sahih al Bukhari* 10:361, and *Sahih Muslim* 7:53" (S. Ahmed 2016, 339n90).

18. I am grateful to Ismail Fajrie Alatas for this insight.

19. On the transmission of spiritual authority through female Sufis in Indonesia, see Birchok 2016.

20. For work that critiques, nuances, and expands Barlas's argument, see the recent Roundtable on Feminism and Islam in the *Journal of Feminist Studies of Religion*, especially the essays by Kecia Ali, Fatima Seedat, and YaSiin Rahmaan (all 2016).

21. See also Seedat (2016) on experience as a site of exegetical authority beyond the text.

CHAPTER 5

1. The Balmikis of Delhi are known for their musicianship. Pehelwan's brother is a classically trained musician who has performed on All India Radio.

2. If connections can be drawn, they would be through the world of practice and oral transmission rather than through text. Dara Shukoh was a follower and patron of many of Delhi's Sufis, including the antinomian Sarmad Shahid. The shrines of these Sufis

continue to be a part of the sacral landscape of Delhi, particularly, as we have seen, for Pehelwan's *qaum*.

3. Ibn 'Arabi is the influential thirteenth-century Sufi shaykh whose philosophy of *wahdat al-wujud*, the unity of all being, underlies much of later Sufi thought and practice.

4. Harry Zohn translates this as "the intended object" and the "mode of intention" (Benjamin 1969a, 74).

5. The association of Shiva with the jinn goes back at least to the seventeenth century, when Shaikh Abdul Rahman Chishti writes of him as the *Abu'l Jinn*, the father of the jinn (Alam 2004, 98).

6. I use *style* here in the sense that Walter Benjamin used *style* to understand style and fashion as being deeply *historical* in their constant reference, through metonymy, resonance, and evocation, to times past, to fashion's constant resurrection of the past in the present. See Benjamin 1999, Convolut B, "*Fashion*."

7. *Mudras*, the symbolic gestures, both static and dynamic, central to Buddhist and Hindu ritual and to Indian classical dance practice, provide a far more resonant metaphor for what I am trying to convey than the prosaic (on paper) "dance moves."

8. The pilgrimage guides at Amarnath have traditionally been local Muslim herdsmen.

9. Presumably, this refers to the Urdu typing and compositing that many imams in Delhi do to supplement their income.

10. This is a reference to the jinn/saint of Firoz Shah Kotla.

11. To go on *tabligh* is a reference to go on a preaching tour with other members of the *Tablighi Jamaat*, a reformist organization dedicated to purifying the ritual practices and ethical lives of Muslims. Given Raju's involvement with jinns and other matters related to the unseen world, he would seem to be a very unusual candidate for *tabligh*, and his desire to participate casts an interesting light on the interaction of different modes of Islamic piety in contemporary South Asia.

12. I am grateful to Allison Busch for the references to the *Ramacharitmanas*.

13. *Gharib nawaz*. This is the first Persian word that has occurred in the poem. (This is Growse's original footnote.)

14. We could see the 'urs as an example of translation that is too successful—so successful in losing its exotic particularities that Muslim reformers see the 'urs as a "Hindu" accretion onto the practice of Islam, whereas its antecedents lie closer to central Islamic lands. See Green (2012, 36–37).

15. On passing in dargah contexts see Bellamy (2011, 61–93).

16. I use the term *modern* in a sense similar to Partha Chatterjee's when he speaks of the "early modern" not necessarily as a period but as recognizable elements of thought or practice (Chatterjee 2012, 67).

17. A deg is a very large vat, in which massive amounts of either sweet or savory rice (the latter with meat) are cooked. Many of the richer members of the Firoz Shah Kotla congregation have degs of rice distributed to the public at large every week at Firoz Shah Kotla. The distribution of degs is modeled on the *langar*, or communal kitchen, common to both more institutionalized Muslim dargahs and Sikh gurudwaras.

CHAPTER 6

1. There is no tradition of autonomous sanctity of this rock that I am aware of. The rock outcropping and boulder that the man from Gaya recognized as Patthar Baba are known traditionally as *Bhim ki Chhatanki*, or the small weighing measure of the mythological warrior Bhim of the *Mahabharata*, renowned for his extraordinary strength. A *chhatank* is a measure of approximately four ounces. The rock outcropping, though a place of wonder, has been treated traditionally as an artifact of other times, or a curio, rather than a place of worship.

2. This parallels Indic ideas of personhood being open to and constituted by the transaction of substances (Marriott 1976).

3. For an intellectual history of Sir Syed Ahmad Khan see Baljon (1958).

4. The title for this section is a phrase borrowed from Bashiruddin Ahmad (1990, 3:29).

5. For mourning and laments related to the fouling of a small river in rural Rajasthan, see Gold and Gujar (2013).

6. For a radical new way of telling the history of the Delhi Sultanate and its urban settlements through precisely such interactions of ecology and technology, see Kumar n.d.

7. See also Gold and Gujar (2013).

8. From ASI, f3/2/D2/11/66 M, "Monuments at Kalkaji, Demolition of."

9. The full moon of Ashad usually corresponds to the end of June, or beginning of July, the beginning of the monsoon in Delhi.

10. The Navratras, the nine days before Dussehra, are one of the biggest festive occasions in Delhi now, especially connected to the worship of Durga and other related aspects of the Mother Goddess.

11. The evidence of Bashiruddin Ahmed is inconclusive because this is one of the times when he copies Syed Ahmad Khan wholesale, and before he speaks of the mela, he has already mentioned that he is citing Syed Ahmad Khan. Neither Zafar Hasan (1997) nor Carr Stephen (1876) mention any festivities related to the Bhuli Bhatiyari ka Mahal.

12. Evidence from *Hari Bhagwan Sharma and Others vs. Badri Bhagat Jhandewalan Temple Society*, Delhi High Court, Feb. 15, 1984, https://indiankanoon.org/doc/990056/.

13. I have no archival evidence for this assertion. But Zafar Hasan, Bashiruddin Ahmad, Syed Ahmad Khan et al. all mention that the Mahal was on the southern end of a very large dam, with Zafar Hasan (1997, 2:233–34) giving the figures of a dam wall five hundred feet long, twenty-two feet high, and seventeen feet broad. Now there is no evidence of such a wall, but immediately to the north of the Mahal, at the southern end of which it now stands, is the large Jhandewalan Reservoir.

14. For a succinct exploration of Nietzsche's thought and the problem of the past see Richardson (2008).

15. See CCO, f354/1915/Home, "Notification of the Kanjars as a Criminal Tribe."

16. The cats had largely vanished by 2014 as a result of extended repair work around the space they formerly inhabited.

17. See also Naveeda Khan (2014) for emergent forms of creaturely interconnectedness and the promise of ecological thought in contemporary Bangladesh.

18. This is my summary of an account given more fully in *Sahih Muslim*, book 26, hadith 5557.

19. A notable exception is David Haberman's (2006) work, which investigates how high levels of pollution affect religious practices connected to the Yamuna River.

20. The ritual is not new, but it is new to this space. David Pinault (2008) writes about similar rituals in Lahore, from where I borrow the phrase.

CHAPTER 7

1. I borrow the title for this section from *Nets of Awareness* (Pritchett 1994), which masterfully describes the end of the precolonial lifeworld of Delhi after 1857.

2. The first Mughal emperor of North India, Babur (r. 1526–30), chose to be buried in Kabul, Afghanistan.

3. For a reading of how Azad and his intellectual legacy were shaped by the events of 1857, see Diamond (2009).

4. Similar sentiments inform the historical writing emerging in Lahore in the second half of the nineteenth century. A new genre of urban history writing in that city transposed the invocation of chains of spiritual ancestors (*silsila*), central to traditions of Indo-Islamic historiographic writing, onto material artifacts and buildings (Glover 2008, 188).

5. For representative examples see CCO, f56/1926/Education, "Correspondence Relating to the Rangrez Mosque"; and CCO, f18/1916/Home, "Preservation of the Mosque and Baoli in Block 20 in the New Capital Area."

6. For the role of the Congress in making Partition legislatively possible, see Bose and Jalal (2004, 135–56). See also Chatterjee 2010a for colonialism and the transformation of elite Hindu histories.

7. Notification F. 4-12/51-A.2, Government of India, Ministry of Education, New Delhi, June 23, 1952.

8. For an excellent analysis of the Bhojshala-Kamal Maula controversy and the ASI's role in muddying the waters, see Bal 2012.

9. CCO, f1(13)/1929/Education, "Correspondence Relating to Mosque at Qudsia Gardens, Delhi."

10. ASI, f5/4/3/69-M.

11. ASI, f33/10/83-M.

12. Order of District Judge Jagdish Chandra in the case of Muntazima Committee Masjid Qudsia Bagh versus the Union of India and Others, June 30, 1983.

13. See, e.g., CCO, f15/1925/Education. In a note dated Oct. 9, 1925, the chief commissioner of Delhi Province informed the finance secretary, Government of India, that, "During the acquisition of land for the Imperial City, the Railway and Cantonments, it was thought desirable to acquire certain mosques in the area under acquisition. The amounts awarded for these mosques were not drawn by anyone as according to Muhammadan ideas mosques are not private property for which compensation can be accepted. As a consequence a sum of Rs. 29,612/8/8 was placed in deposit at various dates between April 1913 and March 1919 subject to the orders of the District Judge, Delhi." As

H. Ahmed (2014, 115–26) discusses, there is legal precedent for the postcolonial state to acquire Waqf properties by classifying Waqf as a "nonessential" part of the practice of Islam. But such acquisition would still not void Muslim customary rights to prayer in such a mosque.

14. "'Muslims' Memo to Jakhar," *Statesman* (Delhi), August 13, 1983.

15. "Mosque Gatecrash Averted," *Hindustan Times*, June 11, 1983, 1.

16. ASI, f34/43/83-M/ASI, "Lok Sabha—Calling Attention Notice in Regard to the Situation Arising Out of Refusal by the Archaeological Department to the Muslims for Offering Prayers in Mosques Under the Survey in Delhi and Other Parts of the Country."

17. "*Muslim neta dhara 144 todenge* [Muslim leaders will violate Sec. 144]," *Punjab Kesari*, Feb. 29, 1984.

18. "Prayers Allowed in 190 Mosques in Monuments," *Indian Express*, March 4, 1984, 7.

19. See "Plea to Govt. on Namaz in Protected Mosques," *Times of India*, Sept. 29, 1986; see also ASI, f34/43/83-M/ASI.

20. "Curfew in Walled City After Violence," *Hindustan Times*, Sept. 8, 1986.

21. See "Tension Prevails in Old City" and "Old Delhi Areas Still Tense," both in *Hindustan Times*, Sept. 9, 1986.

22. "Seeking to Pray in Protected Monuments," *Indian Express*, Sept. 10, 1986.

23. "To Remove or Not to Remove Shoes," *Times of India*, Sept. 11, 1986.

24. "Worship as Business," *Times of India*, Sept. 18, 1986.

25. For details on the Shah Bano judgment and subsequent politics see Pathak and Rajan (1989).

26. The decision to allow unrestricted access to Hindu worshippers was taken by the district judge of Faizabad on Feb. 2, 1986. However, the unprecedented speed with which the decision was taken, after a petition was filed on Jan. 31, and the special attention given the unlocking of the site by state-controlled television and radio, seems to indicate that high-level political calculations influenced the judgment. See H. Ahmed (2014, 219–31).

27. For the law cannot imagine its own demise.

28. See Taneja (2005, 2008) for examples of demolitions and clearances ordered by Jagmohan under the new ASI rules.

29. The BJP government, and Jagmohan, lost power in 2004.

30. In the case of *Archaeological Survey of India v. Narendra Anand* [FAO (OS) 414/2002], the Delhi High Court directed the court to "consider the provision of a mechanism where the prohibition is imposed or relaxed on a case by case basis." Ironically, the ASI filed a Special Leave Petition against this judgment in the Supreme Court in 2005 [SLP(C) no. 1603 and 1604 of 2005] and got a stay on the High Court's directions to review the rules. The Expert Advisory Committee and its permissions in the prohibited area, thanks to this stay, remained entirely outside the law.

31. *EMCA Construction versus Archaeological Survey of India and Others*. LPA 417/2009 in the Delhi High Court. The judgment was passed by Justice S. Muralidhar on Oct. 30, 2009.

32. "Experts: Makeover a Monumental Flaw," *Indian Express*, August 6, 2010.

33. ASI, f1/1/66-M/ASI (my emphasis).

34. This approach can be traced to the work of John Ruskin (1849).

35. For a less colorful and more scholarly exposition of Ratish's views see Nanda (2011).

36. On the anxious everyday coexistence of modern Delhi with its medieval past see Sunil Kumar's (2002) essay on the village of Saidalajab.

37. For succinct histories of the problematic transformations of land tenure in Delhi in the nineteenth and twentieth centuries see Siddiqui (2011) and Chakravarty-Kaul (2011).

CONCLUSION

1. I am grateful to my friend Nauman Naqvi for introducing me to this couplet, and to the entire "inheritance of loss" that it carries with it. For a more detailed discussion on Nasir Kazmi, Intizar Hussain and this particular couplet see Naqvi (2008).

2. I was referring to Benjamin's citation of Flaubert in the *Theses on the Philosophy of History* (Benjamin 1969b, 256).

3. The sentiment that I allude to is perhaps what Svetlana Boym (2001, 2007) characterizes as "reflective nostalgia," which she distinguishes from "restorative nostalgia." Reflective nostalgia, according to Boym, "reveals that longing and critical thinking are not opposed to one another, as affective memories do not absolve one from compassion, judgement, or critical reflection" (Boym 2007, 15).

4. See also Shahid Amin (2015, 98–107) on the transgressive potential of "cooking for a Turkic brother."

5. I deliberately eschew the use of the terms *Barelwi* and *Deobandi*, as these maslak identifiers are not used as terms of self-identity or definition by people at Firoz Shah Kotla.

6. See "New Archaeological Park in Heart of City," *Times of India*, July 3, 2015.

7. For the ways in which South Asian rulers modeled their cities and gardens on the garden of Paradise, see Inden (2012).

POSTCRIPT

1. "Cabinet okays amendment that allows construction within 100 meters of monuments," *Scroll.in*, May 17, 2017.

REFERENCES

ARCHIVAL RECORDS
ASI   Archaeological Survey of India Headquarters, Janpath, New Delhi
CCO   Chief Commissioner's Office Records, Delhi State Archives
DCO   Deputy Commissioner's Office Records, Delhi State Archives

PUBLICATIONS
Abu El-Haj, Nadia. 2001. *Facts on the Ground: Archaeological Practice and Territorial Self-Fashioning in Israeli Society*. Chicago: University of Chicago Press.

Agamben, Giorgio. 1998. *Homo Sacer: Sovereign Power and Bare Life*. Translated by Daniel Heller-Roazen. Stanford: Stanford University Press.

———. 2005. *The Time That Remains: A Commentary on the Letter to the Romans*. Translated by Patricia Dailey. Stanford: Stanford University Press.

Ahmad, Bashiruddin. [1919] 1990. *Waqi'at-i Darulhukumat Dihli*. Delhi: Urdu Academy.

Ahmed, Hilal. 2014. *Muslim Political Discourse in Post-Colonial India: Monuments, Memory, Contestation*. New Delhi: Routledge India.

Ahmed, Leila. 1992. *Women and Gender in Islam: Historical Roots of a Modern Debate*. New Haven, CT: Yale University Press.

Ahmed, Shahab. 2016. *What Is Islam? The Importance of Being Islamic*. Princeton, NJ: Princeton University Press.

Alam, Muzaffar. 2004. *The Languages of Political Islam: India, 1200–1800*. Chicago: University of Chicago Press.

Ali, Kecia. 2016. "On Critique and Careful Reading." *Journal of Feminist Studies in Religion* 32 (2): 121–26.

Ali, Nosheen. 2016. "From Hallaj to Heer: Poetic Knowledge and the Muslim Tradition." *Journal of Narrative Politics* 3 (1): 2–26.

Al-Mohammad, Hayder. 2010. "Towards an Ethics of *Being-With*: Intertwinements of Life in Post-Invasion Basra." *Ethnos* 75 (4): 425–46.

Al-Mohammad, Hayder, and Daniela Peluso. 2012. "Ethics and the 'Rough Ground' of the Everyday: The Overlappings of Life in Postinvasion Iraq." *HAU: Journal of Ethnographic Theory* 2 (2): 42–58.

Amin, Shahid. 2001. "Past Remains." In *The Human Landscape*, edited by Geeti Sen and Ashis Bannerjee, 235–41. Hyderabad: Orient Longman.

———. 2004. "On Representing the Musalman." In *Sarai Reader 04: Crisis/Media*, 92–97. Delhi: Sarai/CSDS.

———. 2005. "Un Saint Guerrier: Sur la conquête de l'Inde du Nord par les Turcs au XIe siècle." *Annales* 60 (2): 265–92.

———. 2015. *Conquest and Community: The Afterlife of Warrior Saint Ghazi Miyan*. New Delhi: Orient Blackswan.

Ammar, Nawal H. 2001. "Islam and Deep Ecology." In *Deep Ecology and World Religions: New Essays on Sacred Ground*, edited by David Landis Barnhill and Roger S. Gottlieb, 193–211. Albany: State University of New York Press.

Argali, Faruq, ed. 2006. *Rekhti: Urdu ke namvar rekhti go sha'iron ke kalam ka mukammal majmu'ah*. Delhi: Farid Book Depot.

Asad, Talal. 1986. "The Idea of an Anthropology of Islam." Occasional Paper Series: Center for Contemporary Arab Studies, Georgetown University.

———. 1993. *Genealogies of Religion: Discipline and Reasons of Power in Christianity and Islam*. Baltimore: Johns Hopkins University Press.

Ashour, Mustafa. 1986. *The Jinn in the Qur'an and the Sunna*. London: Dar Al-Taqwa.

Asif, Manan Ahmed. 2013. "Future's Past." In *South Asia 2060: Envisioning Regional Futures*, edited by Adil Najam and Moeed Yusuf, 46–52. London: Anthem.

Assmann, Jan. 2006. *Religion and Cultural Memory*. Translated by Rodney Livingstone. Stanford: Stanford University Press.

Azad, Abul Kalam. [1910] 1991. "Sarmad Shaheed." In *Rubaiyat Sarmad*, translated by Syeda Saiyadain Hameed, 18–41. New Delhi: Indian Council for Cultural Relations.

Azad, Muhammad Hussain. [1864] 1978. "Dehli." In *Maqalat Maulana Muhammad Husain Azad*. Vol. 2, 221–29. Lahore: Majlis Taraqqi-e Adab.

Bal, Hartosh Singh. 2012. "Setting the Bhojshala Record Straight." *Caravan*, June 1. www .caravanmagazine.in/perspectives/setting-bhojshala-record-straight.

Baljon, J. M. S. 1958. *The Reforms and Religious Ideas of Sir Syed Ahmad Khan*. Lahore: Orientalia.

Barlas, Asma. 2002. *"Believing Women" in Islam: Unreading Patriarchal Interpretations of the Qur'an*. Austin: University Of Texas Press.

Behl, Aditya. 2012. *The Magic Doe: Qutban Suhravardi's Mirigavati: A New Translation*. New York: Oxford University Press.

Bellamy, Carla. 2011. *The Powerful Ephemeral: Everyday Healing in an Ambiguously Islamic Place*. Berkeley: University of California Press.

Benjamin, Walter. 1969a. "The Task of the Translator." In *Illuminations*, translated by Harry Zohn, 69–82. New York: Schocken.

———. 1969b. "Theses on the Philosophy of History." In *Illuminations*, translated by Harry Zohn, 253–64. New York: Schocken.

———. 1986a. "Critique of Violence." In *Reflections: Essays, Aphorisms, Autobiographical Writing*, edited by Peter Demetz, 277–300. New York: Schocken.

———. 1986b. "Surrealism: The Last Snapshot of the European Intelligentsia." In *Reflections: Essays, Aphorisms, Autobiographical Writing*, edited by Peter Demetz, 177–92. New York: Schocken.

———. 1999. *The Arcades Project*. Translated by Howard Eiland and Kevin McLaughlin. Cambridge, MA: Harvard University Press.

Bennett, Jane. 2010. *Vibrant Matter: A Political Ecology of Things*. Durham, NC: Duke University Press.

Bhaskar, Ira, and Richard Allen. 2009. *Islamicate Cultures of Bombay Cinema*. New Delhi: Tulika.

Bhaumik, Kaushik. 2001. "The Emergence of the Bombay Film Industry, 1913–1936." PhD thesis, University of Oxford.

———. n.d. "The Islamicate Miraculous in Bombay Cinema." Unpublished paper.

Bilgrami, Akeel. 2006. "Occidentalism, the Very Idea: An Essay on Enlightenment and Enchantment." *Critical Inquiry* 32 (3): 381–411.

———. 2014. *Secularism, Identity, and Enchantment*. Cambridge, MA: Harvard University Press.

Birchok, Daniel. 2016. "Women, Genealogical Inheritance and Sufi Authority: The Female Saints of Seunagan, Indonesia." *Asian Studies Review* 40 (4): 583–99.

Birla, Ritu. 2009. *Stages of Capital: Law, Culture, and Market Governance in Late Colonial India*. Durham, NC: Duke University Press.

Boddy, Janice. 1989. *Wombs and Alien Spirits: Women, Men and the Zar Cult in Northern Sudan*. Madison: University of Wisconsin Press.

Bonilla, Eduardo Seda. 1969. "Spiritualism, Psychoanalysis, and Psychodrama." *American Anthropologist* 71 (3): 493–97.

Bose, Sugata, and Ayesha Jalal. 2004. *Modern South Asia: History, Culture, Political Economy*. New York: Routledge.

Boym, Svetlana. 2001. *The Future of Nostalgia*. New York: Basic Books.

———. 2007. "Nostalgia and Its Discontents." *Hedgehog Review* 9 (2): 7–18.

Brennan, Teresa. 2004. *The Transmission of Affect*. Ithaca, NY: Cornell University Press.

Butler, Judith. 2004. *Precarious Life: The Powers of Mourning and Violence*. London: Verso.

Carsten, Janet, ed. 2000. *Cultures of Relatedness: New Approaches to the Study of Kinship*. Cambridge: Cambridge University Press.

Chakrabarty, Dipesh. 2000. *Provincializing Europe: Postcolonial Thought and Historical Difference*. Princeton, NJ: Princeton University Press.

Chakravarty-Kaul, Minoti. 2011. "Village Communities and Common Lands: The Rural Foundations of New Delhi." *Indian Archives* 1:67–81.

Chatterjee, Partha. 2004. *The Politics of the Governed: Popular Politics in Most of the World*. New York: Columbia University Press.

———. 2010a. "History and the Nationalization of Hinduism." In *Empire and Nation: Selected Essays*, 59–90. New York: Columbia University Press.

———. 2010b. "The Nationalist Resolution of the Women's Question." In *Empire and Nation: Selected Essays*, 116–35. New York: Columbia University Press.

———. 2010c. "Secularism and Toleration." In *Empire and Nation: Selected Essays*, 203–35. New York: Columbia University Press.

———. 2012. *The Black Hole of Empire: History of a Global Practice of Power*. Princeton, NJ: Princeton University Press.

Chishti, Mufti Shabbir Husain. n.d. *Jinnat ke Purasrar Haalaat*. Delhi: Astana Book Depot.

Cohn, Bernard. 1987. *An Anthropologist Among the Historians and Other Essays.* Delhi: Oxford University Press.

Copeman, Jacob, and Veena Das. 2015. "On Names in South Asia: Iteration, (Im)propriety, Dissimulation." Special issue, *South Asia Multidisciplinary Academic Journal* 12: http://samaj.revues.org/3985.

Crapanzano, Vincent. 1981. *The Hamadsha: A Study in Moroccan Ethnopsychiatry.* Berkeley: University of California Press.

Dalrymple, William. 1993. *City of Djinns: A Year in Delhi.* Delhi: HarperCollins.

———. 2006. *The Last Mughal: The Fall of a Dynasty, Delhi, 1857.* London: Bloomsbury.

Dara Shikoh. 2006. *Commingling of Two Oceans: Majma-'Ul-Bahrain, a Discourse on Inter-religious Understanding.* Translated by M. Mahfuz-ul-Haq. Gurgaon: Hope Publications.

Dargah Quli Khan. 1993. *Muraqqa-i Dehli: Farsi matan aur Urdu tarjamah.* Translated by Khaliq Anjum. Delhi: Anjuman-i Taraqqi-i Urdu.

Darling, Linda. 2002. "'Do Justice, Do Justice, for That Is Paradise': Middle Eastern Advice for Indian Rulers." *Comparative Studies of South Asia, Africa and the Middle East* 22 (1–2): 3–19.

Das, Veena. 1995. *Critical Events: An Anthropological Perspective on Contemporary India.* Delhi: Oxford University Press.

———. 2007. *Life and Words: Violence and the Descent into the Ordinary.* Berkeley: University of California Press.

———. 2010. "Engaging the Life of the Other: Love and Everyday Life." In *Ordinary Ethics: Anthropology, Language, and Action,* edited by Michael Lambek, 376–99. New York: Fordham University Press.

———. 2013a. "Being Together with Animals: Death, Violence, and Non-cruelty in Hindu Imagination." In *Living Beings: Perspectives on Inter-species Engagement,* edited by Penelope Dransart, 17–31. London: Bloomsbury.

———. 2013b. "Cohabiting an Inter-religious Milieu: Reflections on Religious Diversity." In *A Companion to the Anthropology of Religion,* edited by Janice Boddy and Michael Lambek. Hoboken: Wiley-Blackwell.

———. 2015. *Affliction: Health, Disease, Poverty.* New York: Fordham University Press.

Das, Veena, and Deborah Poole, eds. 2004. *Anthropology in the Margins of the State.* Santa Fe, NM: School of American Research Press.

Dasgupta, Rana. 2014. *Capital: A Portrait of Twenty-First Century Delhi.* Edinburgh: Canongate.

Deleuze, Gilles. 1989. *Cinema 2: The Time-Image.* Translated by Hugh Tomlinson and Robert Galeta. Minneapolis: University of Minnesota Press.

Delhi Guide Map: Surveyed 1939–1942. 1945. Dehra Dun: Survey of India.

"Delhi Population Census Data 2011." www.census2011.co.in/census/state/delhi.html.

de Man, Paul. 1985. "'Conclusions' Walter Benjamin's 'The Task of the Translator' Messenger Lecture, Cornell University, March 4, 1983." *Yale French Studies* 69:25–46.

Devji, Faisal. 1993. "Muslim Nationalism: Founding Identity in Colonial India." PhD diss., University of Chicago.

————. 2009. "Illiberal Islam." In *Enchantments of Modernity: Empire, Nation, Globalization*, edited by Saurabh Dube, 234–63. Delhi: Routledge.

de Vries, Hent, and Lawrence Sullivan. 2006. *Political Theologies: Public Religions in a Post-Secular World*. New York: Fordham University Press.

Diamond, Jeffrey. 2009. "Narratives of Reform and Displacement in Colonial Lahore: The *Intikaal* of Muhammad Hussain Azad." *Journal of Punjab Studies* 16 (2): 159–77.

Douglas, Mary. *Collected Works*. Vol. 2, *Purity and Danger: An Analysis of Concepts of Pollution and Taboo*. 1966. New York: Routledge, 2003.

Dreyfus, Hubert, and Sean Kelly. 2011. *All Things Shining: Reading the Western Classics to Find Meaning in a Secular Age*. New York: Free Press.

Dumont, Louis. 1970. *Homo Hierarchicus: The Caste System and Its Implications*. Chicago: University of Chicago Press.

Durkheim, Emile. 1995. *The Elementary Forms of Religious Life*. Translated by Karen Fields. New York: Free Press.

Dwyer, Rachel. 2006. *Filming the Gods: Religion and Indian Cinema*. Oxford: Routledge.

Eaton, Richard M. 2003. "The Political and Religious Authority of the Shrine of Baba Farid." In *India's Islamic Traditions, 711–1750*, edited by Richard M. Eaton, 234–62. Delhi: Oxford University Press.

Eck, Diana L. 2012. *India: A Sacred Geography*. New York: Three Rivers Press.

Erndl, Kathleen. 1996. "Seranvali: The Mother Who Possesses." In *Devi: Goddesses of India*, edited by John Stratton Hawley and Donna Marie Wulff, 173–94. Berkeley: University of California Press.

Ernst, Carl. 1992. *Eternal Garden: Mysticism, History and Politics at a South Asian Sufi Center*. Albany: State University of New York Press.

————. 2003. "Muslim Studies of Hinduism? A Reconsideration of Arabic and Persian Translations from Indian Languages." *Iranian Studies* 36 (2): 173–95.

Ewing, Katherine. 1997. *Arguing Sainthood: Modernity, Psychoanalysis, and Islam*. Durham, NC: Duke University Press.

Fadil, Nadia, and Mayanthi Fernando. 2015. "Rediscovering the 'Everyday' Muslim: Notes on an Anthropological Divide." *HAU: Journal of Ethnographic Theory* 5 (2): 59–88.

Faruqi, Shamsur Rahman. 2006. "From Antiquary to Social Revolutionary: Syed Ahmad Khan and the Colonial Experience." www.columbia.edu/itc/mealac/pritchett/00fwp/srf/srf_sirsayyid.pdf.

Flatt, Emma. 2016. "Spices, Smells and Spells: The Use of Olfactory Substances in the Conjuring of Spirits." *South Asian Studies* 32 (1): 1–19.

Flood, Finbarr B. 2003. "Pillars, Palimpsests and Princely Practices: Translating the Past in Sultanate Delhi." *Res* 43:95–116.

————. 2009. *Objects of Translation: Material Culture and Medieval "Hindu-Muslim" Encounter*. Princeton, NJ: Princeton University Press.

Flueckiger, Joyce Burkhalter. 2006. *In Amma's Healing Room: Gender and Vernacular Islam in South India*. Bloomington: Indiana University Press.

Foucault, Michel. 1977. "Nietzsche, Genealogy, History." In *Language, Counter-Memory,*

Practice: Selected Essays and Interviews, edited by D. F. Bouchard, 139–64. Ithaca, NY: Cornell University Press.

———. 2007. *Security, Territory, Population: Lectures at the College de France, 1977–78.* New York: Picador.

Ganeri, Jonardon. 2011. *The Lost Age of Reason: Philosophy in Early Modern India, 1450–1700.* New York: Oxford University Press.

Gaur, Sushila. 1992. "Jhandewalan ke 'Vaishno Mandir' men Akbar aya tha." *Hindustan*, Sept. 7.

Gayer, Laurent, and Christophe Jaffrelot. 2012. "Introduction: Muslims of the Indian City. From Centrality to Marginality." In *Muslims in Indian Cities: Trajectories of Marginalization*, edited by Laurent Gayer and Christophe Jaffrelot, 1–22. Noida: HarperCollins India.

Ghalib, Mirza Asadullah Khan. *A Desertful of Roses: The Urdu Ghazals of Mirza Asadullah Khan "Ghalib."* Translated and compiled by Frances Pritchett. www.columbia.edu/itc/mealac/pritchett/00ghalib/index.html#index.

Ghufran, Iram, dir. 2011. *There Is Something in the Air*. DVD. New Delhi: Public Service Broadcasting Trust.

Ginzburg, Carlo. 1980. "Morelli, Freud and Sherlock Holmes: Clues and Scientific Method." *History Workshop* 9:5–36.

Glover, William. 2008. *Making Lahore Modern: Constructing and Imagining a Colonial City.* Minneapolis: University of Minnesota Press.

Gold, Ann Grodzins, and Bhoju Ram Gujar. 2013. "A Thousand Nagdis." *Anthropology Today* 29 (5): 22–27.

Goodman, Lenn E. 2009. Introduction to *Epistles of the Brethren of Purity 22: The Case of the Animals Versus Man Before the King of the Jinn*, edited and translated by Lenn E. Goodman and Richard McGregor, 1–56. Oxford: Oxford University Press.

Green, Nile. 2012. *Making Space: Sufis and Settlers in Early Modern India.* Delhi: Oxford University Press.

Growse, F. S., trans. 1887. *The Ramayana of Tulsidas.* Allahabad: North-Western Provinces and Oudh Government Press.

Guha, Ranajit. 1996. "The Small Voice of History." In *Subaltern Studies*, no. 9, edited by Shahid Amin and Dipesh Chakrabarty, 1–12. Delhi: Oxford University Press.

Guha-Thakurta, Tapati. 2004. *Monuments, Objects, Histories: Institutions of Art in Colonial and Post-Colonial India.* New York: Columbia University Press.

———. 2010. "The Many Lives of the Sanchi Stupa in Colonial India." In *The Marshall Albums: Photography and Archaeology*, edited by Sudeshna Guha, 94–135. Delhi: Alkazi Collection of Photography.

Gupta, Akhil. 2012. *Red Tape: Bureaucracy, Structural Violence and Poverty in India.* Durham, NC: Duke University Press.

Haberman, David. 2006. *River of Love in the Age of Pollution: The Yamuna River of Northern India.* Berkeley: University of California Press.

Hali, Khwajah Altaf Husain. 1986. *Voices of Silence: English Translation of Hali's Majalis un-Nissa and Chup Ki Dad*. Translated by Gail Minault. Delhi: Chanakya Publications. www.columbia.edu/itc/mealac/pritchett/00urdu/hali/majalis/03majlis.html?.

Hamilakis, Yannis. 2007. *The Nation and Its Ruins: Antiquity, Archaeology, and National Imagination in Greece*. New York: Oxford University Press.

Hanna, Owen. 2016. "Enchantment and the Uncanny: A Comparative Disambiguation." Unpublished paper, Vanderbilt University.

Hannsen, Beatrice. 1998. *Walter Benjamin's Other History: Of Stones, Animals, Human Beings, and Angels*. Berkeley: University of California Press.

Haraway, Donna. 2016. *Staying with the Trouble: Making Kin in the Cthulucene*. Durham, NC: Duke University Press.

Hasan, Mushirul. 1998. "Aligarh's '*Notre Eminent Contemporain*': Assessing Syed Ahmad Khan's Reformist Agenda." *Economic and Political Weekly* 33 (19): 1077–81.

Hasan, Zafar. [1916–22] 1997. *Monuments of Delhi: Lasting Splendor of the Great Mughals and Others*. Delhi: Aryan Books.

Hashmi, Sohail. 2009. "A Tale of Two Mosques." *Kafila*, August 10. http://kafila.org/2009/08/20/a-tale-of-two-mosques/ (site discontinued).

Hirschkind, Charles. 2006. *The Ethical Soundscape: Cassette Sermons and Islamic Counterpublics*. New York: Columbia University Press.

Ho, Engseng. 2006. *The Graves of Tarim: Genealogy and Mobility Across the Indian Ocean*. Berkeley: University of California Press.

Hodgson, Marshall. 1974. *The Venture of Islam: Conscience and History in a World Civilization*. 3 vols. Chicago: University of Chicago Press.

Hull, Matthew. 2012. *Government of Paper: The Materiality of Bureaucracy in Urban Pakistan*. Berkeley: University of California Press.

Humes, Cynthia Ann. 1996. "Vindhyavasini: Local Goddess yet Great Goddess." In *Devi: Goddesses of India*, edited by John Stratton Hawley and Donna Marie Wulff, 49–76. Berkeley: University of California Press.

Husain, Ali Akbar. 2000. *Scent in the Islamic Garden: A Study of Deccani Urdu Literary Sources*. Karachi: Oxford University Press.

Hussain, Intizar. 2003. *Dilli tha jiska nam*. Lahore: Sang-i Meel.

Ibn Batuta. 1976. *The Rehla of Ibn Batuta: India, Maldive Islands and Ceylon*. Translated by Mehdi Hasan. Baroda: Oriental Institute.

Ibn Kathir. 1998. *The Life of the Prophet Muhammad: A Translation of al-Sira al-Nabawiyya*. Translated by Trevor le Gassick. Reading, UK: Garnet.

Ikhwan al-Safa. 2009. *The Case of the Animals Versus Man Before the King of the Jinn*. Translated by Lenn E. Goodman and Richard McGregor. Oxford: Oxford University Press.

Inden, Ronald. 2012. "Paradise on Earth: The Deccan Sultanates." In *Garden and Landscape Practices in Pre-colonial India: Histories from the Deccan*, edited by Daud Ali and Emma J. Flatt, 74–97. New Delhi: Routledge.

Jaffur Shurreef. 1832. *Qanoon-E-Islam: Or the Customs of the Moosulmans of India*. Translated by G. A. Herklots. London: Parbury, Allen.

Josephson, Jason Ananda. 2012. *The Invention of Religion in Japan*. Chicago: University of Chicago Press.

Kaicker, Abhishek. 2014. "Unquiet City: Making and Unmaking Politics in Mughal Delhi, 1707–1739." PhD diss., Columbia University.

Kakar, Sudhir. 1982. *Shamans, Mystics and Doctors: A Psychological Inquiry into India and Its Healing Traditions*. New York: Knopf.

———. 2009. *Mad and Divine: Spirit and Psyche in the Modern World*. Delhi: Penguin.

Kaur, Naunidhi. 2003. "Building Hatred Around Bhojshala." *Frontline*, April 26–May 9. www.frontline.in/static/html/fl2009/stories/20030509003103700.htm.

Kavuri-Bauer, Santhi. 2011. *Monumental Matters: The Power, Subjectivity and Space of India's Mughal Architecture*. Durham, NC: Duke University Press.

Kesavan, Mukul. 1994. "Urdu, Awadh, and the Tawaif: The Islamicate Roots of Hindi Cinema," in *Forging Identities: Gender, Communities, and the State*, edited by Zoya Hasan, 244–57. Delhi: Kali for Women.

Khan, Naveeda. 2006. "Of Children and Jinn: An Inquiry into an Unexpected Friendship During Uncertain Times." *Cultural Anthropology* 21 (6): 234–64.

———. 2012. *Muslim Becoming: Aspiration and Skepticism in Pakistan*. Durham, NC: Duke University Press.

———. 2014. "Dogs and Humans and What Earth Can Be: Filaments of Muslim Ecological Thought." *HAU: Journal of Ethnographic Theory* 4 (3): 245–64.

Khan, Syed Ahmad. [1847] 2007. *Asar al-Sanadid*. Aligarh: Sir Syed Academy, Aligarh Muslim University.

Kinra, Rajeev. 2009. "Infantilizing Baba Dara: The Cultural Memory of Dara Shekuh and the Mughal Public Sphere." *Journal of Persianate Studies* 2:165–93.

Koselleck, Reinhart. 2002. *The Practice of Conceptual History: Timing History, Spacing Concepts*. Translated by Todd Samuel Presner et al. Stanford: Stanford University Press.

———. 2004. *Futures Past: On the Semantics of Historical Time*. Translated by Keith Tribe. New York: Columbia University Press.

Koshul, Basit Bilal. n.d. "Varieties of the Muslim Response." http://serveislam.com/media/qa//QA_Publications/ariticles/English/BasitBilal/VarietiesMuslimResponseI.pdf.

Krishen, Pradip. 2006. *Trees of Delhi: A Field Guide*. Delhi: Dorling Kindersley.

Kugle, Scott. 2001. "Framed, Blamed, and Renamed: The Reshaping of Islamic Law in Colonial South Asia." *Modern Asian Studies* 35 (2): 257–313.

———. 2007. *Sufis and Saints' Bodies: Mysticism, Corporeality and Sacred Power in Islam*. Chapel Hill: University of North Carolina Press.

Kumar, Sunil. 2002. *The Present in Delhi's Pasts*. Delhi: Three Essays Press.

———. 2010. "The Pir's *Barakat* and the Servitor's Ardor: The Contrasting History of Two Sufi Shrines in Delhi." In *Celebrating Delhi*, edited by Mala Dayal, 47–75. Delhi: Penguin.

———. Forthcoming. "'[And] He Proceeded into the *Mawas*': Reconsidering the Inhospitable Environs of Sultanate Settlements, ca 13th–14th Centuries." *NMML Occasional Papers*. Delhi: Nehru Memorial Museum and Library.

Lahiri, Nayanjot. 2003. "Commemorating and Remembering 1857: The Revolt in Delhi and Its Afterlife." *World Archaeology* 35 (1): 35–60.

————. 2012. "Partitioning the Past: India's Archaeological Heritage After Independence." In *Appropriating the Past: Philosophical Perspectives on the Practice of Archaeology*, edited by Geoffrey Scarre and Robin Coningham, 295–312. Cambridge: Cambridge University Press.

Laidlaw, James. 2002. "For an Anthropology of Ethics and Freedom." *Journal of the Royal Anthropological Institute* 8 (2): 311–32.

————. 2013. *The Subject of Virtue: An Anthropology of Ethics and Freedom*. Cambridge: Cambridge University Press.

Lamb, Sarah. 1997. "The Making and Unmaking of Persons: Notes on Aging and Gender in North India." *Ethos* 25 (3): 279–302.

Lambek, Michael. 2002. *The Weight of the Past: Living with History in Mahajanga, Madagascar*. New York: Palgrave Macmillan.

————. 2003. "Rheumatic Irony: Questions of Agency and Self-Deception as Refracted Through the Art of Living with Spirits." *Social Analysis* 47 (2): 40–59.

————, ed. 2010. *Ordinary Ethics: Anthropology, Language, and Action*. New York: Fordham University Press.

————. 2015. "Living as If It Mattered." In *Four Lectures on Ethics: Anthropological Perspectives*, 5–51. Chicago: HAU.

————. 2016. "On Being Present to History: Historicity and Brigand Spirits in Madagascar." *HAU: Journal of Ethnographic Theory* 6 (1): 317–41.

Lawrence, Bruce. 1986. "The Earliest Chishtiya and Shaikh Nizamuddin Auliya (d. 1325)." In *Delhi Through the Ages: Selected Essays in Urban History, Culture and Society*, edited by Robert Frykenberg, 32–56. Delhi: Oxford University Press.

————, trans. 1992. *Morals for the Heart: Conversations of Shaykh Nizam ad-Din Awliya Recorded by Amir Hasan Sijzi*. Mahwah, NJ: Paulist Press.

Lee, Joel. 2014. "Lal Beg Underground: The Passing of an 'Untouchable' God." In *Objects of Worship in South Asian Religion: Forms, Practices and Meanings*, edited by Knut A. Jacobsen, Mikael Aktor, and Kristina Myrvold, 143–62. New York: Routledge.

————. 2015. "Jagdish, Son of Ahmad: Dalit Religion and Nominative Politics in Lucknow." In "Contemporary Lucknow: Life with 'Too Much History,'" edited by Raphael Susewind and Christopher B. Taylor, special issue, *South Asia Multidisciplinary Academic Journal* 11: https://samaj.revues.org/3919.

Liebeskind, Claudia. 1998. *Piety on Its Knees: Three Sufi Traditions in South Asia in Modern Times*. Delhi: Oxford University Press.

Mahmood, Saba. 2005. *Politics of Piety: The Islamic Revival and the Feminist Subject*. Princeton, NJ: Princeton University Press.

Majoka, Zara Khadeeja. 2016. "Inside Lahore's Royal Quarters." *Herald* (Karachi), July 2015. http://herald.dawn.com/news/1153419.

Majumdar, Rochona. 2009. *Marriage and Modernity: Family Values in Colonial Bengal*. Durham, NC: Duke University Press.

Malik, Aditya. 2016. *Tales of Justice and Rituals of Divine Embodiment: Oral Narratives from the Central Himalayas*. New York: Oxford University Press.

Marriott, McKim. 1976. "Interpreting Indian Society: A Monistic Alternative to Dumont's Dualism." *Journal of Asian Studies* 36 (1): 189–95.

Mattingly, Cheryl. 2012. "Two Virtue Ethics and the Anthropology of Morality." *Anthropological Theory* 12 (2): 161–84.

McGregor, Richard. 2015. "Religions and the Religion of Animals: Ethics, Self, and Language in Tenth Century Iraq." *Comparative Studies of South Asia, Africa and the Middle East* 35 (2): 222–31.

McKean, Lise. 1996. "Bharat Mata: Mother India and Her Militant Matriots." In *Devi: Goddesses of India*, edited by John Stratton Hawley and Donna Marie Wulff, 250–80. Berkeley: University of California Press.

Menon, Nivedita, and Aditya Nigam. 2007. *Power and Contestation: India Since 1989*. London: Zed.

Merleau-Ponty, Maurice. 2002. *Phenomenology of Perception*. London: Routledge.

Mernissi, Fatima. 1991. *The Veil and the Male Elite: A Feminist Interpretation of Women's Rights in Islam*. Translated by Mary Jo Lakeland. New York: Basic Books.

Messick, Brinkley. 1993. *The Calligraphic State: Textual Domination and History in a Muslim Society*. Berkeley: University of California Press.

Metcalf, Barbara, trans. 1992. *Perfecting Women: Maulana Ashraf Ali Thanawi's Bihishti Zewar*. Berkeley: University of California Press.

Mir, Farina. 2010. *The Social Space of Language: Vernacular Culture in British Colonial Punjab*. Berkeley: University of California Press.

Mirza Sangin Beg. 1982. *Sair al-Manazil*. Edited by Sharif Husain Qasimi. Delhi: Ghalib Institute.

Mishra, Ramprasad. 1982. *Dilli, kal aur aaj*. Delhi: Itihas Shodh Sansthan.

Mitchell, Timothy. 1989. "The World as Exhibition." *Comparative Studies in Society and History* 31 (2): 217–36.

Mittermaier, Amira. 2011. *Dreams That Matter: Egyptian Landscapes of the Imagination*. Berkeley: University of California Press.

———. 2012. "Dreams from Elsewhere: Muslim Subjectivities Beyond the Trope of Self-Cultivation." *Journal of the Royal Anthropological Institute* 18 (2): 247–65.

———. 2014. "Bread, Freedom, Social Justice: The Egyptian Uprising and a Sufi Khidma." *Cultural Anthropology* 29 (1): 54–79.

Mody, Perveez. 2002. "Love and the Law: Love Marriage in Delhi." *Modern Asian Studies* 36 (1): 223–56.

———. 2008. *The Intimate State: Love Marriage and the Law in Delhi*. New Delhi: Routledge.

Moin, Azfar. 2012. *The Millennial Sovereign: Sacred Kingship and Sainthood in Islam*. New York: Columbia University Press.

Moosvi, Shireen. 2017. "The Culture Ministry talks not of cultural heritage but of roadways, railway tracks, and private landed interests." *Hindu*, July 21.

Morton, Timothy. 2013. *Hyperobjects: Philosophy and Ecology After the End of the World*. Minneapolis: University of Minnesota Press.

Mufti, Aamir. 2007. *Enlightenment in the Colony*. Princeton, NJ: Princeton University Press.

Naim, C. M. 2013. "The Maulana Who Loved Krishna." *Economic and Political Weekly* 48 (17): 37–44.

Nair, Shankar. 2014. "Sufism as Medium and Method of Translation: Mughal Translations of Hindu Texts Reconsidered." *Studies in Religion* 43 (3): 390–410.

Nanda, Ratish. 2011. "The Archive Based Conservation of Humayun's Tomb." *Indian Archives* 1:1–10.

Nanda, Ratish, Narayani Gupta, and O. P. Jain. 1999. *Delhi, the Built Heritage: A Listing.* Delhi: INTACH.

Nandy, Ashis. 1995. "History's Forgotten Doubles." *History and Theory* 34 (2): 44–66.

Naqvi, Nauman. 2008. "Nostalgia as Critique: Historical Exile and the Fate of Myth and Nation in Intizar Husain." Paper presented at the Fellows' Seminar, Cogut Center for the Humanities, Brown University, Providence, Sept. 23.

Naqvi, S. A. A. 1947. "Sultan Ghari, Delhi." *Ancient India: Bulletin of the Archaeological Survey of India* 3:4–10.

Nasr, Seyyed Hossein. 1996. *Religion and the Order of Nature: The 1994 Cadbury Lectures at the University of Birmingham.* New York: Oxford University Press.

"Natal Friend of the Jinns." 2013. *Ubqari Magazine*, March. www.ubqari.org/article/details/3576?Lang=en.

Nietzsche, Friedrich. 1980. *On the Advantage and Disadvantage of History for Life.* Translated by Peter Preuss. Indianapolis, IN: Hackett.

———. 1989. *On the Genealogy of Morals.* Translated by Walter Kaufman and R. J. Hollingdale. New York: Vintage.

Nizam al-Mulk. 1960. *The Book of Government or Rules for Kings: The Siyar al Muluk or Siyasat-Nama of Nizam al-Mulk.* Translated by Hubert Darke. London: Routledge and Kegan Paul.

Nizami, Khaliq Ahmed. 1992. Introduction to *Morals for the Heart: Conversations of Shaykh Nizam ad-Din Awliya Recorded by Amir Hasan Sijzi*, translated by Bruce Lawrence, 3–60. Mahwah, NJ: Paulist Press.

Page, J. A. 1937. "A Memoir on Kotla Firoz Shah, Delhi, with a Translation of *Sirat-I Firozshahi* by Muhammad Hamid Kuraishi." *Memoirs of the Archaeological Survey of India* 52. Delhi: Manager of Publications.

Palmie, Stephan, and Charles Stewart. 2016. "Introduction: For an Anthropology of History." *HAU: Journal of Ethnographic Theory* 6 (1): 207–36.

Pandey, Gyanendra. 1990. *The Construction of Communalism in Colonial North India.* Delhi: Oxford University Press.

———. 1994. "Modes of History Writing: New Hindu History of Ayodhya." *Economic and Political Weekly* 29 (25): 1523–28.

———. 1997. "Partition and Independence in Delhi: 1947–48." *Economic and Political Weekly* 32 (36): 2261–72.

Pandolfo, Stefania. 2009. "'Soul Choking': Maladies of the Soul, Islam, and the Ethics of Psychoanalysis." *Umbr(a)* 72:71–104.

Pathak, Zakia, and Rajeshwari Sunder Rajan. 1989. "Shahbano." *Signs* 14 (3): 558–82.

Pietz, William. 1987. "The Problem of the Fetish II: The Origin of the Fetish." *RES: Anthropology and Aesthetics* 13 (Spring): 23–45.

Piliavsky, Anastasia, and Tommaso Sbriccoli. 2016. "The Ethics of Efficacy in North India's Goonda Raj (Rule of Toughs)." *Journal of the Royal Anthropological Institute* 22 (2): 373–91.

Pinault, David. 2008. *Notes from the Fortune-Telling Parrot: Islam and the Struggle for Religious Pluralism in Pakistan*. London: Equinox.

Pinto, Sarah. 2014. *Daughters of Parvati: Women and Madness in Contemporary India*. Philadelphia: University of Pennsylvania Press.

Platts, John T. [1884] 2000. *Dictionary of Urdu, Classical Hindi, and English*. Delhi: Munshiram Manoharlal.

Prabhu, Jaideep. 2014. "Why Historians Feel the Destruction of 1.5 Lakh Government Files Is Akin to the Taliban Destruction of the Bamiyan Buddha Statues." *Daily News and Analysis*, Friday, June 27. www.dnaindia.com/analysis/standpoint-why-historians-feel-the-destruction-of-15-lakh-government-files-is-akin-to-the-taliban-destruction-of-the-bamiyan-buddha-statues-1998173.

Prasad, Bhagwati. 2011. *The Water Cookbook*. Delhi: Sarai-CSDS.

Prashad, Vijay. 2000. *Untouchable Freedom: A Social History of a Dalit Community*. New York: Oxford University Press.

Prime Minister's High Level Committee. 2006. *Social, Economic and Educational Status of the Muslim Community of India: A Report*. Nov. http://mhrd.gov.in/sites/upload_files/mhrd/files/sachar_comm.pdf.

Pritchett, Frances. 1994. *Nets of Awareness: Urdu Poetry and Its Critics*. Berkeley: University of California Press.

Purohit, Teena. 2012. *The Aga Khan Case: Religion and Identity in Colonial India*. Cambridge, MA: Harvard University Press.

Qasimi, Ata-ur-Rahman. 2001. *Dilli ki tarikhi masajid*. Delhi: Maulana Azad Academy.

Rahmaan, YaSiin. 2016. "Feminist Edges of Muslim Feminist Readings of Qur'anic Verses." *Journal of Feminist Studies in Religion* 32 (2): 142–48.

Rajagopalan, Mrinalini. 2016. *Building Histories: The Archival and Affective Lives of Five Monuments in Modern Delhi*. Chicago: University of Chicago Press.

Ramberg, Lucinda. 2014. *Given to the Goddess: South Indian Devadasis and the Sexuality of Religion*. Durham, NC: Duke University Press.

Rashid-ul-Khairi. [1938] 2010. *Dilli ki akhri bahar*. Delhi: Urdu Academy.

Ricci, Ronit. 2011. *Islam Translated: Literature, Conversion, and the Arabic Cosmopolis of South and Southeast Asia*. Chicago: University of Chicago Press.

Richardson, John. 2008. "Nietzsche's Problem of the Past." In *Nietzsche on Time and History*, edited by Manuel Dries, 87–111. Berlin: De Gruyter.

Ruskin, John. 1849. *The Seven Lamps of Architecture*. London: Smith, Elder.

Sanyal, Usha. 1996. *Devotional Islam and Politics in British India: Ahmad Riza Khan Barelwi and His Movement, 1870-1920*. Delhi: Oxford University Press.

Sanyal, Saptarshi. 2017. "Disrespecting Heritage." *Indian Express*, July 21.

Sax, William. 2009. *God of Justice: Ritual Healing and Social Justice in the Central Himalayas.* New York: Oxford University Press.

Schielke, Samuli. 2009. "Being Good in Ramadan: Ambivalence, Fragmentation, and the Moral Self in the Lives of Young Egyptians." *Journal of the Royal Anthropological Institute* 15 (S1): S24–40.

Schmidt, Bettina, and Lucy Huskinson. 2011. *Spirit Possession and Trance: New Interdisciplinary Perspectives.* London: Bloomsbury.

Scott, James C. 1990. *Domination and the Arts of Resistance: Hidden Transcripts.* New Haven, CT: Yale University Press.

Seedat, Fatima. 2016. "Beyond the Text: Between Islam and Feminism." *Journal of Feminist Studies in Religion* 32 (2): 138–42.

Seligman, Adam B., Robert P. Weller, Michael J. Puett, and Bennett Simon. 2008. *Ritual and Its Consequences: An Essay on the Limits of Sincerity.* New York: Oxford University Press.

Sells, Michael. 1989. *Desert Tracings: Six Classical Arabic Odes by 'Alqama, Shanfara, Labid, 'Antara, Al-A'sha, and Dhu al-Rúmma.* Middletown, CT: Wesleyan University Press.

———. 1991. "Gentle Now, Doves of the Thornberry and Moringa Thicket." *Journal of the Muhyiddin Ibn 'Arabi Society* 10: www.ibnarabisociety.org/articles/poemtarjuman11.html.

Sethi, Aarti. 2009. "Cinematic Sites: Encountering Film Exhibition in Delhi." M.Phil. thesis, Jawaharlal Nehru University.

Sharan, Awadhendra. 2011. "From Source to Sink: 'Official' and 'Improved' Water in Delhi, 1868–1956." *Indian Economic and Social History Review* 48 (3): 425–62.

———. 2014. *In the City, Out of Place: Nuisance, Pollution, and Dwelling in Delhi, c. 1850–2000.* Delhi: Oxford University Press.

Sharma, Aradhana. 2013. "State Transparency After the Neoliberal Turn: The Politics, Limits, and Paradoxes of India's Right to Information Law." *PoLAR: Political and Legal Anthropology Review* 36 (2): 308–25.

Siddiqui, Sameena Hasan. 2011. "Contours of Power: Urban 'Space' and a Sufi Center." *Indian Archives* 1:11–25.

Sila-Khan, Dominique. 2004. *Crossing the Threshold: Understanding Religious Identities in South Asia.* London: I. B. Tauris.

Simmel, Georg. 1965. "The Ruin." In *Essays on Sociology, Philosophy and Aesthetics*, edited by Kurt H. Wolff, 259–66. New York: Harper and Row.

Singh, Bhrigupati. 2011. "Agonistic Intimacy and Moral Aspiration in Popular Hinduism: A Study in the Political Theology of the Neighbor." *American Ethnologist* 38 (3): 430–50.

———. 2012. "The Headless Horseman of Central India: Sovereignty at Varying Thresholds of Life." *Cultural Anthropology* 27 (2): 383–407.

———. 2015. *Poverty and the Quest for Life: Spiritual and Material Striving in Rural Central India.* Chicago: University of Chicago Press.

Singh, Khushwant, and Raghu Rai. 1984. *Delhi: A Portrait.* Delhi: Oxford University Press.

Singh, Tavleen. 2014. "Election Redux." *Indian Express* (Delhi), May 11. http://indianex-press.com/article/opinion/columns/fifth-column-election-redux/.

Smith, Jonathan Z. 1982. *Imagining Religion: From Babylon to Jonestown.* Chicago: University of Chicago Press.

Snell-Rood, Claire. 2015. *No One Will Let Her Live: Women's Struggles for Well-Being in a Delhi Slum.* Berkeley: University of California Press.

Spadola, Emilio. 2014. *The Calls of Islam: Sufis, Islamists, and Mass Mediation in Morocco.* Bloomington: Indiana University Press.

Steingass, Francis Joseph. [1892] 2000. *A Comprehensive Persian-English Dictionary, Including the Arabic Words and Phrases to Be Met with in Persian Literature.* Delhi: Munshiram Manoharlal.

Stephen, Carr. 1876. *The Archaeology and Monumental Remains of Delhi.* Ludhiana: Mission Press.

Stewart, Tony K. 2001. "In Search of Equivalence: Conceiving Muslim-Hindu Encounter Through Translation Theory." *History of Religions* 40 (3): 260–87.

Sundaram, Ravi. 2010. *Pirate Modernity: Delhi's Media Urbanism.* Delhi: Routledge.

Taneja, Anand Vivek. 2005. "Puratatv ka mithak va mithak ka puratatv: Purana qila." In *Deewan-e Sarai 02: Shehernama*, edited by Ravikant Sharma and Sanjay Sharma, 307–20. Delhi: Sarai-CSDS.

———. 2008. "History and Heritage in the New Urban Fabric: The Changing Landscapes of Delhi's 'First City'; or, Who Can Tell the Histories of Lado Sarai?" In *Patterns of Middle Class Consumption in India and China*, edited by Christophe Jaffrelot and Peter van der Veer, 157–69. Delhi: Sage.

———. 2009. "Muslimness in Hindi Cinema." *Seminar* 598 (June): www.india-seminar .com/2009/598/598_anand_vivek_taneja.htm.

———. 2010. "Stereotyping the Muslim in Bombay Cinema." *Economic and Political Weekly* 45 (4): 30–32.

———. 2015. "Saintly Animals: The Shifting Moral and Ecological Landscapes of North India." *Comparative Studies of South Asia, Africa and the Middle East* 35 (2): 204–21.

Tarlo, Emma. 2003. *Unsettling Memories: Narratives of the Emergency in Delhi.* Berkeley: University of California Press.

Taussig, Michael. 2009. *What Color Is the Sacred?* Chicago: University of Chicago Press.

Taylor, Charles. 2007. *A Secular Age.* Cambridge, MA: Harvard University Press.

Temple, Richard Carnac. 1884. *Legends of the Panjab.* Vol. 1. Bombay: Educational Society Press.

Thapar, Romila. 2005. *Somanatha: The Many Voices of a History.* London: Verso.

"The Real Story of Zafar Jinn." ShiaChat.com, www.shiachat.com/forum/topic/74091 -the-real-story-of-zafar-jinn.

Tlili, Sarra. 2012. *Animals in the Qur'an.* New York: Cambridge University Press.

Tsing, Anna Lowenhaupt. 2015. *The Mushroom at the End of the World: On the Possibility of Life in Capitalist Ruins.* Princeton, NJ: Princeton University Press.

Turner, Victor. 1995. *The Ritual Process: Structure and Anti-structure.* New Brunswick, NJ: Aldine Transaction.

Vanita, Ruth. 2004. "'Married Among Their Companions': Female Homoerotic Relations in Nineteenth-Century Urdu Rekhti Poetry in India." *Journal of Women's History* 16 (1): 12–53.

———. 2012. *Gender, Sex and the City: Urdu Rekhti Poetry in India, 1780–1870.* New York: Palgrave Macmillan.

Vanita, Ruth, and Saleem Kidwai, eds. 2000. *Same-Sex Love in India: Readings from Literature and History.* New York: St. Martin's.

Vij, Shivam. 2009. "Whose Dome Is It Anyway?" *Open*, August 1. www.openthemagazine.com/article/nation/whose-dome-is-it-anyway.

Wadley, Susan. 2002. "One Straw from a Broom Cannot Sweep: The Ideology and Practice of the Joint Family in Rural North India." In *Everyday Life in South Asia*, ed. Sarah Lamb and Diane Mines, 11–22. Bloomington: Indiana University Press.

Weber, Max. 1978. *Economy and Society: An Outline of Interpretive Sociology.* Edited by Guenther Roth and Claus Wittich. Berkeley: University of California Press.

Wehr, Hans. 1976. *A Dictionary of Modern Written Arabic.* Ithaca, NY: Spoken Language Services.

Wescoat, James L., Jr. 1996. "Gardens, Urbanization, and Urbanism in Mughal Lahore: 1526–1957." In *Mughal Gardens: Sources, Places, Representations, and Prospects*, edited by James L. Wescoat Jr. and Joachim Wolschke-Bulmahn, 139–70. Washington: Dumbarton Oaks.

Westermarck, Edvard. 1926. *Ritual and Belief in Morocco.* London: Macmillan.

Wirtz, Kristina. 2016. "The Living, the Dead, and the Immanent: Dialogue Across Chronotopes." *HAU: Journal of Ethnographic Theory* 6 (1): 343–69.

Zaman, Taymiya. 2015. "Nostalgia, Lahore, and the Ghost of Aurangzeb." *Fragments* 4:1–27.

Zamindar, Vazira. 2007. *The Long Partition and the Making of Modern South Asia: Refugees, Boundaries, Histories.* New York: Columbia University Press.

INDEX

Page numbers in *italics* refer to illustrations.

Made in the USA
Columbia, SC
26 March 2018